The Soviet and East European Political Dictionary

THE SOVIET AND EAST EUROPEAN POLITICAL DICTIONARY

Barbara P. McCrea
Jack C. Plano
George Klein
Western Michigan University

ABC Clio Information Services
Santa Barbara, California
Oxford, England

Library of Congress Cataloging in Publication Data

Klein, George.
  The Soviet and East European political dictionary.

  (Clio dictionaries in political science; #4)
  Includes index.
  1. Europe, Eastern—Dictionaries and encyclopedias.
I. McCrea, Barbara P.   II. Plano, Jack C.   II. Title.
IV. Series.
DJK6.K56 1984   947'.0003'21   83-6418
ISBN 0-87436-333-0
ISBN 0-87436-347-0 (pbk.)

10   9   8   7   6   5   4   3   2

ABC-Clio Information Services
2040 Alameda Padre Serra, Box 4397
Santa Barbara, California 93103

Clio Press Ltd.
55 St. Thomas Street
Oxford, OX1 1JG, England

Manufactured in the United States of America

To
Douglas, Ellen, and Sarah McCrea
Jay and Katya Plano
Michael, Kathy, and Karen Klein

Clio Dictionaries in Political Science

SERIES STATEMENT

Language precision is the primary tool of every scientific discipline. That aphorism serves as the guideline for this series of political dictionaries. Although each book in the series relates to a specific topical or regional area in the discipline of political science, entries in the dictionaries also emphasize history, geography, economics, sociology, philosophy, and religion.

This dictionary series incorporates special features designed to help the reader overcome any language barriers that may impede a full understanding of the subject matter. For example, the concepts included in each volume are selected to complement the subject matter found in existing texts and other books. All but one volume in the series utilize a subject-matter chapter arrangement that is useful for classroom and study purposes.

Entries in all volumes include an up-to-date definition plus a *Significance* paragraph in which the authors discuss and analyze the term's historical and current relevance. Most entries are also cross-referenced, providing the reader the opportunity to seek additional information related to the subject of inquiry. A comprehensive index allows the reader to locate major entries and other concepts, events, and institutions discussed within these entries.

The political and social sciences suffer more than most disciplines from semantic confusion. This is attributable, *inter alia*, to the popularization of the language, and to the focus on many diverse foreign political and social systems. This dictionary series is dedicated to overcoming some of this confusion through careful writing of thorough, accurate definitions for the central concepts, institutions, and events that comprise the basic knowledge of each of the subject fields. New titles in the series will be issued periodically, including some in related social science disciplines.

—Jack C. Plano
Series Editor

CONTENTS

A NOTE ON HOW TO USE THIS BOOK

The Soviet and East European Political Dictionary is organized so that entries and supplementary data can be located in several ways. First, concepts are grouped alphabetically within subject-matter chapters. If a reader, for example, wished to find an entry dealing with Marxist theory, he or she could turn to Chapter 2, Ideology and Theory, to find it. In addition, students and general readers can increase their knowledge in a subject area by studying groups of concepts that are related to lectures or textbook assignments. When readers are in doubt as to which chapter contains a term, they can consult the general index. Page numbers for entries appear in the index in boldface type; concepts of lesser significance discussed within entries can be found in the index with page numbers in regular type. Supplementing the index is a Guide to Countries that informs readers where they may find specific information on economic, social, political, and historical topics. Finally, readers can more fully explore topics by using the extensive cross-references provided at the end of the definitional paragraph in most entries. Page numbers have been added for readers' convenience. In these ways, readers have access to broad classes of related information in using this book.

The authors have designed the format of this book to offer the reader a variety of approaches in the quest for information about the Soviet and East European political systems. This design encourages its use as (1) a study guide for introductory courses in the international and comparative fields; (2) a supplement to the textbook or book of readings adopted for use in courses that focus on the Soviet Union and Eastern Europe; (3) as a course aid in cognate fields, such as history, economics, and international relations; (4) a source of review materials for advanced courses in the field; and (5) a reference guide to the specialized language that relates to the Soviet and East European systems.

PREFACE

Precise language is the basic tool of every intellectual discipline. This maxim has served as a guideline and as a challenge in the authors' efforts to define and analyze the main concepts and structures that relate to the Soviet and East European political systems.

With the emergence of the Cold War and the bipolar balance system at the end of World War II, the peoples of Western Europe and the United States were confronted with new situational factors in their relations with Eastern Europe. Over the years, the Cold War intermittently heated up and then cooled into a period of détente. The bipolar system began to erode after Stalin's death in 1953, moving Eastern Europe toward a multipolar or polycentric system. Today, at the center of that region stands the Soviet Union, a giant among states when viewed from geographical, power, and economic perspectives. Within the Soviet sphere of influence are the communist-party states of Eastern Europe: Albania, Bulgaria, Czechoslovakia, East Germany, Hungary, Poland, Romania, and Yugoslavia. Two of these—Yugoslavia and Albania—remain largely free of Soviet hegemony; the rest have limited degrees of sovereignty and have developed unique institutions. Concepts, structures, and institutions relating to all of these political systems are included in this volume, but major attention is given to the central entity, the Union of Soviet Socialist Republics (USSR), or the Soviet Union, as it is commonly called. The authors are aware that this approach of using the Soviet Union as a model may blur the many real distinctions among these complex and individual systems. Students are urged to consult the many fine regional and country studies which have expanded the field of East European studies in recent years.

This book has been designed primarily as a teaching/learning supplement for use by students in their Soviet and East European classes, especially in the introductory course to that region of the world. In addition, the authors hope that others, such as public officials, research scholars, visitors to Eastern Europe, and the general public will find it useful. Definitions, although longer and more analytical than those found in most political dictionaries, are not of a length and

xiii

depth to meet the needs of the serious scholar. The book's value is to be found in the ease with which the reader can locate significant entries that provide basic knowledge about a political concept, structure, or institution and use it to gain a better understanding of the Soviet Union and Eastern Europe. We hope that these "building blocks" will add meaning and interest to all courses that focus on that complex region.

No effort was made by the authors to be exhaustive in their selection of entries for this volume. Each was selected by a sifting and winnowing process in which the authors were guided by several key questions. Does this concept, for example, increase the ability of the reader to communicate in the technical language that applies to the region? Will it contribute to a student's search for knowledge and understanding? How effectively will it supplement other classroom materials? The selection of entries was thus based on our subjective judgment of the basic core of knowledge that can be used as a starting point for understanding the Soviet and East European political systems.

The Soviet and East European Political Dictionary incorporates an unusual format. Although dictionaries have generally remained unchanged in their organization since they first emerged in the fifteenth century, this volume has several unique features. Entries, as already noted, have been selected on the basis of the major foci of the field. The book is divided into chapters in which key concepts are grouped according to the subject matter of the field. In this way, the book can be used in and out of the classroom as a teaching/learning tool, with chapter assignments and topical quizzes, unlike a straight A to Z type of dictionary that is designed primarily for reference purposes. Each chapter in our dictionary is linked through subject matter with a chapter or chapters generally found in leading textbooks in the field. Each entry contains not only a paragraph of definition but also a paragraph of *"Significance."* The latter is used to place the concept in its historical context and provide a contemporary perspective of it within its contemporary environment. Most entries include cross-references in which the reader is encouraged to seek out additional, related information that will add to his or her understanding. Cross-references include page numbers to facilitate and encourage their use. For further reference, the book utilizes a Guide to Countries through which the reader can locate materials pertinent to specific countries in the region. Finally, it incorporates a comprehensive index that includes all of the concepts, events, strategies, theories, institutions, and leading personalities that are defined or described in the book. These features encourage the book's use as a reference tool. An additional unique feature is found in the index: all dictionary entries are identified by page numbers in boldface type, and topics of lesser importance contained within the entries are printed with page numbers in regular type.

As all who have worked in the field know, there is no entirely satisfactory answer to the problem of transliterating Russian words into English. In transliterating Russian and other languages written in the Cyrillic alphabet, the authors have modified the Library of Congress system, especially when a name or word has become familiar to American readers in a simplified form (Trotsky, not Trotskii), and have replaced the Library of Congress's ia with ya (as in *Narodnaya volya*, not *Narodnaia volia*). The Russian soft sign is represented by an apostrophe. Diacritics have been retained for languages such as Polish, Czech, Hungarian, Romanian, and Serbo-Croatian.

Interdisciplinary fields of intellectual and academic interest perhaps suffer more than most disciplines from semantic confusion. This is especially true when beginning students focus for the first time on a region of the world that is unfamiliar to them. Providing some help to students in introductory courses that focus on the Soviet Union and Eastern Europe was one of the primary factors that motivated the authors in writing this book. We hope the book measures up to these expectations, and we would appreciate comments from faculty or students concerning this objective.

The authors recognize the important role played by many scholars who, in their articles and books, have contributed to the enrichment of the language of comparative politics in general and to this region in particular. These efforts and contributions have made *The Soviet and East European Political Dictionary* possible. We also wish to thank our students, who have challenged us over the years in a way that could only add to the value of this book. The authors, however, accept full responsibility for errors, and we invite readers to communicate those of commission as well as of omission to us.

A note of sadness pervaded the usually joyous and relief-filled atmosphere that typifies the completion of a writing project. Early on—December 5, 1981—the project received a setback and the coauthors a great shock with the sudden death of fellow author, Dr. George Klein. Dr. Klein had a long and illustrious career in academia, focusing his scholarly attention on the Soviet Union and Eastern Europe, especially on Yugoslavia and on Czechoslovakia, the country of his birth and early life. He traveled extensively in the region and enjoyed many personal and professional contacts. In many ways, this book reflects the life and times of George Klein, and we, his coauthors and friends, remember him fondly.

—Barbara P. McCrea
—Jack C. Plano
Western Michigan University

GUIDE TO COUNTRIES

The Soviet and East European Political Dictionary

1. Historical Perspectives

Agrarian Populism   Peasant-based political movements that seek to benefit the small-holding peasantry through land redistribution, self-government, and fairer prices for agricultural products. Originally antiauthoritarian and egalitarian, agrarian populism in nineteenth-century Europe focused on securing land reform, and in many societies included a strong socialist bent. Two forms of agrarian populism are important to the political history of the communist-party states: (1) the agrarian-based revolutionary groups in czarist Russia whose adherents believed that Russia could achieve socialism without enduring the miseries of capitalism; and (2) the peasant-based political parties which emerged in the much more liberalized political atmosphere of interwar Eastern Europe. The first group were a major influence in the formation of a Marxist movement in Russia; the second played a major, and sometimes debilitating, role in the interwar Eastern European governments, and were destroyed by the communists after World War II. The Russian populist movement (*narodnichestvo*) arose in the 1860s and 1870s. The various Russian anarchists, nihilists, liberal democrats, populists, socialists, and, eventually, Marxists, arose from the agrarian populist ferment of the postemancipation (1861) decades in Russia. Especially active in the 1870s and 1880s, the populists (*narodniki*) held that by building on the tradition of the self-governing communal peasant village, the *mir*, Russia could avoid capitalism and achieve socialism. After the assassination in 1881 of Alexander II by a populist terrorist group, the *Narodnaya Volya* (People's Will), many Russian populists and socialists were forced to flee abroad to Western Europe, where they came into contact with European Marxists. The fusion of Marxism and populism was largely effected by the exiled Georgi Plekhanov, who had formed the first

3

Russian revolutionary party, *Zemlya i Volya* (Land and Liberty) in 1876. In 1898 Plekhanov played a leading role in the formation of the Russian Social Democratic Labor Party (RSDLP), Russia's first Marxist party, which advocated a proletariat-led Marxist revolt against the czardom. Plekhanov sided with the more gradualist Mensheviks in the 1903 split between the Mensheviks and Bolsheviks. In 1902, the Russian Social Revolutionary Party (SR) was formed out of several loosely defined groups of populists. It advocated a program of agrarian socialism, through revolution if necessary, and, when the czardom fell in March of 1917, was the leading party contending for power until the Bolshevik coup d'etat doomed the Social Revolutionaries. East European agrarian populism was focused differently. The various peasant movements were accorded legitimate status once the Eastern European territory was carved up into individual states by the post–World War I Versailles settlements. In those states that preserved democratic forms, peasant parties in the interwar period played an important political role, one far less revolutionary than the Russian agrarians. Peasant parties were particularly important in Poland, where the Peasant Party constituted a majority in the first Constituent Assembly and pushed through a land reform in 1919, and Czechoslovakia, where the peasant parties took part in the democratic coalition governments of interwar Czechoslovakia. In the poorer Balkan states, agrarian politics were important despite the fact that these new governments soon lapsed into dictatorships. The interwar Yugoslav government was hamstrung by the noncooperation of the Croat Peasant Party. The Bulgarian Agrarian Union, under Alexander Stamboliski, and the Romanian National Peasant Party, led by Iuliu Maniu, accomplished limited land reforms. The East European agrarian movements usually consisted of two wings, a populist one, which sought reform for the benefit of the poorer peasantry, and a wing that represented the richer peasantry, usually the more influential ones. Most East European states carried out some land reform, especially in Czechoslovakia. However, land reform was carried out under the looming shadow of the Bolshevik Revolution next door, so that the rulers permitted land redistribution in order to defuse an agrarian-based revolution. In the 1930s the agrarian parties of interwar Eastern Europe also sought high tariffs against imported food as the worldwide Great Depression worsened. In much of Eastern Europe, the economic stagnation was blamed not only on the Depression but also on the peasant parties, which sought to preserve a traditional way of life in the face of modern technology. *See also* BOLSHEVIK, p. 10; MENSHEVIK, p. 26; MIR, p. 28.

Significance   In the long run, under communism agrarian populism suffered the same fate in Russia and Eastern Europe. Bolshevism was shaped by its agrarian populist heritage. Lenin seized power and then anchored his revolution not only in the miniscule Russian working class but also in Russian peasant populism, appealing to them in the name of "bread, land, and peace." Upon consolidating his power, Lenin turned on the Social Revolutionaries and all other parties, eventually suppressing them. Similarly, when the communists took power in Eastern Europe after World War II, the peasant parties were among the first to be suppressed, as a potential center of competition for power. Some of the strength of interwar communist movements in Eastern Europe may be attributed to the more conservative peasant parties, which were viewed as seeking protection for agricultural producers at the expense of the urban working class. This radicalized the workers and brought some to participate in socialist and communist organizations. The East European peasant parties were also damaged by the fact that some upwardly mobile adherents succumbed to the radicalism of the rightist nationalist movements, which frequently emulated the political style of fascism. However, the East European peasant parties in general, rightist conservative and populist alike, were destroyed by the victorious communists. Despite the efforts of Alexander Stamboliski to create a "Green International" in the 1920s, no true peasant unity existed in the East European states.

Anti-Semitism   The political, social, and religious persecution of Jews that formed a major current in the politics of czarist Russia and Eastern Europe. Anti-Semitism as a sociopolitical philosophy arose in Germany and Austria in the mid-nineteenth century and was quickly carried to czarist Russia where medieval religious anti-Semitism was still an integral part of Russian culture. Imperial Russia included some 5 million Jews, many acquired with the partition of the Polish state under Catherine the Great of Russia. Russia's Jews were confined to the Pale of Settlement in western Russia and the former Polish territories, forbidden to move to the interior, and barred from many professions. In the mid-1800s, the Crown began to sanction, if not sponsor, the widespread persecution and terrorization of the Jews known as the period of the pogroms. Despite European outrage, Alexander III promulgated a series of anti-Semitic edicts which, until the rise of Nazi Germany, were the most anti-Semitic of modern legislation. Bands of marauding reactionaries, criminals, and hoodlums, popularly known as the "Black Hundreds" and tacitly approved by the Crown, mounted attacks on Jews and on those Russians who supported liberal democracy and constitutional reforms. By playing on the endemic anti-Semitism of the Russian people, the Crown sought to discredit the liberal democrats by linking them with the Jews. The pogroms, which resulted in massive destruction of Jewish lives and property, continued throughout the early twentieth century. Officially sanctioned anti-Semitism remained czarist policy until the Bolshevik Revolution of 1917. *See also* BOLSHEVIK, p. 10; INTERNAL PASSPORT SYSTEM, p. 261; REFUSENIK, p. 298; RUSSIFICATION, p. 31.

Significance   Anti-Semitism in Russia and Eastern Europe radicalized many Jews, driving them into underground political movements or into emigration. Jews played a major role in the development of trade unions and in the social democratic movement. Many of the early Bolsheviks were Jewish intellectuals, drawn to bolshevism by its proclaimed internationalism and freedom from narrow nationalistic or religious antagonisms. Anti-Semitic reactionaries in the West identified bolshevism with the Jews, a charge later adopted by Nazi Germany and used to justify the destruction of both Jews and communists in World War II. In the interwar period, the conservative governments of Hungary and Romania followed a policy of official anti-Semitism. Poland's large Yiddish-speaking population fared little better under the highly nationalistic, intensely Roman Catholic government of the new Polish state. During the interwar period, anti-Semitism was frequently a component of right-wing nationalisms which arose in Eastern Europe. Despite bolshevism's early record, Josef Stalin returned in part to the traditional anti-Semitism of czarist Russia. By the late 1930s, almost all Jews had been purged from top party ranks. After World War II, Stalin embarked on a campaign to purge Soviet society of all Western elements, singling out Jews as particular objects of suspicion. Jews were accused of being "cosmopolitans" who tendered their loyalty to worldwide Zionism rather than to Sovietism. Most Jewish cultural institutions were closed and Jewish intellectuals were executed. In Eastern Europe, a wave of Soviet-instigated purges hit especially hard at Jewish communists. At the time of his death in 1953, Stalin was supposedly preparing a new round of purges, hinging on his charges of a "Doctors' Plot," an alleged conspiracy by Jewish doctors to assassinate several top Soviet leaders. Stalin's persecution of the Jews also signalled a shift in Soviet foreign policy, from support of the new state of Israel to support for the Arab states. Although the record since Stalin's death is immensely better, Soviet Jews are still singled out for suspicion and denied their cultural and religious heritage. In the 1970s, with the signing of the Helsinki Accord, many applied for visas to emigrate to Israel. Although the Soviet leadership has permitted over 250,000 Soviet Jews to exit, they have not hesitated to charge Jews with anti-Sovietism and "Zionism," implying disloyalty to the Soviet state. Other East European states have also used their Jewish populations as scapegoats. For example, despite the fact that most Polish Jews perished tragically in World War II, some Polish party leaders both in 1968 and 1980 attempted to blame the upheavals on "Zionists."

Austro-Hungarian Empire   The political unit that dominated central Europe from 1526 until 1918. Ruled by the Habsburg royal house, the Empire was transformed into the Austro-Hungarian Empire (Dual Monarchy) by the Compromise of 1867 which gave Hungary coequal status. Much of what is termed "modern" national- ism developed its distinguishing characteristics among the subject nations of the multinational Empire: the Czechs, Slovaks, Ruthenians, Croats, Bosnians, Slovenes, Serbs, Poles, Romanians. World War I arose out of these national tensions as Austria-Hungary sought to expand into the Balkans. At the end of the War, the Versailles settlements dissolved the Empire into several small states, known as the successor states; these included Austria, Czechoslovakia, Hungary, Poland, Romania, and Yugoslavia. *See also* BALKAN QUESTION, p. 9; OTTOMAN EMPIRE, p. 29.

Significance   All the successor states carved out of the Austro-Hun- garian Empire faced economic and political problems that deepened in the 1920s and 1930s, particularly after the Weimar Republic (Ger- many) succumbed to fascism. These problems contributed heavily to the general instability of central Europe. The industries of the new successor states had been set up as part of a highly integrated economic system with a market of over 50 million, from which the new states were now cut off. In all but Czechoslovakia, Habsburg domination was soon succeeded by varying degrees of authoritarianism. The heritage of the Habsburg lands was nonetheless far more favorable than that of the nations that had been under Ottoman rule for four centuries. As part of the Austro-Hungarian *Rechtsstaat*, the successor states had experi- enced a functioning civil service, universal public education, freedom from arbitrary state action, and a civil law system. As a Western modernizing system, the Empire created the base for industrial development. In several areas, most notably the Czech lands of Bohemia-Moravia, an urban industrial class existed that in the interwar years contained strong elements of Marxism and socialism. Marxism also attracted the ethnic minorities of the new states, who looked to communist ideology for solutions. The breakup of the Empire did not assuage all nationality conflict, as it was impossible to draw national boundaries to coincide perfectly with populations. Thus the creation of the successor states also created nationality problems, such as the Hungarians of Transylvania (Romania), the Slovaks of Czechoslo- vakia, the Polish-Czech population of Teshchen, the multinational mix of Yugoslavia, the Macedonians, and the Slovenes of Carinthian Austria, that still exist under the uniformity seemingly imposed by communism.

Autocracy   The nature of political authority in Czarist Russia which many consider to be the most enduring feature of both Russian and Soviet political culture. Autocracy is an absolutist form of government, unrestricted by any laws or institutions, with all power vested in one man. It is characterized by personalized political authority, a centralized state, intolerance of dissent, and disregard for individual rights. Czarist autocracy developed in the fifteenth century with the formation of the Russian state. Russian society differed from Europe in that Russia never experienced the Renaissance or Reformation. The context in which the Russian state developed, coalescing around the Grand Duchy of Moscow, was one of continual warfare with the Tatar occupiers and constant threat of invasion from the West. Ivan the Terrible (1533–1584) unified the state and assumed the title of Czar and Autocrat of All Russia. Ivan's methods, breaking the power of the nobles and instituting centralized control, protected the new state but also set it on an absolutist course. The rule of law, as it developed in the West, was stifled. Ecclesiastical authority, in the guise of the Russian Orthodox Church, buttressed rather than checked the authority of the Czar. The Autocrat was the symbol of the state; all people and possessions were the possessions of the state. The 1832 Constitution of the Russian Empire, under which Russia was governed until 1906, emphasized the authority of the Czar over all organs of state. Thus, Czarist political authority was absolutist. The small middle class was virtually powerless, the nobles were dependent on the crown, and the remaining 80 percent of the Russian people were bound to the land and the landowners as serfs. Few restraints—legal, social, or economic—checked the absolute power of the Czar.

Significance   Many have argued that it is impossible to understand the nature of Soviet politics without examining what Sovietologist Zbigniew Brzezinski terms "the central reality of Russian history." The Russian philosopher, Nicholas Berdyaev, goes one step further and argues that the Soviet state is merely a reincarnation of the Czarist political order, successful for the very reason that it rests on Russian political traditions. Whether or not one accepts the thesis that the Soviet system is simply Czardom in new ideological clothing, history and its effects on political culture should not be dismissed. The Czarist and Soviet systems share some comparable features: centralism, decision making by a very few or by one man, a strong military and secret police, intolerance and repression of dissent, a fear of external threats, state dominance over property relationships, and lack of institutional restraints. Thomas Hobbes's defense of absolutism as necessary given the depraved nature of mankind perhaps is echoed in Vladimir Lenin's insistence that the masses were incapable of carrying out the revolution by themselves. As an explanation of the nature of the Soviet system, autocracy is a limiting, single-factor analysis, blurring other distinctions between Czarist Russia and the modern Soviet state. Presenting the Soviet system as irrevocably bound to its historical roots allows little hope for evolution. Also, portions of the Czarist Empire, in particular the Cossack lands and the far Eastern peoples, did not experience full-blown Russian autocracy; the writ of Czardom frequently ran small in the borderlands. The argument that Czarist autocracy has been reborn in the Soviet system—especially under Stalinism—assumes that the personalized, unrestrained power of the Czar now rests with the institutions of the Soviet communist party, and ignores the explosion in education and the drastic changes in the class system. The heritage of Czarist autocracy, however much it may have shaped Soviet political culture, is not shared by Eastern Europe, where Soviet institutions imposed after World War II differ from the political cultures of these states.

Balkan Question   The international power struggle among the Great Powers for control of the Balkan area during the nineteenth and early twentieth centuries. The Balkan Question was the product of the erosion of Ottoman power in the Balkans, under Ottoman control since the fifteenth century. As Ottoman power weakened, the Great Powers of Europe contested for control of the strategic Balkan area and, in particular, the Straits of the Dardanelles. The area became a region in which indigenous nationalisms waged a struggle against the Great Powers for the strategic territory which Germany and Austria-Hungary viewed as an avenue to the Near East, and Russia saw as a means of securing warm water ports. Serbia formally achieved autonomy from the Ottomans in 1830. Bosnia-Hercegovina was annexed by Austria-Hungary in 1908. In order to block Teutonic expansion into the Balkans, England followed a policy of shoring up the tottering Ottoman Empire. Macedonia, an area of mixed Slavic population, was claimed by Greece, Bulgaria, and Serbia—and by the Macedonians themselves. Following the Russo-Turkish War, Russia imposed the Treaty of San Stefano on the Ottoman Empire in 1878, giving nearly all of Macedonia to Bulgaria. The Western powers, committed to preserving the balance of power, compelled Russia to renegotiate the treaty and return Macedonia to the Ottomans. Macedonia and what is today southern Yugoslavia remained under Ottoman rule until the Balkan Wars of 1912–13, when the Serbs, Bulgarians, and Romanians finally forced the Ottoman Empire to relinquish its European possessions. *See also* OTTOMAN EMPIRE, p. 29.

Significance   The origins of World War I, which reshaped the map of Europe and brought Bolshevism to Russia, lie in the Balkan Question. On June 28, 1914, Archduke Francis Ferdinand of Austria-Hungary was assassinated in Sarajevo, the capital of Bosnia, by local Slav nationalists. Austria-Hungary used this as a pretext for declaring the war which eventually involved all the Great Powers. The three great empires—Austria-Hungary, the Ottoman, and the Russian—were destroyed by the war. Macedonia, divided between Bulgaria and the new Yugoslav state, remained a source of contention. Bulgaria, which had lost most of Macedonia during the second round of the Balkan wars, continued to claim all of Macedonia, and in pursuit of this fought both World War I and World War II on the losing side. That some of the tensions of the nineteenth-century Balkan Question remain under the surface is apparent from the post–World War II history of Macedonia. In 1945 most of Macedonia remained with Yugoslavia, constituted as a republic within the Yugoslav federation. In August of 1947 Josip Broz Tito, the communist leader of Yugoslavia, and Georgi Dimitrov of Bulgaria apparently agreed that if the Greek communist rebellion were successful, Greek Macedonia would be merged into Yugoslav Macedonia, and Yugoslavia and Bulgaria would form a South Slav federation. Stalin expelled Yugoslavia from the Soviet bloc, essentially for placing national interests above Soviet interests. Most analysts agree that the proposed Balkan Federation strengthened Stalin's resolve to excommunicate a potentially dangerous competitor. Soviet leaderships have periodically supported Bulgaria's claim to Macedonia, using the Macedonian issue to apply pressure against Yugoslavia whenever it has suited their aims. Bulgaria remains an irredentist state and a loyal client of the Soviet Union, and the old Balkan Question remains a barometer of Soviet-Yugoslav relations.

Bolshevik   The Russian word for "member of the majority," the term Vladimir Lenin applied to the followers of his version of Russian Marxism. The Bolshevik Party, which eventually became the Communist Party of the Soviet Union (CPSU), was born out of a split in the Russian Social Democratic Labor Party (RSDLP). Founded in 1898, Russia's first Marxist party was, as with all parties in pre-1905 czarist Russia, a clandestine and persecuted group. The Leninists constituted only a faction within this small movement. Lenin clashed with the more moderate members of the RSDLP over the proper nature and organization of a Marxist party. Lenin insisted on a highly disciplined, selective membership controlled by a core leadership, while the moderates argued for a worker-based, mass party. At the Second Congress of the RSDLP, held in Brussels in 1903, some of the more moderate delegates walked out of the meeting and Lenin was able to claim a majority, dubbing his opponents Mensheviks, "members of the minority." Lenin's designation endured, although at the time and for several years afterwards, the Bolsheviks constituted a minority in the Marxist movement in Russia. The Mensheviks, led by Julius Martov, refused to accept Lenin's organizational strategy and his advocacy of immediate revolution. Lenin's concept of the party, first spelled out in *What Is to Be Done* (1902), posited a select band of professional revolutionaries, bound by party discipline and dedicated to use any available means, including violence, to bring down the czarist regime. In contrast to the Mensheviks' commitment to a worker-based mass party, Lenin argued that the masses could not accomplish a revolution by themselves, but must be led by a dedicated core of professional revolutionaries. Inherent in Lenin's formulation was the implication that the masses would always have to be led, a role he assigned to the Bolsheviks. Although both factions based their ideology on Marxism and Marx's dictum that mature capitalism would be overthrown by revolution, the Mensheviks maintained that capitalist development would have to run its full course in Russia before a Marxist revolution could occur. In this they were closer to the original Marx. The ideological differences between the Bolsheviks and Mensheviks translated into differences in strategy. In 1905 Czar Nicholas reluctantly agreed to set up the Duma, Russia's first and only elected parliament. As gradualists who believed that capitalist democracy must run its course before conditions would be ripe for revolution, the Mensheviks were willing to cooperate in the Duma. Lenin remained committed to the tactics of immediate revolution and was unwilling to cooperate with the burgeoning constitutional movement in Russia. By 1912, the Russian Marxist movement, still small by most standards, had formally split into two parties. Lenin adopted the name of RSDLP-Bolshevik for the small band that was to carry out the Russian Revolution in the name of Bolshevism. The tactics of what became the Bolshevik movement and the political dynamics on which the communist dictatorship was erected were set by Lenin's insistence on an elite, centralized party dedicated to immediate revolution. *See also* BOLSHEVIK REVOLUTION, p. 12; LENINISM, p. 51; LENINISM: DEMOCRATIC CENTRALISM, p. 52; MENSHEVIK, p. 26.

Significance   Lenin's use of the term Bolshevik enabled the Leninist faction of the Russian Marxists to claim to be the true representatives of the working class. Unyielding on the issues of centralism, party discipline, and revolutionary tactics, Lenin's organizational skills proved decisive in 1917. Although the original argument between the Bolsheviks and Mensheviks centered on organization and tactics, portions of a third Russian party, the Social Revolutionaries, were more terroristic and violent than the Bolsheviks. When the czarist government began to collapse in March 1917 under the accumulated disasters of war and incompetency, the Mensheviks cooperated in the hastily constituted Provisional Government. The Provisional Government's reluctance to take Russia out of the war, however, compromised the Mensheviks. The Bolsheviks, as well organized as Lenin had envisioned, were able to take advantage of the Provisional Government's impotence, and deposed it in October of 1917. In the ensuing Civil War period, the Mensheviks became a chief target for Lenin's secret police, the CHEKA. The conflict between the Bolsheviks and the more gradualist Mensheviks foreshadowed a later conflict in international communism. In the 1970s, several western communist parties, such as the Italian Communist Party, argued with the Soviets over whether to cooperate with democratic parliamentary institutions. The movement, labeled Eurocommunism, was resisted strenuously by Lenin's heirs. Today the term Bolshevik has become almost synonymous with communist. In the West it is used critically, to describe a Marxist party that pursues illegal, undemocratic, and conspiratorial tactics. In the Soviet Union it is a term of honor.

Bolshevik Revolution   The uprising that brought the Bolsheviks to power in Russia and transformed the czarist Russian Empire into the communist Union of Soviet Socialist Republics. The Bolshevik Revolution, sometimes called the October Revolution to distinguish it from the February Revolution of eight months earlier that had deposed the Czar, occurred on October 25, 1917. Its guiding spirit was Vladimir Lenin, who had created the Bolshevik party out of the Russian Marxist socialist movement and shaped it as a tightly disciplined instrument of revolution. Since March of 1917, Russia had been ruled by a Provisional Government composed of a group of liberal and moderate politicians in the Duma, Russia's first parliament granted by a reluctant Czar Nicholas II after the Revolution of 1905. In the midst of deepening chaos and military failures on the front, Nicholas had dissolved the Duma in February. The group of Duma politicians who quickly formed the Provisional Government and forced Nicholas's abdication, governed without the imprimatur of either the people, the Duma, or the monarchy; Russia was no longer a monarchy but was not yet a constitutional republic. Essentially self-appointed, the members of the Provisional Government were disturbed by their illegality and hesitated to act decisively. Between March and October, Russia had no effective head of state, no representative body, and, at the end, no effective army. The cautious liberalism of the Provisional Government proved ineffective against the widening anarchy. Meanwhile, the growing power of the Petrograd (Leningrad) Soviet of Workers' and Soldiers' Deputies challenged the waning authority of the Provisional Government, especially over the issue of Russia's participation in World War I. The Petrograd Soviet, and its counterparts elsewhere, was a resurrection of the Petrograd Soviet formed in 1905 to lead the revolutionary movement against the czarist government. At first the Soviet was dominated by Mensheviks and Social Revolutionaries, including Alexander Kerensky, who was also the only leftist in the Provisional Government, since the Soviet officially refused to participate. After April, Lenin and the other Bolshevik leaders exiled by the czar returned to Russia. They then began a steady effort to gain control of the Soviet. In July, the Galician front collapsed and amid severe food crises and growing anarchism, hundreds of thousands of peasant conscripts deserted. In the countryside, the peasants seized the land in hundreds of peasant insurrections. The liberals resigned from the Provisional Government and Kerensky became both Prime Minister and War Minister, ruling through a secret directorate. In August, Kerensky blocked the abortive Kornilov revolt, which he had apparently supported initially, and rearmed the Red Guards of the Petrograd Soviet. The regular army melted away. Thus, from August on the Provisional Government had no credible military support. In September, the Bolsheviks won control of the Petrograd Soviet, Leon Trotsky was installed as head, and the Petrograd Soviet was prepared to become the instrument of the revolution. The final act came on October 24 when the troops quartered in Petrograd and Kronstadt acknowledged the Soviet as the sole leader. The Bolsheviks occupied key points in Petrograd and seized the Winter Palace, the site of the Provisional Government. As the battleship *Aurora* trained its guns on the Winter Palace, the Bolsheviks seized control. Kerensky fled (eventually to the United States) and the Provisional Government ceased to exist. Trotsky, who emerged as the strategist of the Revolution, timed the Revolution to coincide with the second All-Russian Congress of the Soviets, in which the Bolsheviks enjoyed a majority. When the Social Revolutionaries walked out in protest of the Bolshevik coup, the remaining delegates voted to vest power in the All-Bolshevik Council of People's Commissars (*Sovnarkom*) headed by Lenin, and the

Bolshevik Revolution was accomplished. *See also* BOLSHEVIK, p. 10; DUMA, p. 16; KORNILOV AFFAIR, p. 22; LENINISM, p. 51; WAR COMMUNISM, p. 237.

Significance   No other event has had a greater impact on the twentieth century than the Bolshevik Revolution. Despite their initial success in taking control of the capital city, the Bolsheviks were far from controlling Russia; it was in fact initially far more of a coup d'etat than a revolution. Lenin faced an incredible array of problems: peasant insurrections, a disintegrating army, a non-functioning economy, and looming over all, the question of how long—and whether —Russia could continue in the war. That Lenin coped with all these problems while carrying out a Civil War of several years duration is a testament to the superb organizational skills of the Bolsheviks. Russia left the war in March of 1918 with the signing of the Brest-Litovsk Treaty. War Communism, a period of extremely stringent controls, rationing of all materials and food, and requisition of food from the countryside, was effected and the land was turned over to the peasants. Simultaneously, Lenin revived the secret police to punish all those who opposed Bolshevism, reinstated censorship, and, with Leon Trotsky as war commissar, built up a Red Army to fight the anti-Bolshevik (White) forces who ranged over much of Russia. Historically in Europe, red has been the color of revolution, and white of counterrevolution. The Civil War lasted until the end of 1920. In the process, the Czar and his entire family were murdered by Bolshevik revolutionaries. The various anti-Bolshevik forces were doomed by their inability to agree on a common program and to coordinate their actions. An Allied expeditionary force landed at Murmansk and Archangel and provided support for the Whites, an action long resented by the Soviets. By the end of 1920, the Bolsheviks had gained control over the empire, and communism in its Marxist-Leninist variant, was secured in Russia.

Students of Marxism and twentieth-century history have argued endlessly over why the Bolshevik Revolution evolved so quickly into an authoritarian dictatorship. The most common explanations are: (1) Lenin's character itself was essentially dictatorial; he had ruthlessly suppressed opposition whenever possible during his long climb to leadership; (2) the organizational nature of Leninism, particularly democratic centralism, presupposes a rigidly centralized dictatorship; (3) the authoritarian nature of Russian political culture doomed democracy; (4) the rigors of fighting a Civil War against both domestic and foreign enemies forced Lenin into dictatorial methods; and (5) the application of Marxism, designed for developed capitalist systems, to a largely precapitalist system perverted its essential democracy and humanism. The fundamental division is between those who argue for circumstantial causes and those who see in Leninism itself the root cause. The immediate issue faced by the Bolsheviks was how to achieve power; for this Marxism provided no guide. Those who argue that the new Bolshevik leadership was in the beginning democratic, as it did indeed allow for divided opinion and participation of non-Bolsheviks, must account also for the fact that Lenin immediately reinstated the secret police, reimposed censorship, and dissolved the Constituent Assembly, Russia's first and last really democratically elected parliament, in which the Bolsheviks had won barely a quarter of the seats. Russian democratic institutions were too new and too fragile to bear the burden of the sudden collapse of the government amid deepening economic crises and losses on the battlefield. The Bolshevik Revolution was unique in its degree of success but not in its central dilemma: a revolution, ostensibly carried out in the name of democracy and humanism, by a small group of disciplined radicals who then had to consolidate their power over a backward, conservative, and heterogeneous society which had little or no experience in democracy.

Cossacks   The name commonly given to the free frontiersmen who inhabited the borders of the Russian Empire and protected it against outside invasion. The Cossacks were serfs who fled to the borderlands of the Empire to establish their own communitites in the seventeenth and eighteenth centuries. The Cossacks owned their land and were granted tax exemption and other special privileges in return for the obligation to protect the Empire. The Cossacks were constituted into 11 separate branches, the most important being the Don and Kuban Cossacks. During the beginning stages in the development of Cossackdom, the Cossacks participated in various peasant revolts. At the end of the eighteenth century, the Crown recognized their independent status and officially designated the Cossacks as the border guard of the Russian Empire. Their special status ensured their loyalty to the Crown, as did their belief in the legitimacy of the Czar's rule. The Cossacks developed their own cultural traditions and became noted for their military prowess. In the late nineteenth and early twentieth centuries, the elite cavalry units of the Czar's army were drawn from the Cossacks. During the Revolution and ensuing civil war, the Cossacks fought on both sides, but principally with the anti-Bolsheviks. During World War II Stalin once more drew upon Cossack tradition and reestablished special Cossack units in the Red Army.

Significance   The Cossacks initially constituted a multinational grouping which developed a distinct identity and culture. Because of their unique military training, which obligated all Cossack males to military service, a romantic tradition of Cossack military prowess arose. Since the primary unit of Cossackdom was the self-governed village that held its land communally, the collective farm system introduced by Stalin was touted as the social organization preferred by these Russian folk heroes. Since the advent of communism, the Cossack peoples have been merged into the various Soviet administrative divisions, but the romantic tradition of the fiercely independent Cossack remains. A similar situation and tradition developed on the military borderlands of Croatia during the period of Austro-Hungarian rule over northern Yugoslavia.

Duma   The lower house of the czarist legislature, established in 1906 as Imperial Russia's first representative national assembly. The creation of the Duma was a concession forced upon a reluctant Czar Nicholas II during the abortive 1905 Revolution. Although essentially spontaneous and disorganized, the 1905 Revolution constituted the first substantial modern challenge to czarist autocracy. Under the intense pressure of general strikes, military mutinies, defeat by the Japanese Navy, and widespread peasant land seizures, the Czar promulgated the October Manifesto which promised universal suffrage and an elective national assembly. Deriving its name from the elective city councils established under Catherine the Great, the Duma was the lower house of the new parliament, similar in some ways to the United States House of Representatives. The competence of the Duma, however, was severely limited. The Cabinet and Prime Minister were responsible only to the crown, which retained control of the budget, foreign affairs, and the military. Any legislation passed by the Duma could be vetoed by the upper house, the State Council, one-half of whose membership was selected by the Czar. The Czar could also circumvent the Duma when it was not in session by issuing Orders in Council (*Ukazes*), although *Ukazes* had to be submitted for approval at the next Duma session. Electors to the State Council were classified into six categories (large landowners, small landowners, peasants, townspeople, capitalists, and workers), a system resembling the Estates General of the French Revolution, which was assembled under similar circumstances. Direct voting was permitted in only six large cities. The remaining Duma elections were multi-stage and indirect. The voting was heavily weighted in favor of the landowning gentry and urban rich, who were allocated an enormous preponderance of the electoral votes. One electoral vote represented 8,000 landowners while the peasant ratio was 1 to 60,000 and the urban workers, 1 to almost 190,000. The first two Dumas met only briefly, being illegally dissolved by Nicholas who, despite the conservative bias of the electoral arrangements, perceived the deputies as "radical." A new and even more biased electoral law, tailor-made by Nicholas, produced a body that lasted from 1907 to 1912. The new electoral law cut the already miniscule peasant and worker representation by nearly one-half and increased landowner representation by two-thirds. Electoral districts were also gerrymandered so that the representation of the Russian population was increased at the expense of non-Russian peoples. The Fourth Duma, 1912–17, served the Czar by mobilizing support for Imperial Russia's involvement in World War I, but as the war effort faltered and the Czar packed the ministry with incompetent and complacent appointees, the Duma began to play an oppositional role. That the Dumas managed to pass some meaningful legislation is less a testimony to royal cooperation than to the increasing bankruptcy of the czarist system as an agent of governance. In October 1917, the Duma, along with czarist institutions, was swept away by the Bolshevik Revolution. *See also* AUTOCRACY, p. 8; BOLSHEVIK REVOLUTION, p. 12.

Significance   The Duma, and any possibility for the development of representative democracy in Russia, was aborted by Nicholas II's implacable commitment to royal absolutism. The Czar had agreed to the creation of the Duma only in the face of revolution; once the danger waned he insisted that its role be primarily advisory. The electoral rules shut out moderates and liberals; by the Third Duma the landed gentry controlled over 50 percent of the votes while urban workers had only 1 percent. Thus, from the beginning, the representative nature of the Duma was compromised by the Czar's insistence on maintaining royal absolutism and the skewed electoral proceedings he imposed in order to maintain that absolutism. The deputies themselves were hampered by a lack of parliamentary experience, which was exacerbated by the Czar's refusal to establish a working relationship with the Duma. Furthermore, of the major political parties only the Kadets (Constitutional Democrats) were truly committed to a working, democratic parliament. Both the leftists and the rightists sought to bring down the Duma. Thus, by 1917 imperial Russia almost totally lacked experience in representative democracy or constitutional monarchy. The abrupt fall of the czarist monarchy in March 1917 was far less the result of an organized and determined political opposition than of the simple recognition that the sclerotic czarist order could no longer function. Its successor, the short-lived Provisional Government, disintegrated with equal rapidity in the revolution engineered by the Bolsheviks in October 1917.

Great Purge   The mass terror by which Josef Stalin subjected the Communist Party of the Soviet Union to his personal rule and imposed a paralyzing terror on Soviet society in the 1930s. The Great Purge encompasses roughly the period from 1934 to 1938, the peak occurring in 1936–38. The term purge derives from the Russian word *chistka*, literally "cleansing," and originally referred to the periodic evaluation of party loyalty through an exchange of membership cards; in Stalin's time it came to literally mean a cleansing of the party through mass murder. Although the Great Purge was focused on the party, it extended to all of society. There were two components: the staged public "show" trials of party leaders, and the concomitant terror applied to Soviet society by sentencing millions to prison labor camps. The victims ranged from surviving members of Vladimir Lenin's Politburo to hundreds of thousands of ordinary citizens swept into the *Gulag*, the labor camp system. The most prominent target of the show trials was not present: Leon Trotsky, Stalin's chief rival for power in the 1920s. Many of the party leaders tried were charged with complicity in Trotskyite conspiracies. The purge was so pervasive that to list its victims is to describe Soviet society. Included were the "Old Bolsheviks" whose membership dated to prerevolutionary days, ten close associates of Lenin, six Politburo members, half of the 1934 Party Congress, and 70 percent of the Central Committee. By 1938 party membership had declined by 1.6 million. To imagine that all these committed communists had plotted to overthrow the regime is fatuous; their "crimes" were that in some way they appeared to pose a potential challenge to Stalin's dictatorial power. In the purge that swept the Red Army in 1937, three marshals, half the generals, and from 15,000 to 35,000 officers perished. Foreign communists living in Moscow were executed or disappeared. Non-Russian nationalities were especially hard hit, charged as "bourgeois nationalists." Some of the best of Soviet intellectual life died in the camps. Estimates of the toll vary from 3 to 12 million, with some maintaining that as many as 30 million eventually perished. Stalin's chosen instrument was the secret police (NKVD). Special NKVD boards (OSSO) sentenced hundreds of thousands in secret, extralegal proceedings from which there was no appeal. The Gulag became an integral part of the economic plan, providing prison labor for massive construction projects. In the end, Stalin possessed a subservient party whose apparatus owed their positions solely to him. The term Great Purge is usually applied to the worst years of Stalinist terror, but in reality the purges were part of a process begun earlier and continued well past 1938. At the end of World War II, Stalin reapplied the terror. The purges were exported to Eastern Europe where, during the 1950s, they served to rid the East European parties of any suspected nationalists or "Titoists." At the time of his death in 1953, Stalin was apparently plotting a revival of the purge trials, centering around a purported Jewish "doctors' plot" to assassinate the leadership. *See also* COLLECTIVIZATION, p. 185; DE-STALINIZATION, p. 318; GULAG, p.259; KGB, p. 288; KHRUSHCHEVISM, p. 49; STALINISM, p. 78; ZEK, p. 274.

Significance   The extent and horror of the Great Purge attests to the total power wielded by Stalin. Through the purges he achieved control over the party, the army, foreign communist parties, and Soviet society. The purges also offered upward mobility as an entire generation of officials were replaced by Stalin's men. Some analysts maintain that only when Yuri Andropov and his generation pass from the scene will the Soviet party possibly be rid of the heritage of the purges. The terror ended only with Stalin's death. One of the first acts of his successors was to execute Lavrenti Beria, Stalin's NKVD chief. Nikita Khrushchev's de-Stalinization campaign centered on an effort to deal with Stalin's atrocities. Khrushchev however avoided the more fundamental issue of the complicity of the party itself; like Khrushchev, the party leaders had begun their careers under Stalin. Khrushchev's insistence on further examination of the purges may have contributed subsequently to his ouster in 1964. Since then, the party has refused to reopen the issue. Many others besides Khrushchev have struggled to come to terms with the Great Purge and its implications. Explanations vary, including: (1) Stalin was a degenerate madman—a latter day Caligula—possessed by an insatiable desire for power; (2) Once freed from party control, the secret police became a "state within a state"; (3) In a vast, heterogeneous and impoverished society, the party could survive only by an iron dictatorship; (4) Soviet society was not yet sufficiently communized to achieve the sacrifices required for industrialization; (5) State-directed compulsion and terror has always been a fundamental part of Russian and Soviet political culture; (6) The purges destroyed the most staunchly anti-German Bolsheviks, along with most Jews, and thus prepared the ground for Stalin's pact with Hitler's Germany; and (7) Soviet communism is inherently immoral—an argument made by Aleksandr Solzhenitsyn. Since the Great Purge, communism has been characterized frequently by bloody repressions, a feature it shares with other systems labeled as totalitarian. The striking feature about such repressions is that the brutality and terror are directed inwardly, inflicted on the party and the populace. Destructive as the Great Purge was, the Soviet Union of the 1930s cannot be viewed as an unmitigated disaster. Under Stalin it achieved industrialization, largely through its own efforts, and laid the foundation for a modern state. This holds an unfortunate attraction for those who, like the Pol Pot regime of Cambodia, seek to emulate the system of total control through terror.

International Brigades   Volunteer military units that fought with the Spanish Republican Army against General Francisco Franco's forces during the Spanish Civil War (1936–39). The International Brigades were formed in October 1936 as a response to Franco accepting aid from fascist Germany and Italy. The cause of the Spanish Republicans, at the time the legally elected government of Spain, attracted worldwide support as a crusade against the threat of fascism. The signing of the Non-Intervention Pact by most Western nations left the way open for the Soviet Union, through the Comintern, to direct the volunteer brigades. Georgi Dimitrov, head of the Comintern, the Soviet-dominated international communist organization, directed the recruitment. Within the Brigades, communists and socialists dominated; communist parties in many countries and territories sent delegations. The Soviet Union sent equipment and top military personages, including future Marshals Rodion Malinovsky, Evan Konev, and Konstantin Rokossovsky, as advisors. Leadership of the Brigades rested with André Marty, French communist, and Luigi Longo, later Secretary-General of the postwar Italian Communist Party. Participation was by no means confined to communists. Many idealistic young Europeans and Americans made their way to Spain, and were funnelled across the border by the underground network set up in France by Josip Broz Tito of Yugoslavia. Fascist aid proved decisive, however, and the fears of many who served in the International Brigades were realized with the coming of World War II. *See also* COMINTERN, p. 314; YUGOSLAV PARTISAN WAR, p. 35.

Significance   The roster of those who fought in Spain with the International Brigades reads like a list of communist, socialist, and leftist intellectual luminaries of the 1930s and 1940s. Their fates differed dramatically. Many of the communist participants rose to the top after communism came to power in postwar Eastern Europe. Prominent postwar leaders who were involved in the Spanish Civil War include Tito, László Rajk of Hungary, Walter Ulbricht of East Germany, Georgi Dimitrov of Bulgaria, and Palmiro Togliatti of Italy, all of them leaders of their respective communist parties. The Yugoslavs involved with the International Brigades formed the core of the postwar communist leadership in that country; the list includes Tito, Milovan Djilas, Koča Popović, Alexander Ranković, Aleš Bebler, Boris Kidrić, and Veljko Vlahović. Many analysts have attributed the dramatic success of the communist-led Yugoslav Partisan movement against the Axis during World War II to the training its leaders received in conducting guerrilla war in a mountainous country against a better-equipped, mechanized army. At one point, 24 generals in the postwar Yugoslav Army had served in Spain. After the expulsion of

Yugoslavia from the Soviet bloc in 1948, Stalin's paranoia fastened on the Spanish Civil War veterans as possibly tainted by nationalism and Titoism. Most were executed or removed from their positions in the Soviet-directed purge trials which swept Eastern Europe in the early 1950s. The most prominent victims were László Rajk, Rudolf Slánský, Arthur Koestler, and Artur London of Czechoslovakia. The American members of the Lincoln Battalion also suffered. In the 1950s when the anticommunist repression engendered by the Cold War engulfed the United States, Spanish Civil War veterans, many of whom had fought in World War II, were often charged with being subversives. Associations with the International Brigades surfaced once more in Eastern Europe in 1968. Many of the sizable Czechoslovak contingent survived the purges of the 1950s to play a leading role in the 1968 reform movement; prominent in the Prague Spring were: Frantisek Kreigel, member of the 1968 Presidium; Leopold Hoffman, Chairman of the Army Security Committee; Karel Dufek, Foreign Minister; and General Ludvík Svoboda, who served as President of Czechoslovakia. The lessons of the Spanish Civil War extended beyond the testing of military armaments and tactics, or the leadership training it provided for so many communists. The Popular Front, the instrument through which Stalin seized control over postwar Eastern Europe, was launched by the Spanish Civil War and the International Brigades. For the first time, communists were ordered to cooperate with noncommunist parties in a Popular Front against fascism. Operating from a position of strength, the Soviet leadership learned how to manipulate a popular front movement by occupying the leading positions and, one by one, isolating the democratic groups involved, a tactic they were to use in Eastern Europe in the wake of World War II.

Julian Calendar   The calendar used in prerevolutionary Russia, replaced by the Gregorian Calendar in February 1918 by the new Soviet regime. The Julian Calendar, introduced in 46 B.C. by Julius Caesar, differs from the Gregorian Calendar by 13 days. The Gregorian calendar is now used throughout most parts of the world; its adoption by the Bolsheviks brought Russia into line with the modern world.

Significance   The shift from the Julian system to the Gregorian causes confusion in dating events in Russia. The usual method is to retain the Julian dates for all events occurring before February 1918. Thus, the 1917 Bolshevik Revolution occurred in October by the Julian system and is accordingly referred to as the October Revolution, even though its Gregorian date places it in November.

Kornilov Affair   The term that describes the events of August 1917, when General Lavr Kornilov, Supreme Commander of the Russian Army under Alexander Kerensky's Provisional Government, moved troops toward Petrograd (Leningrad) with the announced aim of restoring order to the country. Kornilov's apparent goals were to destroy the revolutionary Petrograd Soviet, which was in effect sharing power with the Provisional Government, and to reorganize the country. Kornilov may have planned a military coup aimed at restoring the czarist regime, which led both Kerensky and the Bolsheviks to oppose his action. No actual fighting occurred; the attempt simply dissipated as Bolshevik agitators persuaded the ranks to desert, and others impeded the march by destroying communications. Kerensky branded Kornilov a traitor and arrested him along with General Anton Denikin and other alleged conspirators. Kerensky played a deceptive role in the Kornilov affair; first he arrested Kornilov, but then he refused to prosecute him. By his duplicity, Kerensky lost the support of the conservatives who had supported Kornilov, but he failed to compensate by gaining from the left wing Social Revolutionaries and Bolsheviks. Kornilov later escaped to the White Army, led by Anton Denikin, and during the civil war was killed at Rostov in March 1918. With his death, the anti-Bolshevik forces lost a major figure. *See also* BOLSHEVIK REVOLUTION, p. 12.

Significance   The consequences of the Kornilov affair were far-reaching. It polarized Russian society and effectively destroyed the Russian army as a military weapon. The Bolshevik slogan, "Bread, land, and peace," aimed at taking Russia out of the war, appealed increasingly to the army rank and file. By his handling of the Kornilov affair, Kerensky lent credence to the Bolshevik claim that the officers were counterrevolutionaries pursing an imperialistic war. The last ties between officers and ranks in the Russian army were severed, desertions became prevalent, and the army began to collapse. The Provisional Government was seriously weakened by the Kornilov Affair. Kerensky formally dissolved the Duma, one of the last sources of legitimacy of the Provisional Government, and dismissed much of the cabinet, enabling him to rule through a secret directorate. The disintegration of the army and Provisional Government was accompanied by increasing anarchy. The Bolsheviks, supported by many Mensheviks and Social Revolutionaries, used the Kornilov affair to unify opposition to the increasingly inept Provisional Government. Kerensky, in a desperate search for allies against Kornilov, released many of the Bolshevik leaders, including Leon Trotsky. The powerful Petrograd Soviet created a Committee for the Defense of the Revolution and armed thousands of workers. Later renamed the Military

Revolutionary Committee and placed under Trotsky's leadership, this Committee played a major role in the October Revolution that brought the Bolsheviks to power. Kornilov's abortive attempt strengthened the Bolsheviks; by September they had gained majorities in the crucial Petrograd and Moscow Soviets. Conditions in the countryside deteriorated as many peasants believed the Bolsheviks' charge that the Provisional Government intended to restore the old regime. Crime and illegal seizure of land by the peasants increased and local adventurers seized power in many provincial centers. By October, the Provisional Government, stripped of any meaningful military capacity, had lost control over large sectors of the society. The better-organized Bolsheviks, backed by increasing numbers of workers and peasants, came to fill the leadership vacuum created by the Provisional Government. Thus, when the Bolsheviks seized power in October, they met with very little organized resistance. Kornilov's attempted coup represents more a catalyst than a direct cause of the Bolshevik Revolution of 1917. His attempt to apply a military solution to what was essentially a political problem only deepened the divisions within the already polarized and chaotic Russian society. Kerensky, in a book by the same title, termed the Kornilov affair "The Prelude to Bolshevism." The Kornilov affair was crucial in shaping the political developments of 1917 that led to the Bolshevik seizure of power.

Kronstadt Revolt   A rebellion in March 1921 against the Bolshevik regime by the sailors stationed at Kronstadt naval base, a fortified island near Leningrad. The Kronstadt sailors set up a Provisional Revolutionary Committee and demanded that the Bolshevik government grant freedom of speech for all workers' and peasants' groups, free all political prisoners, and permit free elections by secret ballot to the Soviets (councils). Essentially, the Kronstadt sailors demanded freedom for all worker-based parties and an end to the political monopoly of the communist party. Under Lenin's direction, the party responded with armed attack and within days took the island fortress and put down the revolt. After the fall of Kronstadt, hundreds were imprisoned or executed without benefit of public trial. *See also* WORKERS OPPOSITION, p. 34.

Significance   The rebellion of the Kronstadt sailors constituted a revolt against the increasingly dictatorial style of the Bolsheviks; their demands were not aimed at dismantling socialism but at implementing the democratic promises of the Bolshevik Revolution. The revolt was a traumatic event for the Bolsheviks because the Kronstadt sailors had provided key support in the 1917 Revolution. The willingness of the

Bolsheviks to use force against their erstwhile comrades demonstrated Lenin's determination to use whatever means were necessary to maintain strict party discipline and suppress all opposition.

Kulak   A Russian word that describes a rich peasant who gained his wealth by hiring and exploiting peasant labor. The *Kulak*s became the main scapegoat of Stalin's drive to collectivize forcibly Soviet agriculture, in which a Kulak often was defined as any peasant who opposed collectivization. The origins of the term lie in the fact that a few Kulaks in prerevolutionary Russia were well enough off to act as village moneylenders; "Kulak" means "fist" and refers to their role as usurers. Although a Kulak was presumed to be a rich peasant, the definition of "rich" was manipulated by the party. They comprised from 5 to 7 percent of the peasantry, although many of these were poor by western standards. At times, a Kulak was defined as anyone who managed to produce a surplus for the market, no matter how small. Before collectivization, Kulak households produced about 20 percent of the total grain harvest, and during the relaxed period of the New Economic Plan in the 1920s they provided most of the surplus for urban consumption. The collectivization of the 1930s brought about the liquidation of the Kulak class. Hundreds of thousands were deported to the far east where many starved to death, and their lands, livestock, machinery and personal possessions were confiscated. *See also* COLLECTIVIZATION, p. 185; GREAT PURGE, p. 17.

Significance   The liquidation of the Kulak class stripped Soviet agriculture of its most productive and innovative farmers. Agricultural production in the Soviet Union lagged behind pre-1929 levels for over a decade. Lenin predicted that the poorer peasants would be vigorous supporters of communism, but the richer ones would oppose it. Thus the labeling of the Kulaks as a class enemy was consistent with Marxism-Leninism. It also had the effect of dividing the peasant class. The extent and brutality of the repression of the Kulaks was not replicated in postwar Eastern Europe when most of those communist states collectivized agriculture.

Left Opposition   A term applied to that wing of the early Soviet Communist Party most devoted to pursuing revolutionary internationalism and a radical transformation of society, usually through rapid industrialization and a centralized planned economy. The Left Opposition and its counterpart, the Right Opposition, are factions that predate the Bolshevik Revolution. In the early prerevolutionary years, this factionalization led to the formation of the left-wing Bolsheviks and the right-wing Mensheviks. Left Oppositionists first became prominent in the Bolshevik party during the conflict over the signing of the Treaty of Brest-Litovsk when elements of the party opposed Vladimir Lenin's negotiations with an imperialist power. The struggle became more acute during the years of Lenin's physical decline (1922–24) as several individuals competed for his position, and became even more pronounced after his death in 1924. The power struggle occurred within the context of the New Economic Policy (NEP) and represented both a political battle for leadership and an internal debate over the proper economic policy. Leon Trotsky assumed leadership of the Left Opposition against the Right Opposition, led by Nikolai Bukharin. Initially, Bukharin was supported by Grigori Zinoviev and Lev Kamenev, who with Josef Stalin as General Secretary of the Party constituted a ruling troika, or triumvirate, after Lenin's death. Despite the implied compromise with the peasants represented by the NEP, Lenin until his death had maintained that a private peasantry and a free market for agricultural products would engender capitalism; however, he mitigated this stand by arguing that the peasants had to be convinced of the advantages of socialism, not coerced into accepting it. Lenin left his successors to wrestle with the underlying problem posed by the NEP: since the market surplus for the cities would inevitably come from the better-off peasants, who would be further enriched by their success, such private agriculture appeared to encourage the growth of capitalism, as any peasant who produced for the market stood to gain personally. Bukharin, who during the Revolution had been a leader of the left wing, became a moderate. As leader of what Stalin later labeled the "right-wing deviationists," Bukharin maintained that the NEP should be continued for at least a generation, arguing that any attempt to coerce the peasants and reinstitute mandatory state grain deliveries would enrage them into rebellion. Bukharin's thesis was countered by the Left Opposition and Trotsky. Trotsky's position centered on the doctrine of "primitive socialist accumulation" and opposition to "socialism in one country." Marx had argued that in the early stages of Western industrialization, the necessary capital had been expropriated from the peasants and from external colonies. Since the Bolshevik Revolution had been "premature"—that is, it hadn't occurred, as Marx had predicted, in a fully industrialized nation—the prime task was to build industrialization, and the crux of the problem was to find the source of necessary capital. Trotsky and his chief theoretician, Evgeny Preobrazhensky, pointed out that Russia had no external colonies, and under the NEP peasant produce couldn't be expropriated. Yet, the newly nationalized industrial sector was too small to provide surplus capital, leaving only the private sector, the peasants. Preobrazhensky couched this in terms of a conflict between capitalism, represented by the peasants, and socialism, represented by the industrial workers. The Left attacked the party majority for being too soft on the rich peasants, the Kulaks, and too timid in pursuing industrialization. Stalin and Bukharin countered with the argument that the policies advocated by the Left Opposition would endanger party control and the newly won stability. Stalin added the formulation of "Socialism in one country," a theory aimed to counter Trotsky's hopes for a worldwide revolution. Socialist revolution in Western Europe, Trotsky held, would create mature socialist systems that would support the Bolsheviks' industrialization programs. Zinoviev and Kamenev, initially supporters of Bukharin, switched sides. Stalin gained control of the party apparatus and by 1925 began to eliminate his opposition, forcing Trotsky, Zinoviev, and Kamenev off the Politburo. By 1928, Stalin had succeeded in destroying both the Left and the Right Opposition. His power secured, Stalin then halted the New Economic Policy, adopted centralized planning and the First Five-Year Plan, and initiated forced collectivization of agriculture, policies originally proposed by Trotsky and the Left Opposition. *See also* NEW ECONOMIC POLICY, p. 218; TROTSKYISM, p. 81.

Significance   The defeat of the Left Opposition signified the end of meaningful intraparty debate and marked the beginning of Stalinist totalitarianism. Stalin began the policy of "building socialism in one country," renouncing Trotsky's internationalism. The secret resolution condemning factions passed by the Tenth Party Congress in 1921 was made public within the party, giving party expulsions for various "deviations" and "factionalism" the imprimatur of Lenin. Trotsky was forced into exile, eventually to be assassinated by Stalin's agents in Mexico in 1940. Stalin's final reckoning with both the Left and Right Oppositions came during the Great Purge of the 1930s when most of the Old Bolsheviks who had at one time sided with either faction were tried and executed. Because the Left Opposition lost the political battle, they have been characterized by Stalin and his successors as antisocialist, anti-industrializing, and defeatist. Yet, neither the Left nor the Right had questioned the primacy of the party, nor the need for rapid industrialization. Although many of the Old Bolsheviks who were executed in the thirties were posthumously rehabilitated during the Khrushchev era, Trotsky and Bukharin are still anathema to the Soviet Communist Party.

Menshevik   A faction of the Russian Social Democratic Labor Party (RSDLP) that in the tumultuous period before and during World

War I opposed Vladimir Lenin's tactics of unconditional party discipline and the need for immediate revolution as the only path to a socialist society. Although the word Menshevik means "member of the minority" in Russian, the more moderate Mensheviks originally constituted the majority in the RSDLP, Russia's first Marxist socialist party. The Menshevik wing of Russian Marxism was formed after a clash with Lenin in 1903; the gulf widened after 1905 when the czar reluctantly agreed to permit the election of an elected parliament, the Duma. Two major issues divided the Mensheviks and Lenin's Bolsheviks: party organization, and whether to participate in the Duma. The Mensheviks opposed Lenin's insistence that a Marxist party must be confined to a small group of professional revolutionaries, bound by hierarchical party discipline to the central leadership. Their preference was for building a party of mass membership among the working class, operated democratically and committed to participating in the electoral system. Essentially, they differed over the proper interpretation of Marxist doctrine. The Mensheviks held that only after capitalism had fully developed in Russia would the proletariat-based revolution that would usher in socialism be possible. When the czarist government fell in March 1917, two members of the Mensheviks took part in the Provisional Government. The Mensheviks opposed the popular Bolshevik policy of taking Russia out of World War I, and thus lost influence and power in the workers' soviets, the *ad hoc* worker assemblies that controlled much of the capital city, where they initially held a majority of seats. The Bolsheviks, who were not bound by gradualism and commitment to democratic forms, rallied the people with promises of "Bread, land, and peace," "All power to the soviets," immediate land reform for the peasants, and the withdrawal of Russia from the war. The inability, if not reluctance, of the Bolsheviks to deliver on these promises made little difference in the events of October 1917, when the well-organized Bolsheviks ousted the Provisional Government. *See also* AGRARIAN POPULISM, p. 3; BOLSHEVIK, p. 10; LENINISM, p. 51.

Significance   Because the Mensheviks ultimately lost the power struggle to the Bolsheviks and Lenin, their true nature has been obscured. In the aftermath of the Bolshevik Revolution and the ensuing Civil War, Lenin cast them in the role of major opponent of the socialist order. The term Menshevik became a term of opprobrium; it was claimed that Mensheviks were responsible for most of the sabotage after the Revolution. Western analysts and opponents of Bolshevism paint them as true democrats, representatives of Russia's lost opportunity to develop democracy consistent with Western forms. They were neither. The Mensheviks were committed to a Marxist, proletarian revolution that would destroy capitalism. They differed from the

Bolsheviks only in their sense of timing, and their interpretation of Marxism. Where Lenin was willing to adapt Marxism to Russian conditions, the Mensheviks supported Marx's original dictum that the revolution would occur only in mature, fully developed capitalist states. Thus, they were willing to maintain democratic forms and cooperate with the Russian constitutionalist movement, accepting Marx's dictum that capitalism is a necessary stage of development. For Lenin, the Mensheviks represented a basic threat to his insistence that the Bolsheviks were the only true interpreters of Marxism. As with any dogma, the heretic is always more of a threat than the unbeliever, and the Mensheviks were persecuted accordingly as traitors and saboteurs. During the Stalinist purges of the 1930s, many of the major victims were cast as Mensheviks, although it is doubtful that many true Mensheviks had survived until then. Leon Trotsky, who originally had vacillated between the Mensheviks and Bolsheviks, was the major *bête noire* of Stalin, and anyone who was remotely connected with Trotsky was accused of Menshevikism. The punitive reaction, first of Lenin, and then Stalin, to the Mensheviks may have rested in the fear that the Mensheviks' attempt to meld Marxist socialism and democracy might prove attractive to the Soviet people.

Mir   The Russian village organization based on joint family and communal ownership of the land. The *mir* (or *obshchina*) was the basic social unit in prerevolutionary Russia. Under serfdom, it functioned as an agent of the landlord to collect taxes and military recruits for the czar. The most important function of the village council (*skhod*), composed of all male members, was the periodic redistribution (*peredel*) of the communal village land. When the serfs were emancipated in 1861, they were still legally tied to the village, subject to the village assembly for justice and land allocation. The mir impeded both modernization of agriculture and the industrialization of the country. In 1906 government legislation encouraged the dissolution of the mir, but such was the attachment of the peasants to this traditional form that by 1913 only 17.7 percent of the peasant households had left the mir. *See also* AGRARIAN POPULISM, p. 3; KOLKHOZ, p. 205; SERFDOM, p. 32.

Significance   The mir was romanticized by the nineteenth century Russian Slavophiles who rejected Western culture and held up the communally based mir as proof of the innate superiority of the Russian people. The idealization of Russian peasant communalism became the basis for several populist movements in the late nineteenth century, including *Chernyi Peredel* (Black Repartition), founded in 1879 by Georgi Plekhanov. A precursor to Russia's first Marxist party, Chernyi

Peredel included many of the original Mensheviks. Some of the early agrarian populists and socialists argued that, thanks to the inherently communal nature of the mir, Russia need not pass through the horrors of Western-style industrialization in order to achieve socialism. Proponents of an agrarian-based revolution (the *Narodniki* and others) drew on the ancient peasant faith in a final *chernyi peredel*, the Black Repartition, which would have given all the land to its rightful tillers. The failure of the mir-based populism under the repressive Alexander II paved the way for the birth of a Marxist socialist movement which focused on revolution by the workers. Although the Soviet communists have advanced the collective farm as a reincarnation of the traditional peasant mir, the analogy is flawed; unlike the peasants of the communist collective farms, the peasants of the mir farmed individually and owned their output, and the mir retained landownership, not the state.

Ottoman Empire   The name given to the Turkish empire, which ruled over the present territories of Albania, Bulgaria, Romania, and Yugoslavia for over four centuries. The name *Ottoman Empire* derives from the Ottoman dynasty, the ruling house of the Empire until 1922. The modern Balkan states achieved their independence as Ottoman power waned during the nineteenth and twentieth centuries, the last territories being liberated as a result of World War I. *See also* AUSTRO-HUNGARIAN EMPIRE, p. 7; BALKAN QUESTION, p. 9.

Significance   Balkan political culture was shaped by centuries of Ottoman domination, emerging in the nineteenth and twentieth centuries as distinct from Western European cultures. The most distinctive feature of the Ottoman Empire was that it was a non-Christian, non-modernizing, non-Western, feudal imperium. The Ottoman Empire was a military-theocratic organization with no concept of Western civil law or administration. Ottoman subjects were classified not by nationality but by religion, the non-Islamic subjects of the Balkans being *reayas*. Ottoman policy was geared mainly toward collecting taxes; the Ottoman lands did not develop a modern agriculture, universal schooling, industrial centers, or the hallmarks of nineteenth-century Western industrialization. When the Balkan states gained independence, they were 80 to 90 percent illiterate, possessed about one-fourth the number of roads as central Europe, and had no native landowning aristocracies. Balkan nationalism emerged in the nineteenth century, fueled by the decline of Ottoman power. As peasant lands, these nationalisms were peasant-based; for example, the leaders of the Serbian revolts of 1815–30 which first freed a portion of the Balkans, were peasants before they were kings. Romania achieved independence in 1859, Bulgaria in 1878, and the remaining Balkan peoples were finally liberated in 1912–18. The divergencies between Ottoman rule and the modernizing Habsburg rule have weighed particularly heavily on the modern Yugoslav state, first constituted in 1919 from portions of the two empires around the core of independent Serbia. The Yugoslav (South Slav) peoples, merged into the new Kingdom of Serbs, Croats and Slovenes, had not only lived under different foreign powers, but in two different worlds—the one European, Roman Catholic, and modernized, the other Orthodox Catholic, Byzantine in heritage, and peasant. The conflict between north and south in Yugoslavia continues to pose severe problems as the cultural cleavages are reinforced by nationality divisions. These differences are replicated in the broader differences between the Balkan states and the central European states; notwithstanding a common experience under communism for almost 40 years, their political traditions and levels of economic development still reflect the centuries-long division of central and southern Europe between two vastly different empires.

PanSlavism   The movement aimed at uniting all Slavic peoples under the leadership of Russia. PanSlavism arose out of the nationalistic ferment that swept Europe after the Napoleonic wars. In their quest for self-determination, the various Slavic peoples of the Austro-Hungarian and Ottoman Empires turned to the idea of a common origin of all Slavs and sought the protection of the Russian Empire. In turn, Czarist Russia used panSlavism to support its expansionist goals, particularly against the Ottoman Empire. By the end of the eighteenth century, as many of the Slavic peoples achieved their independence, the panSlavic movement declined. The ideal of Slavic brotherhood remained, however, and in the interwar period it aided the communist movement in achieving adherents among the Slavs of Eastern Europe. *See also* AUSTRO-HUNGARIAN EMPIRE, p. 7; OTTOMAN EMPIRE, p. 29.

Significance   After World War II the Soviet Union achieved part of the old dream of panSlavism by organizing a state system in Eastern Europe which included the Slavic peoples under the tutelage of the Soviet Union. Residual panSlavic sentiment may have aided the Soviets in achieving power in some parts of Eastern Europe; it is frequently maintained that only the Soviet-led invasion of Czechoslovakia finally eradicated the remnants of panSlavism in that country. Soviet propaganda plays up the Soviet role as protector of all Slavdom by constantly referring to the threat of German revanchism and pointing out that the Western powers failed to protect the Slavic nations from Hitler.

Polish Partitions   Successive divisions of Poland from 1772 to 1796 by which Russia, Prussia, and Austria-Hungary divided up the Polish state. In the last partition, Poland, which had been a political unit for eight centuries, disappeared from the map of Europe. Imperial Russia received the bulk of the Polish lands, which in 1815 (Congress of Vienna) were constituted as Congress Poland and placed directly under the czar. *See also* SOLIDARITY, p. 303.

Significance   The Polish partitions have been a major determinant of Polish political culture, leaving the Poles with an undying hatred of both Germans and Russians, which World War II and the communization of Poland exacerbated. The czars for many years carried out a policy of Russification in Poland, but the 122 years of occupation were marked by recurring nationalistic revolts against the Russians. The Polish Catholic Church became the major carrier of nationalism, a role it continues to play today. Nationalism and religion became fused in Poland. The events of World War II deepened traditional Polish hatreds. In September 1939, World War II began as the German armies invaded Poland from the West and Soviet armies moved in from the East. Although German occupation of Poland was more brutal, many Poles remember that Soviet armies also participated in the dismemberment of the new Polish state that had been reconstituted in 1918, a division some termed the "fourth partition." Thus Poland, of all the East European states, is marked by an endemic bitterness toward the Russians. The imposition of communism in Poland stirred old nationalistic hatreds, evinced in several outbreaks against Soviet control and culminating in the Solidarity movement of 1980–81.

Russification   Czarist policy aimed at assimilating non-Russians into Russian culture and, when possible, converting them to Orthodox Christianity. Russification became official czarist policy as the imperial Russian Empire was expanded in the sixteenth and seventeenth centuries to include millions of non-Russian peoples. In the non-Russian provinces, those who aspired to a position in the civil service, the military, or in the field of commerce had to speak and read Russian. Czarist discrimination against non-Russian peoples produced a sense of grievance, particularly among those who followed a religion other than Orthodox Christianity, the official state religion of the Russian Empire. Groups such as Jews, Armenians, Georgians, and Balts were heavily represented in the early Bolshevik movement. Initially, the new Soviet state won many adherents by encouraging cultural autonomy and by establishing republics for the major nationalities within a federal system. By the 1930s, however, traditional bias toward the major nationality had reasserted itself and Josef Stalin, a Georgian himself, propagated Russian as the language of socialism and purged the party of many minority members. *See also* FEDERALISM: USSR, p. 143; TERRITORIAL DIVISIONS (USSR): UNION-REPUBLIC, p. 174.

Significance   Some analysts maintain that Russification describes the current policies of the Soviet leadership, by which Russians, and to some extent Ukrainians, play a dominant role in Soviet society. Most of the Jews and other minorities have disappeared from the top ranks of the party. Although the Bolsheviks' promise of cultural identity for all nationalities has largely been maintained, the political dynamics of a centralized one-party system continue to disadvantage non-Russians, who constitute just under 50 percent of the population. Soviet schools provide education in the native language for language groups as small as 3,000, but Russian remains the language of politics and the key to success. Of all periodicals in circulation, 85 percent are in Russian. In non-Russian republics and provinces, the common practice is to select either the director or deputy director of an enterprise from the local population while filling the second post with a Russian. Party membership is about 62 percent Russian, and Russian domination of the party apparatus is even more marked. The extent of an official effort to propagate Russian culture remains unclear, but there is little doubt that the Russian nationality dominates party and government, as it did under the czars.

Serfdom   The dominant institution of czarist Russia, by which the peasants were bound in perpetuity to the land and the landowner. Under serfdom, the peasants were essentially chattels, obliged to render taxes and labor to the landlord and to furnish conscripts to the army. In turn the landowner enjoyed the rights of nobility only at the will of the czar. Although such systems have existed since antiquity, only imperial Russia continued into modern times a system of autocracy that rested on the institution of serfdom. At the time of the Emancipation Edict of 1861, approximately 80 percent of the Russian population was bound to the land, half under the authority of the landlords and half as state peasants, tied to crown lands. All were subject to the head (soul) tax and to army conscription and could not legally leave their villages. Serfdom in Russia developed in the fifteenth and sixteenth centuries during the period of czarist centralization, as a series of edicts successively bound the peasants to the land. Under Peter the Great (1689–1725) most of the remaining free peasants were enserfed. In essence, the crown made a bargain with the nobility, protecting their authority over the serfs in exchange for service to the crown. As a result, both noble and serf were essentially dependent on the crown. Except for a small class of "grand nobles" (estimated at about 1,400 families), landownership was extremely fragmented and many nobles were almost as impoverished as the serfs. The heart of serfdom was the village, to which each serf was bound. A village cluster of 400 to 500 peasants might be co-owned by 40 landlords, with the land equally fragmented. Russian agriculture therefore remained extremely primitive. A major impetus to the development of serfdom was imperial Russia's geographic vulnerability to invasion across the vast reaches of its unprotected borders. Lacking funds to support a standing army, serfdom enabled the czarist regime to secure a stable pool of involuntary recruits. The enserfed 80 percent of the Russian population lived essentially without benefits from the system, accorded neither protection of the law nor freedom of movement. Typically, estates were divided into the landlord's land, on which the serf was obliged to labor (*corvée*), and individual peasant plots, a forerunner to the private plot system maintained on today's collective farms in the Soviet Union. No legal, formal edict ever certified the landlord's title to the serfs; the serf was bound not to the landlord but to the land, although authority over serfs rested with the landlord. Russia remained a nation of greatly maldistributed wealth. The possession of 100 "souls" constituted the dividing line between gentry and non-gentry; in 1831, only 22,000 serf-owners qualified as gentry, and 1.5 percent (1,400) of the nobles held over 3 million serfs. After decades of wrangling over how and when to free the serfs, Czar Alexander II signed a limited Emancipation Edict in 1861. The landlords retained title to two-thirds of the land, and the remaining land was transferred to the peasant village (*mir*), to which the peasant was still legally tied. The peasants were obliged to make redemption payments and could not move without permission. The government continued to tax the peasants heavily; by 1913 alcohol taxes provided 28 percent of all government revenues. Not until the Revolution of 1905 was Czar Nicholas II forced to grant the peasants full legal equality. Under emancipation, their condition actually worsened, as few received enough fertile land to maintain decent subsistence, let alone pay redemption and taxes. *See also* KOLKHOZ, p. 205; MIR, p. 28.

Significance   The psychological and political legacy of serfdom bore heavily on the Russian state. Russia was periodically torn by peasant revolts, as in the 1670s (Stenka Razin's revolt) and the 1770s (a revolt led by Emelian Pugachev). Although the peasants usually excused the czar as the "Little Father" who was restrained from freeing the peasants only by the wicked nobility, this minimal allegiance dissolved when the czarist structure was destroyed in 1917. The largely peasant army disintegrated, and by October 1917 Vladimir Lenin was able to ride to power with the support of the land-hungry peasants, who rallied to his promise of "bread, land, and peace". Serfdom in Russia was both exploitative and unproductive, stifling the development of the small landowners and energetic middle class that had fueled modernization in the West. Czarist Russia was essentially prefeudal, as the serf was bound not to the lord, but to the land. No counterpart to Russian serfdom existed in the non-Russian lands of Eastern Europe, varied as these individual countries are. Czechoslovakia, for example, became a country of small peasant landowners; in Yugoslavia an intervening feudal system simply never developed. Marxist-Leninist doctrinarians have chosen to describe these historical discontinuities as a supposedly uniform system of historically determined progression. The fact remains, however, that the system imposed upon Russia by the Bolsheviks, in a condition of prefeudalism, was even less applicable to the countries of Eastern Europe, whose social structures differed so markedly from czarist Russia.

Workers Opposition   A faction within the Soviet Communist Party during the first years of Bolshevik rule that called for increased intraparty democracy. The Workers Opposition, led by Alexandra Kollontai and Alexander Shliapnikov, the first Commissar for Labor, argued for increased autonomy for the trade unions, a greater role for workers in decision making, and collective management in industry. They were opposed most vehemently by Leon Trotsky, who argued for the complete subordination of the unions to the Party and expulsion of all members of the Workers Opposition. Vladimir Lenin adopted a centrist position, stating that the unions should be autonomous but not independent of the Party. At the Tenth Party Congress of 1921, Lenin denounced both sides and called for an end to all factions. Instead of forcing the members of the Workers Opposition to resign, he enjoined them to submit to party discipline. *See also* LENINISM: DEMOCRATIC CENTRALISM, p. 52.

Significance   The Workers Opposition constituted a major block to Lenin's concept of a unified party ruled by democratic centralism enforced through party discipline. Its demise signalled the end of any chance for intraparty democracy. At the Tenth Party Congress, Lenin forced through a secret party statute which provided that the Central Committee, by a two-thirds vote, could expel party members, thus bypassing the Congress that was supposedly the ruling body of the Party. Although Lenin's announced intent was to rid the party of factions, the eventual effect was that the party leadership was permitted to cut off all opposition. Party discipline, as defined by the leadership, became mandatory for all; any suspected "factionalism" came to be equated with disloyalty to communism. The statute, which was not made public until 1924, marks a crucial step in the evolution of the Soviet Communist Party toward rigid democratic centralism. By giving the power of expulsion to the leadership, it set in motion the party machinery for the Stalinist purges of the 1930s.

Yugoslav Partisan War   The name given to the extensive, and successful, guerrilla war that communist-led forces waged against the Axis occupiers in Yugoslavia during World War II. The Partisan forces, initially a communist movement under the leadership of Josip Broz Tito, developed into an army of national liberation that involved all of Yugoslavia's many nationalities. Although leadership remained with the communists, the Partisan army was largely noncommunist, including priests and all sectors of society. The Partisans waged a three-cornered battle for Yugoslavia, contending against both the Axis and the nationalist Serbian Chetniks, under the leadership of Draža Mihailović. The program of the Chetniks was the eventual restoration of the Royal Serbian Monarchy, a policy which forced many Chetniks into opposition to the Partisans and eventual collaboration with the Axis. During the internecine battle which developed, the Partisans stressed the ideal of *bratstvo i jedinstvo,* (brotherhood and unity). Tito emphasized the unity and equality of all nationalities, a condition that had been lacking under the prewar Serbian monarchy's governance of Yugoslavia. In November 1943, the Tito-inspired Anti Fascist Council of National Liberation (AVNOJ) created the National Liberation Movement and proclaimed a Provisional Government headed by Tito. AVNOJ set up civil administrative units for the Partisan-liberated territories and promised to create a federated republic that became a reality at the end of the war. By 1944 the Partisans controlled most of Yugoslavia except for the major cities and the Danubian plain. Belgrade was liberated by joint Partisan-Soviet efforts, but the Soviet army did not remain in occupation. Tito set up a communist government unhampered by the Soviets, and Yugoslavia became the second country since the Bolshevik Revolution to achieve communism through an indigenous revolution. *See also* COMINFORM, p. 313; INTERNATIONAL BRIGADES, p. 20; SEPARATE ROADS TO SOCIALISM, p. 77.

Significance   The Partisan War has become the founding ethos of the Socialist Federal Republic of Yugoslavia, giving the Yugoslav Communist Party a legitimacy which no other party in Eastern Europe possesses. It created a communist state that was not dependent on the

Soviet Union for its existence. During the war the Partisan units remained largely isolated and self-sufficient, a necessity for conducting a guerrilla war in a mountainous terrain. Both the Partisan command and the AVNOJ-initiated civil administrative units developed habits of independent decision making. Evidence exists that Josef Stalin was less than pleased with the independent Partisan leadership; the Soviets criticized the formation of AVNOJ. In addition, from 1943 onwards the British supported the Partisans against both Axis and Chetniks, while little Soviet aid was forthcoming. The independent national power base that the Partisan War created enabled the Yugoslav Communist Party to reject postwar Soviet efforts to reduce Yugoslavia to satellite status, resulting in Yugoslavia's ouster from the Soviet bloc in 1948. The subsequent evolution of Yugoslav communism away from Soviet forms and toward liberalization was based largely on the Partisan War. Essentially, the Partisan War transformed a small conspiratorial Balkan party into a broad-based national movement and created in Tito the only communist leader in Eastern Europe with true legitimacy. A similar resistance movement, led by Enver Hoxha, also developed in Albania. Although recognized by the British, Soviets, and Americans in November 1945, the Hoxha government had difficulty asserting its independence from Tito's Yugoslavia until the 1948 Yugoslav-Soviet split. With the split Albania became the favored protégé of the USSR until the Hoxha government broke with the USSR over the issue of de-Stalinization. Although similar in origin to the postwar Yugoslav system, communist Albania has remained the most Stalinist of the East European states.

2. Ideology and Theory

Atheism   A philosophical orientation, which is promoted by the Soviet and other communist governments, that negates the existence of God or supranatural phenomena as a source of creation, behavior, or knowledge. The roots of atheism are traceable to antiquity, but it received impetus as a philosophical movement under the impact of rationalism and the enlightenment during the eighteenth and nineteenth centuries. Marxism and communism are closely linked with the atheist movement. Marxists regard religious conceptions of life and nature, of the place, role, and purpose of human beings as superstition and prejudice that will ultimately disappear in the construction of the new communist society. Religion will be replaced, according to communist doctrine, "by a sober scientific and materialist view of life." Religion, for Marx, is a weapon in the arsenal of the ruling class; it provides an "opiate for the masses" that helps the poor and downtrodden to forget their unhappy existence. In this way it encourages their exploitation by the ruling class. Marx was convinced that man created God, not vice versa. In the past, Marx noted, religion was strong because of human impotence in the face of natural forces, but in a technically developed society, religion increasingly has become a product of unequal class relationships that encourage exploitation and subjugation. *See also* ALL-UNION KNOWLEDGE SOCIETY, p. 275.

Significance   The Soviet Constitution guarantees freedom of conscience to all members of society, giving each citizen the right to pursue any religious faith and to worship any god he or she pleases. Every citizen is also given the right to be an atheist and to engage in antireligious propaganda. The church is separated from the state, and the school from the church, by the Constitution of the USSR. Although Soviet law provides that all religious and church associations of any

37

faith may function freely as voluntary societies maintained by contributions of their followers, much controversy has arisen over the harsh enforcement of other laws and administrative actions undertaken against religious groups and individual members. As a result, formal church membership in the Soviet Union is very small, whereas in other communist countries, such as Poland, up to 90 percent of the population are at least nominal church members. Although worshippers in the Soviet Union are permitted to attend church and engage in church rituals so long as they do not conflict with state policy, Soviet authorities prohibit or discourage all religious activities that involve expansion of the role of religion, such as building new churches and seminaries. Anyone who professes a religious faith is unlikely to obtain a responsible position in the government and certainly not in the communist party. Soviet youth is the prime target for the communist party's indoctrination program of atheism and antireligion. Marxists believe that all religion will disappear as the final classless, stateless society emerges. Soviet efforts to conduct ideological propaganda campaigns abroad have been weakened by the hostility of governments, religious groups, and millions of individual believers to communism's espousal of atheism.

Bourgeoisie   The class of capitalists opposed to the proletariat or worker's class as described in the writings of Karl Marx and Friedrich Engels. Historically, the bourgeoisie was the European middle class, between the nobility and the workers, which functioned in the early days of the Industrial Revolution as a group of entrepreneurs in the capitalistic system. As a class, it was divided into an "upper" (the nouveau riche group of financiers, investors, and wealthy industrialists) and the "lower" or petite (petty) bourgeoisie (middle class merchants, professionals, and property owners). The term bourgeois is often used to describe an individual or his or her attitude, such as a focus on materialistic things and the maintenance of a certain standard of living and way of life. Bourgeois also connotes conservatism or a reactionary view of politics and economics. For Marxists, the term bourgeois democracy is used to describe a formalistic kind of democracy in which the political superstructure of the state is controlled and manipulated by the bourgeoisie, or ruling class. Karl Marx was convinced that true democracy could only exist under communism because material equality formed the keystone of all democratic rights. The Soviets and other communists have often used "bourgeois democracy" in a pejorative sense to describe the political systems of Western Europe and the United States. Bourgeois nationalism has also been used in a pejorative sense to describe nationalistic tendencies among the minority nationalities of the Soviet Union. Nationalism is viewed by the Soviets as a romantic nineteenth-century force that accompanied the rise of the bourgeoisie in Europe. Advocates of greater autonomy organized along ethnic lines are frequently charged with bourgeois nationalism. *See also* MARXISM: CLASS STRUGGLE, p. 58.

Significance   Marx and Engels were ambivalent about the role of the bourgeoisie. On the one hand, they recognized that capitalism was an essential precursor to socialism, and that the bourgeois class was essential to the development of capitalism. Both the class and the system were part of the evolutionary development of society and must play their proper roles. On the other hand, Marx and Engels despised the bourgeoisie for the commission of economic crimes against the proletariat, holding in contempt not only their economic practices but bourgeois values as well. Yet, interestingly, both men were of the bourgeoisie and their lifestyles were more closely identified with the bourgeois class than with the proletariat. Although communists in the Soviet Union and Eastern Europe still use the terms pejoratively, they recognize that much of the support for communism in Western Europe comes from members of the bourgeois class. Also, they have shown a great propensity for doing business with wealthy capitalists from the West. While the terms bourgeois and bourgeoisie are still used by Marxists, the predictions of class struggle and the dictatorship of the proletariat during a period of socialism that emerged from a Marxist class analysis are given less emphasis today. In propaganda, the Soviets currently focus most of their attention on describing the "successes" of the Soviet system and emphasize its role in economic development and modernization, especially as a model for Third World countries, rather than focusing their attention on the class struggle.

Bureaucratic Model   Explanation of Soviet politics that treats the institutionalization of bureaucratic power as a major determinant of the nature of the Soviet system. The bureaucratic model de-emphasizes ideology as a motive factor in Soviet politics. Instead, it focuses on the hierarchical organization of the state and the communist party's arrogation of all power. Theorists point out that the roots of bureaucracy may be discovered in the Leninist organizational structure, in particular, democratic centralism. Once the revolution was secured, bureaucratic power became the guiding principle for the maintenance of the state. As many Sovietologists, such as Alfred Meyer, T. H. Rigby, and Allen Kassof, point out, Soviet society is bureaucratically organized and managed by a small, cohesive leadership, much in the manner in which the top management of a large corporation operates through a complex of appointed officials whose responsibilities are determined by top management. In Kassof's description, the result is "the administered state." *See also* APPARATUS, p. 88; LENINISM, p. 51.

Significance　　The bureaucratic model describes a system in which the state attempts to direct all activities from the center, via a vast, hierarchical chain of command—to be a member of society is to be under command. The Soviet bureaucratic model is characterized by (1) a single command center; (2) the absence of any mediating institutions between citizen and state; and (3) administration of all aspects of life, most particularly the economy. Some analysts, such as Meyer, maintain that the Soviet bureaucracy represents a new type of bureaucracy, a "sovereign bureaucracy," in which party and state are merged.

Capitalism　　An economic doctrine and system based on private ownership of property and the means of production, a competitive, profit-incentive market economy, individual initiative, and the absence of government restraints on ownership, production, consumption, and trade. Marxists are ambivalent about capitalism. On the one hand, they recall that Karl Marx asserted that capitalism was an essential stage in the evolution of human history, replacing earlier slave and feudal systems, and leading eventually to the higher stage of socialism and, finally, to the ultimate stage of pure communism. On the other hand, communists generally regard capitalism as a great evil that must be destroyed because it warps human nature, alienates workers, and dehumanizes all. Adam Smith, who expounded the sophisticated theories and analyses that comprise modern capitalism in his book, *Wealth of Nations* (1776), can be regarded as the "intellectual godfather of modern capitalism," in the same sense that Karl Marx has been proclaimed the "intellectual godfather of modern communism." He and other classical economists developed the ideas of "individualism" and "freedom" that differentiate capitalism from the collective, state-planning philosophies of Marxism-Leninism. *See also* COMMUNISM, p. 41; CONVERGENCE THEORY, p. 44; MARXISM: CONTRADICTIONS OF CAPITALISM, p. 59.

Significance　　Most of the writings of Karl Marx and Friedrich Engels focused on describing and analyzing the basic nature of capitalism, with very little emphasis on the nature of socialism and communism as the anticipated systems of the future. Marxism thus emerges largely as a destructive rather than constructive philosophy.

Despite the harsh verdict on capitalism reached by Marx, Engels, Lenin and others, contemporary communists in Eastern Europe and the Soviet Union have sought to borrow ideas from the capitalist West to engender higher levels of production and in other ways make their systems work better. Reforms, for example, have reduced central planning and rigid state controls over the economy and have moved most Eastern European economies in the direction of profit incentives for individual industries and workers. In the West, capitalism has also been modified by socialist ideas, some of which were first given prominence in the writings of Karl Marx. Despite these adaptations, both ideologies remain implacably hostile to each other's ultimate goals, and a global ideological-political-military struggle continues between the capitalist and communist worlds.

Communism   A political, economic, and social philosophy that proclaims the ideal of a collective society in which land and capital are socially owned and in which class conflict and the coercive power of the state no longer exist. Although numerous political thinkers and social groups since Plato have proclaimed diverse forms of communism as their ideal, modern forms of communism as alternatives to capitalism began to emerge in the nineteenth century developed by socialists and other reformers, such as Claude Saint-Simon, Robert Owen, and François Fourier. Dismissing this group as well as church communalists as "Utopian socialists," Karl Marx and Friedrich Engels developed an ideology of communism based on what they called "scientific socialism" by which social development proceeds according to certain laws that are recognizable and constant, similar to the laws that govern physics and chemistry. For Marx and Engels, the process by which socialism as the first stage of communism will be ushered in involves a class struggle between the proletariat and the bourgeoisie. That struggle culminates in a revolution in which the institutions of capitalism are progressively destroyed by the victorious proletarians through a socialist program implemented under a "dictatorship of the proletariat." The ultimate stage of human evolution will be pure communism that incorporates a classless, stateless society with full social equality, collective ownership of the means of production, and an abundance of goods and services distributed free in accordance with the communist principle of "From each according to his ability, to each according to his needs." The ideas set forth by Marx and Engels have been interpreted, defined, applied, and modified, and new supplementary theories have been developed over the years since the mid-nineteenth century period of the emergence of the modern doctrine of communism. The main contributors to and interpreters of the ideology of communism during the twentieth century include Vladimir Ilyich Lenin, Josef Stalin, Leon Trotsky, Josip Broz Tito, Mao Tse-tung, Nikita Khrushchev, and Leonid Brezhnev, all of whom have held leadership positions in party and government within their respective nations. Lenin's contributions to Marxism have been recognized by the communist world as the most formidable, with the result that the basic ideology is now generally referred to as Marxism-Leninism in all communist-party states. *See also* LENINISM, p. 51; MARXISM, p. 55; STALINISM, p. 78; TITOISM, p. 80; TROTSKYISM, p. 81.

Significance   In the contemporary world, the term communism has diverse meanings. To many Soviet citizens and some East Europeans, communism is the wave of the future, the scientifically determined highest state of human social evolution. The doctrines of communism for such true believers offer explanations for all human ills, and how they will be corrected through a development of socialism leading to the final stage of communism. Western liberals, on the other hand, regard communism as a system with an ideology that permits and encourages totalitarian rule either by one man (Stalinism) or by an oligarchy (the Brezhnev era). Civil liberties are severely curtailed, and the state, rather than beginning to wither away as Marx had predicted, becomes more powerful with each passing year. The ideal of a classless society has given way, according to Western liberals, to the creation in the Soviet Union and in the communist countries of Eastern Europe of a new class of political and bureaucratic elite. For German and French workers, communism often has implied a defense of lower class interests in systems dominated by the middle and upper classes. For many Third World peoples, communism means a shortcut to industrialization and liberation from Western colonialism. Intellectuals around the world regard it as a potential panacea that could produce a perfect society and change human nature if only its promise were not so tarnished by human greed and the lust for power. Thus communism provides different forms of meaning for each group of its supporters and detractors, and each can find much evidence in the ideology and political applications to support its position and condemn those of others. Western social scientists, for example, accept their societies and the values underlying them pretty much as they are, whereas Marxism-Leninism totally rejects contemporary Western society and its basic value of capitalism. Communism as expounded by Marx and Lenin is an ideology, an ethic, and a general philosophy that contains theories about human beings, their society, their history, and their future. Dedicated communists fervently believe that these theories are scientifically derived, whereas most Western social scientists regard them as subjectively developed analyses topped off with idealistic expectations.

Until World War I, communist theories served only as topics for intellectual debate and as a rallying doctrine for unsuccessful agitators in many countries, starting with the issuance of *The Communist Manifesto* in 1848. The Russian military and political collapse in 1917 provided the historical opportunity for the Bolshevik Revolution and for communists to build socialism in one country. In the interwar period, communism proved mainly to be an ideology that engendered fear in many societies, contributing to the success of fascist regimes that justified their repression as the only means for safeguarding the nation from the threat of a communist takeover. Following World War II, occupation by the Red Army helped bring communist regimes into power in Eastern Europe and in North Korea, while indigenous communist forces won the power struggle in China and in Yugoslavia. Although believed by many to be a monolithic force, the communist world was rent by a major Soviet-Chinese schism as each of the communist giants sought to provide the political and ideological leadership for the world communist movement. In the 1970s and 1980s, the communist world became obsessed with achieving economic growth and material improvement, and a new class of technocrats and bureaucrats assumed the leadership in most communist states. Increasingly, the emphasis in communist ideology has shifted from preaching the gospel of revolution and the destruction of capitalism in advanced, industrialized societies, to a new emphasis on proving communism to be a superior social system that can help Third World nations achieve their modernization goals. Also, increasingly, the collective emphasis in communism has been sapped by a tendency to glorify the national leaders and to govern socialist society not through a dictatorship *of* the proletariat but rather by a dictatorship *over* the proletariat in which a powerful elite group makes all important decisions. The "cult of the individual," rejected in all communist literature, has thrived in communist political systems headed by such dynamic personalities as Vladimir Lenin, Josef Stalin, Mao Tse-tung, Ho Chi Minh, Fidel Castro, and Kim Il Sung. Another major *non sequitur* between ideology and practice relates to the fact that no Western society has had a proletarian or Bolshevik type of revolution, as predicted by Marx, whereas, contrary to Marxist doctrine, revolutions in the name of Marxism have succeeded in a number of backward, peasant societies.

Communist Manifesto   A brief exposition of the theoretical and practical views of Karl Marx and Friedrich Engels, written for the League of Communists as a "call to revolution" against the established institutions of capitalism. Published first in 1848 in German, *The Communist Manifesto* has since been issued in over one thousand editions and translated into almost one hundred languages. For Marx and Engels, the *Manifesto* was the definitive statement of the ideology of communism as they had developed it, with its major theories and objectives summarily expounded. Divided into four major parts, the *Manifesto* includes (1) a summary of the theoretical foundation of communism, including the nature of capitalism, the evolution of class struggle, the program for changing society, and the role of the proletariat in the creation of a new social order; (2) a definition of the role of the communist party and its relationship to the proletariat; (3) a critique of bourgeois and petite bourgeois theoreticians who erroneously offer the proletariat bourgeois socialism or Utopian socialism; and (4) an analysis of the relationship of the communist party with other revolutionary parties and a call for action that includes a description of the immediate program following the revolution, and the ultimate goal of a new, pure society of communism. *See also* MARXISM, p. 55.

Significance   The Communist Manifesto, as a document that calls for and justifies revolution, ranks with the American Declaration of Independence and the French Declaration of the Rights of Man and Citizen in terms of its impact on human history. Marx and Engels believed that the time was ripe for general revolution, and the *Manifesto* first appeared in 1848, the year of revolution and ferment throughout Western Europe. Today, more than one hundred years later, it remains a powerful, provocative document, filled with incisive rhetoric and savage invective. Its appeal to the proletariat—"Workers of the world, unite! You have nothing to lose but your chains"—remains the key revolutionary slogan of communist ideologues everywhere. Marx, however, was bitterly disappointed with its impact during his lifetime. The League of Communists, which had commissioned Marx and Engels to produce the *Manifesto*, lost support and gradually disappeared. The revolution, which Marx was convinced would occur very soon because conditions were ripe for it, failed to materialize during his lifetime, despite the effect of the *Manifesto*.

Convergence Theory   A theory that holds that all states that have undergone industrialization are converging to a point where their social structures and methods of governance will be similar as a result of the imperatives imposed by a commonly shared technology. Convergence theory is based on the Marxist assumption that the prevailing state of technology determines the content of a specific culture and the nature of the governing elite. As applied to the Soviet Union by Western theoreticians, convergence theory predicts that as the Soviet

Union becomes more industrialized and modernized, it will increasingly resemble the leading industrialized nations, especially the United States, with the governing Soviet elite becoming more "rational" in Western terms. *See also* CAPITALISM, p. 40; COMMUNISM, p. 41; DÉTENTE, p. 319.

Significance   If the theory is valid, one can assume that, while not all conflicts between the two superpowers will evaporate, as convergence proceeds ideological differences will diminish. Those who do not accept this form of technological determinism, however, point out that the contents of communist political cultures and those based on Western values are so different that parallel technological development is possible without convergence. Critics also point out that convergence theorists, such as W. W. Rostow, John Galbraith, and Raymond Aron, ignore the fact that technology is neutral and has been used to support such divergent systems as fascism, communism, capitalism, military dictatorships, and monarchies. During the last 60 years the Soviet Union has become a first-class industrial power whose capacities surpass most Western states. Yet, no concrete evidence exists that systemic convergence is present and that the inherent tensions between these rival systems are abated by the approach of technological parity. In fact, in the 1980s parity in technological advances in the arms race has tended to increase tensions and to encourage each to seek superiority.

Deviationism and Revisionism   Two of the cardinal sins against communist orthodoxy. Both deviationism and revisionism involve assuming a position on an important ideological point that is different from or in direct conflict with the officially adopted line of the communist party and state organs. Although revisionism implies a major reinterpretation of Marxist doctrine whereas deviationism has often been used to describe quarrels over the applications of policy, the two terms have often been used interchangeably. In both cases, denunciations and political or legal action are used as pressure techniques in the quest for a slavish acceptance of dogma. When, however, the leadership elite in a communist system "discovers" new truths or interpretations of Marxist-Leninist doctrine, all others in the system are expected to follow that lead. *See also* LENINISM: DEMOCRATIC CENTRALISM, p. 52; GREAT PURGE, p. 17; TITOISM, p. 800; TROTSKYISM, p. 81.

Significance   The definitions, interpretations, and applications of communism as an ideology that permit no deviation or revision apply in the Soviet Union and throughout Eastern Europe. Today, unlike the

Stalinist period, there are many divergences from and revisions of the applications of communist doctrines as they are used in the Soviet Union, but internal harmony and acceptance are generally demanded. Examples include the unique Yugoslav "road to socialism," the return of most land to the peasants in Poland, and the economic reforms in Hungary. Under the Brezhnev Doctrine, if the deviations and revisions appear to threaten Soviet hegemony, the Soviets reserve the right to intervene in the interest of maintaining socialism. Deviationism and revisionism emerged out of Vladimir Lenin's doctrine of democratic centralism, whereby free, democratic participation in policy making must give way, once party policy has been adopted, to acceptance of the decisions as an absolute and binding dogma on the leadership and rank and file members of the communist party, and they in turn would see to it that the new policy is rigidly applied and enforced on the public. Under the Stalinist dictatorship, intraparty democracy became a hollow phrase and every party member who disagreed with Stalin's dictums in the slightest was labeled a deviationist or revisionist. Severe disciplinary action followed, ranging from public reprimand and expulsion from the party to shipment to a slave labor camp or execution. Stalin sought to apply his personal interpretations of Marxism-Leninism to communist parties around the world, expelling those parties and factions that deviated from his views from the Comintern, including in the 1930s the expulsion of Mao Tse-tung and the entire Chinese Communist Party. Departures from communist orthodoxy have often been classified as "right-wing deviationism" (generally, in the direction of capitalism), and "left-wing deviationism" (generally, Trotskyite in nature).

Dogmatism   A pattern of thinking about political, economic, and social matters in which official attitudes are uncritically accepted on the basis of authority without proof or experience. In Eastern Europe, the concept of dogmatism has been used most frequently to describe those communist leaders and movements that have insisted on raising the official philosophy of Marxism-Leninism to the status of a compulsory state religion. The highest expression of this form of dogmatism occurred during the era of Stalin when the dictator fostered a cult of the personality and ruthlessly forced all to accept his policies and decisions. In the ideological arena, an individual has been "captured" when he is absolutely positive on matters of opinion and arrogantly asserts opinions as Truth. Dogmatism is a form of mindset in which the individual, group or society accepts many assumptions on an a priori basis without subjecting them to deductive or inductive reasoning. *See also* DEVIATIONISM AND REVISIONISM, p. 45; IDEOLOGY, p. 48; STALINISM, p. 70.

Significance   Dogmatism in communist systems is a product of communist leaders who insist on raising the official philosophy to the status of a compulsory state doctrine. Once the ideology becomes dogma, repression and terror typically emerge as a means for dealing with the threat of deviationism and revisionism. Although Marxism proclaimed the ideal of collective action and the submergence of the individual will to the group, most communist states have been headed by dynamic, charismatic leaders who have developed their personal interpretations of Marx and Lenin and regard any deviation from their personal views as heretical. Examples include Leninism and Stalinism in the Soviet Union, Castroism in Cuba, and Maoism in China. Although the concept of dogmatism had its inception in Hellenic philosophy and received major attention in German classical philosophy, especially from Georg Friedrich Hegel, the modern communist state with its ideological base has given it a new, practical emphasis. Within the communist world, the Yugoslav communists have frequently utilized the term in their criticism of Soviet practices, from which they sought to distance themselves after their 1948 break with Stalin. In support of their "separate road to socialism," Yugoslav leaders accepted the necessity of publicly rejecting the dogma put forth by Soviet ideological spokesmen that there is only one viable and legitimate model for socialist states, the USSR.

Fascism   The ideology and governing system of the extreme right that establishes an authoritarian society ruled by an elite headed by a supreme leader or dictator. Marxists regard fascism as the highest stage of capitalism. Fascists often win power in a state by exploiting a popular fear of communism, and by propagating fascism as the only effective answer to the threat of a communist revolution. Fascists gain support for their cause by warning the middle class and working class that they will lose everything if the communists win power. Once in power, fascist regimes ruthlessly dispose of their political enemies by labeling them "communists" or "agents of the international communist conspiracy," a charge that leads to a death sentence or long prison term in fascist states. Fascism enunciates the promise of "true socialism" that will end the class struggle by uniting all groups in society in common service to the party, the leader, and the nation. *See also* ANTI-SEMITISM, p. 5; COMMUNISM, p. 41.

Significance   Because fascism and communism are philosophies of the extreme right and extreme left respectively, they have become each other's bitterest enemies. World War II and the atrocities perpetrated by the Nazis in their invasion of Russia added to the hatred and mistrust. Although fascism has no coherent body of theory to support it, it has gained adherents and won power by promising to restore stability to societies threatened by actual or alleged communist revolutions. The fear of communism can be so great that rational people give fascism their support simply because of the terror inspired by the threat of a communist takeover. Adolf Hitler, for example, was regarded by most Germans as a comic figure early in his political career, but when the Great Depression sowed heavy unemployment and mass frustrations in its wake, voters turned to him because he promised to deal effectively with the German communists. In recent years, military or military-supported groups have seized power through coups d'etat in many Third World countries and have established fascist-type regimes that they based on the claim that they were defending the nation against a real or imagined communist threat.

Ideology   A belief system that is used to articulate basic political, economic, and social values that together constitute a body of ideas that serves as the basis for an ideal system. An ideology is involved with fundamental positions concerning the nature of a political system, the way in which the economy functions, who exercises power in the system, the role of the individual and group and their relationship to the state, and the basic goals of society. The concept ideology was originated by an eighteenth-century group of French philosophers and scientists who called themselves "Ideologues." To them, ideology was defined as the "science of ideas," and they used it to achieve a unification of scientific concepts to reflect an understanding of the world. Karl Marx and Friedrich Engels reversed the popular conception of ideology—that ideas can change material conditions—and instead emphasized the impact of materialist conditions on ideational factors. In the contemporary world, social scientists recognize ideology as a philosophy that carries with it some prescriptive practices, beliefs, and sanctions, and is particularly concerned with political, economic, and social beliefs and structures. *See also* CAPITALISM, p. 40; COMMUNISM, p. 41; FASCISM, p. 47; LENINISM, p. 51; MARXISM, p. 55; TROTSKYISM, p. 81.

Significance   As occurred in the 1930s, the world is once again moving toward a polarization produced by global ideological warfare between the "left" and the "center and right." In direct competition for the minds of great masses of human beings are the ideologies of democracy and capitalism and of socialism and communism. Although ideologies are largely intellectual abstractions and rarely serve as precise guidelines to political action, they can be used with great effectiveness to justify and gain mass support for policies and programs undertaken by ideological leaders. Typically, the struggle for power that goes on within a political system encourages charges and countercharges of deviationism and revisionism. Since coming to power in 1917, the Soviets have often been split over issues concerning exactly how the ideas set forth by Karl Marx should be interpreted and applied to actual political and economic conditions. Many Marxist critics feel that the Soviets have so distorted and prostituted Marxism as to constitute absolute heresy and betrayal. Leon Trotsky, for example, lost the political struggle for power to Josef Stalin, was exiled, and thereafter spent his remaining days as arch-critic, charging that the Soviets had completely distorted Marx's ideas by creating a bureaucratic ruling class that betrayed the interests of the workers. Although Stalin no longer needed to fear Trotsky as a political rival, he had Trotsky assassinated in an effort to prevent a major schism in the communist world. Ideology has also been weakened in the communist camp by the spirit of nationalism, creating in its wake in Eastern Europe not only political but ideological polycentrism. The Prague Spring, the Polish Solidarity union movement, and the Yugoslav worker self-management system are examples of nationalistically inspired departures from Soviet-interpreted dogma. Finally, ideology may become outdated by technological developments, such as the impact of nuclear weapons on the ideological heirs to Marx.

Khrushchevism   Interpretations and applications of Marxism-Leninism made by Nikita S. Khrushchev during his seven years as leader of the Soviet Union. The ideas and practices of Khrushchevism were expounded and developed from 1956 when he emerged as the dominant leader in the post-Stalin power struggle to 1964 when he was deposed from power by a faction headed by Leonid I. Brezhnev and Aleksei N. Kosygin. Khrushchev's contributions to communist theory and practice included (1) his attack on Stalin's cult of the individual and the restoration of collective leadership; (2) his denunciation of Stalinist terror and its replacement with less tyrannical policies in the Soviet system; (3) his enunciation of the doctrine of "peaceful coexistence" between communist and capitalist states, with the conviction that communism would prove to be the superior social system by defeating capitalism in a global ideological contest; (4) his call for "wars of national liberation" in the undeveloped world of Asia, Africa, and Latin America; (5) his proclamation of a specific timetable for the transition from socialism to pure communism (within 20 years); and (6) his vision that the communist party will remain as a directing force after the state and its institutions have withered away. Despite his theoretical contributions, Khrushchev was more practical politician than ideologue and theorist, retaining and exuding many of the characteristics and mannerisms of his early peasant life. He engaged in cooperative or confrontational diplomacy with equal skill and vigor, and he provided some bombastic, almost comic, relief on occasion, as when he broke off his summit conference with President Dwight D. Eisenhower after the Soviets had shot down an American U-2 plane, and when he took off his shoe and pounded the table to show his displeasure at a meeting of the United Nations General Assembly. *See also* DE-STALINIZATION, p. 318; STALINISM, p. 78.

Significance   Although many Sovietologists reject the concept of Khrushchevism, holding that his contributions were neither particularly theoretical nor ideological, other analysts defend his contributions as substantial. Either way, they were the product of the internal and external factors that confronted Soviet leaders in the period following Stalin's death in 1953. Moreover, even though no major new interpretations or contributions to Marxism-Leninism were developed, the action of Soviet leaders during the Khrushchev era resulted in new emphases that contributed to the widening of the ideological gap between the Soviets and the Chinese. Although Khrushchev had been a leading accomplice in the Stalinist period of terror, he was able to gain stature and preserve communism in Eastern Europe by denouncing the crimes of Stalin at a time when all communist societies were threatened with popular uprisings. In time, Khrushchev also moved toward one-man rule and was charged by his successors to power with having engendered a "cult of personality" in his efforts to strengthen his rule. In foreign policy matters, Khrushchev is best remembered for his denunciations of nuclear war, for his proposals for "general and complete disarmament" presented to the United Nations in 1960, and for his role in the Cuban missile crisis.

Kremlinology   Analysis of the Soviet system based on the premise that Soviet politics is determined by personalities. Its practitioners, who are termed Kremlinologists, study Soviet political events mainly by looking at the personality shifts within the closed corridors of power in the Kremlin, the unofficial seat of the Soviet government. Such analysis concentrates on the struggle for power and the individuals involved by examining appointments, demotions, public appearances, length of speeches at party congresses, places in official photographs, honorary nominations, and other indicators of

individuals rising and falling in the Soviet power structure. *See also*
"ACTIVE MEASURES," p. 309; PLURALIST THEORY, p. 76.

Significance   Kremlinology is viewed by most political scientists as
far too limited in that it is based on the notion that personality is the
main key to understanding Soviet politics. Most political scientists insist
that policy decisions in the Soviet Union are made on a much more
complex basis than the mere interplay of personalities, and thus
institutions and functions must also be studied. Kremlinology, which
also has become a whimsical term, developed from the fact that
information about policy decisions frequently is so restricted that
western Sovietologists are left with little to analyze except information
about leading personalities.

Leninism   The theoretical interpretations and practical applications of Marxism developed by the Russian revolutionary leader,
Vladimir Ilyich Lenin. The main contributions of Leninism to the
ideology of communism are found in the published works of Lenin,
especially in *What Is To Be Done?* (1902), *Imperialism—The Highest Stage
of Capitalism* (1917), and *State and Revolution* (1918). The main ideological contributions of Leninism include (1) the theory that the highest
and final stage of monopoly capitalism, that of overseas colonialism
and imperialism, results from the actions of trusts and cartels as they
seek investment outlets for surplus capital, markets for surplus production, and sources of cheap raw materials; (2) the belief that, as a
result of imperial competition for investment and market opportunities, war among capitalist states is inevitable; (3) the theory of "combined development," which holds that underdeveloped, colonized
societies that include a mixture of slaveholding, feudalism, and capitalism may be susceptible to a communist-inspired revolution immediately rather than, as Marx predicted, after capitalism had matured; (4)
the theory that the communist party, guided by a small, dedicated elite,
will provide the leadership for the revolution and in implementing
Marx's prescribed "dictatorship of the proletariat" during the period
of socialism; and (5) the method for making decisions in the party that
permits the presentation of individual views during the process of
making decisions, but requires full support of all decisions after they
have been made by the leadership. *See also* LENINISM: DEMOCRATIC
CENTRALISM, p. 52; LENINISM: IMPERIALISM AND COLONIALISM, p. 53.

Significance   Leninism evolved mainly as an attempt by Vladimir
Lenin to explain certain aspects of Marxism and to apply the doctrines
of communism to the changing political and economic environment of

his day. As revolutionary leader and leader of the new Soviet state, Lenin was forced to adapt the ideas of Marxism to the practical problems of running a revolution and running a country. For Lenin, the prime responsibility of the party was to train the masses to respond positively and unquestioningly to whatever decisions were made by the party hierarchy. This for Lenin was the key to the success of the party. Lenin foresaw the contemporary struggles for national self-determination and for economic development and modernization. He predicted the struggles to establish socialism in underdeveloped countries, such as Cuba, El Salvador, Vietnam, Ethiopia, and Angola, and the opposition to these movements carried on by the United States and European countries. In addition to his theoretical and ideological contributions, the doctrine of Leninism recognized Lenin's role as practical political leader. He rallied the Russian people following the disasters of World War I and the Russian Civil War, undertook the political, social, and economic regeneration of the nation at a time when most nations sought its collapse, and charted for it a course of socialism that made it possible for Russia to survive the catastrophe of World War II and emerge as a superpower in the contemporary world. These and other contributions were so substantial that the basic ideology of communism is now generally referred to as "Marxism-Leninism." Lenin, however, differed from Marx on several theoretical points. Lenin placed major emphasis on conducting a successful revolution through a peasant-worker alliance, whereas Marx had pretty much ignored the peasants and placed all hope on the proletariat. Lenin, unlike Marx, believed in the uneven development of the societies of the world. Lenin also, as a practical matter, rejected Marx's idea that progress toward socialism would be automatic or predetermined by economic factors. For Lenin, the hope for revolution was greatest for undeveloped countries and territories where a two-stage revolution could occur, with a bourgeois revolt preceding a revolution engineered by the workers. He especially counted on revolutions in colonial countries that would destroy imperialism and cut off the sources of many raw materials and markets for capitalistic societies.

Leninism: Democratic Centralism   The doctrinally sanctioned method used for decision making and administration within communist parties. Democratic centralism was developed by Vladimir I. Lenin to be followed in all interpersonal relationships within vertically integrated organs of complex organizations, with special emphasis on its application within communist parties. Lenin incorporated two basic principles in his advocacy of democratic centralism: (1) the democratic origin of decisions through election with the continuing responsibility of those individuals involved in decision making; and (2) the subordination of lower party organs to higher party organs in the decision process. Lenin also emphasized that in discussion and decision making, all should participate equally in being able to present their point of view, but once the decision was made, its acceptance was obligatory on all and no dissenting minority was to be tolerated. *See also* BOLSHEVIK, p. 10; BUREAUCRATIC MODEL, p. 39; COMMUNISM, p. 41; PARTY LINE, p. 115; WORKERS OPPOSITION, p. 34.

Significance   In moving from theory to practice, many communist regimes perverted Lenin's idea of democratic centralism, using it to justify antihumanistic actions. Josef Stalin, for example, acting under the banner of democratic centralism, imposed a system of bureaucratic centralism and individual dictatorship upon the communist party and the government. Lenin had sought to establish an ideal system by fusing the practical and psychological advantages of rank and file participation with the need for ideological unity and bureaucratic efficiency. The system aimed at securing the internal cohesion and efficiency needed in the struggle to win power and to implement the socialist program after the revolution had succeeded. Currently, there is a trend in the Soviet Union and in some of the countries of Eastern Europe to restore the applicability of democratic centralism in the decision processes of national communist parties.

Leninism: Imperialism and Colonialism   The theory advanced by Vladimir Lenin that economic contradictions that grow out of the nature of capitalism lead states into undertaking policies of expansionism and exploitation. Although the theory that capitalism produces imperialism and colonialism can be inferred from the writings of Karl Marx, it remained for Lenin to develop a full-bodied theory in *Imperialism: The Highest Stage of Capitalism* (1917) and *State and Revolution* (1918). For Lenin, imperialism exists in two forms: (1) one in which capitalist states establish their rule over overseas territories and peoples; and (2) another in which advanced capitalist states establish their dominance over underdeveloped areas of the world through the export of capital. In this way, investment becomes a means for the exploitation of foreign peoples and for the extraction of wealth through cheap labor and low prices for raw materials. For communists, the mere presence of foreign capital in such countries and territories represents exploitation and, hence, all capitalist states by definition are imperialist. Lenin's analysis explained imperialism as essential for capitalist states as a means for finding new investment outlets for surplus capital, for finding new markets for excess production that cannot be consumed on the home market because of the increasing impoverishment of the workers, and as a means for securing cheap raw materials to feed the domestic factories. These factors, Lenin held, became more important motivators of state and corporative overseas policies of conquest and control as capitalism moved from its early competitive stage to a "monopoly stage" dominated by cartels and trusts. *See also* LENINISM, p. 51.

Significance   In developing his theories of imperialism and colonialism, Lenin borrowed heavily from the analyses of the English economist, J. A. Hobson, as set forth in his book, *Imperialism* (1902). Hobson developed the thesis that Western imperialism could be attributed mainly to the tendency of capitalist systems to oversave, thereby creating the need to cope with the problem of overproduction/underconsumption in the domestic market by securing overseas markets. Lenin, however, focused his attention mainly on the problem of oversavings creating huge amounts of capital, with few domestic opportunities for investment. Lenin's theories on imperialism and colonialism predicted increasing imperialist rivalry that would lead to major wars among capitalist states. Lenin altered Marxism by predicting that proletarian revolutions need not necessarily take place only in the most highly developed capitalist states. Instead, he foresaw political and economic revolutions taking place in the underdeveloped societies of Asia, Africa, and Latin America dominated by monopoly capitalism. His predictions have proved to be somewhat more reliable in this area than were Marx's. His prediction, however, that upheavals and revolts against Western capitalism would deny raw materials and markets to capitalist states has proved false, because Third World states have strived to expand their exports of primary commodities and trade has flourished. In most cases, capitalist states have granted independence to their colonies, but economic imperialism in the form of control over most investment and technology in the developing countries continues. In many cases, capitalist states have prospered after granting independence to their colonies. Within the colonies, independence has been achieved not as a result of class struggle but as the product of nationalism and an indigenous mass movement. These historical facts, critics assert, have tended to negate most Leninist theories of imperialism and colonialism.

Lysenkoism   The genetic theory named for Soviet agronomist, Trofim Lyšenko, who claimed that by changing the environment it is possible to induce changes in organisms that can be genetically transmitted to future generations. Lysenkoism rejects Mendelian genetics and the essential differences between somatic and germ cells, and it holds that it is possible for humans to direct evolutionary change by manipulating the environment. Since this belief in the transmission of acquired characteristics fits Stalin's ideology of the building of a new socialist society and the "new Soviet man," Lysenkoism became the official biology in the Soviet Union. Lysenko claimed that wheat strains that had been hardened in the north kept and passed on these acquired characteristics when moved to more moderate climates. Stalin promoted Lysenkoism as proof that the Soviet man, raised under conditions of socialism, was a superior being who could pass on this superiority to future generations. Lysenko's theories became mandatory in Soviet biology, and other forms of genetic research were blocked. After Stalin's death, Mendelian genetics again became acceptable in Soviet biology, but Khrushchev supported Lysenkoism when he launched his Virgin Lands Project and awarded Lysenko the Order of Lenin, the highest government award. *See also* NEW SOVIET MAN, p. 107; VIRGIN LANDS, p. 236.

Significance   During the years when Lysenkoism dominated Soviet biology, great havoc was wreaked in the Soviet scientific community. Scientific departments were purged of members who could not accept Lysenko's theories, and it became impossible to pursue research that did not advance Lysenko's theories. Lysenkoism also was used to justify the postwar Soviet exploitation of Eastern Europe on the grounds that the peoples of Eastern Europe were inferior because they had not had the same exposure to a socialist environment as Soviet citizens. Lysenkoism also accorded with Stalin's claim that Russian was the language of socialism and therefore should be accepted as a second language throughout Eastern Europe. The imposition of Lysenko's theories, which Stalin called "the only genuine materialistic theory," set Soviet biological research back many years. Lysenkoism is frequently cited as an example of how a totalitarian state can subordinate science to the false imperatives of ideology and power in the face of incontrovertible scientific proof.

Marxism   A set of theories developed originally by Karl Marx, a nineteenth-century philosopher and economist, with his collaborator, Friedrich Engels, to explain scientifically and to predict economic, social, and political phenomena. Marx drew from three sources in developing his broad theories of human society: (1) the German philosophical revolution, especially that fostered by the Hegelians; (2) the French political revolution; and (3) the English industrial revolution. Marxism as an ideology concentrated mainly on the evils and predicted collapse of capitalism, but in *The Communist Manifesto* of 1848

Marx spelled out the nature and structure of socialism and communism as he envisioned them for the post-capitalist world. Marx started his analysis with a materialist interpretation of history, using the dialectic to chart the ultimate union of opposing forces in all human relationships. Class struggle, for Marx, was the major force that gave movement to history through the dialectical process. In his analysis of capitalism, he recognized certain basic, irreconcilable conflicts that foreordained the ultimate collapse of capitalism as a result of class struggle involving a victory by the proletariat or working class over the bourgeoisie or capitalist class. This analysis started with the idea of "surplus value," which is taken as profit by the capitalist, divesting the proletarians of much of the value of the products they make, with the result that capitalism breeds overproduction and underconsumption, and these in turn tend to produce economic depressions, wars, and above all, intensifying class struggle. A typical capitalist economy, according to Marx, also suffered from progressive growth in the size of business enterprises, which tended to stifle competition, and from an increasing impoverishment of the workers leading them to begin to recognize themselves as a class. Although Marx preferred that the workers win the battle of the ballot box, he predicted that the capitalist elite would not give up their power peacefully, and a violent revolution would be necessary to usher in the new era. For Marx, a transition period of socialism would follow the seizure of power, a period in which society would be governed by a "dictatorship of the proletariat." Many changes would occur during this period, with the institutions of capitalism progressively destroyed and replaced by collectives based on social cooperation. Ultimately, Marxism foresees that the changing social environment would produce a substantial change in human nature and a "new communist man" would emerge to replace the hostility-prone, conflict-ridden capitalist man. As a result of these massive structural and human changes, the class struggle would end, government, which for Marx had always served as an instrument of the dominant class, would wither away, and a new classless, stateless society of pure communism would emerge. In communism, the basic creed of socialism ("From each according to his ability, to each according to his work") would change to the new formulation ("From each according to his ability, to each according to his need"). For Marx, this would mean the end of social change through the dialectical process, since the energizing force of class struggle would no longer exist. Marx's theories were developed in *The Communist Manifesto* and in his principal work, *Das Kapital*, first published in 1867. *See also* COMMUNISM, p. 41; LENINISM, p. 51.

Significance   Marxism has had a profound effect on the history of the twentieth century. In addition to the Soviet Union and China, many smaller countries of Eastern Europe, Asia, Africa, and Latin America have established communist systems as a result of internal upheavals or external pressures. Marxist-oriented socialist and communist parties overtly or covertly challenge the established order in many other countries around the globe. Interpretations and applications of Marxism remain major elements of contention in the world power struggle between Moscow and Peking, with pro-Soviet and pro-Chinese parties competing with each other for power in most capitalist states. In all communist states, leaders have flexibly interpreted and pragmatically applied Marxism, but none has repudiated the doctrine or overtly amended it. The denouement of the communist plan through the remaking of man's nature and the "withering away" of the state has not taken place in any communist society despite periodic predictions of progress. Little concrete evidence exists to support the emergence of the new society. In the Soviet Union, for example, a new class of technocrats and bureaucrats operate the machinery of the state, which, far from withering away, has become a more pervasive force under communism. The main target of Marxism in the contemporary world is the developing societies of the Third World. Here communist propaganda has changed from the Marxian dogmas of historical inevitability and the inner contradictions of capitalism to promises that Marxism can provide shortcuts to economic development and social modernization for developing societies. Despite its many doctrinal permutations and interpretations in the contemporary world, Marxism remains a powerful ideological force that attracts peasants, workers, intellectuals, and others to its banner. Many Marxists are "true believers" who study the writings of Marx and Lenin with religious zeal and try to apply them with political fanaticism.

Marxism: Alienation   The estrangement of workers from society that occurs, according to Karl Marx, as a result of the method of production in a capitalistic economy. Marx determined that, under capitalism, human beings were increasingly alienated by being treated like inanimate objects—like things or commodities. For Marx, a worker produces an object that becomes, in effect, part of his or her own being. But the worker does not own the object, and it is thus alienated from the worker as creator. The worker has put part of his or her life into the object produced, but that part of his or her life no longer belongs to the worker. The object then reaches the market and becomes subject to the laws of the marketplace. As compensation for contributing part of his or her life to the product, the worker derives some measure of compensation. The worker creates the object with the means of production but merely used them because they are owned and controlled by the capitalists. The owner of the means of production, the capitalist, is also estranged, both from the process of production, and from its key ingredient, namely, work. Insofar as the owners are alienated from the workers and the production process, they become strangers within the same house, and the alienation of one individual from another becomes a dehumanizing fact of life. For Marx, workers will be free and no longer alienated when they can plan their work and organize the work process under their own initiative. Under capitalism, he noted, everything is rationed, measured, and planned for the workers. Thus each worker becomes a prisoner of others who decide his or her working conditions, allotted time, and the methods of work to be employed. All of these factors contribute to the alienation of workers in capitalistic societies, according to Marx. *See also* MARXISM, p. 55; MARXISM: HUMANISM, p. 65; WORKERS' SELF-MANAGEMENT, p. 239.

Significance   Economic alienation, according to Marx, is the basis for other forms of alienation, including political and ideological. He believed that mass alienation was partly a product of the new technology of the Industrial Revolution, but he was also convinced that much of the problem could be solved by the destruction of capitalism and its replacement with a collectivized system of production in which the workers would also be the owners. The ultimate solution, for Marx, will occur only after the triumph of socialism, when the state has withered away and all production is for use rather than for profit, with a distribution system based on need rather than on wealth. Most evidence today indicates that Soviet workers are just as alienated from society as those in the West, resulting in low productivity, poor work attitudes, and widespread alcoholism. In Yugoslavia, however, emphasis on the Worker Self-Management System in which the workers manage each enterprise and reap the benefits from high levels of production and good sales indicates that this kind of direct participation in decision making in the workplace may tend to reduce worker alienation. Marx's theory of alienation and dehumanization became the core of the critique of Marxism-Leninism that developed in Eastern Europe after Stalin's death. These "Marxist humanist" philosophers, such as Karel Kosík, Ivan Sviták, and Leszek Kołakowski, have generally been silenced or exiled because the humanist critique threatens the party's monopoly of power. In Yugoslavia, the Marxist humanists so vocal in the 1960s also have been suppressed and their theoretical journal, *Praxis*, prohibited.

Marxism: Class Struggle   The conflict in society between a dominant class and a subordinate class that leads to the creation of a higher social order. Karl Marx expounded the idea of class struggle to explain the evolutionary movement of society from lower to higher orders and, ultimately, to a final classless, stateless society of pure communism. In capitalism, Marx observed that the conflict and contradictions between the proletariat and bourgeoisie was a product of the increasing impoverishment of the workers and a polarization engendered by a growing class consciousness. The inner contradictions of capitalism would lead, according to Marx, to a revolution, which would usher in the era of socialism as a transition period leading to communism. Marx pointed out that the class struggle in capitalism is part of a broader canvas that, through the application of the dialectic and his materialist conception of history, explains mankind's earlier evolution from primitive, slave, and feudal social systems. Marx's doctrine of class struggle assumes that only two classes exist in a capitalist society, the bourgeois and proletarian (or, put another way, the rich and the poor), that the two have absolutely contradictory interests, and that each will become implacably hostile to the other. *See also* MARXISM, p. 55.

Significance   Marx of course did not discover the existence of classes, nor the struggle between them. He recognized that bourgeois historians and economists as well as socialist thinkers had discussed the role of classes in society extensively. Marx summarized his special contributions as (1) providing proof that the genesis of class struggle is and always has been tied to a definite historical phase in economic development and production; (2) predicting that the class struggle in capitalism would inescapably lead to the dictatorship of the proletariat; and (3) predicting that such dictatorships are a transitional phase leading to the destruction of all classes and the evolution of a classless society. To encourage these developments, communist party leaders in many countries have sought through various forms of agitation to develop a militant class consciousness among the workers, with revolution against the established system as its major objective. Critics of Marxism reject the idea that class struggle is predetermined and inevitable. In capitalist societies, critics point out, most people have begun to think of themselves as "middle class." It is also increasingly evident that the progressive impoverishment of the workers leading to a sharpening of class consciousness, as predicted by Marx, has not occurred in modern industrial societies. In the United States, for example, many workers have reached the goal of a good standard of living and some have topped it off with luxury products.

Marxism: Contradictions of Capitalism   The irreconcilable conflicts inherent in the nature of capitalism that, according to Karl Marx, will bring about its collapse. For Marx, the contradictions of capitalism start with the labor theory of value, which holds that all wealth is produced through the mixing of labor with the raw materials of the earth. In producing goods and other forms of wealth, however, the worker receives only a portion of the value of the goods produced in the form of wages, with the remainder taking the form of profit or surplus value. The result is that workers produce large amounts of mass-produced goods but receive only part of the value of those goods in wages, resulting in underconsumption and overproduction. The consequences flowing from these conditions, according to Marx, include imperialism, colonialism, economic depressions, world wars growing out of intense capitalistic competition for markets, a class struggle between the rich and poor, and ultimately a revolution that overthrows capitalism and ushers in the era of socialism. *See also* MARXISM, p. 55; MARXISM: SURPLUS VALUE, p. 72.

Significance   Most of Marx's writings dealt with weaknesses and inner contradictions of capitalism based on his "scientific" analysis of existing European systems, especially those of Germany, France, and England. Marxists firmly believe that the basic nature of capitalism contains the seeds of its own destruction, and that the denouement leading to revolution will occur within such societies as capitalism matures. This process cannot be unduly hastened from outside, however. Soviet leaders from Vladimir Lenin to Leonid Brezhnev have echoed these Marxian thoughts with the claim that "revolution cannot be exported, it must be indigenous." Many non-Marxist economists have identified the same contradictions in capitalist society that Marx found led to underconsumption and overproduction. Keynesianism, for example, is based on the assumption that oversaving is a natural phenomenon of capitalist societies, and that it leads to underconsumption and underinvestment. To overcome these contradictions, economist John Maynard Keynes called for a vigorous role by government to stimulate the economy back to healthy growth and to a point where consumption and investment would equal production. Increasingly severe economic slumps that culminated in the Great Depression of the 1930s were believed by many Marxists to be the arrival of the Marx-predicted apocalypse of capitalism. Since World War II, however, Western democratic systems have been able to avoid a major collapse of their economies through the use of monetary and fiscal policies that have averted the kinds of catastrophes that Marx predicted.

Marxism: Dialectical Materialism   A general theory and method of philosophy expounded by Karl Marx to explain the process of social evolution as the product of contradictions, a process in which all aspects of reality are viewed as a whole. The dialectic, developed by Plato and Aristotle and refined by Immanuel Kant and G. W. F. Hegel, was used by Marx in the development of his general theory of social evolution. Unlike Hegel, who focused on pure reason in the application of the dialectic, Marx emphasized the materialist nature of the dialectic, holding that thinking exists not in the abstract but only as the product of a specific social environment. The dialectic postulates a process by which each idea (thesis) produces a contradictory idea (antithesis), resulting in a conflict out of which emerges a new, higher idea (synthesis). Marx adapted the dialectic to his materialist outlook and used it to describe the ongoing conflict between the servile and dominant classes in every society that, he held, inescapably produces contradictions and conflict, resulting in the eventual emergence of a new, more perfect social order. The dialectically fostered historical evolution for Marx had moved mankind from its earliest primitive systems to a slave society, then to a feudal system, and then to capitalism. In capitalism, the seeds of conflict and contradiction involve the struggle between the bourgeoisie and the proletariat, with the eventual transition into socialism as a product of that class struggle. The climax of the dialectic process, Marx predicted, would involve a social evolution from socialism into pure communism. Because class conflict would no longer exist, the dialectic process as a means for achieving social evolution would no longer work or be needed, since human beings would live in a perfect society free of conflict and contradictions. *See also* MARXISM: MATERIALIST CONCEPTION OF HISTORY, p. 66.

Significance   The concept of dialectical materialism is central to the philosophy of communism because Marxists regard it as a science of society that reveals the laws of social change. Dialectical materialism is the starting point for Marx in developing his general theory of the materialist conception of history. A dedicated communist, using the dialectic process developed by Marx, accepts Marx's diagnosis of the internal conflicts of capitalism and fervently believes in the inevitability of the transition from capitalism to socialism, and from socialism to communism. By inverting Hegel's dialectic, ideas for Marx became a reflection of material reality, rather than the reverse. Critics of Marx's dialectical materialism reject as a gross oversimplification the idea that all material things are interrelated with the social environment. The processes and predictions of social evolution set forth by Marx as a key to understanding the dialectic contain elements of mysticism, and, some would charge, the dialectic resembles a religious faith despite its claim to be scientific. In using the dialectic to predict that Germany was ripe for revolution, followed by France and Britain, Marx fell far short, yet Russia, apparently far removed from the culmination of the dialectic process, had a revolution. Marx and his colleague, Friedrich Engels, foresaw the denouement of the dialectic process during their lifetimes, but again history demonstrates that they were much more adept at reading the dialectic into phenomena *after* they had occurred than in predicting future events.

Marxism: Dictatorship of the Proletariat   The means advocated by Karl Marx for governing a state during the period of socialism following a successful proletarian revolution. For Marx, the dictatorship of the proletariat meant that the workers would control and operate the machinery of the state and would use it to reorganize society and convert the means of production from private to public ownership. The power of the state should also be used during this transitional period to stamp out the remaining vestiges of bourgeois power and to put down counterrevolutions. The dictatorship of the proletariat was to be aimed at consolidating communist power, eliminating the bourgeoisie as a class, and establishing the basic framework of socialism as prescribed in *The Communist Manifesto* (1848). For Vladimir Lenin, Josef Stalin, and other Soviet leaders, the dictatorship was vested in the Communist Party of the Soviet Union and its leaders as the representatives of the proletariat. *See also* MARXISM, p. 55; PEOPLE'S DEMOCRACY, p. 330.

Significance   The concept of the dictatorship of the proletariat was a key component of communist ideology for Marx and his colleague, Friedrich Engels, and they frequently speculated about its nature and what its role would be following the anticipated revolution. When the Bolshevik Revolution occurred in Russia, ideological speculation had to give way to the practical matter of governing. Lenin viewed the dictatorship as a means for implementing democracy by bringing the workers and the poor into the governing process. He also referred to it as a means for bringing about "the oppression of the oppressors" and "their exclusion from democracy." A sharp conflict soon arose between the ideologues of the Second International and the Russian Revolutionary Workers' movement, highlighted by the famous polemic between Lenin and Karl Kautsky, with the latter charging that Lenin's concept of "dictatorship" was repugnant to democracy. The Polish, later German, revolutionary, Rosa Luxemburg, rejected both Lenin's and Kautsky's views, holding that Marx and Engels had actually called for the *direct* political participation of the masses. These and many other interpretations by scholars and political activists tend to obscure the fact that Marx left the concept purposely vague and general, concerned more with substance than with means. For many years, Josef Stalin's application of the dictatorship of the proletariat was based on the theory that the class struggle becomes sharper as the building of socialism sweeps away the remnants of bourgeois power, leading to the use of violence on a mass scale, not only against the bourgeoisie but against the working class itself. For Stalin, it proved to be a dictatorship *over* the proletariat rather than *of* the proletariat. Critics point out that in all communist states it is a case of dictatorship *over* the proletariat carried on by a single party leader or group of oligarchs. Currently, the term proletarian democracy is substituted in the Soviet Union in state and party propaganda for the less appealing dictatorship of the proletariat.

Marxism: Economic Determinism   The postulate set forth by Karl Marx that the nature of the economic system, especially the mode of production in a society, determines that society's political, legal, moral, religious, and cultural superstructure. In his economic interpretation of history, Marx predicated the existence in every economic system of divisive classes that provide the historical force that guides the emergence of new modes of production as the society moves from lower to higher stages, i.e., from feudalism to capitalism to socialism. Marx's materialist conception of history starts with the assumption of "economic man," that is, that the basic activity of human beings relates to the production and acquisition of the means of subsistence. The ownership, organization, and operation of these productive forces and the means for the consumption of food and material wealth produced by them determines, according to the Marxian dialectic, the nature of society. Class conflict engendered by this system provides the motive power for the society's evolution. In his analysis, Marx identified three economic factors of production as the ones most directly related to social evolution and historical development: labor, raw materials, and the instruments of production. *See also* MARXISM, p. 55.

Significance   Although Karl Marx is often referred to as an economic determinist, many Marxian scholars regard this as a shallow description of his philosophy and ideology, which involved far more than a simplified cause and effect relationship. Yet, he did emphasize the fundamental role that the nature of the economic system plays in the shaping of all social institutions. According to Marx, the contradiction between modern productive techniques and bourgeois ownership leads to an inescapable conflict in the form of a class struggle. Rather than a function of determinism, Marx preferred to think of this conflict as an evolutionary, historical process. Marx and Marxists have focused on the economic interpretation of history as a means for explaining how workers can recognize their identity and be politicized to engage in a class struggle that ultimately results in revolution. For Marx, only the powerful motivating force of class self-interest could provide the explanation for the movement of history. Vladimir Lenin, on the other hand, placed greater emphasis on making things happen by taking advantage of a historical circumstance or crisis, rather than sitting back and waiting for the denouement of the historical process. For many Marxian critics, the victory of communism in most if not all communist states occurred as a result of special political or national conditions resulting from war or postwar situations, not from economic factors or from the culmination of the class struggle.

Marxism: Final Stage of Communism   The ultimate stage of the dialectical process of history, as predicted by Karl Marx. Under communism, according to Marx, a "new communist man" will live in a classless, stateless society, free from the competitiveness and hostility that characterized the lives of human beings in all previous social systems. A new and higher morality will guide individuals in the final stage, and spontaneous cooperation will replace the coercion of government and the economic elite. Marx predicted that, following the worker-led revolution in which a society overthrows capitalism, a transitional era of socialism will be ushered in with a "dictatorship of the proletariat" serving as the instrument of government. During this period of proletarian dictatorship, massive changes will occur in the way society functions. Marx expected that in time pure communism will replace socialism as the proletarian state simply "withers away." Communism will constitute the final and highest stage of social evolution. Since it will be a condition of near perfection, Marx could see no reason why further evolution should or would occur. Moreover, the energizing force of class conflict will no longer exist to provide the motive power for societal change. Under communism, the production and distribution of material wealth will change from the socialist basis of "from each according to his ability, to each according to his *work*" to a communistic basis of "from each according to his ability, to each according to his *needs*." Marx's main ideas concerning communism as the final stage of the social evolutionary process were set forth in *The Communist Manifesto* in 1848. *See also* MARXISM, p. 55.

Significance   Marx's Utopian vision of a future society of pure communism free of the conflicts and antagonisms of capitalist society has helped to attract intellectuals around the world to support communist ideology. The doctrine gives Marxism the anticipatory quality of a religious faith since it postulates that human beings in effect will be reborn and cast in an earlier, uncorrupted form guided by a new and higher set of moral values. The elimination of government as a major goal of communism linked Marx with his rival, Mikhail Bakunin, and the philosophical anarchists of his day, who also regarded the state as the major instrument of oppression and sought to destroy it. While political leaders and ideologues in communist states have never repudiated the doctrine of the evolution of societies to pure communism, they have often rationalized it as a distant objective attainable only after the entire world accepts communism. So long as a "hostile capitalist encirclement" exists, the changes in society that will lead to the ultimate goal of pure communism cannot be instituted. In the 1960s, however, Premier Nikita Khrushchev announced to the representatives of 81 communist parties convened in Moscow that the Soviet Union was completing the building of socialism and would be the vanguard in the movement of all socialist societies to communism. Many of the writers, artists, and others who have been inspired by the Marxist vision of an ultimate society free of war and class hostility have been thoroughly disillusioned by the harsh discipline, rigid thought control, and police state methods they have found in communist states. Critics of Marxism hold that the ideology of communism has flunked its empirical test. There is no evidence, they point out, that society has changed dramatically under socialism, or that human nature can be molded in such a way as to provide for revolutionary societal changes that will lead to the realization of Marx's vision of a pure society.

Marxism: Humanism   An interpretation of Marxism, especially influential in the 1950s and 1960s, that stresses the early works of Marx, particularly the Paris Manuscripts of 1844 that center on Marx's examination of human alienation. Marxist humanism, particularly as articulated by East European philosophers, was a means of reexamining the basic tenets of Marxism-Leninism on which the official ideologies of the ruling communist parties rested. Although orthodox Marxists in essence reject Marx's early works as intellectually immature, basing their own thought on *Das Kapital* and later works, the Marxist humanists argue that Marx's early works contain the core of Marxism, an ethical doctrine which deals with the unity of humankind. Marxist humanists argue that Marxism is not a science, but rather is a moral doctrine. Marxist humanism also has its origins in Hegel's concept of man as a self-creating being, and emphasizes the creative role of man. The leading philosophers of this school of philosophy, such as György Lukács and Leszek Kołakowski, argue that mankind can be just as alienated under state socialism as under capitalism; that the reduction of human relations to relations between commodities or things posits a mechanistic view of humanity that is just as alienating as capitalist commodity-labor. Essentially, most Marxist humanists maintain that humans must be fully involved in their own fate, and that they must possess control over the means of production. Some also point out that automation, whether or not within the context of capitalist conditions, is especially dehumanizing. *See also* MARXISM, p. 55; MARXISM: ALIENATION, p. 57.

Significance   Marxist humanism deemphasizes the scientism of classic Marxism, and in particular, the foreordained role of the proletarian class struggle in the evolution to socialism. From their conclusions, the Marxist humanists mounted a broad-based philosophical critique of the contemporary practices of the communist-party states, and their major preoccupation with economic growth. By the early 1960s the humanist movement had spokesmen in most of the East European countries, particularly in Yugoslavia where a freer intellectual atmosphere and the institution of workers' self-management permitted more open questioning of classic Marxism-Leninism. The movement included such diverse individuals as Ivan Sviták and Čestomir Cisar of Czechoslovakia, Ernst Bloch of East Germany, and Kołakowski of Poland, as well as intellectuals of Western Europe and the United States. In Yugoslavia, the philosophers Svetozar Pejović, Veljko Korać, Predrag Vranicki, Gajo Petrović, and Rudi Supek grouped themselves around the journal *Praxis*. Long after the other East European Marxist humanists had been expelled or suppressed, their Yugoslav counterparts continued to question the verities of Marxism-Leninism. Although workers' self-management embodied many of the humanist arguments put forward by the *Praxis* philosophers, they continued to reiterate their right to criticize its implementation, pointing out the persistence of "Stalinist dogmatism" in the Yugoslav party while warning of the dangers of "immature self-management," market capital, and growing class differences. As a counterforce, the Yugoslav Marxist humanists were disbanded in 1975 when eight leading members of the Belgrade Faculty of Philosophy were fired and *Praxis*, after 11 years, ceased publication. Thus ended the most extensive, open debate over the meaning of Marxism ever carried on within a communist-party state.

Marxism: Materialist Conception of History   The central thesis of Karl Marx's doctrine of social evolution. For Marx, the materialist conception of history was based on phenomena that followed a recognizable evolutionary process to its logical conclusions, with all causes and effects capable of being studied in a scientific manner. In identifying these evolutionary laws, Marx at the same time rejected other theories of prime movers of history, such as the "great man" theory that the personal whims and decisions of kings and political leaders create history, or that, on the other hand, history is the accidental product of circumstantial events, or, conversely, foreordained by God. Marx's materialist conception of history starts with the assumption that human beings are involved in productive enterprises that collectively comprise the society's mode of production, which in turn determines the social, political, and spiritual processes of life for that society. It is not the way human beings think that determines their social system, but rather it is their social existence that channels their thinking. The mode of production or basic economic system, however, inescapably produces conflict in society. Using dialectical materialism as a guide, Marx recognizes that the existing economic order, the thesis, tends in time to produce new, challenging productive forces, the antithesis. The conflict that grows out of this contradiction is ultimately resolved by revolution, resulting in the creation of a new productive system, and a new synthesis is achieved. Central to this process, and therefore providing the dynamism that gives movement to history, is the Marxian idea of class struggle. Thus historical evolution, according to Marx, has resulted from the contradictions embedded in society's mode of production, which pitted the servile class against the exploiting class in capitalism and in preceding primitive, slave, and feudal patterns, producing an evolutionary movement from one stage to the next. For Marx, history will ultimately lose its momentum when rival classes are eliminated during the period of socialism and a final product of history, communism, will emerge in a classless, stateless society. *See also* MARXISM: DIALECTICAL MATERIALISM, p. 60; MARXISM: ECONOMIC DETERMINISM, p. 63.

Significance   By placing his ideas of revolution and socialism within the broad matrix of a materialist conception of history, Marx sought to give his theories a scientific and intellectual base that would lend them support in his constant ideological wars with other socialist thinkers and activists. Marx combined his role as economist with his role of historian to produce what he preferred to describe as "scientific socialism." While some scholars refer to it as a general theory of economic determinism, most Marxists reject that as too simplistic a description of Marx's theory of historical evolution. A dozen years before Charles Darwin published his monumental *Origin of Species*, which sought to explain the process of biological evolution, Karl Marx published his *Poverty of Philosophy* (1848) and *The Communist Manifesto* (1848), which sought to do for the social world what Darwin would do

for the biological. His evolution, unlike Darwin's, predicts the historically inevitable triumph of socialism, which gives communism the
mystical, anticipatory quality of a religious faith for its supporters.
Although Marx believed that the means for achieving socialism may
initially be peaceful and democratic, in the unraveling of the historical
process a violent revolution becomes unavoidable. Although many
economists, historians, philosophers, sociologists, and political scientists have criticized Marx's general theory of the materialist conception
of history, it has also been accepted as gospel by many who have studied
his theory and accepted its explanatory power. The popularity of
Marx's theories with many intellectuals throughout the world as a
means for social regeneration gives it a pragmatic support not enjoyed
by most other ideologies. Yet popularity is not a proper test of scientific
proof. Proletarians, who for Marx were to play the key role leading to
the historically inevitable triumph of socialism, lack understanding and
have demonstrated little interest in Marx's complex theories. Regardless of the esteem or contempt that rival ideologues have for Marx's
materialist conception of history, it stands as a major effort in the social
sciences to develop a philosophy of society based on historical evolution.

Marxism: Means of Production   The state of technology and
the control of production that, according to Karl Marx, determine the
nature of the economic, political, and social system within a society.
The means of production are also defined by bourgeois economists as
capital goods used in the production of wealth, along with land and
labor. In antiquity, slave labor was essentially the means of production,
resulting in the dominant position of the slave-owning class. In the
eighteenth and nineteenth centuries, capital equipment produced by
the Industrial Revolution provided the means of production, resulting
in the dominance of the capitalist class. This dominance, according to
Marxist theory, ensures class control over the entire society. Within the
socialist state, Marxism distinguishes between two kinds of property,
personal and social. Personal property, as defined by the party and the
state, remains by right with the individual. Social property, conversely,
must never be permitted to be placed under the control of individuals
because private ownership could lead to its use for exploitation and
enslavement of other individuals. *See also* MARXISM, p. 55; WORKERS'
SELF-MANAGEMENT, p. 239.

Significance   Marxism's emphasis on the role of the means of
production is central to communist ideology. Exploitation within slave,
feudal, and capitalistic societies was for Marx a natural outgrowth of

systems that placed control over the means of production in private hands. In his socialist program set forth in *The Communist Manifesto* (1848), Marx called for a changeover from private control to social ownership and control over the means of production. The assumption here was that this action would destroy the capitalists as a class by eliminating their power base. Socialist states have generally walked a thin line in distinguishing between personal property and the means of production. An automobile, for example, may be an individual's personal property in the Soviet Union, but when it is used as a taxi it becomes a means of production. Private farm plots are another exception to the Marxian rule that all means of production should be social property and not used for private gain. Communist states have demonstrated increasing flexibility in wrestling with the problem of maintaining social control over the means of production, fixing variable limits on the right to own property and to employ other human beings in using the property. Patterns of ownership run the gamut from the pattern in the Soviet Union to Hungary, which permits a sizable private sector to flourish.

Marxism: New Communist Man   An assumption by Karl Marx that the basic nature of human beings can be changed from hostile, competitive, conflict-ridden beings to cooperative, gregarious, public-spirited ones through a process of evolution produced by changing the social environment. The concept of "the new communist man" assumes that human nature has been warped by the social environment of capitalism. By changing that environment during the period of socialism, Marx believed that human nature would change as well, not just in response to immediate stimuli, but permanently. The new characteristics would be passed on to succeeding generations. For Marx, private property and the exploitation of the labor of others for profit creates an environment that induces hostility and conflict. Most of the pathologies ascribed to "industrial man" by Marx and others are traceable to the perverting influence of capitalism. These range from greed induced by the profit motive to criminality that afflicts the industrial proletariat because of ignorance and poverty. By replacing capitalist institutions and practices with socialist designs, Marx believed that the potential virtue in human nature would prevail. The Marxian vision of human beings living under communism is essentially an elitist one, in which proletarians adopt codes and manners similar to those of the elite. *See also* LYSENKOISM, p. 54; NEW SOVIET MAN, p. 107; STAKHANOVITE, p. 232.

Significance   According to Marx, the new communist man will be a product of the sweeping economic and social changes that occur during the transitional period of socialism. These structural and human changes will ultimately produce a new society, free of the hangups of the past, with institutional and human components in perfect harmony. The doctrine of the new communist man has given Marxism a religious cast, since it postulates that human beings will be "born again" in an uncorrupted form guided by new and higher moral values. For Marx, a change in human nature as well as human institutions was essential in the final historical stage of pure communism when man will live in a classless, stateless, cooperative society free from arbitrary restraint and coercive power. Critics of Marxism point out that, after almost 70 years of socialism in the Soviet Union, there is no clear empirical evidence that human nature is changing for the better. Instead of voluntary cooperation and greater freedom, Soviet citizens are in many ways exploited and controlled by their government. Critics also point out that there is no lesser propensity to commit crimes in the Soviet Union than before. Soviet penal law, for example, applies heavy penalties for varied offenses against socialist property, and citizens also continue to commit ordinary "bourgeois" crimes at a bourgeois rate. The split in the world communist movement between Moscow and Peking has changed the ideological references about the new communist man to "the new Soviet man" and "the new Chinese man," respectively. Soviet leaders at times in the past have supported the genetic theory, Lysenkoism, that the nature and characteristics of living organisms are shaped by their environment, a position influenced by Marx's ideological theory of changing human nature by changing the environment.

Marxism: Permanent Revolution   A process described by Karl Marx that is carried on in a particular historical setting which leads ultimately to the victory of the proletariat, within individual countries and worldwide. Permanent revolution, according to Marx, is an outgrowth of successful bourgeois revolutions that usher in an era of capitalism. With the establishment of capitalism, the proletarian class can begin its long process of revolutionary development. The term is also used to describe the social transformations that occur in the transition period following a successful proletarian revolution, a period referred to by Marx as "socialism" based on the "dictatorship of the proletariat." This period is part of the continuum of revolutionary changes that links the prerevolutionary era to the postrevolutionary era. By making revolution a dynamic, continuing process, Marx tried to prevent the institutionalization of revolution, especially through the bureaucraticization of the postrevolutionary situation. Marx and Lenin both accepted bourgeois revolution as a true revolution, essential in that it must play its proper role in the historical sequential process. The final and decisive revolution during the period of socialism would transform society and produce a new human being as a product of the changed environment. *See also* MARXISM, p. 55; TROTSKYISM, p. 81.

Significance   The concept of permanent revolution has created many divisions within and among communist systems and parties as various leaders and ideologues have tried to define what Marx actually meant in applying the term to concrete situations. The question of permanent revolution, for example, was at the heart of the ideological and power contest in the 1920s between Josef Stalin and Leon Trotsky following the death of Vladimir Lenin. Trotsky took the position that Marx's dictum of permanent revolution should guide the Russian rulers into using the Soviet Union as a base to promote worldwide revolution. Stalin stressed the necessity of building socialism in one country, the Soviet Union, holding that Trotsky's position amounted to pure adventurism; the gains of the Bolshevik Revolution should not be risked but rather consolidated and protected. Trotsky's idea that a socialist revolution in one country should be used as a spark or catalyst to carry the revolutionary movement onto the world stage retained support with various communist parties in different countries, even after his defeat in the power struggle, exile, and assassination in Mexico. When Mao Tse-tung headed the Chinese Communist Party, he proclaimed the goal of uniting all communist parties in the world in a common revolutionary campaign, but his successors to power have placed major emphasis on building socialism in China. The notion of permanent revolution has usually been expounded by the militant left wing of communist parties. Frequently they have been considered to be out of step with the party and have been expelled or punished as "Trotskyites," one of the most serious accusations in the communist lexicon.

Marxism: Socialist Program   The fundamental changes that, according to Karl Marx, will occur after the workers seize power and begin the process of transforming society from capitalism to socialism, preparing it for the eventual transition into the final classless, stateless stage of pure communism. The tenets of the socialist program set forth by Marx in *The Communist Manifesto* of 1848 include (1) abolition of the private ownership of land; (2) ending of all inheritance rights; (3) levying of a sharply progressive income tax; (4) state ownership and operation of all communication, transport, banking and credit; (5) collectivization of agriculture and the establishment of "industrial armies"; (6) obligation of all citizens to work; (7) abolition of child labor; and (8) free education for all children in public schools. Marx provided that the socialist program would be instituted during the period of socialism under a governing system he described as the "dictatorship of the proletariat." *See also* MARXISM, p. 55.

Significance   The socialist program, considered a radical, unworkable social program in Marx's day, has been largely implemented by the Soviet Union and by many other communist governments in East Europe. In addition, many of the program's objectives—progressive income taxes, limits on inheritance rights, state control of banking and credit, state ownership of communication and transport, abolition of child labor, and free public school education—have been adopted partly or wholly as public policy in democratic, capitalist states, such as the United States, Britain, and France. In many ways, Marx's socialist program resembles the campaign platform of a political party in the West. Marx and other early communist leaders believed that the fundamental changes proposed in the socialist program could never be implemented without a successful proletarian revolution because of the implacable opposition of the bourgeoisie to any changes that might threaten their dominant position. In recent years, the socialist program in the Soviet Union has been substantially altered from Marx's views by an increased dependence on sales taxes rather than a progressive income tax, by the increased use of market mechanisms to determine production goals, by the emergence of a massive military-industrial complex, and by the evolution of a new class of technocrats and bureaucrats. Many Third World countries have adopted modified forms of socialism that resemble both Marx's program and the platforms of Western democratic socialist parties.

Marxism: Surplus Value   The idea, postulated by Karl Marx, that under capitalism the price of every product includes not only the "socially necessary" cost of the labor that produced it, but also the profit for the capitalist who financed and directed its production. The latter for Marx is "surplus value" because he believed it to be an unnecessary cost of production. Surplus value, Marx opined, is the means under capitalism by which the bourgeois class is able to dominate and exploit the proletarian class. Moreover, surplus value is the key ingredient among the inner contradictions of capitalism. There is a natural tendency for capitalists to expand the production of surplus value or profits, according to Marx's analysis, leading to an increasing impoverishment of the workers, unemployment, underconsumption, and surplus production. These conditions lead to imperialism, colonialism, economic depressions, wars resulting from capitalist rivalry, and the stagnation of national economies. The ultimate result is a class struggle between the exploiters and the exploited that, for Marx, leads to revolution and the victory of socialism. *See also* MARXISM, p. 55; MARXISM: CONTRADICTIONS OF CAPITALISM, p. 59; TURNOVER TAX, p. 235.

Significance　　The theory of surplus value was developed by Marx by combining the labor theory of value expounded by such classical economists as Adam Smith, John Locke, and David Ricardo with the mercantilist doctrine of subsistence wages. The labor theory of value held that all value is based on the mixing of human labor with the raw materials of the earth, and the mercantilist doctrine expounded the philosophy that workers should be paid extremely low wages to provide them with an incentive to work by making their lives a continuing struggle for sustenance. Marx was ambivalent about the concept of surplus value. On the one hand he asserted that the worker who contributes all the value to a product is cheated out of his just compensation whereas the capitalist profits by exploiting another's labor. On the other hand, Marx believed that surplus value was the fatal flaw of capitalism that would bring about its collapse when the workers finally rose up in revolution, a result which he would applaud, and one he hoped would occur during his lifetime. For Marx, it was self-evident that, if the workers receive only a portion of the value of a product in the form of wages, there would not be enough purchasing power in that society to consume the mass-produced goods that typified the Industrial Revolution of his day. Defenders of capitalism reject the Marxian analysis, holding that profits are essential to reward risk-taking and entrepreneurial ability on which economic growth and societal well-being are based. Moreover, critics of communism emphasize that capitalist states have higher standards of living and the life-style of workers has improved more rapidly than that of workers in communist states where surplus value goes to the state. In most capitalist states, purchasing power has been maintained and oversavings avoided through governmental fiscal and monetary policies, and by the transfer of funds from those who have it to those who will spend it in the form of massive consumer credit systems. Vladimir Lenin expanded on the consequences of surplus value by holding that it produced not only overproduction and underconsumption of products but huge surpluses of investment capital as well, leading to overseas competition among capitalist states through their imperialistic policies aimed at securing investment opportunities through colonization.

Marxism: Withering of the State　　The doctrine expounded by

Karl Marx that, during the period of socialism, there will be a progressive disappearance of the state and its agencies and offices, leading ultimately to the emergence of a classless, stateless society of pure communism. For Marx, the withering away of the state was to be the supreme culmination of his ideology of communism. In the Marxist view, the state has always been an instrument of coercion, used by the dominant class to maintain and exercise its power and control over the subservient class or classes. The state, for Marx, will begin to disappear during the period of socialism when under the dictatorship of the proletariat a genuine classless society begins to emerge. Since the state's only reason for existence is to serve the interests of the ruling class, the elimination of classes will result in its withering away like a useless appendage. *See also* MARXISM, p. 55; SOCIALIST LEGALITY, p. 271.

Significance   The doctrine of the withering away of the state put Marx in a league with the anarchists of his day, who also considered the state to be an instrument of oppression that should be destroyed. Whereas the anarchists regarded the state itself as the supreme evil that perverted human nature, Marx believed the state and its apparatus to be a mere superstructure of capitalism and the class structure it created. If capitalism and classes were eliminated, then the superstructure of the state would also disappear. In addition, some of the utopian socialists discussed the passing of the state as a human institution. Marx believed that his predictions were different from those of the anarchists and socialists because his prophecies were based on scientific analysis. In practice, the socialist state in the Soviet Union and other communist countries manifests little tendency to wither away. Almost 70 years after the Bolshevik Revolution the Soviet state and its bureaucracy are stronger and more pervasive than ever. These years have seen the building of a huge bureaucracy that not only embraces those elements that are in the traditional purview of the state in all societies, but state decision making has been extended to the entire economy and to the individual pursuits of citizens that are considered to be private in most societies. Nevertheless, claims are occasionally made by communist leaders that the process of withering has begun. Nikita Khrushchev, for example, informed Americans on television during his visit to the United States in the 1960s that "within 20 years" the final stage of communism would be ushered in and the state would disappear. Departing from Marx's vision of the final state, Khrushchev determined that while the state would wither away, the communist party would remain as a guiding and directing force for the classless society. In Yugoslavia during the 1950s and 1960s communist theoreticians declared that the institution of the workers' self-management system was a major step toward the disappearance of the state. Despite these and similar claims, no empirical evidence exists to support the Marxian doctrine that the state will begin to wither during the period of the dictatorship of the proletariat.

New Class   A term applied to the ruling elite of a communist-party state, taken from the book by the same title, authored by Milovan Djilas and first published in New York in 1957. *The New Class* constitutes the first systematic political and sociological analysis of communism in power by a member of the party elite. The book had a dramatic impact because its author, a former vice-president of Yugoslavia in the early postwar years, played a major role in bringing the Yugoslav communists to power. Produced and smuggled abroad while the author was imprisoned for openly criticizing the Yugoslav regime, *The New Class* argues that communist-party states are ruled by a "new class" of party bureaucrats which arrogate all power to themselves. Djilas asserted that communism, rather than destroying the class system, merely substitutes a new elite for the old bourgeoisie. Djilas characterized the new class as an elite whose power is defined not by direct ownership of the means of production, as in capitalism, but by their control of and access to special privileges stemming from their monopoly of all power. Once in power, the revolutionary leadership gives way to an elite that becomes a privileged class whose morality is constantly eroded by the privileges it enjoys. Djilas vividly described the life-style of the new party elite, the access to special stores, cars, vacation villas, and all the appurtenances of power so much in contrast to the impoverished life of the workers in whose name they claimed to rule. *See also* MARXISM: HUMANISM, p. 65; WORKERS' SELF-MANAGEMENT, p. 239.

Significance   The term new class in the West has become synonymous with the ruling elite of a communist-party state. The use of the term implies the arrogance, venality, and corruption that Djilas attributes to those who betray the revolution. Although methodologically weak, Djilas's scathing critique of communist power has been supported by many, Marxist and non-Marxist alike. From Hungary in 1956 to Poland in 1980–81, various would-be reformers have demanded that party functionaries give up their privileges. Djilas was the first influential communist to call for the party to relinquish its monolithic power. His most striking contribution is in the dramatization of the usurping power of communist leaderships, a process in which he played a dominant role as a Partisan hero and Josip Broz Tito's second-in-command. In Yugoslavia, although Djilas was imprisoned until 1967, the Yugoslav party quietly adopted many of

Djilas's original arguments and embarked on a program of decentralization and liberalization in the 1960s. A key component of Djilas's critique of Soviet-style communism is his identification of the centrally controlled communist economy as "state capitalism," just as exploitative of the workers as bourgeois capitalism. Many of Djilas's arguments have been expanded by such Marxist critics as the Marxist humanist philosophers, the Czechoslovak reformers of the Prague Spring, and the Polish Solidarity movement.

Opportunism   A pejorative term used by communists to describe the actions of socialists with whom they disagree. In its narrowest meaning, opportunism implies a deliberate effort to adapt one's thoughts and actions to short-term trends, seeking acceptance and advantage at the expense of ideological purity. The Bolsheviks, for example, termed the democratic socialists *political opportunists* because they were willing to abide by majority rule. Since the communists base their ideology on the revolutionary concept of class struggle, such cooperation with the class enemy was viewed as the betrayal of class interests and scorned as opportunism. *See also* DEVIATIONISM AND REVISIONISM, p. 45; DOGMATISM, p. 46.

Significance   In practice, all individuals, parties, movements, and states that disagree with the Soviet party line at any time are labeled opportunists. In the 1920s, those who followed Leon Trotsky were called "left opportunists" and those who followed Nikolai Bukharin were labeled "right opportunists." The use of the term in a pejorative sense is in keeping with the general propagandistic approach of the Soviets in describing their political enemies in words and phrases that connote evil actions or sinister motives.

Pluralist Theory   An approach to understanding the dynamics of Soviet politics that emphasizes the role of contending interest groups in the policy-making process. Rather than treating the Soviet Union as a totalitarian state governed by a single, monolithic party, pluralist theory posits the existence of various interest groups within the polity that contend for policy decisions favorable to their interests. This approach to the policy process stresses bargaining among groups, as opposed to the totalitarian model that assumes a single, hierarchical bureaucracy that operates free of any political pressure. Western analysts, such as Gordon Skilling, have identified growing numbers of political groupings within the polity. Groups studied thus far include the military, voluntary mass organizations, regional interests, scientists, nationality groups, and bureaucratic groups. The pluralist approach permits a much more sophisticated analysis of the Soviet policy-making process by identifying demand sectors and the opinion leaders who articulate the demands of a specific sector. Vernon Aspaturian has identified six such "demand sectors" in Soviet society: (1) ideological; (2) security; (3) producers; (4) consumers; (5) agricultural; and (6) public service and welfare. Other scholars have concentrated their analysis on the military, socioeconomic interest groups, or interest groupings within the bureaucracy itself. *See also* CITIZEN PARTICIPATION, p. 275; MASS ORGANIZATIONS, p. 291.

Significance   The pluralist approach to understanding Soviet politics developed out of the growing recognition that the application of the totalitarian model to Soviet politics does not adequately explain the policy process. Where the totalitarian model examines only the outputs of the system, the pluralist approach places attention on the input portion of the system as well. This approach stresses political conflict and conflict resolution rather than political control, and has proved valuable in explaining both the policy process and bureaucratic politics in the Soviet Union. Earlier studies of the Soviet polity, based almost entirely on the totalitarian model, implicitly assumed that the system rested almost entirely on overt threats, coercion, and terror. By the 1960s, however, Western scholars began to recognize that the system is based at least partially on popular support, both within the broad reaches of the party and extending to the many voluntary mass organizations that enroll many nonparty members. Pluralist theory recognized that many interest groupings exist within this popular support, and as with their counterparts in Western polities, they contend for policy decisions that support their interests. Since the totalitarian model posits a single, closed system that receives no inputs from the outside, pluralist theory has provided a useful corrective to this single-factor analysis, which did not adequately explain policy shifts. Pluralist theory has also proved to be relevant in analyzing the communist systems of Eastern Europe, which more clearly than the Soviets diverge from the totalitarian model.

Separate Roads to Socialism   The claim that each nation has the right to choose its own path to socialism without regard for the interests or dictates of any foreign power. The concept of separate roads to socialism was the fundamental issue in the break between Yugoslavia and the Soviet Union in 1948. Josef Stalin insisted that the new communist government of Yugoslavia, under Josip Broz Tito, accept Soviet hegemony. When Tito refused, Stalin expelled Yugoslavia from the Cominform. The conflict clearly centered on the issue of national sovereignty versus Soviet domination. The concept has since been described as "national communism," the placing of national interests above the interests of the Soviet Union. It became the formulation under which Yugoslavia has pioneered an innovative form of communism, based on decentralization of power and workers' self-management. Subsequently, other communist states such as China and Albania have rejected Soviet domination. *See also* COMINFORM, p. 313; POLYCENTRISM, p. 331; SOCIALIST INTERNATIONALISM, p. 335; TITOISM, p. 80; WORKERS' SELF-MANAGEMENT, p. 239.

Significance   With Yugoslavia's successful defense of its right to develop a separate road to socialism outside of Soviet control, the image of a Soviet-dominated international communist movement was shattered. Stalin's insistence on domination gave credibility to the charges that Soviet communism is imperialistic, and revealed to the world the true relationship between the Soviet Union and Eastern Europe. Although the Soviet Union effected a limited rapprochement with Yugoslavia in 1955, Yugoslavia has remained outside of the Soviet bloc, refusing to become a member of the Warsaw Treaty Organization. Its independent stance has enabled it to play an international role out of proportion to its actual power base. Tito, with India's Jawaharlal Nehru and Burma's U Nu, was a founder of the nonaligned movement of Third World nations, and Yugoslavia continues to be an attractive model for new nations who wish to avoid both capitalism and Soviet-controlled communism. Nations such as Algeria have been influenced by the worker self-managed socialism that Yugoslavia developed once it was free of Soviet dominance.

Stalinism   The theoretical and practical interpretations and applications of Marxism by Josef Stalin, who in his roles as party secretary and premier dominated the communist party and governmental machinery in the Soviet Union from 1928 until his death in 1953. Unlike Marxism-Leninism, Stalinism does not represent a comprehensive philosophy or ideology. Stalinism consists mainly of the techniques and practices of governance during a critical period of Soviet history. After coming to power, Stalin seized upon the Leninist instrument of democratic centralism and proceeded to use it as a means to gain absolute power through his control of the party secretariat. Lenin just before his death supposedly warned his comrades of Stalin's mode of operations in a Testament, but Stalin nevertheless was chosen as Lenin's successor to the post of party secretary, which he used to secure complete personal power. After building his power base, Stalin's main contributions were in the methods he used in organizing the Soviet people for achieving industrialization, expanding agricultural production, defense of the nation against the Nazi attack, and the reconstruction of the war-devastated nation. In the major efforts to achieve rapid industrialization and collectivization of agriculture, opposition was ground under by a massive secret police system that employed terror as a routine instrument for gaining compliance and conformity. In the process, Stalin perverted the collective decision-making machinery of the party and government, and all major decisions became subject to one man's will. During these years, public adulation of Stalin on a massive scale led to what Nikita Khrushchev later called "the cult of the individual" and "the cult of personality." Through his purge of the "Old Bolsheviks" in the 1930s, Stalin destroyed all who had political legitimacy but were not unconditionally loyal to him. These actions also weakened the communist party as a viable, self-sustaining institution. No party congress, for example, was called into session between 1939 and 1952. The application of Stalinist principles to Marxism-Leninism created a system which permitted no dissent or opposition. *See also* COMMAND ECONOMY, p. 187; DE-STALINIZATION, p. 318; GREAT PURGE, p. 17; LENINISM, p. 51.

Significance   Stalinism has come to be equated with left-wing dictatorship in the spectrum of politics and power, and with the total bureaucratization of a political system when viewed from the perspective of administration. Yet, Stalin showed considerable flexibility and pragmatism in his leadership. His unchallengeable stand, for example, that domestic development with emphasis on heavy industry must take precedence over the international revolution that Leon Trotsky argued for, helped save the Soviet Union from defeat by the Nazis. When Stalin discovered during World War II that Soviet soldiers were less inclined to fight for proletarian internationalism than for the nationalistic objective of defending the Russian motherland, he borrowed from the old czarist traditions to inspire the troops. Stalin also demonstrated that, in addition to Marxist-Leninist prescriptions for the victory of communism, military occupation by a communist great power, as demonstrated in Eastern Europe after the war, could accomplish that goal if international conditions were favorable. Stalin also functioned effectively in the international milieu of diplomacy, successfully defending Soviet national interests in negotiations with President Franklin Roosevelt and Prime Minister Winston Churchill and other wartime and postwar leaders. Fundamentally, Stalinism incorporated a paranoid system of ubiquitous surveillance and punishments, on a scale perhaps unprecedented in the modern world. Human life became an expendable commodity in Stalin's plans to transform Soviet life as millions of individuals fell victim to the terror. The effects of Stalinism will be felt in the Soviet Union for many years. Stalin built autocratic party and governmental institutions of totalitarian control that extended Russian traditions of absolutism into the latter half of the twentieth century. Most such institutions constructed during the Stalinist years are still in place, even if on a modified basis. Despite the denunciation of Stalinism, many theoretical and practical applications of communist theories carried out over the 25-year period of Stalin's rule remain basic to the contemporary doctrine of Soviet communism. Those which have had the largest impact on communist ideology include his idea of "socialism in one country," Five-Year Plans for fostering industrialization, and the collectivization of agriculture.

Titoism   The theory and practice of national communism as developed by Josip Broz Tito, communist leader of Yugoslavia. Titoism is a Western term that appeared in the late 1940s to describe the process by which nations take separate roads to the building of socialist society. In the Soviet lexicon, Titoism and national communism are used pejoratively to describe a form of deviationism or revisionism. Titoism emerged as a new communist theory in 1948 when President Tito rejected the hegemonic and monolithic approach to world communism imposed by Josef Stalin. National communism as a movement arose as a reaction to Soviet insistence that all Eastern European communist states follow the Soviet model of development utilizing models devised in Moscow. Almost all communist parties of Eastern Europe had wings or factions that sought to reject this Soviet dictation. In Hungary, for example, Imre Nagy led the group in the party that rejected Soviet hegemony, in Poland it was Władysław Gomułka, and in Bulgaria, Traicho Kostov. Yugoslavia came to symbolize national communism, especially after the Soviets had succeeded in expelling Yugoslavia from the Cominform in 1948. Following that event, a purge of suspected Titoists occurred throughout Eastern Europe under Soviet direction. Those accused of Titoism were suspected of placing national interests before the interests of the Soviet Union. For Tito and other supporters of national communism, nationalism and communism are complementary doctrines that should be melded into a new approach that would permit each communist state to develop its political independence and its own road to socialism. *See also* SEPARATE ROADS TO SOCIALISM, p. 77; WORKERS' SELF-MANAGEMENT, p. 239; YUGOSLAV PARTISAN WAR, p. 35.

Significance   Titoism provided a schism within the ranks of world communism that shattered the unity of the Eastern European communist bloc and reduced the hegemonic role of the Soviet Union as the leader of world communism. The national communism movement has had some impact on all the countries of Eastern Europe, with Romania and Albania taking the lead in proclaiming their independence from Soviet dictate. Two communist states—Bulgaria and the German Democratic Republic—have been affected the least by the impact of national communism in Eastern Europe. The United States has sought to encourage the basic schism created by Titoism by trade benefits, credits, and investments for those countries perceived as most effectively defying Soviet policies and demands. Soviet military interventions occurred in Hungary and in Czechoslovakia when the Soviets determined that the trend toward national communism had gotten out of hand and might result in the restoration of a pluralist system that would dilute party control and erode Soviet hegemony. Yugoslavia, however, has pursued a policy of nonalignment, has carried on extensive trade with both the East and the West, and has developed its political and economic system pragmatically, free from external ideological or political controls. When Nikita Khrushchev came to power in the Soviet Union, he denounced Stalinism and reached a temporary rapprochement with Tito in 1955. Nevertheless, national communism has been generally accepted by most of the communist world, with each communist state interpreting Marx and Lenin in a manner compatible with the pragmatic interests of the state. Eurocommunism as practiced in Western Europe, especially in Italy, Spain, and France, has developed its own forms of Titoism in rejecting Soviet leadership, in openly criticizing Soviet policies, and in joining in coalitions with the democratic socialists. Thus, Titoism has destroyed the homogeneity of the Soviet bloc and the unquestioned supremacy of the Soviet Union as the first country of socialism. The Soviets have recognized this and today try to operate on the principle of *primus inter pares*, first among equals, although this position is rejected by the Chinese communists who have sought to take the leadership role in the world communist movement.

Trotskyism   Communist theories expounded by Leon Trotsky, a leader in the Bolshevik Revolution and Civil War period, who contested Josef Stalin for power in the Soviet Union following Lenin's death in 1924. Trotsky took the position that the success of the revolution in Russia presaged the achievement of world revolution, and that the communist base in Russia should be used to promote it. For Trotsky, the success of the revolution depended upon its ability to ignite revolutions in the countries of Western Europe. The new Soviet state could not exist in a hostile capitalist encirclement. Stalin on the other hand rejected the idea of trying to "export the Russian revolution," holding that revolutions must develop out of indigenous conditions just as the Russian experience did. Stalin called for a policy of building socialism in one country, the Soviet Union, to give communism an impregnable base. The success of communism in Russia, Stalin held, would spill over into the rest of the world in the form of encouragement of revolutions by following the Bolshevik example. In his writings, Karl Marx had clearly expected the communist revolution to be international in scope, although "the proletariat of each country must of course first of all settle matters with its own bourgeoisie." Lenin, too, stated that communism and capitalism could not long coexist in the same world, and, unless Germany had a successful revolution, communism could not be sustained in Russia. Trotsky interpreted Marx and Lenin quite literally in calling for world revolution and criticizing Stalin's policy of "socialism in one country." In addition to their ideological conflict, Trotsky and Stalin became locked in a struggle for power after Lenin's death in 1924, a struggle won by Stalin. Trotsky fled and, after spending years in exile severely criticizing Stalin for sacrificing the ideals of the revolution and creating a bureaucratic hell in the Soviet Union, he was assassinated in Mexico in 1940, allegedly by a Stalinist agent. *See also* LEFT OPPOSITION, p. 24; LENINISM, p. 51; MARXISM, p. 55; STALINISM, p. 78.

Significance   Trotskyism became a synonym in the Soviet Union for revisionism and deviationism, two of the cardinal sins against communist orthodoxy. Although his major criticisms of Stalin—that he had sacrificed world revolution for Russian nationalism, and that he had created a bureaucratic ruling class that exploited the workers and betrayed their interests—were often cited as the reason for his break with Stalin, he grieved mainly about Stalin's victory over him in the power struggle. Trotsky failed in that struggle despite the fact that he was a brilliant Marxist theoretician and author, and a first rank military tactician who had saved the revolution by forging the Red Army into a first-class fighting force. He was, however, outmaneuvered by the crafty Stalin, who used his post as Party Secretary to consolidate his power base. Trotskyism remains a viable political force in the world today, with Trotskyite parties active in several countries. As Soviet critics, they continue their martyred leader's opposition to the idea of socialism in one country, to the bureaucratization of communism in the Soviet Union, and to the tendency to create a new ruling class in Soviet-style communist systems.

3. Communist Party Structures and Processes

Activist   A party member or non-party person who voluntarily devotes his or her free time to civic affairs, serving in various community or public organizations. The activist is often rewarded by election to the executive committee or department of the local party. Communist party policy promotes the image of the activist as the ideal party member, serving society while conveying the meaning of communism to his peers. The core group of such politically engaged individuals within each party unit is known as the *aktiv*. The term has also come to mean the core group of the most active members within a sociopolitical organization. *See also* CADRE, p. 88, MASS ORGANIZATIONS, p. 291.

Significance   Activists are the communist version of the "good citizen," those who take on the responsibilities of leadership, organization, and implementation in public groups. An activist may be a nonparty member who volunteers to take part in public affairs, which in a communist system includes practically all aspects of life, since all organizations operate under party surveillance. Such nonparty activists usually fall into three categories: (1) ambitious people who hope to be asked to join the communist party; (2) people who use voluntary activism as a way of "paying one's dues" to the system without joining the party; and (3) retirees. The party encourages citizen participation in the myriad public organizations and rewards the activist accordingly with career benefits, prestige, or advancement within the party. Although at one time most party members were probably activists out of a sense of enthusiasm, today they probably view activism as more of a route to social mobility.

Agitator   The official party spokesman whose chief function is to dispense political information and serve as a link between the party and the masses. Agitators, who are trained in party schools, typically operate on the local levels, addressing neighborhood meetings or workers on the shop floor. The task of the agitator is twofold: (1) to explain party policy in concrete terms; and (2) to create a sense of involvement in carrying out party goals. A major task of agitation work is exhorting the workers and farmers to fulfill the production targets of the economic plan, thus pointing out to the citizens their role in building communism. During periods of major political events, such as party congresses, agitators explain the proposed party platform and policy shifts, again relating these to the individual. The number of agitators is difficult to estimate since many function only seasonally, at harvest time or during elections, but analysts maintain that over 3 million agitators operate on a semi-permanent basis. During elections, when agitators mount an intense effort to bring every citizen to the polls, they may number over 8 million. Although the vast majority are party members, many non-party members volunteer and are accepted since agitators are selected for their status and respect in the local community as well as for political reliability. The Agitprop Department of the Central Committee determines the issues and themes of agitation work, but the local party organization is directly responsible for the agitators and sets their work schedules. Most large primary party organizations have teams of agitators, grouped into an agit-collective. *See also* AGITPROP, p. 85; PARTY SCHOOLS, p. 116; POLITINFORMATOR, p. 121.

Significance   The institutional role of the agitator developed logically from Marxist-Leninist philosophy, which stresses the participation of the masses in running the state. Agitators played a key role in the Bolsheviks' preparation for the Revolution, particularly in the czarist army and among the peasants, where they gained many adherents for Bolshevism. Despite the negative connotation attached to the term in the West, agitation work is aimed at explanation, not incitement. By bringing ideology and party policy down to the grassroots level, the agitators buttress the party's claim to legitimacy as the servant of the people. The agitator is supposed to provide a sense of citizen involvement in the system, a key element in Soviet theories of the relationship between state and society. Although the spread of mass media has rendered some aspects of the agitators' functions anachronistic, the agitator remains an important link between party and people. Because agitation work is conceived as a dialogue, part of the agitators' responsibility is to elicit responses from their audiences. They must be prepared to field questions and answer criticisms. If properly carried out, the agitators' work provides a sense of the public mood concerning the party and its programs.

Agitprop   An acronym for Agitation and Propaganda Department. Agitprop is the communist party organ charged with mobilizing broad public support for party programs and ensuring that all forms of public expression and communication conform to the party line. Agitprop has played a key role in the maintenance of the Soviet system since its inception in 1920 as one of the functionally specialized departments of the first Secretariat of the Central Committee. Agitprop's role rests on the proposition that every form of public expression and communication is relevant to the party, and therefore must be under the direct control of the central party authorities. Agitprop departments exist in all republic, regional, city, and local party units. At the local level, Agitprop's functions are carried out by *Agitpunkty* (agitation points), local offices blanketing the country that disseminate official information and attempt to mobilize the citizenry in support of the system, especially during elections. Agitprop is the agency through which the party molds public opinion and mobilizes public support. One of its chief tasks is to explain party policy to the masses, giving concrete form to party ideology as it applies to specific situations. Agitprop's vast responsibilities include determining the content of all official information, propagating the party line, overseeing the political education carried out in the hundreds of party schools and in the regular educational system, and supervising the content of all media communication and cultural activities. The State Committee for Publishing, Printing, and Book Trade and the State Committee for Television and Radio are directly responsible to the Agitprop Department of the Secretariat. Agitprop supervises the content of the many newspapers published by the central organs of party and government, including *Pravda* (Central Committee), *Izvestiya* (Presidium of the Supreme Soviet), *Trud* (Central Council of Trade Unions), and *Literaturnaya Gazeta* (Union of Soviet Writers). In the area of creative activity, Agitprop promotes the politically favored forms of expression and condemns all others. Agitprop's all-pervasive presence extends into education, science, culture, and the party itself; the posters and filmstrips at local *agitpunkty* are selected by Agitprop. At the local level, teams of agitators (party-trained spokespeople) function as the chief vehicle of face-to-face contact between the party and the masses. *See also* AGITATOR, p. 84; MEDIA, p. 293; POLITINFORMATOR, p. 121.

Significance   Agitprop is the key element in the maintenance of the party's monopoly over ideology and all legal forms of expression. As the party has always maintained that all communication and expression have ideological import, it was apparent from the beginning that ideological purity, and the party line, could be maintained only if the party controlled communications. However, Agitprop is a dual-function organ. At least since 1902, when Lenin accepted Georgi Plekhanov's distinction between propaganda and agitation, the party has distinguished between these two functions. In the Bolshevik lexicon, propaganda involves communicating many ideas to a relatively small number of people, such as indoctrination of party members; agitation is the explanation of a few ideas to the many. The Bolsheviks were innovators in the art of mass communication. Bolshevik agitators were especially successful in the Army in 1917 and after the Revolution when the task of the agitators was to acquaint the citizenry with the new system. Agitation now is especially concerned with elections, when teams of agitators explain the issues and candidates to voters and make sure that they vote, with each agitator usually responsible for 20 to 40 voters. Agitation is thus aimed at the masses, as part of the intense effort to involve and mobilize the entire citizenry for participation in the building of communism. Although the term Agitprop has acquired a pejorative meaning in the West, it is a mistake to reduce Agitprop's activities to simplistic propaganda, an endless repetition of meaningless ideological cant. Just as the early Bolsheviks were pioneers in mass communication and molding public opinion, a substantial proportion of Agitprop's responsibilities include what in the West would be termed "public relations." Agitprop operates much as do the specialized public relations bodies attached to governmental departments in the United States, such as the Department of Defense's information agency. Since the 1960s Agitprop has shifted from the less sophisticated tactics suitable to a semi-industrialized, substantially illiterate society to a focus on dissemination of information, citizen involvement, upgrading of the status of the agitators, with less emphasis on mass political indoctrination. Nikita Khrushchev, in his attempt to revitalize the party apparatus, replaced Agitprop with the Ideological Department. After his ouster, Agitprop was revived, under the name of Propaganda Department, although Agitprop is still its usual designation. Agitprop's key role in the political education and training of party members can be deduced from the fact that after Khrushchev's ouster, propaganda and mass communication were the only areas to suffer large-scale personnel changes. The common practice that a member of the party's ruling body, the Secretariat, serve as head of Agitprop attests to its key role in system maintenance.

Anti-Party Group   Members of the Soviet Presidium (Politburo) who in June of 1957 voted to oust Nikita Khrushchev from the First

Secretaryship of the communist party. The Anti-Party Group, led by Vyacheslav Molotov, Lazar Kaganovich, Dmitri Shepilov, Georgi Malenkov, and Nikolai Bulganin, were foiled when Khrushchev succeeded in calling the Central Committee to Moscow for a vote. The Central Committee reversed the Presidium action and passed a resolution condemning Khrushchev's opponents as an "anti-Party factionalist" group. Most were removed from positions of major importance. *See also* DE-STALINIZATION, p. 318; KHRUSHCHEVISM, p. 49.

Significance   The Anti-Party Group's attempt to oust Khrushchev has several important facets. The first of these is that Khrushchev won by calling the Central Committee into session, marking one of the few times in Soviet political history when the Central Committee has fulfilled its statutory duty of selecting the party leadership. Secondly, the defeat of those who opposed Khrushchev's reforms and de-Stalinization campaign, enabled Khrushchev to reconstruct the party's leading bodies and continue reform. He enlarged the Presidium to 15 full members and increased the power of the Central Committee by expanding its representation on the Presidium from 1 to 9 full members. The 9 new members on the Presidium included Leonid Brezhnev and Marshal Georgi Zhukov, who according to unofficial sources provided the military aircraft to fly the Central Committee to Moscow for the crucial vote. Nonetheless, Zhukov, the first professional military officer to achieve full membership on the Presidium, was expelled from that body within months, as Khrushchev apparently thought that he might compete for power. Unlike Stalinist times, neither execution nor imprisonment was meted out to the conspirators. They remained within the party and, as Khrushchev's policies threatened more and more members of the party apparatus, gained support. By 1964 the dissidents, who now included Leonid Brezhnev, raised a majority of the Central Committee to support ousting Khrushchev. The massive changes that Khrushchev had made in the realm of both party and economic policy threatened many careers, a probable explanation for the determination of the opposition to effect his ouster. That a number of Khrushchev's supporters, such as Leonid Brezhnev, Aleksei Kosygin, and Nikolai Podgorny, turned against him indicates that Khrushchev's control of the party apparatus through reform and appointments was not sufficient to guard against the threats to individual members raised by reform of the party apparatus and by de-Stalinization. Once the secret police had been curbed, it appears that a Soviet leader cannot pursue policies that directly challenge the interests of the party and other established institutions without risking opposition. Having abjured terrorism by the emphasis on de-Stalinization, Khrushchev could not resort to the purge as a means of overcoming bureaucratic opposition.

Apparatus (*Apparatchiki*)   The corps of full-time, paid communist party officials who are responsible for the day-to-day operations of the party at all levels. Members of the party apparatus are termed *apparatchiki*, "people of the apparatus," and are responsible for implementing party policy. As with any modern bureaucracy, positions are functionally specific and the chain of command hierarchical. In a communist state, the party apparatus resembles a government bureaucracy in both size and functions. The apparatus is not a decision-making body; it implements party policy. If the Politburo decides to increase the working class membership of the party, it is the local apparatchiki who must implement this. Some apparatchiki may work as heads of such organizations as trade unions or the *Komsomol* rather than within the party organization. Entrance into the apparatus, especially in the USSR, is increasingly determined by education and attendance at party schools, rather than by ideological fervor. Apparatchiki are typically well represented in the administration of local soviets. Most communist parties are loath to reveal the numbers of such full-time, career party bureaucrats. For the Soviet Union, the size of the apparatus has been estimated at between 100,000 and 500,000. *See also* NEW CLASS, p. 75; NOMENKLATURA, p. 109.

Significance   The party apparatus is the mechanism by which central party policy is implemented at all levels. The apparatus has become the key element in the maintenance of party control in communist-party states. The apex of the apparatus is found at the Central Committee, where an impressive number of apparatchiki staff the departments of the Secretariat and the various committees. The most publicly obvious members of the apparatus are the regional and district party secretaries, who serve as the local representatives of the central party hierarchy. The term apparatchiki has acquired a negative connotation, coming to mean a typical mindless bureaucrat. In addition, the apparatchiki is frequently resented by ordinary citizens because members of the apparatus receive special privileges. Their position also gives them an important voice in filling *nomenklatura* positions, ensuring that all important jobs in society are delegated to politically reliable citizens.

Cadre   A term used in communist systems to refer to those individuals who occupy key positions in all sectors of society. The cadre, or key personnel, constitute the political, economic, administrative, and intellectual elite of the system and are selected by the party leadership. Party control of the cadres enables the party to penetrate all sectors and segments of society. In the Soviet Union, the leading cadres, (*rukovodiashchie kadry*) are estimated at about 3 million people, all of whom essentially owe their positions to the party. Essentially, a member of the leading cadres can occupy his or her post only with the approval of the communist party, a situation which is replicated in the Eastern European states. Only Yugoslavia, where a decentralized economic system and workers' self-management permit other leadership criteria to be considered, has abandoned total party control over cadre policy. The term itself implies a small, highly selective core group that leads by virtue of its knowledge, skills, and prestige. In its illegal, prerevolutionary period, the Bolsheviks were by necessity a cadre party. Cadre policy, the determination of who is politically reliable and qualified, has been a crucial concern of communist leaderships since the Bolshevik Revolution. In the Soviet Union, cadre policy is directly controlled by the Central Committee Secretariat. Cadre policy thus determines the qualifications of a rector of a university, manager of an economic enterprise, director of a ballet company, or chairman of a local soviet. Central party control over the recruitment of these key personnel ensures that all policy and implementation will be carried out in line with party directives. *See also* APPARATUS, p. 88; KHARAKTERISTIKA, p. 105; NOMENKLATURA, p. 109.

Significance   Cadres permeate all aspects of a communist system and constitute a crucial component of party monopoly of power. Communist leaderships use their control over cadre policy to create a base of support; a shift in cadre policy may signal a change in political direction. As First Secretary of the Communist Party of the Soviet Union, Nikita Khrushchev attempted to broaden cadre policy and reorganize the party apparatus by a massive turnover in leading personnel. Khrushchev's plan to rotate leading positions and create two separate party hierarchies, one for industry and one for agriculture, demoralized the leading cadres as well as the party functionaries and probably contributed to his ouster by the Central Committee in 1964. His successor, Leonid Brezhnev, repeatedly stated, "Trust in cadres," which was interpreted as "no more reorganizations." Cadres in all communist party systems have become increasingly well educated and trained, leading to the criticism that communism has betrayed its proletarian heritage by developing into technocracies, or rule by the technocrats. The criticism recognizes the fact that through control of cadre policy, the party ensures total penetration of the system, setting in place a virtual army of reliable personnel who administer all aspects of the system.

Candidate Member   A probationary member of either the communist party or of a party organ. A candidate member of the party serves a probationary period of one to three years, during which time he or she receives training through party courses before being admitted to full membership. Candidate party members are admitted by the Primary Party Organization, the basic party unit, and are largely recruited through the *Komsomol,* the official youth organization. Candidate members must be recommended by three party members, but a Komsomol recommendation may be substituted for one recommendation. A candidate party member has the right to participate in party work and discussion but cannot vote. The principle of candidate membership is applied to all levels of the communist party hierarchy, from the Politburo and Central Committee on down. Candidate members of higher party organs are co-opted from lower levels of the party. As with candidate party members, such probationary members of party organs may participate in discussion but do not vote. All party bodies usually contain from one-third to one-quarter candidate members, who are full party members of their primary party organizations. *See also* CO-OPTATION, p. 98; KOMSOMOL, p. 290; PRIMARY PARTY ORGANIZATION (PPO), p. 122.

Significance   The principle of candidate membership is in line with the Leninist precept that the communist party, as the advance guard of the proletariat and the leading element of society, must be highly selective and confine decision-making power to a small core group. The application of candidate membership to all party organs means that the division between full membership and candidate membership places a portion of the party on probation even after they have achieved positions of major influence. Similarly, the elevation of a candidate to full membership in such vital bodies as the Politburo signals that the member has attained the peak of political power.

Central Auditing Commission   The financial inspection agency of the Communist Party of the Soviet Union (CPSU), named at the party congress. The Central Auditing Commission is charged with verifying and auditing the finances of the party. It submits a report to the congress, which is the closest thing to a financial statement of the party, and during its tenure, is responsible for supervising party finances and accounting.

Significance   Since the finances of the CPSU and other communist parties are largely secret, the details of the work of the Central Auditing Commission are not public knowledge. The Commission does issue a partial financial statement, from which can be gleaned such information as the fact that party publications account for an increasing share of party income, or that CPSU party dues now constitute about 65 percent of party income. The Auditing Commission generally confines its criticism to local party units.

Central Committee   According to party statutes, the most authoritative continuing body in a communist-party system. The Central Committee is formally charged with the direction of the party between party congresses, supervision of all party organs, and representation of the party domestically and internationally. The Politburo (Presidium) and Secretariat in theory report to the Central Committee and are selected by it. Major party resolutions and decisions are issued in the name of the Central Committee. In reality, the power and authority of the Central Committee are severely limited by its relatively large membership and infrequent meetings. Responsibility for policymaking and implementation are delegated to the much smaller Politburo and Secretariat, the true locus of power in a communist system. The Central Committee provides a forum for publicizing the party line and formally ratifying party policy; it has little policymaking power. The Soviet Central Committee totals 426 full and candidate (nonvoting) members and usually meets twice a year in full (plenary) sessions for several days. Plenary sessions are held before major events, such as the introduction of the economic plan, or to discuss current issues of import in foreign or domestic affairs. Plenary sessions are not regularly scheduled and generally only a report is issued rather than a full account of the proceedings. At party congresses, the most important event is the report of the Central Committee, in effect a "state of the union" address. Such crucial decisions as the draft five-year plan must be formally approved by the Central Committee. All resolutions issued by the Central Committee are binding on party members; the major function of the Central Committee is to give formal authorization of party policy. The Central Committee has been a critical part of the communist party structure since its inception at the First Party Congress in 1898. Originally the governing body of the party, the Central Committee became the instrument by which Vladimir Lenin maintained control over the party. By 1919 the Central Committee had been expanded from its original core group and it possessed two permanent bureaus, the Organizational Bureau (Orgburo) and the Political Bureau (Politburo). The increase in the size of membership and the creation of functionally specific departments contributed to the decline of its power; the Politburo became the party's inner ruling group. During the first decade of Bolshevik rule the Central Committee, however, continued to play an important role, even as late as 1932 occasionally outvoting Josef Stalin. Stalin purged the Central Committee, installing his own supporters, and reduced its role to that of formally ratifying the policy of the leadership, a function it retains today. The Central Committees of the Eastern European parties, with a few minor exceptions, are modeled after the Central Committee that evolved under Lenin and Stalin. All have relatively large memberships, although the Hungarian Central Committee does not include candidate members, and all meet infrequently, having delegated authority to the party's inner bodies. All possess a sizable permanent staff that is divided into functionally specific committees, such as cadres, security, and ideology, which function under the direction of the Secretariat. Members are carefully selected so as to represent the leading elements in the system, a type of representation that lends further legitimacy to the pronouncements of the Central Committee. As with all party and government bodies in a communist system, the Central Committee is controlled by the party leadership through the principle of interlocking memberships, whereby a substantial proportion of its members also hold important state or party positions. The Central Committee typically includes members of the Politburo, Secretariat, Council of Ministers, and deputies to the Supreme Soviet as well as key republican and provincial party leaders. This duplication of offices ensures that the major function of the Central Committee is confined to advice and legitimization. The Central Committee does have an important formal legislative function because decrees (*postanovleniya*), which are binding on legislative organs, are issued in its name. *See also* POLITBURO (PRESIDIUM), p. 118.

Significance   Although largely shorn of its original policymaking power, the Central Committee can provide information about the political dynamics of a communist state. The representation of the various institutional and party interests on the Central Committee is a political question the analysis of which can provide insight into group politics. As its role is to present an official consensus on all policy issues, its membership must include representatives of all key elements in the system. Analysis of this membership can provide some clues to communist politics; for example, if the proportion of military members increases, analysts may assume that the military is wielding increasing power in the country. The membership of the current central committees in the Soviet Union and Eastern Europe is highly trained and technical, indicative of the importance attached to scientific and economic development. The timing of plenary sessions is important. At times, the Central Committee may become the ultimate political arbiter. In June of 1957, the Central Committee of the Soviet Union outvoted the Anti-party Group that had tried to remove Nikita Khrushchev, and a subsequent Central Committee, in 1964, removed him. In Czechoslovakia in 1967 the Central Committee became the focal point of dissent, finally stripping Antonín Novotný of the leadership after much open debate. As demonstrated by Khrushchev's experience, the top leadership cannot operate without the support of the Central Committee. Party leaders usually try to "pack the membership," one common tactic being to enlarge it. Thus, Todor Zhivkov in 1962 ensured his leadership of the Bulgarian party by enlarging the Central Committee. János Kádár of Hungary, as another example, enlarged the Hungarian Central Committee before presenting the New Economic Mechanism (NEM), a fairly radical economic liberalization, for ratification. Elevation from candidate to full membership signals that a party official is at the topmost level. Central Committee members may advance into top government posts, or into the Politburo or Secretariat. The Central Committee comprises the elite of a communist system. Only in Yugoslavia, where rotation of office is more common and the economic managership freed from mandatory central economic planning, is the roster of the Central Committee less a guide to the top elite. Central committees function as the chief agency of legitimization for the party leadership. All important decisions, from the annual May Day slogans to the party statutes are issued in its name; the Central Committee formally ratifies party policy and conveys a sense of consensus for the system.

Collective Farm Party Organization   An organization that is responsible for most of the day-to-day operation of a collective farm (*kolkhoz*) in the Soviet Union. The organizational unit of the collective farm party is the Primary Party Organization (PPO), the basic unit of the communist party. PPOs now exist in practically all the collective farms in the Soviet Union. In Eastern Europe, party penetration of the rural sector has been far less successful, especially in Poland where over 80 percent of the land is privately owned. The workforce of a Soviet collective farm may total 500 or more, of which 30 to 40 typically will be party members. Since the workforce on a collective farm tends to be divided by functions, the kolkhoz PPO is usually subdivided into party groups by function of the various members. Each party group is headed by an organizer (the *partgruporg*). The partgruporgs coordinate their activities with the kolkhoz party secretary who frequently is the farm manager. The general membership elects a party bureau, as in other PPOs, that directs the smaller units. The major function of the collective farm party organization is to carry out the directives of the economic plan, and much of its work is devoted to agitprop. *See also* AGITPROP, p. 85; KOLKHOZ, p. 205; PRIMARY PARTY ORGANIZATION (PPO), p. 122.

Significance   The collective farm party organizations that now blanket the Soviet countryside represent a major achievement of Nikita Khrushchev, who as First Secretary and leader of the state made Soviet agriculture a priority. His predecessor, Josef Stalin, had concentrated on collectivizing Soviet agriculture, a brutal process that left millions dead and an alienated peasantry. Stalin's methods in the countryside were to control the agricultural sector by coercion and terrorism. Khrushchev substituted more subtle means of control, namely organizing the collective farms and bringing them into the party process. Once party penetration of the farms was attained, Khrushchev disbanded the Machine Tractor Stations (MTSs), Stalin's favored method of control over the peasantry. There is little doubt that under Khrushchev the lot of the Soviet peasant was bettered. The increased party presence on the farm has meant that the individual collective farms have had some input into economic decision making when production targets are drawn up by planners upon the advice of regional and local representatives. The *kolkhoz* party secretary reports directly to the party bureau of the district (*raion*) and may be able to successfully argue for an adjustment in production targets. The record in Eastern Europe is spottier; few of the East European systems have achieved anywhere near the degree of party presence in the rural areas as in the Soviet Union. As the communist party has been a worker-based urban phenomenon, this may have increased the alienation of the rural sector in Eastern Europe.

Collective Leadership   The principle of sharing central decision-making authority. The Communist Party of the Soviet Union claims to follow the principle of collective leadership in all major political decisions, particularly those taken by the Politburo. Collective leadership, in Soviet terminology, means that the central authority is shared equally among a small collective of leaders rather than being exercised by one man, as it was under Josef Stalin. In contrast to one-man rule, or decision making by a chief executive, collective leadership implies leadership by compromise and consensus, with no major action taken until unanimous agreement of the collective leadership is reached. Stalin's heirs have stressed the principle as a corrective to the abuses perpetrated by Stalinism and the "cult of personality."

Collective leadership is viewed as a fundamental principle of Leninism and an advance over both one-man rule and the chief executive system of Western democracies. In theory, communist collective leadership resembles the consensual style of decision making practiced in traditional societies, ranging from the Iroquois Federation to the stateless societies of precolonial Africa. *See also* POLITBURO, p. 118; YUGOSLAVIA: COLLECTIVE STATE PRESIDENCY, p. 176.

Significance   The principle of collective leadership has its ideological roots in the egalitarianism of Marxism and the doctrine of the "withering away of the state." In the early days of the tiny, illegal Bolshevik Party, consensual leadership was practiced, although Vladimir Lenin remained "first among equals." While the method of Soviet political decision making is not divulged, some Western analysts maintain that there is some validity in the claim to collective, or consensual, decision making. It is apparent that debate does occur within the Politburo, and that since Stalin no one person can unilaterally override the rest of the Politburo. Politburo decisions may indeed be the result of compromise, and may differ from the action originally proposed. The stress on collective leadership has enabled the Soviet leadership to criticize both the Chinese and Yugoslavs as revisionists who have abandoned the Leninist model of intraparty democracy. The Soviets also pointedly maintain that the President of the United States has more autonomous power than the General Secretary of the CPSU. One person, the President, for example, can legally make a decision to undertake a nuclear war whereas in the Soviet Union such a decision would be made collectively in the Politburo. The term collective leadership also has been used to describe the interim period immediately after Stalin's death in 1953 when Georgi Malenkov, Nikita Khrushchev, and Vyacheslav Molotov (later replaced by Nikolai Bulganin) shared power until Khrushchev consolidated his power in 1956. The degree of collective leadership values has varied both from communist country to communist country, and within a country over time. Neither Romania nor Albania can be cited as examples of collective leadership, while, since the death of Josip Broz Tito, Yugoslavia has moved into a period of collective leadership.

Congress   According to communist-party statutes, the supreme organ of a communist party, charged with setting policy and electing a central governing committee responsible for directing party work between congresses. National party congresses, now usually held every four to five years in communist-party states, are theoretically the highest party authority. In practice, the large number of delegates—

almost 5,000 in the Soviet Union—and infrequent meetings preclude any meaningful policymaking role. The policymaking responsibilities of the central committee have also atrophied, being replaced by the inner party leadership who sit on the Politburo and Secretariat. The agenda of a party congress and the membership of the central committee are predetermined by the party leadership, with the party congress acting as a ratifying agent. National party congresses are preceded by local and regional congresses, or conferences, where a central committee is also ratified by the participants and delegates to the next highest level congress selected. At the lower party levels, party conferences serve mainly to validate the decisions of higher party authorities and under careful supervision, name the delegation to the next highest party conference. At the middle levels, party conferences may deal with more substantive matters, particularly economic, where delegations may articulate local concerns. Local members, however, through the system of indirect delegation from level to level, have no input into the selection of the party's central bodies. Communist party congresses date from the early days of the Bolsheviks, when they wielded considerable policymaking powers. Between 1903 and 1917, seven party congresses or conferences (the latter differed only in that they were not empowered to elect a new central committee) were held. Top leaders delivered reports on their work and were truly accountable to the congress in the early days of the Bolsheviks. Until 1925, congresses of the Communist Party of the Soviet Union (CPSU) met annually. Stalin first breached the party statutes by delaying the 15th CPSU Congress; by 1952, no CPSU Congress had been held since 1938. Since then, Stalin's successors have convened congresses every four to five years, a pattern generally followed by the Eastern European states. The agenda of a national party congress is publicized months in advance. The major event is the report of the Central Committee, delivered by the General Secretary, followed by dozens of speeches praising him. Thus, the party congress has become a ceremony, whose major function is to convey unity with the leadership. In Yugoslavia, where during the 1960s much political power devolved to the republican level, republican party congresses have at times taken conflicting stances, which then had to be resolved by the federal party congress. In Yugoslavia, the republican parties also directly elect representatives to the central party bodies and each republic is assured representation on these bodies. Otherwise, the party congress in the Soviet Union and Eastern Europe is usually a predictable event, orchestrated by the party leadership. *See also* CENTRAL COMMITTEE, p. 91; SECRETARIAT, p. 126; WORKERS OPPOSITION, p. 34.

Significance   The party congress functions not as a policymaking body, as intended by its Bolshevik founders, but as an instrument to validate and legitimize the decisions of the party leaders. Since it formally approves the membership of the central committee, it also legitimizes major personnel changes, giving them the aura of democratic election. Attendance at party congresses is a means of rewarding the party regulars, much as political conventions in the USA are used to reward the party faithful. Although shorn of its original policymaking and elective functions, the party congress is still of value to the political analyst. The speeches frequently provide insight into party policy and can indicate shifts in priorities. At times party congresses have been crucial. Soviet policy toward intraparty opposition was determined by the Resolution on Unity passed by the Tenth Party Congress in 1921, when Vladimir Lenin suppressed the Workers Opposition movement and decreed that factions within the party would not be tolerated. The Tenth Congress was the last Soviet congress that played an active role in policymaking, although congresses throughout the 1920s were still enlivened by open debate. After Josef Stalin seized undisputed power in the Soviet Union, the party congress as a meaningful body atrophied even further. The 1934 Congress, dubbed the "Congress of the Victors," was orchestrated by Stalin to proclaim the triumph of the first Five-Year Plan and the "success" of agricultural collectivization. Stalin's successor, Nikita Khrushchev, used the 1956 20th CPSU Congress to deliver a speech revealing the inhumanity of Stalinism. Khrushchev's "secret speech" constituted a clear signal that Khrushchev was embarking on a program of de-Stalinization. Immediately after the Soviet Union expelled Tito's Yugoslavia from the Soviet bloc in 1948, the Communist Party of Yugoslavia met at the Fifth CPY Congress and defiantly endorsed Tito's refusal to bow to Soviet hegemony. In Czechoslovakia in 1968, as the Soviet-led Warsaw Treaty troops invaded the country, delegates met secretly at the 14th (Vysočany) Congress in Prague to set the official seal of approval on what became the Soviet-aborted Czechoslovak liberalization. Some analysts have speculated that the Soviet invasion was timed to prevent the Vysočany congress, which was later declared illegal and replaced in the official histories by a hastily-convened pro-Soviet congress. The postponement of a scheduled party congress may signal internal dissension, economic problems, or any number of reasons why the leadership may wish to avoid a public mass meeting. The Polish congress of 1981 was marked by many delegates' insistence that at least one-third of the Polish Central Committee be democratically elected. Conversely, congresses have been held ahead of schedule, usually indicating major changes which the leadership wishes to formalize. Party congresses are attended by delegations of foreign communist parties from around the world. The composition and actions of these delegations can illuminate relations between the various communist parties. The rift between the Soviet Union and China became evident from the actions of the Chinese delegation at the 21st CPSU Congress in 1961. In 1971, the Italian and Romanian delegations to the 24th CPSU Congress were outspokenly critical of Soviet actions in Czechoslovakia, giving impetus to the Eurocommunism movement that was aimed at separating the European parties from Soviet practice. A communist party may refuse to send a delegation, the host congress may refuse to accept it, as has happened to Yugoslav delegations, or a party may register its disapproval by sending a delegation of insultingly low status. Thus, while the congress of a ruling communist party may bear little resemblance to the original Bolshevik institution, the party congress remains a useful tool for political analysis.

Co-optation   The method by which communist parties typically select their leading personnel. The practice of co-optation means that, at each level of the party, key personnel are selected by the next highest level of party leadership. Thus, although all party officers and bodies are formally elected by their members, the elections are predetermined by higher party bodies. Lower party units do not usually have the power to refuse an official nominee nor the power to elect one not approved from above. The practice extends throughout the hierarchy of the party bodies, to the topmost level of Politburo and Secretariat where the membership is co-opted from lower party bodies. *See also* DUPLICATION OF OFFICE, p. 100; ELECTORAL PROCESS: USSR, p. 140; NOMENKLATURA, p. 109; PARTY ASSIGNMENT, p. 110.

Significance   Co-optation of party bodies and leading personnel resembles the electoral process in a communist-party system, where the party selects the candidates for public office, who then usually run unopposed. Both systems rely heavily on the *nomenklatura* system and the extensive personnel files used to identify reliable potential leadership. Co-optation is closely tied to party assignment, wherein a party member will be given a designated party assignment, which may be accepting nomination to a party body. Although the term implies absolute and unilateral control by higher party bodies, in reality the selection process is more complex. Lower party units may be consulted and discussions held, and members at times may refuse a party assignment. In a sense, because the party controls the staffing of all important positions through nomenklatura, co-optation applies to the staffing of all key posts, party or nonparty.

Criticism and Self-Criticism (*Kritika i samokritika*)   The duty of all communist party members to point out the faults and mistakes of their fellow members and to publicly confess their own errors. Criticism and self-criticism is part of party discipline and is meant to be a constructive means of ensuring conformity to the party line. The practice is consistent with Marxism's doctrine of the perfectability of humankind through constant reeducation, but it has frequently been used to discipline and punish individuals. Although communist parties constantly enjoin their members to engage in criticism and self-criticism, it frequently has become a mere formality. The principle of democratic centralism, which mandates obedience to the centrally determined party line, restricts it to criticism of the means of execution of policy; criticism of policy itself is not permissible. *See also* LENINISM: DEMOCRATIC CENTRALISM, p. 52; PARTY LINE, p. 115; PARTY STATUTES, p. 118.

Significance Criticism and self-criticism, prescribed by party rules, provide a means by which individual officials can be singled out and conformity ensured. In periods of political stability, much of it becomes a ceremonial recital of petty lapses, but it can also become a vehicle through which a group may enhance its power by discrediting rivals. The practice was used during the Stalinist purge trials of the 1930s and again in Eastern Europe in the early 1950s to persuade the victims of the purges to publicly confess their predetermined "crimes," as a last testimonial of faith in the communist party. Some analysts have pointed out that the concept has roots in the *auto-da-fé* of the Spanish Inquisition, when the condemned participated in a final ceremony as a means of cleansing themselves of sin before the inquisitional court. Although discredited by the purge trials, criticism and self-criticism is used to bolster the party's claim to intraparty democracy. Since Stalin, the use of public self-confessions has waned. An increase in criticism and self-criticism still may signal a shift in personnel or major policy changes. Such intraparty practice usually remains secret but may be reflected publicly in newspaper and journal articles pointing out errors and mistakes, which thus illuminate internal party politics for the analyst.

Dual Accountability Principle applied to the party bodies of the Soviet and East European communist parties whereby each party organ is responsible both to its parent party unit and to the next highest party unit. Dual accountability applies to all party organs except those at the top of the hierarchy. Beginning with the Primary Party Organization (PPO), each party unit under careful direction "names" an executive committee and from the membership of the executive committee, a party bureau or secretariat, led by the local party secretary. Each party organ must report both to its parent party unit and to its counterpart at the next highest level of party organization. In effect, under dual accountability the membership of party organs is selected by the party leadership at two levels, and it is responsible to both. The process extends to the topmost level where the central party authorities are responsible only to their own memberships. Mandated by party statutes, dual accountability is maintained by the principles of democratic centralism and party discipline. *See also* LENINISM: DEMOCRATIC CENTRALISM, p. 52; PARTY STATUTES, p. 118.

Significance   Dual accountability, also called dual subordination, provides a network of horizontal and vertical responsibility that enables the central leadership to control the party structure. Originally intended by the Bolshevik leaders to maintain accountability, the subordination of party organs to two units provides a system of checks that creates tight central control over the party apparatus. Relations among the party units and organs at the various levels are determined by dual accountability and the principle of democratic centralism. Party statutes, binding on all party members, mandate this. For example, the relevant party statutes of the Polish communist party states: (1) "All party authorities are required to report to the party organizations that elect them"; (2) "Maintenance of party discipline is required and the minority is subordinate to the resolutions of the majority"; and (3) "Resolutions and directives from higher party authorities must be carried out by lower ones." Such rules set up a hierarchical control system that allows only the central party authorities freedom of action; dual accountability reinforces the lack of intraparty democracy.

Duplication of Office, "Interlocking Directorates"   The practice common to communist systems whereby party leaders at all levels simultaneously hold government and party posts. This duplication of office guarantees that party policy will be executed by the government. All party members are bound by party discipline to observe and implement party decisions, whether they act as a party official or as a government official. Thus, the party controls all state agencies through duplication of office. All nongovernmental organizations, such as the trade unions, youth organizations, residence committees, or cultural organizations are also staffed by party leaders. At the highest levels, duplication of office is all-pervasive, with top party officials holding several government and party posts. In the Soviet Union, members of the Politburo may also hold seats in the Secretariat, the republican or provincial party leaderships, the Presidium of the

Supreme Soviet, or the Council of Ministers. All are members of the Central Committee. Comparable duplication of office exists at all levels. Key members of the basic party units, the Primary Party Organizations (PPOs) sit on the local soviet (assembly), hold party positions, and frequently manage local enterprises or head other organizations. The membership of the local soviet usually includes the head of the local police, the Procurator, the managers of local enterprises, heads of cultural institutions, and local party officials. Because the party controls the nomination process to all elected bodies and controls the appointments to all key nongovernmental positions through the *nomenklatura* system, a series of what can be termed interlocking directorates exists. This can be envisioned as a series of overlapping party/government positions with the party supreme and the functional separations blurred. The only separation of powers which exists is found in the generally accepted principle that the party determines the policies that the government executes. Government subordination to party is ensured through party discipline and democratic centralism; duplication of office assures this. *See also* NOMENKLATURA, p. 109; PARTY ASSIGNMENT, p. 110.

Significance   The effects of the Soviet practice of duplication of office are far-reaching. The interlocking party/government directorates integrate policymaking and implementation, much as the chief executive officer of an insurance corporation who serves on the board of directors of a major New York bank protects the interests of the insurance industry and integrates insurance policy with banking policy. As the government is subordinate to the party, government initiative is stifled. It weakens the soviets and local administrative bodies, erodes public confidence in governmental bodies, and renders sizable sections of the constitution meaningless. Since the principle of duplication of office was first introduced by Vladimir Lenin, as part of the party's prerogative as the leading agency in society, party officials have constantly tended to usurp the proper functions of government. Administrators become reluctant to make decisions without checking with party officials, abdicating more and more responsibility to the party. *Podmena*, the substitution of party for government, is increasingly recognized as a problem by Soviet analysts. As long as the party insists on duplication of office, however, podmena will continue. Many western Sovietologists, such as Merle Fainsod, have maintained that the "overlapping and parallel" functions are necessary to the maintenance of a Soviet-style communist system. The efforts of the Yugoslav League of Communists to avoid this duplication of office so common to Soviet and East European states is a feature which markedly distinguishes Yugoslavia from the other communist party systems. The Yugoslav reforms of the 1960s, which decentralized decision making and freed the economy from mandatory central planning also decreased the overlap between party and government officeholding. Elsewhere in Eastern Europe, the leading cadre in all government and non-party organizations are always party members. Local assemblies, the party units, youth organizations, trade unions, and government agencies all share personnel. In reality, the elaborate government structure does not exist independently of the party. The interlock of party and government is assured by duplication of office, and party directives carry the force of law.

General Secretary   The highest office in a communist party state. The General Secretary, sometimes called the First Secretary, is the dominant political figure and the leader of party and state. Although officially only the head of the party, in reality the General Secretary is also the titular head of state and the symbol of national authority. The formal legal arrangements of the various ruling communist parties give little indication of the true power of the General Secretary of the party. According to party statutes, he is elected by the central committee and serves as head of the party secretariat, where his vote is supposedly equal in weight to the votes of the other individual members. As chief executive of the party, he oversees the implementation of party policy, determines key appointments, and controls the party apparatus. The General Secretary also heads the Politburo, the chief policymaking body for the system. As all government institutions are in practice subordinate to the party, he also functions as the head of state. There is no limitation on term of office, nor any institutionalized means of removing the General Secretary. Since 1922, when Josef Stalin became the first General Secretary of the Communist Party of the Soviet Union, only four men—Stalin, Nikita Khrushchev, Leonid Brezhnev, and Yuri Andropov—have occupied the position. The actualities of the position are minimal, and have differed from time to time and from state to state. Some party Secretaries have also served as the formal head of the government, as Leonid Brezhnev served as the Chairman of the Presidium of the Supreme Soviet and Gustáv Husák is President of Czechoslovakia. Others have not followed this practice, or only have adopted the formal state office after several years, as did Brezhnev. Whether or not the party Secretary also serves as titular head of state makes little actual difference. For example, Brezhnev conducted the negotiations for the Helsinki Accord for the Soviet Union even though at the time Aleksei Kosygin was officially the Soviet head of state. As the symbol of national leadership, the General Secretary is the repository of the party's self-assigned role as the leader of society and the ultimate authority. His role in policy initiation is difficult to measure, but as chief of the party he obviously determines basic policy. Although Stalin exercised dictatorial control during at least his last 20 years, all available evidence indicates that consensual decision making was the dominant style of the Khrushchev and Brezhnev leaderships. As chief conciliator, the General Secretary is responsible for creating acceptable compromises, thus determining much of the policy that guides the nation. Current party Secretaries probably do not possess enough power to dismiss a Politburo member, as an American President can simply dismiss a cabinet member. In foreign affairs, the General Secretary probably does not possess the power to determine foreign policy without previous consultation and information, as did Stalin. Periodically, the General Secretary delivers reports to the Central Committee that indicate the importance he attaches to a particular issue. For example, Brezhnev's May 1982 report to the Soviet Central Committee on agricultural policy constituted a clear sign that the Soviet leadership considers agricultural shortcomings a crucial issue. The General Secretary is essentially responsible for the overall leadership of the country, and when he speaks, all the power and authority of the party stand behind him. The selection of a General Secretary is a political mystery. In many cases, the Soviet leadership appears to have played a major role in determining who shall head the East European states. Vulko Chervenkov, the First Secretary of the Bulgarian party, was forced to give way to Todor Zhivkov in 1962 when Khrushchev pressed for the removal of the most Stalinist of the East European leaders. János Kádár was installed in Hungary in 1956 with the approval of the Soviet authorities; Gustáv Husák replaced the reformist Alexander Dubček as Czechoslovak First Secretary after the Soviet-led invasion of Czechoslovakia in August of 1968. Only Josip Broz Tito of Yugoslavia has ever succeeded in naming a successor, by setting up a collective state Presidency. Although the "elective" role of the Central Committee is usually confined to rubberstamping the collective co-optation made by the inner party elite, at times it has fulfilled its statutory function. When Khrushchev was ousted in 1964, the Soviet Central Committee vote was the determining fact, and in 1968 a reformist Czechoslovak Central Committee voted to depose Antonín Novotný. Usually the successorship is decided by the leading figures on the politburo and secretariat, however, thus illuminating where the locus of power lies in a communist system. With the current exception of the decentralized and federalized Yugoslav state, the dynamics of political succession in other communist party systems almost presupposes a single leader. The strict hierarchical flow of power, the concentration of party and government functions at the topmost party level, and the domination of party over government almost necessitates the presence of a supreme leader, the party Secretary, who has come to symbolize:the authority of the party and its unrestrained power. *See also* COLLECTIVE LEADERSHIP, p. 94; DUPLICATION OF OFFICE, p. 100; POLITBURO, p. 118; SECRETARIAT, p. 126.

Significance   The importance of the General Secretary can be ascertained by the fact that any change in the incumbency of.this office is viewed as crucial to a communist-party state. With each change in the General Secretaryship, the Soviet system has changed. Historically, the nature and style of the Soviet leader have influenced the system more than in any other industrialized nation. The overwhelming importance of the General Secretary is borne out by the intense speculation that develops whenever a change seems imminent, as in the early 1980s when Brezhnev's failing health spurred speculation about his probable successor. The problem of succession is a major weakness of Soviet-style systems because there is no institutionalized method of deposing or replacing a General Secretary. The lack of any legal or constitutional means promotes secrecy, factionalism, and conspiracy. Democratic centralism, party discipline, and censorship dictate that no criticism of the national leader is permitted. Although the days are past when an Aleksandr Solzhenitsyn could be imprisoned for derogatorily referring to Stalin and his mustache, the General Secretary is still sacrosanct. Even the liberal Yugoslav system never permitted overt criticism of its charismatic leader, Tito. On those rare occasions when public opinion is so adverse as to bring down a party Secretary, as in Czechoslovakia in 1968 or Poland in 1980, it is the party, not the people, who make that decision and select a successor. Two party secretaries have succeeded as the result of what amounted to domestic revolution in 1956, Władysław Gomułka in Poland and János Kádár in Hungary. The Poles appear to have stumbled into an *ad hoc* method of changing the top leader—every ten years or so the workers take to the streets and so discredit the leadership that the party bows and names a new First Secretary, namely in 1956, 1970, and 1980. Thus, the party Secretary may serve as the ultimate scapegoat for the shortcomings of his party and the system. Lacking true elections and any legal claim to national leadership, party Secretaries have traditionally pursued two methods of legitimizing their power: (1) by manipulating the symbols of office so that "the people" accept him as national leader; and (2) by control over appointments, creating a power base of local party officials who owe their positions to him. A few, most significantly Tito, have been able to base their power on charisma and service to the nation, but for most the charismatic approach rapidly degenerates into what Khrushchev termed the Stalinist "cult of personality." Since Khrushchev's revelations about Stalin's brutality, party leaders have generally avoided the mandatory hero-worship, ubiquitous propaganda, and mass manipulation associated with Stalinism, preferring to base legitimacy on economic and military achievements. János Kádár of Hungary, the most low-key of party Secretaries, achieved legitimacy as the leader of Hungary's economic successes. The Romanian leader, Nicolae Ceauşescu, while maintaining internal controls that were stricter than elsewhere in Eastern Europe, pursued a certain degree of independence from Moscow internationally, which brought trade and cooperation from the noncommunist countries. Both Brezhnev and Khrushchev used economic promise as legitimization. Such legitimizing devices are a double-edged sword if the economy falters; Edward Gierek of Poland was forced out in 1980 by the workers' revolt catalyzed by the glaring discrepancies between Gierek's promises and the faltering Polish economy. The dynamics of legitimization and succession in Yugoslavia have differed substantially since Tito's death in 1980 (after 35 years as national leader). In a federation characterized by devolution of power, political competition among the eight constituent units of the Yugoslav federation, and the lack of a majority nationality, no one political figure can claim legitimacy as a national leader. The mechanism set up by Tito, a Collective Presidency composed of the heads of the eight federal units plus the Secretary of the Yugoslav party, rotates the Presidency among its members each year, in an order set forth by law. This mechanism has functioned and for several years has avoided one-person dominance. That no heir to Tito has emerged is probably due to the decentralized nature of Yugoslav politics, where the eight republican and provincial leaders base their power in their respective national constituencies and each possesses effective veto power over the rise of a single dominant leader. In the Soviet Union and Eastern Europe, the position of party Secretary reveals the true nature of politics and power in a communist-party system. The power of the party Secretary as national leader lies not in legal institutions but in his control over the party. Party control means control over the nation, thus making it clear who rules in a communist state. Although communism in theory speaks only of "collective leadership," the office of General Secretary has tended to elevate an individual charismatic leader into the key role in each communist state in the decision-making processes.

Kharakteristika   A personal information file maintained by Soviet authorities on party members, citizens of some importance, and those who are involved in a major relocation from one part of the country to another. The *kharakteristika* contains not only personal data, such as education, but also deals extensively with an assessment of the individual's political attitudes and reliability. The content of the kharakteristika becomes extremely important when an individual is a candidate for a high-level position included in the *nomenklatura* system or if he applies for a visa for foreign travel. *See also* NOMENKLATURA, p. 109.

Significance   The kharakteristika is an important element of party control, enabling the party to ensure that individuals deemed politically unreliable are not permitted to play important party or nonparty roles. Since the content of the file is secret and is based on numerous reports, the individual has little control over an instrument which may exercise a crucial influence on his life. The kharakteristika constitutes an important element in the filling of nomenklatura positions, which include almost all of the important positions within Soviet society. It thus is crucial to maintaining the party's predominant influence over most aspects of Soviet life.

Main Political Administration (MPA)   The chief agent of political indoctrination and control of the Soviet armed forces by the communist party. The Main Political Administration reports directly to the Central Committee and is supervised and instructed by the Politburo. The MPA reviews the political reliability of military personnel and supervises the numerous Primary Party Organizations (PPOs) and Komsomol organizations based in the armed forces. Members of the MPA hold military rank and are responsible for both supervising and directing all political work in the Soviet armed forces. At each level of operation, from the company to the division, the chief MPA official is the political officer, the *zampolit*. Zampolity have sizable staffs; the overall size of the MPA is estimated at 40,000. The MPA originated during the Civil War period as a means of ensuring the loyalty of the many former Czarist officers who served with the Red Army. An April 1918 decree instituted a system of political commissars attached to the Red Army. During the Civil War all military orders had to be countersigned by a commissar and the commissars were held responsible for the actions of all military men. The MPA is a direct continuation of this tradition of civil control over the military. As party membership in the Soviet armed forces increased, to an estimated 20 percent today, the role of the MPA became supervision of military party units as well as political indoctrination. The MPA is also responsible for the military press; an important function of the zampolit is agitprop work. The political officers are trained in military party schools, the highest of which is the Lenin Military Political Academy. The MPA also includes a

Main Military Council, charged with supervising national party policy in the military. *See also* PARTY SCHOOLS, p. 116.

Significance   The Main Political Administration is a crucial agency in the party's ability to maintain control over the military. Unlike many one-party systems, communist systems have largely avoided the perils of military control. The MPA has remained subordinate to the party leadership, which has effectively used this mechanism to ensure that only the most politically reliable officers advance in rank. The MPA also serves to recruit new members into party units in the military, thus ensuring a ready pool of politically reliable officers. The military, however, has considerable independence of action on matters of strategy, organization, and discipline. Rather than being in an adversary position, the military and the party maintain a close working relationship. The Brezhnev leadership (1964–82) was marked by the increasing representation of the military in high party bodies. Some observers, such as Dimitri Simes, maintain that the military exerts *de facto* control over Soviet foreign policy.

New Soviet Man   The belief that an evolution in human nature can be produced by changing the social environment. In Marxist-Leninist terminology, the concept of "the new Soviet man" or "the new communist man" assumes that most of the pathologies of industrial society are traceable to the perverting influence of capitalism. These pathologies range from selfishness and greed created by the all-pervasive profit motive to criminality induced by the deliberate stimulation of wants that the capitalist system cannot meet. Humankind's true nature—altruistic, cooperative, and egalitarian—has been warped by the competitive, conflict-ridden environment of capitalist society. Only when private property is abolished and capitalist institutions are replaced by socialist designs, according to communist theoreticians, will humanity's potential virtue prevail. *See also* COLLECTIVE (KOLLEKTIV), p. 278; LYSENKOISM, p. 54; MARXISM: NEW COMMUNIST MAN, p. 69.

Significance   Marxist-Leninist theoreticians originally spoke of "the new communist man"; Stalin amended this to the "new Soviet man," and used the concept as the linchpin in the massive social engineering effort undertaken by the regime. The new Soviet man (or person; the word can be translated both ways and is meant to refer to the entire population) was to be the chief product of "building socialism in one state," as Stalin termed his policy of pursuing national interests over the goals of international communism. From nursery school to retirement, Soviet citizens are socialized to think in terms of the collective society and their responsibility to it. Stalin's use of the term became even more ethnocentric after World War II when it was used to justify Soviet domination over Eastern Europe. Stalin maintained that the new Soviet man was clearly superior not only to capitalist man, but also to those who had only recently come under socialism. The teaching of Russian was made mandatory in Eastern Europe, on the grounds that Russian was the natural language of socialism. Thus, the doctrine was used to justify political and economic hegemony in Eastern Europe as well as compulsory instruction in the Russian language. Stalin's use of the doctrine of the new Soviet man as rationalization for the political, economic, and cultural control of Eastern Europe was buttressed by the theories of the charlatan scientist, Trofim Lysenko, who maintained that characteristics acquired from one's environment could be genetically transmitted. Thus, Lysenko's theories were used to support the claim that a socialist environment would produce a superior socialist human being. This ethnocentric use of the doctrine discredited it, particularly after Khrushchev's de-Stalinization campaign revealed some of the worst excesses of Stalin's control of Eastern Europe, and it is rarely referred to today. Similarly, official efforts to produce a "new Bulgarian man" or a "new Romanian man" have subsided. The doctrine itself, that of socialism producing "a new man" remains part of the appeal of Marxism-Leninism, congruent with Marx's insistence that the substructure (the economy) shapes the social and political superstructure. In Marxist thought, the new communist man will be the product of the sweeping social and economic changes that occur during the transitional stage of socialism to communism. The doctrine lends to Marxism a religious cast, since it postulates a Utopia in which humanity will be reborn and recast in an earlier, uncorrupted form, guided by a higher set of moral values. According to Marxist theory, the new man would appear in the final historical stage of pure communism, when humanity will live in a classless, stateless cooperative society free from arbitrary restraint and coercive power. This utopian image of the good future society, free from the evils of industrial society, accounts for much of Marxism's appeal to intellectuals. Critics of Marxism and the Soviet system point out that there is no evidence that human nature is changing under conditions of Marxist socialism, or that there is less greed and criminality. The Soviet Union and other socialist states continue to have police forces, a criminal substratum that continues to commit "bourgeois" crimes, widespread alcoholism, and criminal courts and prisons to deal with these seemingly indestructible remnants of capitalism.

Nomenklatura   Secret lists of party, government, and other prestigious positions in the Soviet system that require all appointments to
be confirmed by the communist party. *Nomenklatura* positions constitute the elite of Soviet office-holders in every sphere of society and may
be filled only with party approval or by direct party appointment. Each
party organization, from the level of *raion* (district) to the Central
Committee in Moscow, has a specific list (nomenklatura) of posts for
which it is responsible. The candidates for these posts are apparently
selected from lists of promising citizens, based substantially on the
kharakteristika (dossier) maintained on each individual. The more
important the position, the higher the party organ that must confirm
the appointment, with the most important appointments being part of
the Central Committee's nomenklatura. Nomenklatura positions may
be found in every level of human activity, including, for example, the
industrial sector, collective farms and the military. The power to make
nomenklatura appointments is distributed among party units, by
geographical region, and vertically according to the level of prestige
and power of the position. Some organizations, like the KGB, the
Komsomol, or the trade unions, appear to have their own nomenklatura, but all are subject to eventual party confirmation. Because so
much of the operation of the nomenklatura system is secret, with many
Soviet citizens themselves being unaware of its existence, it is difficult to
estimate the number of such positions. The Central Committee
probably has direct control over several hundred posts and is responsible for confirming many more, while some analysts estimate that the
central committees of the republics are responsible for about 2,000
each. A Soviet citizen, however, may receive appointment to a nomenklatura position without party membership. Positions that require a
high level of technical knowledge or special skills are frequently
awarded on the basis of competence alone. For this reason, many of the
brightest Soviet students who are not politically motivated enter the
hard sciences, an area in which they can succeed with minimal political
participation. However, ultimately the party must approve all nomenklatura appointments, party or non-party. *See also* KHARAKTERISTIKA,
p. 105.

Significance   The nomenklatura embraces the elite of Soviet society
and the operation of the system provides an important key to the
understanding of elite maintenance in the Soviet Union. Although it
resembles the patronage system in Western societies, and in another
sense is a continuation of Peter the Great's Table of Ranks (which was
used to fill military, civil service, and judicial posts), nomenklatura
offers tight party control at all levels and maintains the party's ultimate
control over staffing. Appointment to a nomenklatura post brings not

only prestige, power, and higher pay, but also provides many secondary benefits to the occupants of these posts. These may include extra pay and bonuses, sometimes termed the "thirteenth month" (an extra month's pay); the "Kremlin ration" (so-called "gold" rubles worth several times their official face value because they may be used to purchase goods in state-run hard currency shops); and special access to scarce consumer goods, holiday facilities, private transport, special medical services, and better housing. The system provides the communist party with a key lever of control over Soviet society in all important spheres.

Partiinost' **(Party-Mindedness)**   The basic principle that according to Marxism-Leninism should be the organizing philosophy of a party member's life. The correct application of *partiinost'* means that party members will at all times shape their lives and actions toward achieving the goals of Marxism-Leninism. Partiinost' combines elements of a world view, penetrating all aspects of life, with the practical direction of a party member's activities. Partiinost' creates members so instinctively party-minded that service to the party and the building of communism is the motive force of their lives. The principle is derived from Marxian dialectical materialism; Marx maintained that partiinost' is a necessary condition for the building of a classless society, and develops along with class consciousness. *See also* CADRE, p. 88; PARTY LINE, p. 115.

Significance   Partiinost' is both a theoretical concept and an organizing principle for party members. According to Marx, partiinost' is based on objective laws of social evolution. In practice, partiinost' means that the party member must at all times be an active partisan. Furthermore, the world view presented by partiinost', as interpreted by the party, is the reality. Any views or actions that diverge from this reality are criticized as "subjectivism," "relativism," or "idealism," all terms of condemnation in the communist vocabulary. A correct spirit of partiinost' involves accepting reality as defined by the party as well as a heightened sense of commitment. Exhortations to party members to observe the spirit of partiinost' usually signal the leadership's determination to tighten party discipline. Both Soviet and East European party leaders publicly exhort their members to a heightened sense of partiinost'. Leonid Brezhnev emphasized partiinost' as a crucial component of correct leadership. Josip Broz Tito once chastised Yugoslav communists suspected of harboring nationalist tendencies as lacking in partiinost'.

Party Assignment   The specific task or political work which a communist party member is directed to fulfill as part of his or her individual responsibility for carrying out party policy. Party assignments are made by the local unit (the PPO), by the various party secretaries, or by higher party organs. Upon joining the party as a probationary candidate member, each new candidate is given a specific party assignment. How well he fulfills his party assignment may determine whether he will be accepted as a full party member. This process continues throughout a party member's career, with the assignments increasing in responsibility as he progresses through the party hierarchy. Party assignments may be either long term or short term, and include both work within the party structure and work in community and government organizations, such as trade unions, Komsomol units, and cultural organizations, or in organs and committees of local government. A party member is expected to fulfill enthusiastically each assignment and to take new assignments at the direction of party authorities. This system enables the communist party to penetrate all sectors of society, from the shop floor and residential unit to the federal parliament, ensuring implementation of party policy and obedience to the party line. The party member may be directed to serve as a deputy in the local soviet (assembly), join the *Druzhiny* (volunteer militia units), deliver a lecture, write a short article, or lead party-arranged discussion groups. In addition, the committed party member is expected to volunteer for numerous community tasks. *See also* CADRE, p. 88; CANDIDATE MEMBER, p. 90; DUPLICATION OF OFFICE, p. 100; MASS ORGANIZATIONS, p. 291; PARTIINOST', p. 110.

Significance   The party assignment is the means by which the party trains its future leadership cadres while simultaneously providing the mechanism through which the party directs the day-to-day activities of all sectors of society. Those who best fulfill their party assignments are earmarked as potential leaders and are usually given further training in party schools, eventually becoming full-time functionaries in party or government organs. Party assignments provide a way of charting the rise and fall of potential leaders. Soviet analyst John Reshetar has identified four routes to the top of the party hierarchy: (1) through the central party apparatus; (2) by ideological expertise; (3) by technical expertise; and (4) through leadership positions in provincial organizations. The obligations which the party assignment system places on all members can be so time-consuming and burdensome that it provides a method of self-selection; only the most dedicated and ambitious usually seek party membership. Training in party leadership begins with the Komsomol, where selected members are assigned additional tasks, such as leading Pioneer units for schoolchildren. Because party members saturate all non-party organizations, there is little spontaneity in Soviet public life; in fact, the very word has a negative connotation for the communist. The time obligations placed upon a party member, particularly at the lower levels, are great. Many analysts of communist party politics feel that failure to fulfill party assignments constitutes a major reason why "less deserving" members are dropped from the party during the periodic membership reviews. The burden placed upon party members means that although membership carries with it special privileges, it also entails a sizable obligation in terms of time and commitment.

Party Bureau   The executive committee of a local or territorial party unit, responsible for carrying out the daily work of the party on its territory. The party bureau has four major functions: (1) supervising the implementation of party policy on its territory; (2) managing local party affairs; (3) gathering and evaluating information for policymakers; and (4) approving appointments to important positions, party and non-party, which are on its *nomenklatura* list. A typical party bureau includes around a dozen local party leaders, many of whom also occupy important posts in local government and economic bodies. If it is a rural district, collective farm managers will be included. The party bureau is headed by the first secretary, who is the most important political official in the territory. Party bureaus typically meet about once per week. In the Soviet Union, the party committees of the districts (*raikoms*) or cities (*gorkoms*), which have been elected by the at-large party membership, directly approve the party bureau. Above this district level, at regional or republican levels, the party committee (or conference) elects a party bureau that in turn selects a smaller secretariat. At the lowest level of party organization is the Primary Party Organization (PPO) or cell, based in the workplace or residence, where the entire membership elects the party bureau. The party bureaus and secretariats are a key element in the complex party administrative hierarchy, bound by party discipline and democratic centralism to implement all decisions of the central party hierarchy. PPO bureaus report directly to the party bureau of their respective districts, the district (raikom or gorkom) party bureaus report to the provincial (*obkom*) party bureau; the provincial to the union-republic, and the union-republic to the federal. Although in theory the party bureau is elected by the party committee, which in turn has been selected by the membership at large, the reverse is usually the case. The general practice is that higher party leaders select the membership of lower party bureaus, frequently utilizing the party assignment system—in effect, the manager of a local enterprise, who is already a party member, will be directed to serve on the raikom party bureau. Names are then presented to the party committee for ratification, which is usually by a show of hands. Some raikoms and gorkoms at least discuss the candidates and conduct a more genuine election; however, any potential conflict has already been resolved with local party leaders before the committee meeting. At the territorial level, the bureau has several full-time secretaries and a sizable staff. The smaller raikom and gorkom bureaus usually include four departments: (1) organizational; (2) general; (3) industry-transport or agriculture; and (4) propaganda and agitation (agitprop). The major responsibilities of the PPO bureaus are agitprop, supervision of economic activity, and party affairs. The composition of the party bureau, which includes the leading figures from all sectors, facilitates the coordination of party policy with all of society. At the raikom or gorkom level, party bureaus resemble the nonpartisan city council of a medium-sized midwestern town—local businessmen, politicians, bank officials, union leaders, community civic leaders, a sprinkling of workers and educators. At the provincial level, the larger party bureaus generally include the provincial first party secretary, several other party secretaries, leading government officials, local newspaper editors, the head of the police, trade union chiefs, leaders of the youth organizations, the procurator, the provincial KGB chief, and the secretaries of the most important district parties in the province. The party's control over appointment to all important posts, party or non-party, means that these leading local or provincial figures have already been preselected for leadership positions by the party, and deemed reliable. *See also* PARTY ASSIGNMENT, p. 110; PRIMARY PARTY ORGANIZATION (PPO), p. 122; VERIFICATION (PRAVO KONTROLYA), p. 129.

Significance   At every level the party bureau is the primary coordinating mechanism on its territory. All Soviet institutions, be they party, economic, government, citizen, cultural, or whatever are essentially components of a single party-controlled bureaucracy. This is not to imply complete, totalitarian control by the bureaucracy; local interests frequently conflict and the local party bureau becomes the chief resolver of conflict in such instances. The party bureau is charged with allocating the resources of the community or territory, a highly political and potentially conflictual responsibility. Party bureaus also play an important role in economic planning. Soviet economic planning is carefully constructed to consider the resources and needs of the various territorial units. The party bureaus transmit this crucial information to the central planners, and in turn criticize the draft plans that are presented to the regional authorities. In rural districts, the raikom party bureau is charged with allocating the agricultural production targets for the district among the collective farms. The main function of a workplace-based PPO is to monitor the implementation of the economic plan and mobilize the workforce. Such on-site supervision in the enterprise has led many to equate the PPO bureau with an enterprise board of directors. Since most important enterprise personnel are generally included in the PPO bureau, the effect is one of fusion rather than usurpation. The right of verification (*pravo kontrolya*) that permits the party to oversee the implementation of party policy everywhere in society deeply involves the party, and especially the party bureaus, in local decision making. As part of its party work, the party bureau approves appointments to important local positions and nominations to the local soviet. Thus, for the politically ambitious and upwardly mobile, the local party bureau is the first gatekeeper. In all, the party bureau serves as the executive arm of the local party unit as well as the first step in the hierarchical ladder of party power. Its executive function involves it in local conflict resolution as well; the bureau cannot simply operate by dictate, but must coordinate and adjudicate.

Party Control Committee   Disciplinary organ of the communist party, responsible for maintaining and enforcing party discipline. The Party Control Committee, which today is attached to the Central Committee, supervises the vast party bureaucracy and ensures conformity to the centrally determined party line. The Party Control Committee also serves as a court of appeal for members expelled from their local units. A key organ for the maintenance of central control, it is formally attached to the Central Committee but is not part of the Central Committee apparatus, with some evidence indicating that it operates under the direct control of the Politburo and Secretariat. Each party unit of the Communist Party of the Soviet Union (CPSU), from local to republican, has a similar disciplinary agency. These control committees, operating under the central Party Control Committee, investigate complaints about officials and possible violations of party statutes and check on compliance with the party line by all members. Set up by Vladimir Lenin as the Central Control Commission, this specialized agency of discipline originally guarded against abuse of power by party officials. Under Josef Stalin, it became a major instrument through which he purged the party of all suspected of opposing his one-man rule, including dozens of Central Committee members. It was increasingly penetrated by the secret police and became an instrument of Stalin's personal power. After Stalin's death, the Party Control Committee reverted to its function of supervising party discipline. Its major function today is to oversee the work of the lower control agencies and to review their decisions, especially cases of expulsion from the party, which by party statute must be carried out by the local party unit. *See also* GREAT PURGE, p. 17; NOMENKLATURA, p. 109.

Significance   The Party Control Committee functions as a key element in the maintenance of central party control over all lower units. As the guardian of the party line, the Committee and its subordinate agencies are responsible for supervising the conduct of individual members as well as mediating complaints. Because party control penetrates practically all aspects of Soviet life, the Party Control Committee is ostensibly involved in non-party areas as well. Managers of economic enterprises have been expelled from the party for bad management practices, as well as local government bureaucrats who fail to fulfill party directives. The Party Control Committee also plays an important role in the selection of personnel for politically sensitive posts, as it keeps voluminous records on the performance and reliability of personnel. The Committee may mediate for party members who feel victimized by local authorities, but in general it enforces conformity to central party policy.

Party Line   The sum total of current policy determined by the central leadership of a communist party. The party line is a combination of current objectives and the policies the party enacts to implement them. It is not a single policy statement, therefore, but comprises all the policies currently in effect. As a tactical guide based on political realities, it may change as the political requirements change, but the long-range goal of achieving communism remains the same. At any given time, the party line is the official attitude toward any goal or problem. Observance of the party line is binding; only in Yugoslavia have party members been permitted to question specifics of the party line. Elsewhere, any departures are viewed as deviation if not treason. Party members are encouraged to transmit the party line to the masses by agitation and propaganda work. *See also* LENINISM: DEMOCRATIC CENTRALISM, p. 52; POLYCENTRISM, p. 331; WORKERS OPPOSITION, p. 34.

Significance   The party line is closely tied to the concept of democratic centralism and party discipline. It is important both as a guide to party actions and because it carries the force of law for party members. On specific issues, Soviet-style communist parties distinguish between ideology and long-term goals, and the short-term strategies shaped by political necessity. Thus, the party line may direct communists in noncommunist countries to cooperate with the local bourgeoisie while at the same time the ideology scorns them as the class enemy. Perhaps the most brutal shift in the party line occurred when Josef Stalin signed the 1939 Non-Aggression Pact with Nazi Germany. For East European communist parties, the guidelines of the party lines are set by the Soviet party. Some East European parties are permitted greater latitude in adjusting the party line to national conditions than others. The most open critics of the sanctity of the party line have been the Yugoslavs. The peak of this movement was reached at the Ninth Congress of the League of Communists of Yugoslavia in 1969, which officially permitted individual dissent from the party line on issues of conscience. In Soviet-controlled states, any discussion of following the Yugoslav example, such as occurred in Czechoslovakia in 1968 and Poland in 1980–81, has been suppressed. The Soviet party line is no longer the unquestioned course of action for communist parties in the rest of the world, because there is no longer a unified world communist movement.

Party Program   A comprehensive statement of the goals of a communist party, usually adopted at a party congress. Similar to the platform of a West European political party, the party program is both a programmatic statement of tasks and strategy and an ideological statement. Unlike the party statutes, which are essentially party rules, the party program is an all-inclusive document that sets the course of the party for the next four or five years. The party line is derived from the party program. Frequently the party program will present the ideological justification for the goals to be pursued. Once enacted, a new party program supersedes all past programs and is binding on all party members. *See also* PARTY LINE, p. 115; PARTY STATUTES, p. 118.

Significance   The party program has been an important element of the strategy of ruling communist parties since Vladimir Lenin presented the 1919 Party Program to the victorious Bolsheviks. Party programs can signal important changes in policy, as in the 1969 Yugoslav Party Program, or the 1968 Action Program of the Czechoslovak Communist Party, which spelled out the goals, tasks, and objectives of the liberalizers. Because no alternative to the party program is permitted public consideration, the ruling party assumes that it has a mandate of support from the populace.

Party Schools   An extensive system of specialized schools devoted to training citizens in a communist state for party and community work. Party schools are found in all East European communist states, including Yugoslavia, and are the major instrumentality of political instruction for adults. The higher level party schools train the future party elite in advanced management and ideology, while the ordinary citizen can improve his skills and prepare for volunteer community work at the lower level party schools. In the Soviet Union, the party schools are organized at three levels; primary, intermediate (the Schools of Marxism-Leninism), and advanced (the Universities of Marxism-Leninism). The curriculum includes an introduction to Marxism-Leninism, party history, basic economic principles, and a variety of ideologically oriented programs. Potential party functionaries, selected by the relevant party unit, attend regional or republican party schools that offer lengthier, more politically specialized instruction. The capstone of the system is the Academy of Social Sciences in Moscow, attached directly to the Central Committee, whose counterpart in other communist-party states is usually called the Higher Party School. The party schools train most of the future middle level government functionaires in public administration as well as preparing a pool of potential elite communists at the Academy of Social Sciences. A similar high party school trains the functionaries of the Main Political Administration (MPA), the party organization that maintains party control over the military. Currently, an estimated 20 million Soviet citizens are enrolled in party schools, including about 8 million who are not party members. One of the major functions of the lower and middle level party schools is to train citizens, both party and nonparty, for agitation and propaganda work in the local communities. *See also* AGITPROP, p. 85; APPARATUS, p. 88; INSTITUTE OF THE USA/CANADA, p. 324.

Significance   The party schools were originally developed to prepare a largely semiliterate Soviet citizenry for building communism and to ensure a pool of trained, ideologically aware recruits for the communist party. Much of the early work of the party schools centered on adult literacy and vocational education. Today, in particular the Yugoslav and Romanian party schools at the lower levels retain this function. The first text developed for the party schools was Nikolai Bukharin's *The ABC of Communism* (1919), a pamphlet that put Marxist theory into everyday language. Translated into many foreign languages and read by millions, it remains a striking example of the early party schools' ability to popularize Marxism-Leninism. Most party schools today are devoted to training future bureaucrats and, at the lower levels, propaganda workers. Although many graduates privately admit that political instruction, especially at the lower levels, is frequently boring, attendance is viewed as a means of achieving upward mobility in the system.

Party Statutes   The governing document, or rules, of a communist party, binding on all members and organs of the party. The party statutes are the constitution of the party, delineating its organizational structure and the areas of competence of the various institutions enumerated. Party statutes govern such matters as the admission of new members, the conditions of expulsion or other forms of discipline, and the structure of the basic units. In particular, they enshrine democratic centralism as the keystone of party practice. *See also* LENINISM: DEMOCRATIC CENTRALISM, p. 52; PARTY PROGRAM, p. 116.

Significance   The party statutes are the constitutional framework which governs the conduct of a communist party and lays out its institutional organization. At times they are observed more in spirit than in form, as during the long period when Stalin operated without convoking a party congress, contrary to the statutes of the Soviet communist party. The usual communist practice of filling party posts through co-optation from above is also extra-statutory, although the correct form may be observed by holding after-the-fact elections. Party statutes in a one-party communist state may be as important a source of law as the constitution itself.

Politburo (Presidium)   The abbreviation for the Political Bureau of the Central Committee, the chief policymaking organ and dominant political institution in the Soviet Union. Composed of the most powerful leaders of the communist party, the Politburo makes all important policy decisions for party and state. First constituted by Vladimir Lenin in October 1917 to direct the Bolshevik Revolution, the Politburo has been the true locus of power throughout most of Soviet history. In reality, the Politburo makes policy for both government and party, although technically its mandate extends only over the party. This fusion of power stems from the fact that leading party personnel hold important government posts, and party discipline assures the implementation of party policy by all government organs. As chief policymaker, the Politburo functions somewhat as a cabinet in a parliamentary system, but without any institutional restraints. Although it is the dominant political institution in the Soviet system, only two concrete facts are known about the Politburo: its membership and the fact that all important policy decisions originate there. It is a self-selected oligarchy, whose members are co-opted by their fellow oligarchs. The selection process is secret; technically responsible to the Central Committee, its membership is formally approved by the Central Committee. Its decisions may be formally announced by other bodies, such as the Central Committee or the Presidium of the

Supreme Soviet, but if it is a policy decision of importance, involving a long-term commitment, allocation of resources, or a change in state policy, it can be safely assumed that the decision originated in the Politburo. According to Leonid Brezhnev, the Politburo met at least once a week during his tenure on it. Much of the work of the Politburo is apparently concerned with international affairs, national security, and the economy. Information on policy issues under discussion by the Politburo is supplied by the specialized departments of the Central Committee apparatus, and officials may be invited to deliver reports. Decisions, when announced, are presented as unanimous. The Politburo has no set size, no formal membership selection process, and no set agenda. It has no effective responsibility to any other organ of party or government. Traditionally, its members also hold posts on the Council of Ministers, the Central Committee, the Secretariat, the Supreme Soviet Presidium, and republican party committees. Although it has no formally designated head, in practice the General Secretary (or First Secretary) of the party is the leading figure on the Politburo and thus the ultimate repository of political power in the Soviet state. As is common with all party organs, Politburo members include both full and candidate, or nonvoting, members. Since Josef Stalin the size of the Politburo has ranged from 14 to 25 full and candidate members. Only one woman in all of Soviet history has ever been named to the Politburo. All Politburo members customarily sit on the Central Committee, now reduced to the role of official legitimator of Politburo policy and in the Supreme Soviet. In rare instances, however, the Central Committee has adjudicated Politburo decisions, as when Nikita Khrushchev was deposed in 1964. How Politburo meetings are conducted, how votes, if any, are taken, and how compromises are achieved, are unknown, but they remain matters of much speculation. It seems probable that in addition to regular meetings the Politburo or smaller *ad hoc* group will be in almost continual session during a national crisis. Disagreements over policy can usually be ascertained only through rumor or sudden shifts in membership. Under Stalin, the power of all party organs, including the Politburo, atrophied. Stalin's successor, Nikita Khrushchev, restored the power of the Politburo and, as a corrective to the evils of Stalinism, emphasized its consensual collective nature, a policy continued by Brezhnev. On the basis of current knowledge, it is evident that the Politburo functions as the chief power instrument for the system, acting as a collective policymaking body responsible for determining the priorities of the state and allocating its resources accordingly. *See also* ANTI-PARTY GROUP, p. 86; CENTRAL COMMITTEE, p. 91; DUPLICATION OF OFFICE, p. 100; LENINISM: DEMOCRATIC CENTRALISM, p. 52; SECRETARIAT, p. 126.

Significance   The Politburo is the dominant political institution in a communist-party system, epitomizing the concentration of power common to these systems. Because almost all important policy decisions are determined by a small body whose operations are shrouded in secrecy, analyzing the political dynamics of a communist system can be difficult. The unpredictability and lack of concrete data has permitted ideologically motivated assumptions that cannot be checked out against fact. Analysts who study communist systems frequently focus on the Politburo, a concentration that may conceal other important aspects of communist politics. Nonetheless, membership on the Politburo is the most tangible sign of power. Appointment to and demotion from the Politburo signify both the political power of an individual and the priority attached to the sector he is viewed as representing. Thus, the inclusion of the then head of the secret police (KGB), Yuri Andropov, and the Minister of Defense, Andrei Grechko, in 1973 was taken as indicative of the increased weight of the military and the Politburo's own priorities. Sudden demotions, such as that of Agriculture Minister Dmitri Polyansky may signify either a loss of personal power, failure to achieve the goals set for that sector, or both. Since Stalin, Politburo membership has apparently been selected with the aim of representing the most important sectors and constituencies of the Soviet polity. Representatives of key government functions, such as Foreign Affairs and important territorial units such as the Moscow and Leningrad parties or the parties of Georgia, the Ukraine, and Kazakhstan are usually included. In Eastern Europe, the Politburo may also be called the Presidium or Executive Committee, but whatever the name it is the dominant political institution. The Romanian system is directed by a 38-person Executive Committee that delegates some policymaking to the 9-member Permanent Bureau (Permbureau); both bodies are headed by party leader Nicolae Ceauşescu. Only Yugoslavia, where government institutions possess some measure of autonomy, deviates somewhat from the practice initiated by Lenin. The Yugoslav state has devolved economic decision making to the individual enterprises, abandoned mandatory central planning, permitted the republican and provincial parties substantial autonomy, and abjured party control through duplication of office, measures that have eroded the power of the central party policymakers. The Yugoslav party is headed by a 24-person Presidium of the Central Committee, whose members are selected by the constituent party units of the Yugoslav League of Communists (i.e., the eight republican and provincial parties) rather than by self-selection. The Yugoslav Presidium in turn apparently delegates much of its routine work to a smaller Executive Committee, selected from within its own ranks. The Presidium, however, apparently retains some policymaking functions, especially in the area of conciliation of diverging republican interests. A Soviet-style Politburo usually contains an inner group of 3 to 5 of the most powerful figures, usually identifiable because they are also members of the party Secretariat. Thus, when Andropov was named to the Soviet Secretariat in 1982, this indicated that he had joined this inner group and was in line to succeed Brezhnev. Again, an exception to this is Yugoslavia, where by party statute members are to avoid duplication of executive and administrative posts. The practice of policymaking by a small inner group was formally instituted at the Eighth Party Congress of 1918, which named Lenin, Leon Trotsky, Nikolai Krestinsky, Lev Kamenev, and Josef Stalin to the first Politburo. The fact that the Politburo operates largely in secret with no institutional restraints contributes to the pervasive judgment that Marxist-Leninist systems are oligarchies. The Politburo operates as the classic oligarchic system: rule by the few, generally in their own political interests; almost total arrogation of power; and membership through self-selection. The rank and file party members have no voice in the selection of the Politburo; there are no elections and no alternatives. The concentration of power, oligarchic nature, and secretiveness of the Soviet Politburo and its East European replicas symbolizes for many the nature of communist party rule.

Politinformator   The political information officer in the Soviet system whose responsibility is to explain and expand upon party policy and ideology in specific topical areas. Whereas the local party "public relations officer," the agitator, works only at the local level in an informal fashion, the *politinformator* normally deals with a specific topic in much more detail in a lecture setting and is responsible for a much broader geographic area. Politinformators receive rigorous training in party schools and typically specialize in four areas: domestic policy, economics, international relations, or cultural affairs. The politinformator system was instituted in the 1960s in response to the criticism that the agitator system had become outmoded. Agitation work was criticized as simplistic and boring, conveying superfluous information which the worker could easily glean from television or the radio. Politinformators were intended to revitalize party-to-people communication with a trained corps of specialized information officers conducting in-depth discussions of current issues. Even more advanced are the lecturers (*dokladchiki*), intellectuals, professionals, and senior party officials of the regional or republic party committees who supplement the politinformator work. Although the responsibilities of politinformators may appear to overlap those of agitators, the former are more specialized political information officers who offer more sophisticated information to a well-educated Soviet citizenry. *See also* AGITATOR, p. 84; AGITPROP, p. 85.

Significance   The politinformator has added technical expertise and professionalism to traditional Agitprop work. During periods of news blackout, such as the 1968 Soviet-led invasion of Czechoslovakia, the politinformator may play a major role in the field of communications. Frequently, shifts in party policy may be ascertained by examining the work of these specialized information officers. The debate in the 1960s over whether politinformators should supplement or replace traditional agitation work is revealing about bureaucratic interest-group politics in the Soviet Union. Initially, Nikita Khrushchev proposed substituting politinformators for what he charged was a moribund agitation system. The agitators remained in place, however, causing some confusion over the proper division of responsibilities. After Khrushchev's ouster from power in 1964, the politinformators' role was more clearly defined and expanded, but the long-entrenched agitator apparatus succeeded in preserving its traditional role as the local communicator of party policy.

Primary Party Organization (PPO)   The basic organizational unit of the communist party, commonly termed the party cell. In the Soviet Union, PPOs number over 390,000. Every party member, no matter what his or her rank, must hold membership in a Primary Party Organization. Only the PPO can accept candidate members, admit new members, and expel members, although the latter proceedings may in actuality be initiated by higher party authorities. Unlike higher party units, which are territorially based, the PPO is based on the place of work or economic function of its members. By party statute, every workplace or institution that employs three or more party members must form a PPO; about 40 percent are based in the economic enterprises. PPOs range in size from 3 members to thousands, with about 95 percent with memberships under 100. Above the PPO level, the party organization replicates the territorial organization of the government. Immediately above the PPO is the district (*raion*) or city (*gorod*) party committee, followed by the national area (*okrug*), the province (*oblast'*) or territory (*krai*), the union-republic, and finally, the federal level. Thus, the Communist Party of the Soviet Union, like the government, is organized on a federative structure. The PPO provides a major mode of political participation. Of the over 16 million members enrolled, more than 4.5 million are directly involved in PPO work. The structure and functions differ with the size of the PPO. About 40 percent have fewer than 15 members and are highly informal; frequently the members rotate the secretaryship and share leadership duties. The major function of such small PPOs, especially in rural areas, is usually communications and agitprop work. Those enrolling more than 15 elect an executive committee of 3 to 9 members to direct party work between the monthly meetings. In the largest PPOs, numbering over 1,000, an executive committee of 50 is elected and a smaller, inner bureau directs the day-to-day work. All PPO officials must be confirmed by higher party organs. The jurisdiction of the PPO is limited to the PPO itself; all decisions of higher party bodies are binding upon them. The larger PPOs, of 50 or more, are usually subdivided into party groups that function as PPOs at the shop floor or department level. Every member is assigned party work, either within the party structure or in the mass organizations, such as the Komsomol, the trade unions, and the comrades' courts. The major functions of the PPO may be broadly categorized as (1) selecting and training members; (2) mobilizing and ensuring adherence to the party line; (3) electing delegates to higher party organs; (4) assessing public opinion; (5) recommending key personnel to the work unit; and (6) coordinating and supervising the administration of the work unit in which the PPO is based. The last is a key function. In all but government units the PPO is charged with supervision of administration. In larger factory units, the PPO committee functions somewhat as a board of directors. Recommendations made by the PPO are key to advancement within the enterprise or institution. This includes advancement by nonparty members; for example, promotion within university ranks is determined by party recommendation as well as by academic merit. Most PPO meetings are open and nonmembers are invited to attend, although they do not vote. *See also* CANDIDATE MEMBER, p. 90; COLLECTIVE FARM PARTY ORGANIZATION, p. 93; LENINISM, p. 51.

Significance   The Primary Party Organization is the basic organizational unit of every communist party around the world. Nonruling communist parties, however, usually call their basic units cells. The PPO embodies the Leninist definition of the basic unit, or cell, as the direct link between the worker and the leading party organs. The structure evolved from Lenin's organizational blueprint first explained in the article "What Is to Be Done," published in the Bolshevik paper, *Iskra*, in 1902. According to Lenin, a network of secret party cells were to infiltrate all sectors of society. The secret cell system was designed to foil the czarist secret police by ensuring that even in cases of police penetration the damage to the party would be minimal, as few members knew the entire network. The PPO system is a continuation of the cell system under conditions of communist party rule; since there is no longer any need for secrecy its functions have changed substantially since Lenin. It remains true to the Leninist definition of the cell as the link between party and people. The supervisory-control function of the PPO is particularly significant to understanding Soviet politics. It constitutes both a brake on bureaucratic fiat and a method of applying party policy to concrete situations. The local PPOs have the right to question all administrative decisions and to review all policy implementation in the work units in which they are based. Thus, it functions as the local arm of the party, reinforces party control at local levels, and enables the party to maintain authority over the complex administration of a vast centralized economy. Because the party work assignments frequently involve positions within the mass organizations, the PPO is the primary instrument through which the party penetrates all sectors of society. Membership in a PPO has become a prime path for upward mobility, and undoubtedly many join for reasons of professional ambition rather than out of ideological conviction. Generally, membership in higher party organs comes through co-optation from the lower levels. Thus, higher party officials can keep close track of the talent within the PPOs under their jurisdiction and use them as a recruiting ground. The PPO also functions to articulate interests and demands within the Soviet system. In larger units, a specific officer, the *partinformator*, is charged with assessing public opinion and transmitting this to the higher decision makers. The PPO constitutes a primary mode of participation, permitting millions of Soviet citizens to perceive themselves as part of the decision-making process. Typically, the PPO is severely constrained by the rules of party discipline and democratic centralism, leaving it with little autonomy in decision making. Its importance, however, is far broader than as a servile instrument of mobilization for the top party hierarchy, which is a stereotypical Western view of the PPO.

Purge (Exchange of Party Cards)   Periodic review of party personnel with the aim of "cleansing" the party of unreliable or unworthy members. The original meaning of the term purge (*chistka*) simply refers to the standardized practice of "purifying" the party organization by a periodic review of party members. All party members are interviewed, their qualifications reviewed, and new party cards are exchanged for old with all who pass the review. Josef Stalin debased both the term and the practice in the 1930s when he used the purge as an instrument of terror. The term became synonymous with terror, as those who were purged were imprisoned, executed, or subjected to other drastic punishment. This period of terror, which has become known as the Great Purge (1934–38), affected millions of Soviet citizens, both party and nonparty, and discredited the mechanism.

Since Stalin's death the present communist leaderships have strenuously avoided the use of terror in intraparty relationships and confined such periodic reviews to an exchange of party cards. The preferred method today is an administrative procedure, carried out by the Primary Party Organizations (PPOs), which issue new party cards based on a successful review. Such periodic reviews are used to weed out the non-activists who refuse to carry out their assigned party duties as well as those who refuse to live by the rules of the party. *See also* GREAT PURGE, p. 17; PARTY CONTROL COMMITTEE, p. 114.

Significance   The exchange of the party cards, or purge, enables the party to periodically review the qualifications of its membership and retain its image as the vanguard of society. An exchange of party cards may be local, as occurred in the Soviet Republic of Georgia in 1972–74 following revelations of widespread corruption there, or it may be national, as in the USSR in 1974. Such national purges are now usually limited in scope; it is estimated that the 1974 party card exchange affected about one percent of the total party membership. On the other hand, an exchange of party cards can restructure the nature of the membership by tightening requirements. If ordered after a political upheaval, as in Czechoslovakia following the Prague Spring of 1968, it may involve several hundred thousand party members. Although postwar communist leaderships have abjured the use of terror in connection with such membership reviews, to be purged from the party still carries penalties, as the numerous high-level Czechoslovak officials discovered in 1970 when they were dropped from the party and placed in menial jobs. In more liberal communist systems, such as Yugoslavia, members are permitted to resign without fear of reprisal. Resignation frequently serves the same purpose as a purge in tightening party discipline. At times, a party membership may simply purge itself, as occurred in Poland, where in the wake of the 1981 imposition of military rule, thousands of disaffected party members resigned. Thus, both the meaning of the term purge and the method of implementation has changed since Stalin. Stalin essentially attempted to create a revolutionary, charismatic movement that would build the perfect communist society. In pursuit of "perfection" and revolutionary goals, he repeatedly purged the party, exacting severe penalties on those purged, using the purges to prevent the emergence of a conservative, privileged bureaucracy. Post-Stalin leaderships have largely given up on the pursuit of perfection and have created stable, secure bureaucracies. There have been no large-scale purges on the model of the 1930s since Stalin's death, with the possible exception of Albania, the various leaderships confining themselves merely to demanding obedience to the rules.

Secretariat   The central executive body of a communist party, responsible for overseeing the execution of all party decisions and the direction of party affairs. In the Soviet Union, the Secretariat is presently composed of ten top party administrators, the Party Secretaries, headed by the official leader of the party, the General Secretary, the leader of the nation. A small inner elite of three to five members, including the General Secretary, usually sits on both the Secretariat and Politburo and in effect constitutes the ruling elite of a communist state. The Secretariat constitutes the executive office of the communist party; through its control over the extensive party apparatus it ensures that all party policy is properly implemented in conformity with party directives. As chief administrative body, the Secretariat oversees the entire party strucure and allocates party resources. A major source of the Secretariat's power is its control over appointments to all important posts through the *nomenklatura* system. The Secretariat receives reports from all lower party units and issues directives that are binding upon them. The control of the Secretariat is extended to all governmental and economic institutions through the party members who occupy leading positions in non-party bodies. By virtue of their party membership, all these top government and economic officials are subordinate to the centralized hierarchy of party control. Party directives are thus binding on the government. Technically, if a party directive is in conflict with government practice, the party directive takes precedence, but because all government organs are led by party officials, conflict does not occur. East European communist parties follow the Soviet model, with minor exceptions. The decentralized Yugoslav system has, however, freed government and economic officials from strict party control. In all other communist systems, the General Secretary (or First Secretary) heads the Secretariat and is the leader of the nation. The Yugoslav League of Communists has a much larger executive body, a 39-member Presidium that delegates much of its work to a 12-member Executive Committee elected by the Presidium from among its own members. Because Yugoslav party statutes specifically discourage duplication of party and government offices, and because power is decentralized, the Yugoslav Executive Committee enjoys less unilateral power than its counterparts. The Secretariat elsewhere is responsible for overseeing all party affairs and for the general execution of national policy. Party Secretaries oversee broadly related functional areas; the actual division of responsibilities among Secretaries is not known. Subject areas delegated to one or more Secretaries usually include all important sectors of the economy, agriculture, cadre policy and appointments, ideology, culture, defense, foreign relations, national security, and party affairs. Little is known about the political processes of the Secretariat. Membership is through co-optation by the party elite, with appointments being confirmed *ex post facto* by the Central Committee. The number of members in recent years has varied from 5 to 14 full members. Little of its work is publicized. Many Secretariat decisions are announced as decisions of the Central Committee, to which it is in theory responsible. With the Politburo, the Secretariat constitutes the apex of power in a communist system; there are no effective institutional checks on either. The major functions of the Secretariat include (1) monitoring the implementation of party policy as determined by the Politburo; (2) approving all important appointments; (3) preparing and proposing policy for the Politburo; and (4) overseeing the activities of all party units. Since the party penetrates all activities, the power of the Secretariat extends over all society. A crucial function of the Secretariat is monitoring the implementation of the legally binding economic plans for the nation's economy. Only Yugoslavia, which has abandoned compulsory central economic planning, permits enterprise managers any autonomy from central party control. Although Secretariat properly refers to the handful of top party administrators, the party Secretaries, the term is also used to denote the central administrative apparatus of the Central Committee. Directed by the Secretariat, the Central Committee apparatus constitutes its support staff and is divided into functionally specific departments. In the Soviet Union, this central administrative staff is estimated at around 1,500. The exact number of departments (*otdely*) is not known but is currently assumed to number 21 or 22, down from the 30-some under Nikita Khrushchev. Departments are headed either directly by a Party Secretary or by a department head who is responsible to a Secretary. Departments are divided into sections (*sektory*). Sovietologist Jerry Hough estimates the number of such sections in the Soviet apparatus at 150 to 175, with 3 to 15 assigned to each department. According to Hough, in addition to the departments concerned with the major sectors of the economy, such as heavy industry and transportation, the Soviet Central Committee departments include (1) administrative organs (KGB, Procuracy, Ministry of Justice); (2) agriculture; (3) culture; (4) defense; (5) foreign cadres; (6) general intrasecretarial affairs; (7) information (TASS and press secretaries); (8) international; (9) planning and finance; (10) Main Political Administration of the armed forces; (11) agitation and propaganda; (12) science and education; (13) other socialist countries; and (14) organizational party work. Each of these departments report directly to a Party Secretary and is responsible for a number of related ministries, state committees, and other institutions. The central apparatus of East European systems tends to follow the Soviet model with the occasional exception of Yugoslavia. The Central Committee apparatus, under the direction of the Secretariat, prepares reports for the

Politburo and may supply expert testimony on various policy issues under consideration. As the institution that has assumed ultimate responsibility for the nation, the party needs an all-pervasive monitoring and record-keeping system, a function which the Secretariat performs. *See also* CENTRAL COMMITTEE, p. 91; GENERAL SECRETARY, p. 102; POLITBURO (PRESIDIUM), p. 118.

Significance   The Secretariat is the single most important instrument of party control and the mechanism through which the party extends this control over all of society. Each party unit, from republican to local, possesses a comparable executive organ that is ultimately subordinate to the Secretariat. The relatively small size, general administrative oversight function, and power over key appointments has caused some analysts to compare the Secretariat to the Executive Office of the President (EOP) of the United States. As with the EOP, the Secretariat and its chief administrator, the General Secretary, can restructure the central administrative apparatus at will. However, the political dynamics obviously differ vastly, as there are no political competitors and no institutional checks in a Soviet-style system. The Secretariat plays a key role in foreign relations. Relations between the Soviet Union and the Eastern European states are generally carried out by the Secretariat on a party-to-party basis rather than through diplomatic channels. The effect is to limit the sovereignty of the East European states, since according to the tenets of Marxism-Leninism as interpreted by the Communist Party of the Soviet Union, all other communist parties are subordinate to the Soviet party. Thus, during the 1980–81 Polish crisis, most of the debate between Soviet and Polish authorities over how to handle the challenge of Solidarity was conducted through the Soviet party apparatus. Only the Yugoslav state, by breaking with Soviet ideological hegemony, has freed itself from conducting diplomacy through party channels. The Secretariat evolved out of the first major party organization instituted by Lenin in 1919, which created the Politburo and an Orgburo, charged with the internal administration of the party. Originally the Secretariat was the support staff of the Orgburo. The Secretariat gradually took over the functions of the Orgburo as Josef Stalin used his position as the only party leader on both Politburo and Orgburo to achieve power. Stalin used his control over the party apparatus to consolidate power, eventually destroying his rivals and achieving undisputed power. Stalin's successors, Nikita Khrushchev and Leonid Brezhnev, followed a comparable although far less violent path to supreme power. Shifts in the membership of the Secretariat are an important indication of the rise and fall of party leaders and the policies they espouse. For example, Nikolai Podgorny was removed from the Soviet Secretariat in

1965 probably because he supported a consumer-oriented economic reform, a position unacceptable to Brezhnev. The Secretariat and Central Committee apparatus are the key instrument in the party's ability to fulfill its self-appointed role as the leading element of society. The centralized hierarchy of control that is characteristic of communist systems reaches its apex in the Secretariat. With the Politburo, the Secretariat epitomizes the bureaucratization of communist party systems whereby all important decisions are made and implemented by party functionaries rather than by elected officials.

Verification (*Pravo kontrolya*)   The communist party's self-determined right to verify the compliance of all institutions and officials with party policy. The right of verification (*pravo kontrolya*) involves the party with the routine management of all economic enterprises and institutions, as well as party and government agencies. Most pravo kontrolya is performed by the local party unit (PPO), which is charged with determining whether local managers and officials carry out party directives. All local decisions must be verified prior to implementation for compliance with party policy and then afterwards, to ensure that they have been correctly implemented. *See also* PARTY BUREAU, p. 112; PARTY LINE, p. 115; SECRETARIAT, p. 126.

Significance   As practically all aspects of a communist system are considered to be in the public sector and thus subject to guidance by the party, there is very little that is not subject to party verification. As Sovietologist Jerry Hough has theorized, the party's right to verify economic decisions may make the local party bureau the *de facto* board of directors of an economic enterprise. In cases of conflict between management and party authorities, the party may override the management, although since most enterprise managers are party members this is infrequent. The communist party views the right of verification as part of its moral duty to enforce standards of efficiency, professionalism and public morality. Pravo kontrolya has been increasingly emphasized by the Soviet party leadership; the 24th Party Congress in 1971 formally extended the right of verification by local party units to all local assemblies and to scientific, cultural, and other institutions. For the party, verification ensures that all economic plans, party directives, and government orders are implemented in conformity with party policy.

4. Governmental Structures and Processes

Collegial Head of State   A collective body charged with executing the laws and exercising the ceremonial functions of state. The collegial head of state is an institution common to communist-party states. It exercises the functions that in democratic systems are normally performed by a president or head of state. In theory elected by the national parliament and responsible to it, the collegial head of state in communist-party systems is comprised of top party officials who exercise the prerogatives of state power when parliament is not in session. As communist parliaments meet only a few days each year, the collegial head of state is in reality the chief executive and legislative organ of government. These bodies, usually called Presidium or Council of State, legislate by unilateral decree and represent the country internationally. Most legislation in communist-party states originates in the collegial head of state rather than in parliament. The Chairman of the presidium or Council of State fulfills most of the ceremonial functions of state, signing international treaties, receiving diplomats, and representing the state in international negotiations. The collegial executive organs of the East European states are modeled after the presidium of the Supreme Soviet, and, as is true of the Soviet Presidium, wield considerable power. Most East European systems combine the office of Chairman with that of party Secretary, a practice followed by the Soviet Union since 1977 when Leonid Brezhnev assumed the chairmanship of the Presidium of the Supreme Soviet, thus becoming both head of party and head of state. Two East European states diverge from the Soviet pattern. Czechoslovakia has a one-man Presidency and Yugoslavia possesses a Collective Presidency whose powers are limited by responsibility to the Yugoslav Federal Assembly. Elsewhere, the collegial heads of state are essentially instruments of party policy, with

131

little responsibility to the government. The collegial organs of state are as follows: (1) Albania: Presidium, headed by party secretary Enver Hoxha; (2) Bulgaria: Council of State, headed by party secretary Todor Zhivkov; (3) East Germany: Council of State, headed by party secretary Erich Honecker; (4) Hungary: Presidential Council, not headed by the party secretary; (5) Poland: Council of State, not headed by party secretary; (6) Romania: Council of State, headed by party secretary Nicolae Ceauşescu, who also holds the title of President; (7) USSR: Presidium of the Supreme Soviet, headed since 1983 by party secretary Yuri Andropov; (8) Yugoslavia: Collective Presidency, Presidency rotates in set order each year. *See also* DUPLICATION OF OFFICE, p. 100; PRESIDIUM OF THE SUPREME SOVIET, p. 158; YUGOSLAVIA: COLLECTIVE PRESIDENCY, p. 176.

Significance   The vesting of formal state functions in a collegial head of state is patterned after the principle of collective leadership espoused by communist parties. Communist theory promotes the idea that the collegial head of state is superior to the one-man presidencies of bourgeois democracies. The members of these collective bodies typically hold top party positions, thus making the formal responsibility to parliament a fiction. The chief function of the collegial heads of state is to translate party policy into legal form and to represent the state on ceremonial occasions. Whether or not state authority is exercised by a parliament or delegated to an inner collegial body actually makes little difference since the party controls the government apparatus through duplication of party/government posts. When the Czechoslovak Communist Party seized power in 1948, it chose to retain the office of President rather than instituting a collegial head of state—most probably in order to usurp the prestige of that office, held by Tomáš Masaryk in the prewar period when Czechoslovakia was the only functioning parliamentary democracy in Eastern Europe. Except for a brief period of liberalization, the Czechoslovak Presidency has been held by the party secretary, now Gustáv Husák, and the dynamics of party control are thus comparable. The Yugoslav Collective Presidency differs substantially from the Soviet model. Set up to provide a successor to Josip Broz Tito, its powers are limited by responsibility to the Yugoslav Federal Assembly. With Tito's death, the office of President, which is mainly a ceremonial title, rotates in set order each year. Unlike its East European counterparts, the Yugoslav Federal Assembly is a functioning parliament, meeting in lengthy sessions and originating most of the federal legislation. To date, the Collective Presidency has functioned as intended, a truly collective body with responsibilities to the parliament.

Council of Elders The parliamentary body composed of the most experienced deputies in the Supreme Soviet that apparently is responsible for coordinating the work of the federal legislature. Little is known about the functions and composition of the Council of Elders. Each of the two chambers of the Supreme Soviet has a Council of Elders, chaired by the chairman of the chamber and comprised of about 150 deputies. Its prime function appears to be setting the agenda. In this, the Council of Elders resembles a parliamentary steering committee of leading deputies. The only public function of the Council is the approval of the standing orders at the opening of each session. It apparently also recommends the candidates for the chairmanships of each of the standing committees. The Council of Elders meets prior to each session of the Supreme Soviet, determining the order of business and scheduling speeches and reports, functioning much as the Rules Committee of the United States House of Representatives. It may also be responsible for the final review of draft legislation before placing bills on the agenda. Its membership is said to include the leaders of the parliamentary delegations from each of the republics and territories. Although most of the members are party functionaries, the Council of Elders also includes nonparty members with tenure, estimated at about 20 percent. *See also* LEGISLATIVE PROCESS, p. 149; SUPREME SOVIET, p. 166.

Significance The Council of Elders is composed of leading party deputies and those deputies who have accumulated tenure as experienced legislators. Frequently, these are the same. The party controls nominations to the Council. The normal practice is that about two-thirds of the deputies to the Supreme Soviet serve only one term; those returned for more than one term are usually party functionaries; thus the Council is generally staffed by leading party members. The practice of including the leading deputy from each republican and territorial delegation serves to buttress the federal principle in the Supreme Soviet.

Council of Ministers The highest executive and administrative organ in the Soviet government. Constitutionally the Council of Ministers is a collective (collegial) head of government, charged with implementing the laws and exercising the ceremonial functions of state. The Council of Ministers constitutes the apex of the vast government bureaucracy, numbering about 2 million officials, which administers all economic, political, cultural, and social activities of the state. Although sometimes compared to a parliamentary cabinet, the

Council of Ministers is far too large to act as a working cabinet; most of its assigned functions are probably exercised by its Presidium and by the individual ministries and departments. As of 1978, the top 106 administrators who comprise the Council included the Premier, or Chairman, 2 First Deputy Chairmen, 11 Deputy Chairmen, 62 Ministers, 12 heads of state committees, and 3 heads of national administrative agencies. The 15 chairmen of the republican Council of Ministers are *ex officio* members, thus assuring coordination with the republican Councils of Ministers. Below the level of the Autonomous Republic, the chief administrative body is called an executive committee. In terms of size and scope of jurisdiction, the Soviet Council of Ministers and the government it presides over are unique. Few if any other governments attempt to regulate so much of the activities of the polity; the additional fact that almost all economic activity in the Soviet Union is nationalized and under government control makes almost every decision an administrative one. Well over half of the ministries and interdepartment State Committees represented on the Council of Ministers are economic or industrial in nature. Each Minister heads a functionally specific Ministry, charged with adminstering a specific branch of economic or political activity. Ministries and State Committees may be divided into three categories: political (education, culture), industrial (construction, engineering), or economic (finance, banking). The Council of Ministers issues binding decrees (*postanovlenie*) and orders (*rasporyazhenie*). The Council is charged with drawing up and implementing the national economic plan. Additional statutory functions include directing monetary and fiscal policy, overseeing the military, maintaining public order, and appointing important officials. The division of responsibilities between the Council and the Presidium of the Supreme Soviet is obscure; the Presidium exercises functions that are normally the prerogative of the head of state. The full Council usually meets only quarterly, to hear reports. Its relationship with the party is not defined; presumably most policy decisions originate in the party leadership and are implemented by the Council. Ministers, who always hold top party posts, are formally appointed by the Supreme Soviet but in reality are undoubtedly selected by the party leadership. The Council also possesses substantial legislative power. Many decrees issued in its name are really policy decisions, clearly far broader in scope than its constitutional responsibility of elaborating already existing law. Such decisions are usually issued jointly with the Central Committee. As chief administrator, it supervises the vast Soviet civil service. Its economic duties are far-reaching, including drafting, coordinating, and implementing the economic plan, and overseeing the major industrial branches of the nationalized economy. Its jurisdiction extends into all levels and sectors of Soviet life. Its control over the vast bureaucratic apparatus of the state makes it a key adminstrative institution. Every Soviet citizen, from the kolkhoz farm manager who wishes to change his assigned production quota to the student seeking entrance to a university must deal with an administrative agency that is ultimately supervised by the Council of Ministers. *See also* GOSPLAN, p. 196; LEGISLATIVE PROCESS, p. 149; MINISTRY, p. 151; PRESIDIUM OF THE COUNCIL OF MINISTERS, p. 157; STATE COMMITTEE, p. 164; YUGOSLAVIA: FEDERAL EXECUTIVE COUNCIL, p. 177.

Significance   The Council of Ministers is a major instrument for translating party policy into law. Little concrete is known about the actual work and division of responsibilities of the Council. Given the fact that it regularly includes important party leaders, analysts assume that it plays a role in the policy process in addition to its formal administrative responsibilities. Many of the decrees and orders issued by the Council of Ministers regarding the execution of laws are similar to the regulations issued by the various administrative agencies of the U.S. executive branch that explain how laws passed by Congress should be implemented. However, many of the Council's acts are actually lawmaking. The acts of the Council of Ministers do not have to be published unless normative in content (lawmaking) or of general significance, a determination that is made by the issuing agency itself. Some Western analysts believe that this "secret" legislation outnumbers the published legislation, meaning that many of the technical decisions that regulate so much of Soviet life are not public. Of the published legislation, an estimated three-fourths emanates from the Council of Ministers. Frequently policy decisions made by the party leadership will be translated into law by the Council; thus a party decision to increase funding for the agricultural sector will be translated into legally binding decisions by the Council of Ministers and its coordinating bodies. As such, it serves then as a major allocator of resources for the system. The executive arms of the governments of the East European states are patterned after the Soviet Council of Ministers. The exception is the Federal Executive Council of the Yugoslav government, which more closely resembles a true parliamentary cabinet. The Yugoslav Federal Executive Council is more responsible to the national parliament. But it differs in another crucial aspect. In Soviet-style systems, there is no provision for a parliamentary vote of no confidence, nor for the resignation of a cabinet. In Yugoslavia, FEC officials may be questioned by the parliament and, in 1967, a republican cabinet resigned, in the best Western parliamentary tradition over a difference with federal authorities. The Soviet Council of Ministers and its East European counterparts admit to no such possibility; their major functions are to implement party policy, supervise the administrative bureaucracy, and preserve the party monopoly of power. Stripped of its legislative functions, the Council may be envisioned as the chief administrator of the state, the supreme executive authority. The top administrators, although operating under the direction of the party, have substantial powers as chief administrators and enjoy considerable discretion in managing the government and allocating its resources.

Defense Council   An important interdepartmental body attached to the Council of Ministers and, in the early 1980s, headed by the General Secretary and leader of the party, Yuri Andropov. The existence of the Defense Council (*Sovet Oborony*) was first publicly acknowledged in 1975. The 1977 Soviet Constitution states that the Defense Council is named by the Presidium of the Supreme Soviet. Little is known of its functions; it must be assumed from its title and the fact that the General Secretary heads the Council that it is the preeminent coordinating body for defense policy. Observers believe that it includes the General Secretary, who also serves as Commander-in-Chief of the Armed Forces, two or three top Politburo members, and representatives of the Ministry of Defense and related agencies. It should not be confused with the Military-Industrial Commission, a subordinate body of the Council of Ministers that coordinates the work of the Defense Ministry, ministries involved in military production, and those scientific institutes engaged in military research and development. *See also* PRESIDIUM OF THE COUNCIL OF MINISTERS, p. 157.

Significance   The Defense Council is typical of the Soviet pattern wherein some of the most crucial institutions are the least publicized. The inclusion, however brief, of the Defense Council in the 1977 Constitution marks a step forward in public visibility. It also probably reflects the fact that the Defense Councils of the East European states have operated far more publicly. All seven of the East European states possess comparable bodies; those of Poland, Czechoslovakia, and Yugoslavia were created by public legislative acts in 1967, 1969, and 1973, respectively. By 1983, with the accession of Yuri Andropov to the party leadership, Andropov assumed leadership of the Defense Council.

Deputy   An elected member of a national, regional, or local legislature. In the Soviet Union, more than 2.2 million deputies serve in over 50,000 legislatures, called soviets. Soviets range from the bicameral federal legislature, the Supreme Soviet, down to small village soviets. Deputies are elected by universal suffrage of all persons over 18. Deputies exercise legislative authority at each administrative level; the scope of their authority is determined by the federal and republican constitutions. Although the party controls the nomination process, many nonparty members whom the party deems reliable are permitted to serve as deputies. Deputies are responsible to the soviet to which they are elected, to the relevant party unit, and to their constituents. However, the bulk of legislative work of any soviet is actually carried out by the executive bodies of the soviet, under party direction. In recent years, the role of the deputy has acquired more substance as the party has encouraged the deputy to act as the chief link between citizen and government. Deputies can request information from any state agency (the *spravka*), file complaints against state agencies, and request necessary legal aid. Ministries are now required to reply within one month. The role of the deputy traditionally has been viewed as an honorary function, since the executive bodies perform most of the legislative work; however, recent developments have strengthened the office. Deputies have come to play a major role as ombudsmen for their constituents: cutting red tape, protecting them against bureaucratic malfeasance, and answering requests for information. *See also* ELECTORAL PROCESS: USSR, p. 140; NOMINATIONS PROCESS: USSR, p. 153; PEOPLE'S COUNCILS, p. 157; SOVIET, p. 160; SPRAVKA, p. 162.

Significance   A deputy typically performs a wide range of services for his or her constituents, in the course of which many have found it necessary to employ a staff of paid help and volunteers to answer questions and render aid. A 1972 Soviet law further emphasized the function of the deputy as the link between citizen and government. Deputies at the district (*raion*) level in particular are expected to be the chief contact; they are responsible for explaining government decisions to their constituents. Since upper-level soviets usually meet only a few days per year, the nonprofessional nature of the Soviet deputyship offers time to enlarge the ombudsman function. The strengthening of the constituent work for the deputy has created legitimacy for the system—and additional work for the deputy, who in some cases must begin to feel like the beleaguered freshman Representative in the United States Congress who is trying to build a constituency base. Serving as deputy also provides a major mode of political participation open to many, and with the increase in the representative function, has involved many citizens in the system.

Dual Subordination   The administrative principle applied to all Soviet and East European organs of government that involves both vertical subordination to the next highest government body, and horizontal subordination to the appropriate soviet (elected assembly) or its executive committee. Dual subordination rests on democratic centralism (a principle first applied by Vladimir Lenin to the communist party), which mandates the strict subordination of all lower organs of government to the superior organs in the government hierarchy, and on the other hand, gives democratic responsibility to the local electoral body. Thus, the departments of the soviets are responsible to their parent soviet and its executive committee, and to the corresponding department in the next highest level of government. Similarly, the executive committees are responsible to their local soviets and to the executive committee of the next highest soviet, i.e., a district (*raion*) executive committee is responsible to the district soviet and to the executive committee of the provincial soviet. The process extends to the central organs, with the Supreme Soviet and Council of Ministers at the top. The Minister of Education of a republic, for example, is subordinate to the republican Council of Ministers, and to the USSR Minister of Education. *See also* LENINISM: DEMOCRATIC CENTRALISM, p. 52; DUPLICATION OF OFFICE, p. 100; KGB, p. 288.

Significance   Dual subordination ensures unity and central control. In practice, it has meant that all final determinations are made by higher authorities while local issues are decided by the local elected bodies. Two key Soviet institutions, the secret police (KGB) and the Procuracy, are exempt from the principle of dual subordination, being responsible only to the central authorities. This exemption, it can be argued, proves that horizontal responsibility to local authorities is not meaningless. Dual subordination was introduced by Lenin in 1918 in the immediate chaos following the Bolshevik Revolution when the relatively small Bolshevik party somehow had to find a way of controlling a huge empire. East European states after World War II adopted many Soviet administrative practices including dual subordination. In its application, dual subordination tends to erode the authority of local governments, since their subordinate units can always appeal upwards.

Electoral Process: Eastern Europe   The party-controlled process by which candidates are nominated and elected to the representative bodies, from local councils to national parliaments. The electoral process in Eastern Europe differs from the Soviet in that nominations are made in the name of a national front organization and all candidates run under its banner. Such national fronts include the mass organizations and the communist-controlled remnants of prewar political parties. The process is modeled after the Soviet: direct universal suffrage, no write-ins, and total party control over nominations. The main difference is that the party operates in all Eastern European states through a national front. Some differences among these countries have emerged. Hungary and Poland, for example, have permitted a limited number of contested seats, although no candidate is permitted to run as the representative of an opposing political party. Poland, despite its adherence to the general pattern, has recorded some shockingly low voting turnouts for communist systems, which usually manage a 98–99 percent turnout of eligible voters. Also, since the 1960s a handful of independent Polish Catholic activists have been permitted to run for the parliament (*Sejm*), in tacit recognition of the fact that it is to church rather than party that the Polish populace tenders its allegiance. Hungary has recently experimented with a few contested elections where the candidates actually may take differing viewpoints on issues. At all levels throughout Eastern Europe, candidates are selected from names proposed by the various members of the national fronts and approved by party-controlled electoral commissions. All run as individuals, in the name of the national front rather than the communist party. *See also* ELECTORAL PROCESS: USSR, p. 140; ELECTORAL PROCESS: YUGOSLAVIA, p. 141; MASS ORGANIZATIONS, p. 291; NATIONAL FRONT, p. 325.

Significance   The electoral processes of the East European states, which operate through party-controlled national front organizations, echo the mechanism through which communism came to power in postwar Eastern Europe. In the immediate postwar chaos, in a measure of compliance with the Yalta Agreement, national fronts composed of all leading non-Fascist elements were constituted as interim governments. The various communist parties achieved dominance of the national fronts by clever manipulation of their position as the liberators of Eastern Europe. After they consolidated power and destroyed the opposing democratic parties, they retained the facade of the national front as a means of legitimacy. The East European fronts differ somewhat, although the results have been basically the same. In Czechoslovakia, the National Front includes the remnants of three prewar political parties, thus drawing on the credibility of the prewar democratic coalition that ruled Czechoslovakia. The Polish United Front contains two rump parties, the United Peasant Party and the Democratic Party, and similarly nurtures the fiction of a national front. In Poland, this apparently has been less successful, as Polish voting levels have been surprisingly low, falling to 55 percent in Warsaw in 1961, and in 1976 again declining in the seaport towns of Gdańsk, Gdynia, and Szczecin. Thus, elections in Poland have some predictive value, at least in terms of indicating the level of alienation.

Electoral Process: USSR   The method in the Soviet Union by which representatives to legislative bodies are selected. The electoral system is structured so as to provide total party control over who is elected to the various legislative bodies (soviets) from the federal level down to local village councils. Voters are presented with a ballot listing only one candidate for each office; there are no contested elections. Voters have only the choice of affirming the entire list of candidates or striking candidates' names; a write-in will invalidate the ballot. In order to strike a candidate's name, the voter must use a special voting booth, available only in polling places that are usually manned by party officials. Understandably, most voters simply place the unmarked ballot in a box, which certifies approval of the candidate list. Since only a single list of candidates is presented, nomination usually means election. At all levels, candidates may be proposed at voters' meetings called by five types of social organizations: the party, trade unions, cooperatives, youth organizations, and cultural organizations. Party control over the latter four ensures that the party retains control over the final list of candidates. Elections are based on single-member territorial voting districts; for the territorial legislatures electoral districts are divided into wards of about 500–3,000 voters. Western observers question whether Soviet elections constitute true elections or are merely symbolic exercises that include an element of coercion. Electoral campaigning in the Soviet Union is conducted with great seriousness and voters are constantly exhorted to fulfill their duty as citizens. Nonvoting is viewed as a political act; about 99 percent of eligible voters regularly turn out for elections. It is maintained by many that the lower the level of government body, the more open the process. Despite the obvious elements of coercion involved, some candidates' names are struck by voters. The authorities monitor election results closely and consider the invalidation of a candidate by several percentage points as indicative of widespread dissatisfaction. Nonparty members are included on the candidate lists, although only with party approval. The proportion of nonparty members in the Supreme Soviet is usually around one-fourth; the proportion increases in city and regional assemblies. *See also* DEPUTY, p. 136; ELECTORAL PROCESS: EASTERN EUROPE, p. 138; ELECTORAL PROCESS: YUGOSLAVIA, p. 141; NOMINATION PROCESS: USSR, p. 153; SOVIET, p. 160; SUPREME SOVIET, p. 166.

Significance   The usefulness of the complex and lengthy Soviet electoral system is frequently questioned. The logical question that arises is: why does the government incur the expense of massive campaigns for elections with predetermined outcomes? The answer, for many analysts, is that Soviet elections constitute a crucial legitimizing device by which citizens publicly affirm their allegiance to a system whose ideology proclaims it to be the "people's government." Soviet elections are clearly designed to enhance the sense of individual political participation and to give citizens a sense of involvement in the system. This explains why almost every adult citizen is contacted personally prior to an election by an election worker and urged to vote. These election workers number in the millions, and for the many nonparty members, such work is one of the most common forms of political participation. Thus, in Soviet elections the crucial aim is not selection of representatives, but *involvement* and *mobilization* of the citizenry. The electoral system also provides a method of entry for nonparty members who are considered loyal and capable, and frequently may provide an avenue of upward mobility for the ambitious. Holding elections also enables the leadership to insist that the system is democratic and based on the will of the people. Moreover, since the party controls the crucial nomination process, elections provide a means of maintaining ethnic parity in government.

Electoral Process: Yugoslavia   The complex system by which deputies to the local, republican, and federal legislative assemblies are selected. Until 1974 the Yugoslav electoral process was so open that it resembled elections in a parliamentary democracy. Modeled after Soviet practice following World War II, by 1969 it had evolved into a freewheeling system which featured contested elections, open discussions of issues, criticism of the party, and most crucially, the rise of politicians who based their power in their ethnic constituencies rather than with the national communist party. The 1974 electoral laws substituted a system of indirect election, by which deputies are delegated from other bodies rather than directly elected. The system is a three-stage process. Every two years delegations of between 10 to 30 voters are elected at "pre-election" meetings of the working organizations—the more than 65,000 Basic Organizations of Associated Labor (the basic units of the self-management system in the enterprises), agricultural cooperatives, army units, and other working collectives from hospitals to universities. Nominations to these delegations are made by the Socialist Alliance, the more than 8 million strong mass organization that operates under party tutelage. Simultaneously, similar voters' delegations are selected in the 12,000 local communities (*mesne zajednice*), the smallest territorial subdivision. About 1 million Yugoslavs, 7 percent of the eligible voters, serve on these delegations. These delegations then elect the delegates to their respective communal (county) assemblies. The communal assemblies are tricameral:

the Chamber of Associated Labor is chosen by the working organization delegations, the Municipal Chamber by the mesne zajednice delegations, and the Socio-Political Chamber by the party itself and the organizations it directs (youth federation, Socialist Alliance, trade unions, et al). The communal assemblies then delegate from their membership the deputies to the six republican and two provincial assemblies. At the final stage, deputies are selected to the bicameral Federal Assembly (*Skupština*). The 510 communal assemblies elect the deputies to the Federal Chamber from nominations proposed by the voters' delegations. Each republic sends 30 deputies and each autonomous province, 20. Federal law stipulates that at least half of the deputies must be from Basic Organizations of Associated Labor (BOALs). The republican and provincial assemblies elect from their membership the deputies to the second federal chamber, the Chamber of Republics and Provinces, 12 from each republic and 8 from each province. *See also* ELECTORAL PROCESS: EASTERN EUROPE, p. 138; ELECTORAL PROCESS: USSR, p. 140.

Significance   The Yugoslav electoral system is basically one of indirect delegation with the Socialist Alliance, and, ultimately, the party directing the process. The open political competition that developed in the 1960s coincided with the devolution of power from federal to republican and local organs, and the strengthening of parliamentary autonomy. When the Croat crisis of 1971 erupted, it was viewed as a manifestation of the increased power of republican politicians who based their power in their ethnic constituencies. To the party leaders and their charismatic chief, Josep Broz Tito, the Croat push for greater autonomy threatened the always fragile Yugoslav federation, one in which no one nationality enjoys a majority. The central party authorities were determined to staunch the tide of nationality-based competition by tightening party control. One of the major sacrifices was the free-wheeling, competitive elections that had evolved during the 1960s. The indirect role allotted to the ordinary voters buttresses party control; the special role allotted to the party preserves it. Yugoslav theorists, such as Edvard Kardelj, maintained that the delegate system is more responsive than a "representative" system, since the delegations are responsible to their neighborhoods or working organizations. Delegations are supposed to meet periodically with their deputies to discuss all questions on forthcoming agendas, and the deputies, while not bound by vote of their delegation, are supposed to pursue their decisions. The complexity of the system and the number of person-hours it demands add up to a substantial amount of voluntary participation. As a general rule, however, only professional politicians —i.e., party authorities—have the time to devote more than cursory attention to the many complex issues involved. The 1974 electoral laws did not change the essentially confederal nature of Yugoslav politics. Communal assemblies still retain considerable powers and most federal issues require the prior agreement of the republican and provincial assemblies. Because Yugoslav legislative assemblies are meaningful bodies, the electoral process, indirect as it is, is still more important to the policy process than elsewhere in Eastern Europe. Many major investment decisions are made at the local and republican levels. Thus, the makeup of the voters' delegations can be crucial to the working organizations, and participation in them is a meaningful form of political participation, with direct payoffs to the enterprise. The specific representation allotted to the BOALs strengthens the self-management system.

Federalism   A united system of government composed of two or more component units that retain certain constitutionally allocated rights and functions. Federalism is distinguished from unitary systems by the fact that in unitary systems the territorial subunits of the government function only as administrative subdivisions of the central government. In a federal system, the federal government exercises specific powers, such as control of the military, foreign affairs, the economy, and banking, while other powers are reserved solely to the constituent units of the federation. Among communist-party systems there are three federal systems: The Union of Soviet Socialist Republics (USSR), Czechoslovakia, and Yugoslavia. Federalism in the USSR, as in Czechoslovakia and Yugoslavia, is based on the multinational composition of the state. According to the Soviet Constitution, the USSR is a voluntary federation of 15 sovereign union-republics. The union-republics are: The Russian Soviet Federated Socialist Republic (RSFSR), Ukrainian Soviet Socialist Republic (SSR), Byelorussian SSR, Kazakh SSR, Uzbek SSR, Georgian SSR, Azerbaidzhan SSR, Lithuanian SSR, Moldavian SSR, Latvian SSR, Kirgiz SSR, Tadzhik SSR, Armenian SSR, Turkmen SSR, and Estonian SSR. In all but two of the union-republics (Kazakh and Kirgiz SSRs), the "leading" nation is the majority population. Most of the powers exercised by the union-republics are concerned with the preservation of local languages and cultural identities. As in the state-based U.S. federal system, the union-republics also possess considerable administrative authority. The highest legislative organ of the federation, the Supreme Soviet, is bicameral, one chamber representing the population at large and the second comprised of directly elected representatives of the component territorial units of the federation. Soviet federalism operates on two levels, the federal to republic level, and the union-republic level, the latter involving the relationship between the union-republics and their constituent units, the autonomous republics, autonomous provinces, and national areas. These smaller units, contained within the union-republics, serve to recognize the numerically smaller nationalities and ethnic groups with homelands in the interior. Not all union-republics contain such subdivisions; the bulk are located in the huge and heterogeneous Russian Union-Republic. In all, there are 53 ethnically based political-administrative units in the USSR, all of whom are represented in the Supreme Soviet. Union-republics and autonomous republics possess their own constitutions, citizenship, and organs of state power, as is true of the U.S. states. The autonomous provinces and national areas possess administrative autonomy but do not have constitutions, citizenship, or higher organs of government, these being mandated by the constitutions of the union-republic. Union-republic constitutions differ in degree, with the differences usually being accommodations to the culture of the majority population. All use the native language in administrative affairs, education, and judicial processes. All-Union (federal) law takes precedence over all other laws and all laws of the Supreme Soviet are binding throughout the federation. *See also* FEDERALISM: CZECHOSLOVAKIA, p. 145; FEDERALISM: YUGOSLAVIA, p. 146; TERRITORIAL DIVISIONS (USSR), p. 168.

Significance   Federalism in the USSR is inextricably tied to the multinationality of the state, a cultural mosaic of some 100 separate nationalities. Originally, both Karl Marx and Vladimir Lenin opposed federalism, arguing that it perpetuated "bourgeois nationalism" and delayed the development of socialism. Marx, however, never envisioned the revolution occurring in a semideveloped, multinational state. Caught up by the realities of the Russian situation, Lenin conceded the inevitablity of federalism as a means of containing the growing separatism of the many non-Russian nationalities that had chafed under the Russian dominance of the Czar. After the October Revolution in October 1917, the Bolsheviks were faced by a civil war. Lenin's endorsement of federalism was a means of uniting the various non-Russian nationalities. Federalism provided a way to destroy Czarist-Russian dominance while curbing the centrifugal tendencies implicit in national self-determination. Thus, Marx to the contrary, the adoption of the federal principle established Bolshevik control while accommodating the Leninist principle of self-determination. Federalism was formally instituted with the 1919 Constitution of the Russian Soviet Federal Socialist Republic. As the Bolsheviks consolidated their power, other Soviet republics were created and joined to the RSFSR by treaties that recognized them as sovereign republics. The 1924 Constitution formalized the federal structure of the USSR. The key to understanding the nature of Soviet federalism is that it is cultural, rather than political, in substance. The centralized Communist Party of the Soviet Union (CPSU) exercises all political power in the state; Lenin had no intentions of permitting any dilution of the party's political monopoly. As the party controls all state institutions, the union-republics are not permitted political autonomy. The fact that the constitution grants the right of succession to the union-republics is a meaningless guarantee. The true nature of Soviet federalism lies in its acceptance and nurturing of differing national and ethnic identities. Federalism has defused the major cause of nationality strife, the denial of national self-identity and unequal treatment. Conversely, the overarching central authority of the CPSU has protected the USSR from the inherent fragility of many nationality-based federal systems. Since Lenin, Soviet federalism has been posited on the theory of many diverse nationalities that will form a single proletarian culture while retaining their national self-identities. Those who predict the dissolution of the USSR from ethnic strife ignore the fact that most non-Russians have fared far better under communism than under the czars. Although nationality-based dissent has increased during the past decade, it is most in evidence in the western regions, in the formerly independent Baltic states and the Ukraine. As in many multinational systems, a major problem in the next decades may be the leaders' ability to counter rising nationalist expectations while preserving the unity of the system.

Federalism: Czechoslovakia   The most recently instituted federal system in the communist-party states. The change from a unitary system to federalism has been termed the only lasting reform wrought by the 1968 Czechoslovak liberalization movement. Commonly called the Prague Spring, the reform movement was characterized by two major demands: a more liberalized political system, and the Slovak demand for equal status. The Soviet-led invasion of August 1968 blocked the attempt to divorce Czechoslovakia from Soviet-style communism, but the Slovak demand for a federal system was implemented. In January 1969, two constituent units, the Czech Socialist Republic (ČSR) and the Slovak Socialist Republic (SSR), were constituted and the organs of government were federalized. Both republics possess their own parliaments, organs of government, and administration. The federal legislature is bicameral, one chamber representing the population at large and the other the two republics, with 150 members each. Federal law is supreme. The communist party, however, is not federalized. Only Slovakia has its own republican party structure; the Czechs operate within the national party. In terms of political impact, federalism has had little effect. Set up under the direction of the Soviets, the federal system has operated as in the USSR, where the highly centralized party actually controls all levers of power. *See also* FEDERALISM, p. 143; FEDERALISM: YUGOSLAVIA, p. 146; PRAGUE SPRING, p. 295.

Significance   The major result of the institution of federalism in Czechoslovakia has been psychological satisfaction for the Slovaks. Although the two nationalities have coexisted within the same state for decades, the more industrialized, educated, and numerically superior Czechs dominated the predominantly rural Slovaks. Communism did little to change the Slovaks' perceptions of unequal treatment. Many argued that Czech-determined investment policies neglected Slovakia. In addition, the Slovaks suffered disproportionately from the Soviet-instigated purges of the early 1950s, when many leading Slovak communists were persecuted for "Titoism" or "bourgeois national-ism." Slovak national aspirations thus played a key role in the Prague Spring. The current party leader, Gustáv Husák, is a Slovak who, with the support of the Soviets, replaced the reformist Alexander Dubček. Some analysts maintain that Husák, and other Slovak communists who cooperated with the Soviets after the invasion, were co-opted through the promise of federal equality for Slovakia.

Federalism: Yugoslavia   A distinctive institutional feature of the complex governmental structure of the Socialist Federal Republic of Yugoslavia (SFRY). On November 29, 1945, the Yugoslav state was reconstituted as a federation of six republics and two autonomous provinces, the latter attached to the Republic of Serbia. The six republics are Slovenia, Croatia, Serbia, Macedonia, Montenegro, and Bosnia-Hercegovina.The first five are homelands for a major national-ity; Bosnia-Hercegovina is an area of mixed Slavic Moslem—Croat—Serb population. Of the two Autonomous Provinces, the Vojvodina is an area of mixed Hungarian—Serb—Croat population and Kosovo contains the bulk of Yugoslavia's Albanian population. All possess their own parliaments, powers of taxation, judicial organs, universities, police, and so forth. All federal organs are constituted on the basis of ethnic parity, a principle that is extended to federal party organs. The parliaments of the eight constituent units delegate members to the federal Chamber of Republics and Provinces; the second chamber of the bicameral Federal Assembly is delegated from local assemblies. The competency of the federation is limited. The 1974 Constitution reserves all powers to the Republics except those expressly granted to the federation; specifically, foreign policy, national defense, and the national economy. At the federal level, decision making is structured so as to necessitate a republican consensus. This is usually achieved through the Federal Executive Council, the parliamentary cabinet. Republics, Provinces, and local units of government are responsible for the development of their own territories, for local administration, possess their own tax base, and manage their own resources. A federal fund for aid to the less developed regions represents an attempt to equalize economic development. *See also* YUGOSLAV PARTISAN WAR, p. 35; WORKERS' SELF-MANAGEMENT, p. 239; YUGOSLAVIA: COLLECTIVE STATE PRESIDENCY, p. 176; YUGOSLAVIA: FEDERAL EXECUTIVE COUNCIL, p. 177.

Significance   Unlike federalism in the Soviet Union, which is designed to protect cultural identity in a multinational state, federalism in Yugoslavia is a substantive political institution. It has been the instrument through which the system has effectively devolved political power, and with the unique system of self-management has created a decentralized state that differs vastly from the other communist bloc states. Postwar political developments have been characterized by a fluctuating balance between the federalized state institutions, the dynamics of ethnically based politics, and the centralizing tendencies of the communist party. Until 1950 most political power and administration rested with the central party apparatus. Political power and administration were subsequently devolved to republican and local governments, authorities, and to the enterprises, which under self-management were freed from central control. The process was carried further by the 1963 Constitution and the 1965 economic reforms, aimed at creating a socialist market economy. In 1971, demands for further autonomy in Croatia caused the party to reassert control, and in 1974 a new constitution replaced direct contested elections with a system of delegation from local bodies. The party emphasized its intent to remain the "leading force" and, by cracking down on the Croat nationalists, defined the limits of the permissible. Nonetheless, politics remains based in the constituent units of the federations, and local government and party leaders continue to contend for favorable allocation of resources. The Yugoslav Federation is a delicately balanced mechanism that must operate in the most diverse of states— the classic description of Yugoslavia runs: one political party, two alphabets, three religions, four major languages, five major nationalities, six republics, and seven bordering states. Of the 22 million citizens, no one nationality enjoys a majority as do the Russians in the Soviet Union. In addition to Serbs, Croats, Macedonians, Montenegrins, Slovenes, Hungarians, Bosnians (Moslem Slavs), and Albanians, it includes a host of small nationalities; many of these peoples have a long history of conflict and outright fratricide. In a meaningful federal system, nationality and economics inevitably become intertwined with the politics of resource allocation. Such has been the case in Yugoslavia. The 1971 Croat crisis centered on economic demands, the demand that the richer republics be taxed less for the development of the poorer republics, the demand for greater republican control over foreign currency earnings, and so forth. Yugoslavia's most recent nationality conflict, the demand of the Albanians of Kosovo for elevation to republican status, is fueled by the Albanian perception of Serbian hegemony and a failure to deliver on economic equality. The frequently shifting political arrangements in Yugoslavia usually spring from nationality problems; institutional change has become an institution in itself. The politics of ethnicity cannot be erased from Yugoslavia as long as it retains self-management and a federal structure.

Functionary   A full-time paid worker in the party or state bureaucracy. In a communist-party state, the term generally refers to the civil service, or officialdom. *See also* APPARATUS, p. 88.

Significance   Functionary is the preferred term in the Soviet Union for any full-time official of the party or government. Those who work in the party bureaucracy are often popularly referred to as *apparatchiki*, a term the party discourages. In the West, the term functionary also connotes "faceless bureaucrat" and is used to describe a low-level official who is expected to carry out the policies of a superior, but not engage in decision making or undertake initiatives.

Legal Enactments   The laws, regulations, rules, and orders constituting the body of legally binding acts that regulate much of the Soviet polity. As with most other governments, legal enactments in the Soviet Union emanate from several governmental sources and take several forms, ranging from federal law that applies to the entire state to regulations issued by local agencies that regulate a specific administrative function. Party decisions by themselves are not law. They must be translated into legal enactments by various state authorities. Legal acts are hierarchically ranked by their source and scope of mandate; laws (*zakony*) passed by the federal Supreme Soviet take precedence. The complex system of legal enactments and their promulgating bodies is as follows: (1) Zakon (statute or basic law), Supreme Soviet and republican soviets; (2) *ukaz* (edict), Presidium of the Supreme Soviet; republican presidiums; (3) *postanovlenie* (decrees), Supreme Soviet, Presidium, Council of Ministers, individual ministries, state committees, analogous republican and territorial organs; (4) *rasporyazhenie* (decisions or regulations), Council of Ministers, individual ministries, state committees, other analogous organs; (5) *prikazy* (orders), state committees, local soviets, courts; and (6) *reshenie* (decisions), courts, local soviets. Ministries and departments also issue instructions (*instruktsiya*), which regulate internal agencies, or *polozhenie*, which delineate the scope and authority of subordinate agencies. All these are legally binding acts of government. The most important are zakony and ukazy, which are "normative" acts, creating fundamental law or altering it. They differ only in that zakony are enacted by the Supreme Soviet and ukazy are issued by the Presidium when the Supreme Soviet is not in session. Laws must be published within seven days in the State Gazette (*Vedomosti SSSR*); most of the legislative enactments listed are ukazy. The bulk of the day-to-day regulations that govern so much of Soviet life are issued in the form of decrees, regulations, orders, or instructions and published in the Collection of Decrees (*Sobranie Postanovlenii Pravitel'stva SSSR*), the equivalent of the United States Federal Register. *See also* COUNCIL OF MINISTERS, p. 133; LEGISLATIVE PROCESS, p. 149; SUPREME SOVIET, p. 166.

Significance   As the Supreme Soviet meets only briefly, most of the important normative enactments are initially promulgated as ukazy, edicts of the Presidium, and usually are ratified later as zakony by the Supreme Soviet. Both the practice and the name derive from Russian history when the Czar ruled largely by ukaz, a unilaterally proclaimed edict. Only the most important legislation, such as draft legal codes, originate as zakony. All other legal enactments are not normative, and may be annulled by the Presidium of the Supreme Soviet. Much in the manner of the myriad regulations issued by the quasi-legislative administrative agencies of the U.S. government, they are largely regulatory or procedural in nature. At the provincial and regional levels, legislative and regulatory powers are vested in the local assemblies (soviets) and agencies, which adopt decisions and issue orders within the limits allowed by the laws of the federation and republic.

Legislative Process   The process by which party policy is translated into legal enactments. The legislative process is essentially the creation of legally binding laws and rules promulgated by the state authorities in whom national sovereignty is constitutionally vested. In communist-party states, despite the party's monopoly of power, legal theory has always distinguished between political authority, reserved to the party, and state authority, vested in the organs of government. Therefore, in the Soviet Union and other communist-party states, party decisions are not by themselves law. They must be translated into legal enactments by the various organs of state authority. Party control over the legislative process is maintained by the duplication of jobs for key party and government personnel, and the application of the principle of democratic centralism, which mandates that each party member must observe and implement all party decisions. It is difficult to ascertain where legislative proposals in the Soviet system actually originate, and how much change is permissible during the drafting stage. The legislative process in the Soviet Union is roughly as follows; (1) policy decisions are made by inner party organs; (2) party members serving in the various organs of government transmit these decisions in the form of legislative proposals; (3) draft legislation is prepared by the appropriate legislative committees or by the staffs of the various ministries; (4) the inner bodies of the legislature (Presidium or State Council) approve the draft bills; and (5) draft legislation is presented for vote. Although it is clear that no legislative issue can be initiated without party direction, the details are worked out by various governmental bodies. Draft bills are presented to the Supreme Soviet by the Council of Ministers, the Presidium, or the Council of Elders; individual deputies do not initiate legislation. This legislative process is repeated at all lower administrative levels, within the limits of the powers allotted to them by the constitution. An increasing number of important laws are circulated in draft form and technical-expert comments solicited; key draft bills have been published in the press and citizen responses (which are usually substantial) collated. Thus, important legislation may pass through these stages: (1) party proposes; (2) proposals transmitted to government; (3) draft legislation prepared by committees and staff; (4) drafts circulated among experts and possibly published; (5) draft may be adjusted according to responses; (6) Presidium reviews; (7) bill drafted in its final form; (8) presented to Supreme Soviet or Presidium for enactment; (9) Presidium instructs lower soviets to enact conforming laws. If the Supreme Soviet is not in session, the bill will be enacted as a *ukaz* (edict) by the Presidium and later ratified by the Supreme Soviet. *See also* COUNCIL OF MINISTERS, p. 133; DUPLICATION OF OFFICE, p. 100; LEGAL ENACTMENTS, p. 148; PRESIDIUM OF THE SUPREME SOVIET, p. 158.

Significance   Because the Supreme Soviet meets only briefly for a few days each year, debate over legislative proposals is not public; the real nature of the legislative process in the Soviet Union is obscure. Any important legislation must involve some debate over specifics but this is not conducted in public view. With key legislation, the decisions are probably made by the inner party organs; in other instances the locus of debate is more difficult to pinpoint. The outstanding feature of the Soviet legislative process, which is mirrored in East European systems, is the fact that although policymaking is reserved for the party, the regime has maintained a complex institutional process to legally translate policy into law. All important decisions are enacted as law by the Supreme Soviet or its Presidium, which is indicative of the importance the regime places on maintaining the semblance of popular sovereignty. Federal law is also important because it is through these acts, binding on the entire territory of the Soviet Union, that republican compliance with federal law is assured.

Ministry   A functional executive department that adminsters a specific branch of state adminstration. The ministry is the chief executive organ of the government, in command of the federal, regional, and local administrative agencies charged with implementing policy decisions. Comparable to a cabinet-level executive department, a ministry is headed by a minister. In the Soviet Union, ministries exist at three levels: (1) the all-union federal ministry (usually heavy industry); (2) the union-republic ministry, federal ministries with counterparts in the republics and autonomous republics; and (3) the republican ministry. The all-union federal ministries directly administer their subordinate units from Moscow, and in addition directly supervise certain key heavy industries. The union-republic ministries direct the personnel under their jurisdiction through the republican, territorial, and local administrations. Soviet ministries are found at three governmental levels: federal, republican, and autonomous republic; below this level the equivalent is an executive department. Ministers are appointed by and are technically responsible to the Presidium of the Supreme Soviet. Effective control, however, is probably exercised by the Council of Ministers, and, ultimately, by the party, thus rendering the adminstrative apparatus an almost independent branch of government. Most all-union federal ministries are economic in nature. Most union-republic ministries are economic, political, cultural, or social in nature, directing such sectors as public order, justice, or education. Ministries set their own general rules of order, appoint personnel, and are empowered to issue legally binding orders (*prikazy*) and instructions (*instruktsiya*) to agencies and departments within their jurisdiction. Each ministry is headed by a minister, one or more first deputy ministers, several deputy ministers, and a collegium of its leading officials, all but the minister being appointed by the Council of Ministers. Ministries, which may have staffs of 700 to 2,000, are divided into functionally specific departments (*otdely*). Ministers are almost always members of the party Central Committee; deputy ministers also typically hold high party posts. The personnel of a ministry, including the leading officials, generally constitute a highly specialized, professional group of career administrators who have progressed through the ranks. Although the Soviet Union has no formal civil service, performance rather than political criteria appears to dictate advancement. It is estimated that approximately one-third of the civil servants are not party members; the minister and his deputies, however, are invariably party members. The professionalization of the ministry means that even ministers are rarely shifted; it would be unthinkable for a former economic minister to suddenly resurface as Minister of Foreign Affairs. Each ministry has an educational institution that trains middle-level personnel in public administration. The vast bureaucracy is hierarchically organized; each administrator is responsible to his own executive unit and to the relevant department or ministry in the next highest government level, on up to the federal level, where the ministries direct the activities of all under their organizational jurisdiction. The ministry thus forms a crucial element in the bureaucratic control system. Because the Soviet economy is nationalized, and almost all social and cultural activities are controlled by the state, practically every Soviet citizen is employed by an institution or an enterprise that ultimately is supervised by a ministry. *See also* BUREAUCRATIC MODEL, p. 39; PRESIDIUM OF THE COUNCIL OF MINISTERS, p. 157; PLURALIST THEORY, p. 76.

Significance   Most Soviet ministries are concerned with directing a particular branch of the economy, a major responsibility of the Soviet administration. The concentration of ministries devoted to heavy industry at the federal level reflects the long-time priority of Soviet industrialization. The ministries typify the bureaucratization of society, where almost all decisions are made by appointed officials rather than by elected representatives. East European administrative systems are modeled after the Soviet, with the exception of Czechoslovakia, which is a federal state and thus has republican ministries as well as federal. The Yugoslav system of public administration is substantially different, for two reasons: (1) much power has been devolved to local governments, including the control of the administration; and (2) the economy is decentralized, each enterprise competing in the market, free of any mandatory central economic plans. Federal and republican ministries have substantial autonomy; investment decisions and production targets are the responsibility of the enterprise workers' councils and local government. In the Soviet Union and other East European states, the ministries are thought to play an important role as bureaucratic interest groups. Analysts, both communist and noncommunist, maintain that the ministries frequently represent the interests of their constituency in policy debates. As chief executors of policy, the ministries frequently make policy. The party ultimately may control, but the details of party directives are filled in by the various ministers, thus making them the focus of this process. For example, a Ministry of Agriculture may argue for greater investment in agriculture, while the representatives of heavy industry—commonly called "metal-eaters" —continue to push for more investment in defense and heavy industry. The ministries serve as an important allocator of state resources. The sheer size and scope of responsibilities of the Soviet bureaucracy has, in the opinion of some, impeded the efficiency of the ministries. Others, such as Allen Kassof, have referred to the Soviet Union as "the administered society," arguing that bureaucracy has replaced terror as the chief method of control. Whatever the degree of efficiency or control, the ministry is the key element in an almost all-pervasive bureaucratic system of control.

Nomination Process: USSR   The crucial stage in Soviet legislative elections that determines the membership of the various elected soviets, from the federal Supreme Soviet to local village assemblies. The Communist Party controls the nomination process, presenting a single list of candidates to the voters. Thus, nomination to the final candidate list almost ensures automatic election. The party usually does not directly nominate candidates. Instead, nominations are made in general citizens' meetings, held in each district or polling precinct that elects a deputy to a soviet. Millions of citizens are involved in these general meetings, which formally select over 2 million deputies to the federal, regional, and local legislatures. Nominations at the general meetings are made by representatives of the many official mass organizations. Any legally constituted public organization, that is, any organization that has received the permission of the government to organize, can nominate a candidate. These include trade unions, youth groups, collective farms, military units, working cooperatives, and working collectives of such institutions as universities and hospitals. The right to nominate candidates is apportioned among the organizations; the intent is to give each sector of society a voice in the nomination process. Party control over nominations is maintained through the mass organizations and working collectives, whose key posts are staffed by reliable party members. The most crucial stage in candidate selection is the pre-nomination discussion when party officials meet with local leaders and screen possible candidates. At this stage, the party leaders present their choices and solicit opinions from the community leaders, and may adjust their proposed slates accordingly. At the local levels, there is apparently much more input from nonparty leaders than at republican and federal levels, where the predetermined slates of party favorites are almost always endorsed. Electoral commissions, again selected by a party-controlled system resembling the nomination process, are formed for each territorial unit that elects deputies to an assembly. Candidates must be formally registered with the relevant electoral commission. All candidates run without opposition as representatives of the "Bloc of Party and Nonparty People." At the higher levels, many seats are by practice reserved on an *ex officio* basis, that is, the occupant of a high political or administrative office is automatically entitled to a legislative seat. *See also* ELECTORAL PROCESS: EASTERN EUROPE, p. 138; ELECTORAL PROCESS: USSR, p. 140; ELECTORAL PROCESS: YUGOSLAVIA, p. 141; MASS ORGANIZATIONS, p. 291.

Significance   The widespread citizen involvement in the nomination process serves as a legitimizing device for Soviet elections while the single-candidate list preserves party control and the sense of universal support for the system. As upwards of 9 million citizens are involved in the general nomination meetings, and about 1.3 million serve on the myriad electoral commissions, the nomination process constitutes a major avenue of political participation, however carefully controlled by the party. At times, candidates are rejected at the local general meetings, implying that citizen input is permissible. Because the party controls the process, it is able to present a more representative list of candidates than those prevailing in most democratically elected legislatures. Thus, of the deputies to the Supreme Soviet, 30 percent are women, 20 percent are under 30 years old, and a sizable number are workers and peasants. The party also controls the tenure of deputies; the usual practice is that nonparty representatives serve only one or two terms while party functionaries are returned to office, thus creating a core of party leaders, who constitute the experienced legislators of the system. The real bargaining probably occurs during the prenomination discussions. Thus, the Soviet nomination process probably resembles the process by which candidates were selected in the once-solid Democratic South of the United States, where election was actually determined in the preelection caucuses of the Democratic Party.

Parliaments: Eastern Europe   Elected national assemblies that constitutionally are the highest organs of legislative authority and the embodiment of popular sovereignty. East European parliaments, with the exception of the Yugoslav Federal Assembly, are modeled after the Supreme Soviet of the USSR. The political dynamics of all but Yugoslavia are comparable. Elections are controlled by the communist party. Parliaments meet for only a few days each year, delegating their work to small inner bodies, the presidiums or state councils, staffed by high party officials. The council of ministers, or cabinet, is drawn from the membership of the parliament and is responsible for executing the laws. They too are staffed by party officials. These party-dominated and directed bodies assume almost all of the functions of the parliaments. Thus, although the larger membership of the parliaments typically contains upwards of one-third nonparty members, party control is assured through the mechanism of overlapping party/government offices. Unlike the USSR, a few multicandidate elections have been permitted, in East Germany, Hungary, Poland, and Romania. Candidates, however, run as individuals and never in opposition to the party. In any case, all candidates must be approved by the party. The role of the parliaments in actually determining law is minimal. Most legislation originates in the party-dominated inner parliamentary bodies; the presidiums and state councils are empowered to legislate by decree when the parliaments are not in session—which is most of the time. The exception is Yugoslavia, where the Federal Assembly enjoys true subsystem autonomy. The two federal systems, Czechoslovakia and Yugoslavia, possess bicameral parliaments; all others are unicameral. The parliaments of the East European states are (1) Albania: People's Assembly, 250 members; (2) Bulgaria: National Assembly, 400 members; (3) Czechoslovakia: Federal Assembly: House of Nations, 150 members (75 Czechs, 75 Slovaks); House of the People, 200 members elected from equally apportioned electoral districts; (4) East Germany: People's Chamber, 500 members; (5) Hungary: National Assembly, 352 members; (6) Poland: *Sejm*, 462 members; (7) Romania: Grand National Assembly, 369 members; (8) Yugoslavia: Federal Assembly: Federal Chamber, 220 members (30 delegates from each of the six constituent republics, 20 from the two autonomous provinces); Chamber of the Republics and Provinces, 88 members (12 delegates from each republic and 8 from each province, all elected by secret ballot of the chambers of the 8 assemblies meeting in joint session). *See also:* COLLEGIAL HEAD OF STATE, p. 131; ELECTORAL PROCESS: EASTERN EUROPE, p. 138; SUPREME SOVIET, p. 166.

Significance   East European parliaments share certain common characteristics, stemming from the fact that the ruling communist parties in those states derive their legitimacy from an ideology that validates the party's role as the sole leading force in society. Government institutions serve the fundamental goal of building communism, a goal which according to Marxism-Leninism cannot be achieved if political power is shared. Parliaments represent the masses, for which the party is the vanguard; the will of the vanguard party and the interests of the masses inevitably coincide. The party's monopoly of political power has created parliamentary institutions that are little more than facades for party control. Outside Yugoslavia, these parliaments do not serve as instruments for the articulation of interests; Leninism and the principle of democratic centralism preclude any meaningful pluralism or interest articulation outside party channels. Essentially, the parliaments serve primarily to ratify decisions made by the party. The Yugoslav system does permit interest articulation across a wide spectrum; most is based in the interests of the various republics and is focused in the parliamentary institutions. East European parliaments do differ somewhat from the Soviet model; their parliamentary committees generally have been more active in the legislative drafting process. The differences in parliamentary activism appear to be related to the degree of subordination exacted by the USSR and the varying historical experiences of these states. The political cultures of East Germany, Bulgaria, and Romania appear to be most congruent with communist-party systems. Conversely, Poland, Hungary, and Czechoslovakia possess a parliamentary tradition. During the interwar period Czechoslovakia was the only functioning democracy in East Europe and is the heir to a strong democratic tradition. Limited parliamentary activism at times has developed in the latter three states, but always within the framework of Soviet hegemony. The Hungarian Communist Party, which under the New Economic Mechanism (NEM) has broadened decision making, has permitted multicandidate elections and committee debate of draft legislation. During the brief period of liberalization in 1968, the Czechoslovak parliament reasserted itself as a deliberative body, a development cut short by the Soviet-led invasion that reimposed Soviet control over Czechoslovakia. Throughout the 1960s and 1970s the Polish *Sejm* possessed an active committee structure, which debated and amended many draft bills. The Polish parliamentary revitalization was terminated by the imposition of military rule in December 1981. The most internally authoritarian states, East Germany, Bulgaria, and Romania, have exhibited the least parliamentary activism. Yugoslavia, which is in a class by itself, has an ethos centered on resisting foreign dominance, from the Ottoman Turks to the Soviets. The successful resistance to Soviet dominance in 1948 has left Yugoslavia free to develop its own parliamentary institutions, albeit within the framework of a single-party state. The major difference in Yugoslav parliamentarianism lies in the fact that in Yugoslavia, federalism has true institutional impact in terms of pluralism. Elsewhere, the likelihood of an evolution to a parliamentary system embracing elements of interest articulation and pluralism is slim. As long as the Soviet Union perceives control of East Europe as a political and military priority, any such development threatens the party's monopoly of power and thus threatens Soviet hegemony. For all but Yugoslavia, the Soviet communist party still defines the internal limits of the system.

People's Councils   Local organs of government in Eastern European states, modeled after the local soviets (councils) of the Soviet Union. The People's Councils (in Czechoslovakia called National Committees) possess administrative authority over local governmental units. Election is controlled by the communist party. Reliable non-party members, upon party approval, are typically allotted some seats. The Councils generally do not meet frequently, delegating most of their tasks to the local administrative apparatus. *See also* RAION, p. 172; SOVIET, p. 160.

Significance   People's Councils were set up in Eastern Europe after World War II as the commnist parties strengthened their hold on these states. The title is meant to indicate popular backing for communist governments. These local councils are generally responsive to local issues, frequently serving as a source of input to the policymakers, but they must operate under central control. Most powers rest not with the councils, but with the permanent administrative apparatus and the local party executive committee that directs their work. The organs of local government in Yugoslavia, the communal (county) assemblies, are much different. Their origin lies in the Partisan War, when the communist-led Partisan Army set up Committees of National Liberation on territories liberated from the Axis occupiers. The Committees were responsible for local self-government and frequently operated almost independently. As self-management and decentralization were applied to the Yugoslav system, the communal assemblies came to possess meaningful power. They essentially manage the assets of the commune, have an independent tax base, and are responsible for many administrative and social welfare functions.

Presidium of the Council of Ministers   The inner body of the much larger USSR Council of Ministers, comparable to a working cabinet. Little is known about the Presidium of the Council of Ministers, but it appears that most of the formal powers of the Council of Ministers are exercised by its Presidium. Given the size of the Council of Ministers, 106 currently, and its infrequent meetings, there is little doubt that most of the decisions announced in the name of the Council of Ministers are actually the decisions of the Presidium. Its membership, frequency of meetings, and responsibilities are not known. Only with the 1977 Soviet Constitution was the existence of the Presidium of the Council of Ministers formally announced; the Constitution refers to it as "the working organ of the Council of Ministers," which is empowered to decide "all urgent questions" and to "speak in the name of the government of the USSR." Translated, this means that the

Presidium (not to be confused with the Presidium of the Supreme Soviet) is probably the most important organ of central administrative authority, responsible for the overall direction of the national economy and the state administration. Its membership apparently includes the Chairman of the Council of Ministers, the First Deputy Chairman, and about twelve Deputy Chairmen, and possibly other members. It includes the heads of such important economic ministries and committees as state planning (Gosplan), Science and Technology, Construction, Economic Ties with Foreign Countries, Agriculture, Energy, and Defense. Thus, its major function appears to lie in the area of economic planning and coordination. *See also* COUNCIL OF MINISTERS, p. 133.

Significance   The Presidium of the Council of Ministers is typical of Soviet practice, both in party and government, of delegating responsibility to small, inner bodies, about which little is known. There is probably substantial duplication of responsibility between the Presidium of the Council of Ministers and the Secretariat of the party Central Committee, but how responsibilities are divided is not clear. The composition of its membership, mainly top economic administrators, and the nature of its decisions indicate that the Presidium may also function as a Council of Economic Advisers to the party Politburo. As almost all economic decision making in the centralized Soviet system is ultimately the responsibility of the party leadership, the Presidium of the Council of Ministers is undoubtedly a major institution, despite its obscurity. Its two top members, the Chairman and the First Deputy Chairman, have also typically been members of the party Politburo, and the Deputy Chairmen are inevitably members of the party Central Committee. As East European Councils of Ministers are also typically large bodies, it can be assumed that there, too, the real administrative responsibility is delegated to similar cabinet-like inner bodies. The function and role of the Presidium of the Council of Ministers conform with the elitist principles that govern decision making throughout the Soviet system.

Presidium of the Supreme Soviet   According to the Soviet Constitution, the "permanently functioning organ of the Supreme Soviet," empowered to act as the highest organ of state authority when the Supreme Soviet is not in session. The Presidium of the Supreme Soviet is in effect the highest legislative body of the Soviet Union. The Supreme Soviet meets only briefly, delegating its powers to the Presidium during the interim. The Supreme Soviet is empowered to issue legally biding edicts (*ukazes*); most of the law (*zakon*) that governs the Soviet Union originates as ukazes, which are later ratifed as zakons by the Supreme Soviet. The Presidium also functions as the ceremonial head of state. Although elected by and responsible to the Supreme Soviet, in theory, the Presidium in practice acts independently. The Presidium includes the Chairman, a first deputy chairman, 15 deputy chairmen, and 29 other members. As with the membership of the party Secretariat, an obvious attempt is made to balance the membership by including representatives of the major nationalities and crucial sectors of the system. The 15 chairmen of the republican presidiums are *ex officio* members. The powers of the Presidium are extensive. It apparently plays a major role in the drafting of legislation, working closely with specialized party and government agencies and with the committees of the Supreme Soviet. The Presidium may (1) issue binding decrees (*postanovlenie*); (2) set up or abolish government ministries; (3) restructure the administrative apparatus; (4) issue orders to the judicial organs; (5) appoint key government officials; and (6) ratify border changes between the republics. The military powers of the Presidium include the authority to (1) declare war; (2) mobilize the armed forces; (3) proclaim martial law, either throughout the nation or for a specific area; and (4) appoint military commanders, all without approval of the Supreme Soviet. Its judicial functions include the powers to (1) supervise the federal Supreme Court; (2) grant pardons and issue amnesties; and (3) elaborate on or interpret existing laws for the judiciary. It is therefore the only source of judicial review in the Soviet system. The Presidium also grants and revokes citizenship and is the only body that can grant the right to renounce citizenship, an act upon which the permission to emigrate hinges. As formal head of state, the Presidium (1) ratifies treaties with foreign nations; (2) appoints and receives ambassadors; and (3) represents the USSR abroad. According to international protocol, the Chairman of the Presidium is the ceremonial head of state, and is sometimes referred to as the President of the USSR, (not to be confused with the Premier of the Council of Ministers, who is head of government). Thus, the Presidium constitutes the supreme legislative, executive, and judicial authority of the formal state apparatus. The vesting of legislative, executive, and judicial powers in one body is consistent with Soviet doctrine, which treats separation of powers as a devious feature of bourgeois democracy. *See also* LEGAL ENACTMENTS, p. 148; LEGISLATIVE PROCESS, p. 149; SUPREME SOVIET, p. 166.

Significance   The extensive powers of the Presidium of the Supreme Soviet is consistent with the Soviet practice of delegating the powers of larger bodies to smaller inner bodies, which frequently operate away from public view. Since the exact role and functions of the Presidium are unknown, it is assumed to be a major instrument through which party policy is transformed into law. Although the communist party retains a monopoly over policy decisions, the actual legal implementation of party decisions is carried out by the formal apparatus of the government; party decisions by themselves are not law. The Presidium appears to be the major instrument of this process. Soviet doctrine maintains that the true locus of popular sovereignty rests with the elected soviets (assemblies); the Presidium and its republican and regional counterparts function as transmitters of party policy into law. In the process, as they draft legislation, they fill in the details of party directives and may even institute some change. The elected soviets at all levels delegate most of their functions to inner working bodies, at the republican level also called presidiums and at the lower levels, executive committees. As with much of the Soviet governmental apparatus, the true scope of the Presidium is not known. Given its size, it is unlikely that the full membership meets frequently; most probably the work is carried out by an inner working group of top officials, all of whom hold high party posts. For some years, Leonid Brezhnev held the post of Presidium Chairman and Party Secretary, the first time in Soviet history that both positions have been occupied by the same person, although this has been standard practice in several East European states. When Brezhnev assumed the Chairmanship in 1977, it indicated the party's concern with maintaining power over the government. In 1983 Yuri Andropov became Chairman. The legislatures of the East European states, with the exception of the Yugoslav Federal Assembly, follow Soviet practice. All meet infrequently, and all delegate true legislative power to a nonelected inner working body that operates under party control.

Soviet   The Russian word for council or assembly. The term soviet was applied to the workers' councils that arose in Russia during the Revolutionary period. Today soviet is the formal title of the 51,482 local and regional legislative bodies, the parliaments of the 15 republics, and the national parliament, the Supreme Soviet. The importance which the ruling Communist Party of the Soviet Union attaches to maintaining the facade of representative democracy is implied in the formal title of the federated state that succeeded Russia, the Union of Soviet Socialist Republics (USSR). In all there are 41,746 rural soviets, 3,751 village soviets, 634 borough (city ward) soviets, 2,103 city soviets, 3,101 district soviets, 10 soviets of the autonomous regions, 8 soviets of the autonomous republics, 6 territory soviets, 120 province soviets, and the 15 soviets of the union-republics. Only the Supreme Soviet is bicameral; all others are single-chamber bodies. Deputies to the soviets are elected at general elections from a single-candidate list, nominations to which are controlled by the party. Each soviet is responsible to the authorities at the next highest level as well as to its own constituency, and according to the USSR Constitution exercises legislative authority on its territory. Most of the work of a soviet is delegated to an inner working body, the executive committee or presidium. According to the Constitution, the soviets are the locus of popular sovereignty and the "political foundations of the USSR." Although less than half the deputies of local soviets are party members, party control over nominations and the delegation of most responsibilities to an inner body means that the soviets function chiefly as an instrument of legitimation for party decisions, which are transmitted to the soviets for formal legislative approval. The primary function of the soviets is to implement policies set out by the supreme organs of the state, under party direction. A major responsibility of the soviets is the implementation of the economic plan. *See also* BOLSHEVIK REVOLUTION, p. 12; DEPUTY, p. 136; ELECTORAL PROCESS: USSR, p. 140; PEOPLE'S COUNCILS, p. 157; TERRITORIAL DIVISIONS (USSR), p. 168.

Significance   The initial slogan of the Bolshevik Revolution was "all power to the soviets." In October 1917, the Bolshevik leader, Vladimir Lenin, toppled the Provisional Government that had ruled since the Czar's abdication in February 1917. Claiming to act in the name of the workers' and soldiers' soviets, Lenin instituted communist-party rule in Russia. Workers' soviets had first emerged spontaneously during the 1905 revolution that forced Czar Nicholas II to grant limited constitutional reform. The Petrograd (Leningrad) Soviet, a loose organization of workers in the czarist capital city, assumed leadership of the 1905 general strike. In 1917, as the accumulated strains of Russia's war effort and czarist ineptitude plunged Russia into near-anarchy, the Czar was forced to abdicate. Workers' and soldiers' soviets arose throughout the country. The early soviets were a combination of strike committees, self-governing workers' councils, action groups, and debate societies. After the Czar's abdication a hastily formed Provisional Government formed. The soviets in the key cities refused to cooperate with the Provisional Government, and as the Provisional Government proved to be largely ineffectual, the soviets assumed more and more importance. Initially the soviets were dominated by Mensheviks and Social Revolutionaries, but by the summer of 1917 the Bolsheviks, by clever manipulation and the espousal of such popular stances as withdrawal from the war and land redistribution to the peasants, controlled the key soviets of Petrograd and Moscow. In September 1917, Leon Trotsky won leadership of the Petrograd Soviet. Bolshevik control of the Petrograd Soviet proved crucial. In October 1917, the Bolsheviks seized power in the name of the soviets, claiming to act as the spokesmen of the workers. The Bolshevik dominance over the soviets was the key to the bloodlessness of the October Revolution that brought communism to Russia. In the power vacuum created by the ineffectual Provisional Government, Lenin was able to use the soviets as the front for the Bolshevik seizure of power. Once in command, the network of soviets gave the Bolsheviks a ready instrument of legitimation. At the Second All-Russian Congress of the Soviets of Workers and Soldiers in November 1917, the Bolsheviks announced that the Provisional Government had been succeeded by a Soviet of People's Commissars (*Sovnarkom*) headed by Lenin. Most of the Menshevik and Social Revolutionary delegates were forced out of the Congress and the Bolsheviks set up a Central Executive Committee to act as an interim legislative body. A Constituent Assembly election was announced for January 1918, but the Bolsheviks, who drew only one-quarter of the votes in Russia's first and only genuine democratic election, refused to allow it to meet. Lenin and the Bolsheviks continued to rule in the name of the *Sovnarkom* and the soviets. By 1920, most of the Mensheviks and Social Revolutionaries had been forced out of the soviets and Lenin had succeeded in breaking the independent power of the soviets. The initial slogan of the Bolsheviks, "all power to the soviets," has become one of the most hollow promises of the Revolution. As Hannah Arendt has pointed out, one of the first priorities of the victorious Bolsheviks was to eradicate the soviets as independent decision makers; whenever similar bodies have spontaneously arisen in communist-controlled lands, such as in Hungary in 1956, these heirs to the original soviets have also been suppressed. Since 1917 the CPSU has consistently claimed to rule in the name of the soviets, a claim which gives legitimacy to the party's monopoly of political power. Such is the ideological value attached to the soviet that the name has come to stand for a citizen or, collectively, the people of the USSR, surely one of the few times a political institution has given its name to an entire nation. The term Soviets is also used to denote the leadership of the Soviet Union.

Spravka   A certificate signed by a government official that supports a citizen's right to have a request fulfilled by some authority. A *spravka* may be a request for information, a residence permit, validation of information requested by an authority, duplication of lost documents, a request for additional fuel during a hard winter, or daycare for a child. Spravkas may also be complaints about government nonfeasance, misfeasance, or malfeasance. They constitute a formal acknowledgment of the citizens' request and complaints. Officials must first screen all requests for spravkas, and then, once signed,

rank them in order of priority and direct them to the proper authority. In urban areas, housing concerns are the most frequent subject of
spravkas; overall, information on pension rights ranks high. All levels
of Soviet officialdom are involved in the system, from deputies of the
Supreme Soviet to local soviets. Generally, the higher the status of the
petitioner, the higher the authority contacted. If refused, the petitioner has the right to appeal to a higher authority. The volume of
requests, which may range to 30,000 yearly, is so heavy that deputies
maintain staffs and local soviets use volunteer public councils (*ob-
shchestvennyi sovet*) to screen the applications. Once signed by an
official, the spravka means that an adminstrative department must
honor the citizen's request. *See also* DEPUTY, p. 136.

Significance   The spravka is one of the ways in which the Soviet
system maintains the links between citizen and regime. It has become
a key element in ensuring that the regime penetrates all aspects of
Soviet life. However, the spravka system also provides a way of
preserving the sense of community, making the official the servant of
the local community. The local official has become the mediator for
the citizen. Since the 1960s, deputies to the Supreme Soviet have
come to play an increasing role in the issuing of spravkas, and the
effect has been startlingly similar to what has happened to American
congressmen as government agencies have proliferated. Like his
American counterpart, the Soviet deputy's staff spends much of its
time on constituency work. Most deputies maintain local offices,
staffed by both professionals and volunteers who assist citizens with
paperwork, screen spravka requests, answer questions, and in general, serve as the main point of contact between the citizen and the
bureaucracy. In some senses, the Soviet deputy, like the congressman,
has come to serve as the citizens' ombudsman, a role enhanced by the
spravka system.

Standing Committee of the Supreme Soviet   A functionally
specific legislative committee of the USSR Supreme Soviet. Standing
committees review draft laws and monitor the activities of government agencies in their specific areas of responsibility. The 30 standing
committees are selected by the coordinating body of the Supreme
Soviet, the Council of Elders, which also sets the agenda. The committees review only draft laws (*zakony*), the legislative acts of the Supreme
Soviet; they have no review powers over the Presidium's edicts
(*ukazy*), which constitute the bulk of Soviet normative law. The bills
reviewed by the committee originate elsewhere, usually with the
Council of Ministers or the Presidium of the Supreme Soviet, and are

frequently issued in conjunction with the party Central Committee. Each committee is headed by a chairman and includes 35 deputies (Planning-Budget has 45). Thus, about two-thirds of the total membership of the Supreme Soviet sits on a committee. The number of committees may vary from session to session. In 1978 there were 15 standing committees in each chamber: (1) Agriculture; (2) Conservation; (3) Construction; (4) Consumer Goods; (5) Credentials; (6) Education, Science, and Culture; (7) Foreign Affairs; (8) Health and Social Security; (9) Industry; (10) Legislative Proposals; (11) Planning-Budget; (12) Trade; (13) Transportation-Communications; (14) Women's Affairs; (15) Youth Affairs. Recently, an Energy committee was added. The substance of committee jurisdiction is a good indication of major fields of Soviet governmental operations. Because there is so little information about the legislative process, the role of each committee is difficult to ascertain. Full committees meet infrequently; most work is carried out in subcommittees. Votes are by a show of hands and require a quorum. Committees also possess investigatory powers: they may issue recommendations to lower organs of government, require reports, call witnesses, and question government officials. Reviews of major bills are publicized in the daily press. It is at the committee stage that legislation is most apt to be amended. Once the bill is in final form, it is presented to the Supreme Soviet and invariably passed by a unanimous vote. *See also* LEGISLATIVE PROCESS, p. 149; PARLIAMENTS: EASTERN EUROPE, p. 154; SUPREME SOVIET, p. 166.

Significance   The standing committees are a recent development in Soviet legislative practice. A 1967 Law on Committees institutionalized the committees and they have since become increasingly active; throughout the 1970s their numbers steadily increased. The committees may represent one of the more democratic aspects of the Soviet system. Expert witnesses are heard by the committees and much fine-tuning of legislation apparently takes place in committees. Their increased activity has enhanced the role of the deputies. Their membership includes important regional officials, suggesting that bargaining among regional interests may be possible during the draft bill stage. East European parliaments also possess standing committees; their role varies from state to state, with the committees of the Polish *Sejm* being the most active, until 1981.

State Committee   An administrative agency, usually attached to the federal Council of Ministers, whose work is interdepartmental. State committees can be distinguished from the individual and functionally specific ministries by the nature of their work, which typically overlaps the work of several ministries. Their administrative powers are also broader. A specific ministry, such as the Ministry of Agriculture, is empowered to issue orders and regulations binding only on its own subordinate units. A state committee can issue orders binding on any relevant agency, including other ministries. For example, the State Committee for Prices can issue orders binding on any relevant agencies. Two crucial agencies of control in the Soviet system are state committees: the State Planning Committee (Gosplan) and the Committee for State Security (KGB). Although they are in theory subordinate to the Council of Ministers, it is likely that they operate far more under the direct control of the central party organs. The most important state committees in the Soviet Union include: Gosplan, the KGB, the State Committee for Construction, the State Committee for Supply, the Committee of People's Control, the State Committee for Labor and Wages, the State Committee for Foreign Economic Relations, the Board of the State Bank (Gosbank), the State Committee for Radio and Television, and the State Committee for Prices. State committees are instituted by the Presidium of the Supreme Soviet, which also names their chairmen. Other members are appointed by the Council of Members. They usually possess smaller staffs than the regular ministries, indicative of their function as decision-making and coordinating bodies rather than as line administrative agencies. Because their orders are binding on other ministries and agencies, they are in some ways superior to the ministries. State committees usually have three functions: planning, coordination, and supervision. Comparable state committees usually exist at the republican and territorial levels. *See also* COUNCIL OF MINISTERS, p. 133; GOSPLAN, p. 196; KGB, p. 288; MINISTRY, p. 151.

Significance   State committees coordinate the work of the state in several broad areas, particularly in the area of economic affairs and state security. State committees have proliferated in the postwar years, probably as the result of the increasing complexity of government responsibilities in an industrialized state, which increasingly requires coordinating mechanisms. Because they generally deal with vital areas, it is assumed that they frequently operate under the close control of central party organs. For example, the priorities set by the economic plans and the budget are set by the Politburo and Secretariat, and although the legislation which implements these priorities is presented by the Council of Ministers, it is clearly the work of Gosplan and its related state committees. Gosplan itself has been the source of several new state committees that began as subordinate departments but later acquired independent status as the need for coordination increased.

Supreme Soviet   According to the Constitution of the Soviet Union, the highest organ of state authority, responsible for enacting basic laws, amending the Constitution, appointing high government officials, and monitoring the work of the administrative agencies. In reality the size of the Supreme Soviet, 1,500 members, and extremely brief sessions preclude it from acting as the supreme legislative body. Most of its work is delegated to the Presidium of the Supreme Soviet, which is empowered to act for the Supreme Soviet when it is not in session. The Supreme Soviet is a bicameral body that, like the United States Congress, is divided into one chamber that represents the constituent units of the Soviet federation, and a second chamber elected on the basis of equally proportioned single-member electoral districts. Unlike the Congress, the two chambers are of equal size, each with 750 member deputies. The Chamber of Nationalities represents the union-republics and territories that are based on nationality, the goal being to give each of the Soviet nationality groups representation at the national level. Each union-republic elects 32 deputies; each autonomous republic, 11; each autonomous region, 5; and each national district, 1. Thus, it resembles the United States Senate, where each state, regardless of population, is accorded the same representation. The overrepresentation is even more marked in the Soviet system: the smallest union-republic, Estonia, possesses only one percent of the population of the largest, the Russian Republic. The Council of the Union is similar to the U.S. House of Representatives, being based on single-member electoral districts of equal size. All deputies are elected for five-year terms. The Supreme Soviet usually convenes for two brief sessions per year, lasting from two to five days. Voting is unanimous, by show of hands; there is no debate on legislation. Full sessions of the Supreme Soviet are therefore ceremonial in nature, setting the constitutional seal of approval on policy initiated elsewhere. When the Supreme Soviet is not in sessions, the Presidium is empowered to issue binding edicts, *ukazy*, which must be ratified subsequently by the Supreme Soviet. The enactment of ukazy into law (*zakon*) is a formality; typically over 50 percent of the laws enacted by the Supreme Soviet originate as ukazy of the Presidium. The major functions of the Supreme Soviet are: (1) enacting fundamental laws (zakony); (2) approving edicts (ukazy) of the Presidium; (3) amending the Constitution; (4) ratifying economic plans and budgets; (5) defining the jurisdiction of state organs; (6) electing the Presidium from its membership; (7) electing the federal Supreme Court; (8) appointing ministers; (9) supervising the work of all other soviets; and (10) monitoring the work of state agencies. The Supreme Soviet can amend the Constitution or interpret it through law. As no independent judicial review agency exists, the Supreme Soviet therefore makes constitutional law, as is true in the other East European states. Since the 1960s, the Supreme Soviet has become increasingly specialized, being divided into functionally specific committees that apparently accomplish much of the legislative work. Legislation is usually initiated by the Council of Ministers or the Presidium. Frequently, a legislative proposal will be enunciated first by a joint declaration of the Central Committee of the party and the Council of Ministers. Since party members occupy all leading government positions, the legislative process is obscure. Whether a particular legislative proposal originates in the Politburo, Presidium, or Council of Ministers is difficult to ascertain and probably not important, given the duplication in membership. Legislation is proposed in the form of draft bills, which in the instance of especially important acts will be published in the leading newspapers for public discussion, and then set in its final form by the relevant legislative committee. Although the Supreme Soviet does not function as a deliberative parliament in the Western sense, its role as legitimator of policy is crucial to the system. Legal acts of the Supreme Soviet take precedence over all other acts of goverement. Its power to amend or reinterpret the Constitution gives it added authority. That the Soviet leaders feel the necessity for a constitutional organ of state authority is evident, or else it would not be necessary for all important norms to possess the legislative seal of approval. As the chief institution for translating party directives into official law, the Supreme Soviet lends legitimacy to the authority of the communist party. *See also* COUNCIL OF ELDERS, p. 133; DEPUTY, p. 136; LEGISLATIVE PROCESS, p. 149; PRESIDIUM OF THE SUPREME SOVIET, p. 158; STANDING COMMITTEE OF THE SUPREME SOVIET, p. 163.

Significance   As the institutional bearer of the federal principle, the Supreme Soviet is the chief forum for the articulation of national interests, particularly in the economic arena. Because of the real effort the Communist Party makes to balance the social composition of its membership, the Supreme Soviet is the most representative body in the soviet political system. Its membership includes nonparty members, workers, peasants, young citizens under 30, and women, all in substantial numbers. Leading positions, however, are occupied by party members. The Supreme Soviet is characterized by a high rate of turnover; generally only party functionaries build up enough experience to act as effective legislators. The widespread perception that the Supreme Soviet is no more than a rubberstamp for party policy is an oversimplification. The committees play an active role, and criticism of government officials is regularly scheduled on the agenda of full sessions of the Supreme Soviet. Although the Soviet Union lacks a parliamentary heritage, the Supreme Soviet derives legitimacy from several strands in Russian history. These include: (1) Marx's glorification of the Paris Commune of 1871; (2) the communal heritage of Russian peasant life, centered in the self-governing village *mir* or council; (3) the assembly, the *zemsky sobor*, of early czarist times; and (4) Lenin's use of the spontaneous revolutionary worker soviets of 1905 and 1917 as the instrument by which he secured the Bolshevik Revolution. Although individual differences exist among the legislatures of Eastern Europe, with the exception of the Yugoslav Federal Assembly all are modeled after the Supreme Soviet. They too meet infrequently and delegate their power to an inner body, a presidium or state council. The recent expansion in the importance of the committee system is also a feature of East European legislatures, with a concomitant increase in parliamentary visibility. In some communist-party states where the prewar parliamentary heritage is much more meaningful, legislatures have surpassed the Supreme Soviet in legislative capabilities. The Polish *Sejm* has permitted open floor debate and negative votes; before the imposition of martial law the *Sejm* debated many of the issues raised by the Solidarity labor organization. Hungarian parliamentary committees have rejected several government bills and conducted policy debates before the actual drafting of bills. The Yugoslav Federal Assembly is another excellent example of a legislative body in a communist state that exercises real power. It meets in lengthy sessions with open debate, originates legislation, and amends government proposals. The largely ceremonial role of the other communist parliaments does not mean that these institutions are devoid of meaning or the potential for evolution. Various of the non-Russian nationalities in the Soviet Union have cautiously indicated interest in strengthening the role of the Supreme Soviet. The major role of the Supreme Soviet and its sister communist parliaments, as constitutional instruments for legitimizing policy, renders them potentially important. In each instance of dissent from Soviet control in Eastern Europe—Poland and Hungary in 1956, Czechoslovakia in 1968, and Poland in 1980–81—the national legislatures had begun to function as forums of debate until suppressed.

Territorial Divisions (USSR)   Administrative or territorial divisions of the Soviet Union which exist either to preserve the cultural identity of a specific nationality or to decentralize administrative functions, or both. The territorial divisions of the Soviet Union are as follows: 15 union-republics, 20 autonomous republics, 8 autonomous provinces, 6 territories (*krais*), 10 national districts (*okrugs*), 120 provinces (*oblast's*), and 3,478 *raions,* the last being the local unit of administration. The oblast's and raions are administrative units; the others are both administrative units and national homelands. The vast territory and complex multinational composition of the Soviet Union has dictated an intricate structure of territorial divisions. Most of the territorial divisions are located within the Russian Soviet Federated Socialist Republic (RSFSR), which includes over half of the population and two-thirds of Soviet territory. *See also* FEDERALISM, p. 143.

Significance The problem of administratively decentralizing a country as huge as the Soviet Union is complicated by the ethnic and physical diversity of the country. In general, the Soviets have managed to accommodate most of their approximately 100 nationalities into some type of territorial units. This represents the Bolsheviks' major compromise with the reality of governing a vast multinational empire. Although Marxism-Leninism eschews federalism, the Bolsheviks rapidly discovered that in order to hold their country together they had to make some compromise with the drive for cultural autonomy. This was accomplished by the plethora of territorial divisions designed to give most of the Soviet Union's diverse peoples a homeland. Similarly, the vast territory necessitates administrative decentralization. This the Bolsheviks accomplished by a system of provinces and county-like units, the *raions,* which replicate a good part of the old czarist structure. The reforms of Peter the Great introduced the *guberniya* (government) as the basic administrative unit; the 119 czarist *gubernii* are not too far removed from the 120 oblast's of the Soviet Union, particularly in central Russia. For political purposes, the territorial divisions are important because each contains its own party organization, and is the locus of politics in its district.

Territorial Division (USSR): Autonomous Province A Soviet administrative unit that possesses administrative autonomy within a union-republic, but that is not accorded the full status of a union-republic in the Soviet federation. At present there are eight autonomous provinces in the Soviet Union: five in the Russian republic (Adygei, Mountain-Altai, Jewish, Karachai-Cherkes, Khakas) and one each in the republics of Azerbaidzhan (Karabakh), Georgia (South Ossetian), and Tadzhik (Mountain Badakshan). The autonomous province should not be confused with the much smaller province, the *oblast'.* Only the autonomous province has the power to delineate the boundaries of the *raions* (counties) on its territory and, as a nationally based administrative unit, it has specific federal representation (five deputies) in the Council of Nationalities of the Supreme Soviet. The administrative structure of an autonomous province is similar to the other administrative subdivisions of the Soviet Union. Each has an elected assembly (soviet), an appointed executive committee, courts, procurator, and administrative agencies. In the areas of education, administration, social services, land management, and justice, the autonomous province is relatively independent; the national language is used for these activities, except for the Jewish (Evrei) province. The autonomous province is directly subordinate to the union-republic within which it is located. *See also* FEDERALISM, p. 143; TERRITORIAL DIVISIONS (USSR), pp. 168–174.

Significance   The autonomous provinces attest to the Soviet Union's commitment to the maintenance of national identities in the Soviet federation. Although there is little political autonomy to match the cultural autonomy, the granting of territorial homelands to so many nationalities has helped the Soviet system cope with its multinationality. The status of autonomous province has been granted generally to the smaller nationalities that occupy remote stretches of territory. The exception to this policy was the formation of the Jewish autonomous province, which appears (unsuccessfully) to have been created to contain Soviet Jews in a bleak area on the Chinese border remote from urban European Russia; less than 10 percent of its population is Jewish. The granting of official status for the major language of the autonomous province has been an important adjunct in the preservation of the national identities of these smaller groups. By these and other means the Soviet Union has sought to maintain a diverse, multinational population within a politically integrated and highly disciplined country.

Territorial Division (USSR): Autonomous Soviet Socialist Republic (ASSR)   A Soviet administrative unit, established along nationality lines, located within a union-republic. The Autonomous Soviet Socialist Republic (ASSR) forms an official part of the Soviet federal system, ranking just below the union-republic, and above the autonomous province in the scale of Soviet federalism. The status of ASSR has generally been granted to national groups whose members are too small to warrant union-republic status. The 20 ASSRs are located within union-republics and are directly subordinate to them. They have their own constitution, local administration, supreme soviet, supreme court, council of ministers, and many of the other formal trappings of statehood. Currently there are 16 ASSRs in the Russian Republic, one each in the Republics of Azerbaidzhan and Uzbek, and two in Georgia. Each ASSR constitution is subject to confirmation by its union-republic, but may take into effect the specific features of its major nationality. Each ASSR sends 11 deputies to the

Council of Nationalities of the Supreme Soviet, and the Presidium of the Supreme Soviet contains representatives of the ASSRs. Among the larger ASSRs are the Tatar, Bashkir, Chuvash, Chechen-Ingush, and Karelian. *See also* FEDERALISM, p. 143; TERRITORIAL DIVISIONS (USSR), pp. 168–174.

Significance   As the Bolsheviks established a federal system with the announced aim of protecting and encouraging national identities, the Autonomous Soviet Socialist Republic developed as a logical extension of the principle of granting a home territory to each discrete, relatively homogeneous national grouping. ASSRs use the national language for all administrative and judicial operations. Since most ASSRs are located within the huge Russian Republic (RSFSR), it has been argued that the Russian Republic is in effect a subfederation within the Soviet federation. This theory, however, does not stand up to the fact that the ASSRs within the Russian Republic are neither coequal nor autonomous, nor are they granted specific national representation within the legislature of the Russian Republic, nor do they have the theoretical right to secede as do the union-republics.

Territorial Division (USSR): National District (*Okrug*)   A territorial subdivision within the Russian Soviet Federated Socialist Republic (RSFSR). The national district, or *okrug*, was instituted for the purpose of providing administrative and cultural autonomy for a specific small nationality. There are ten okrugs, all located within the far reaches of the Russian Republic. Okrug boundaries may be changed by the republican government; they are not enumerated in the Constitution. Administratively, the okrug is subordinate to the republic, and implicitly also to the *krai* or *oblast'* within which it is located. Each okrug possesses an elected assembly, executive committee, and district court. It is represented by one deputy in the Soviet of Nationalities of the federal Supreme Soviet. *See also* FEDERALISM, p. 143; TERRITORIAL DIVISIONS (USSR), pp. 168–174.

Significance   Administratively, the okrug has little autonomy. The main reason for its existence is to protect the cultural identity of the small nationalities found in the vast, sparsely settled areas of non-European Russia. It should not be confused with the krai, a larger and even more remote subdivision of the RSFSR.

Territorial Division (USSR): Province (*Oblast'*)   A territorial administrative unit, of which there are 120, of the larger union-republics of the Soviet Union. The *oblast'*, usually translated as province or region, is the intermediate administrative unit between the union-republic and the local administrative units, the *raions*. The smaller union-republics (Azerbaidzhan, Armenia, Estonia, Georgia, Latvia, Lithuania, and Moldavia) lack oblast's. Typically, an oblast' numbers between 1 and 4 million inhabitants. Each oblast' has an elected assembly, executive committee, and judiciary. The oblast' executive committee usually includes departments for social services, general affairs, organization and instruction, construction, finance, industry, agriculture, planning, and trade. A typical oblast' will have a provincial capital, a territory of between 7,700 and 38,000 square miles (20,000 and 100,000 square kilometers), and between 10 and 40 raions on its territory. Moscow and Leningrad are accorded oblast' status and thus are directly subordinate to the union-republic. *See also* FEDERALISM, p. 143; TERRITORIAL DIVISIONS (USSR), pp. 168–174.

Significance   The oblast' is the key administrative and political unit, for it is here that much federal policy must be coordinated with regional interests and implemented. The oblast' leadership must mediate between conflicting interests, coordinate regional planning, and resolve competition over resource allocation. The party secretary of the oblast' executive committee (*obkom*) is a key figure in Soviet politics; many party leaders have begun their careers as obkom secretary.

Territorial Division (USSR): *Raion*   The basic administrative unit of Soviet local government, similar to a county or a municipal borough, territorially based on a rural or urban district. In the smaller union-republics, the *raion* is directly subordinate to the union-republic administration; the raion soviet (assembly) is subordinate to the republican soviet. In larger union-republics which are divided into provinces (*oblast'*s), the raion is subordinate to the province in which it is located. Cities with a population of more than 100,000 are divided into urban raions, similar to a city borough, and each has its own administration and soviet. The lowest territorial unit is the rural town or village, which is subordinate to the raion. The importance and functions of the raion tend to vary with its degree of industrialization and location. Remote rural raions maintain fewer commissions to carry out social services, while a municipal raion may be responsible for a wide variety of public services, ranging from sewage and water to cemeteries, laundries, and concert halls. *See also* FEDERALISM, p. 143; PRIMARY PARTY ORGANIZATION (PPO), p. 122; TERRITORIAL DIVISIONS (USSR), pp. 168–174.

Significance   The raion presents a seeming paradox in that this local unit occupies such an important place in what is one of the most centralized political systems. The key is that the system enforces standardization on all levels while granting local government some meaningful functions. A raion council must approve the annual budget and economic plan for its territory and is responsible for determining the use of all raion land. Raions oversee the administration of economic enterprises on their territories and are responsible for providing local public services. The local council also directs the militia (police) on its territory and maintains official records. Most of these functions are handled by the executive committee of the local council. In party matters the raion is even more important. Because the Communist Party of the Soviet Union is organized territorially, the raion party is the crucial organ for ensuring political conformity at local levels. The raion party supervises all Primary Party Organizations (PPOs) on its territory. The *raikom*, the executive committee of the raion party (the municipal equivalent is the *gorkom*), is the major instrument of supervision; in fact, supervising the PPOs is one of the major functions of the raikom or gorkom. Raion party secretaries can often be powerful figures, dispensing political favors and selecting protégés, much as do many county party chairpersons in the United States. Indicative of the power of the raikoms is the result of Nikita Khrushchev's efforts in the early 1960s to dissolve these local party organs. Khrushchev came under much criticism for "destroying the cadres," i.e., cutting away at the base of local politics, and after he was ousted in 1964, the new regime immediately restored these workhorses of local politics. In general, although administratively the powers of the raion are not well defined and may be abridged by higher authorities, it remains important as the basic unit of government and party and is the most visible component of the complex system for most Soviet citizens.

Territorial Division (USSR): Territory (*Krai*)   A large administrative subdivision located within the territory of the Russian Soviet Federated Socialist Republic (RSFSR), of which there are six in all. The territory, or *krai*, is a vast, sparsely populated area located far from any major population center. Five of the krais contain autonomous provinces; they may also include national areas (*okrugs*). Krais are established by the Constitution; thus their numbers cannot be changed, but the Russian Republic can change the boundaries. The krai possesses an elected assembly (soviet), administrative apparatus, and a judiciary. *See also* FEDERALISM, p. 143; TERRITORIAL DIVISIONS (USSR), pp. 168–174.

Significance   The krai mainly resulted from the huge expanse of the Russian republic, itself larger than the United States, which requires some form of administrative decentralization. Krais are generally located in areas of mixed populations, and provide a means of uniting several small ethnic groups into an administrative unit.

Territorial Divisions (USSR): Union-Republic   Constituent unit of the Soviet Socialist Federated Republic (USSR). The Soviet federation contains 15 union-republics: The Russian Soviet Federated Socialist Republic (RSFSR); Ukrainian Soviet Socialist Republic (SSR); Byelorussian SSR; Kazakh SSR; Uzbek SSR; Georgian SSR; Azerbaidzhan SSR; Lithuanian SSR; Moldavian SSR; Latvian SSR; Kirgiz SSR; Tadzhik SSR; Armenian SSR; Turkmen SSR; and Estonian SSR. All of the union-republics are constituted on the basis of nationality. In all but two (Kazakh and Kirgiz SSRs), the "leading nation" or national group constitutes the majority population. The huge Russian union-republic includes a number of minority nationalities in addition to its Russian majority population. Union-republics differ widely in size and population. The RSFSR embraces two-thirds of Soviet territory and just over one-half of its population; Estonia contains only .55 percent of the total population. All have equal representation in government organs, such as the Supreme Soviet. Each union-republic has its own constitution, Supreme Court, governmental organs, and in theory enjoys the rights to secede from the federation and to negotiate international treaties. Union-republics have their own planning apparatus and budgets, but the republican budgets are controlled by the federal authorities. Union-republics have the full array of communist party structures, from politburos and central committees to party congresses. An exception is the huge Russian union-republic, which does not have a separate republican party apparatus. The RSFSR operates within the federal (all-union) CPSU organization where ethnic Russians enjoy a disproportionate percentage of high party positions. The First Secretary of a union-republic party is automatically a member of the federal Central Committee and is usually a national of the union-republic. The post of Second Secretary is generally occupied by a Russian national. In practice, union-republic autonomy is largely confined to the preservation of cultural autonomy. Despite the guarantees of secession and negotiation, Article 77 of the 1977 Soviet Constitution gives the federation virtually unlimited power over the constituent units. At the Dumbarton Oaks Conference in August 1944 the Soviet delegation demanded United Nations representation for each of the union-republics. A compromise agreement, essentially the price of Soviet adherence to the United Nations, led to separate membership and representation in the United Nations for Byelorussia and the Ukraine. *See also* FEDERALISM, p. 143; CENTRAL COMMITTEE,

p. 91; POLITBURO, p. 118; RUSSIFICATION, p. 31; TERRITORIAL DIVISIONS (USSR), p. 168.

Significance   The union-republics represent the major compromise made by Vladimir Lenin between Marxism's scorn for federalism as a vehicle for bourgeois nationalism and the realities of governing a vast multinational empire. Immediately after the Bolshevik Revolution in 1918 all the nationalities within Russia were subsumed into a highly centralized Russian Socialist Federated Soviet Republic. Nationalist movements arose in protest, especially in Georgia and the Ukraine. The attempts to establish truly independent Soviet republics were put down by the Red Army in 1920–21. By 1922, in a series of treaties with the various nationalities, the Union of Soviet Socialist Republics (USSR) was established. From their inception the independence of the union-republics has been constrained by the centralization of the Soviet system and the primacy of the communist party. Nationalism in the USSR has frequently been expressed through demands for greater cultural autonomy and protests against perceived Russification. In the 1960s and 1970s some dissent coalesced around the issue of cultural autonomy for non-Russians, particularly for the expanded use of national languages. Such dissent has been most apparent in the Ukraine, the Baltic republics, and in Georgia. The Soviet leadership remains most sensitive to nationality-based dissent; the only dissenters to be executed in the post-Stalin period have been Georgian nationalists. Politically, the central party organs dominate the union-republics. Party membership is disproportionately Russian; the RSFSR, which includes just over 50 percent of the population, accounts for 62 percent of the membership. Apparently, effort is made to ethnically balance the composition of top party organs by including representatives of the major union-republics, but in practice the union-republics are controlled by the central party organs.

Voters' Mandate   An important part of the Soviet electoral process through which voters present demands for specific action to the authorities. A Voters' Mandate can be adopted only at a pre-election voters' meeting, by a majority vote. At that point, the mandate is recognized as a "general demand" and is transmitted to the local or regional Soviet (assembly). However, the soviet does not deal with the mandate until after the election. If the authorities decide that a mandate can't be fulfilled, they must explain to the voters. Local soviets are regularly presented with thousands of such mandates, and answer most. Mandates often deal with specific requests, such as new schools, better medical care, extra fuel allotments, or repair work. In cases where the request is minimal, such as landscaping apartment buildings or building a playground, the local soviet may donate the equipment and the local residence committees usually provide the volunteer labor. *See also* ELECTORAL PROCESS: USSR, p. 140.

Significance   Voters' Mandates serve as a device to underline the importance of the citizen in the electoral process. They also represent a form of demand articulation officially structured into the Soviet political system, in that the authorities are required to answer all such mandates. Also known as Imperative Voters' Mandates, they supposedly date from the 1905 Revolution when, according to Lenin, the Decree on the Land was drawn up in response to 242 such mandates presented by local peasant assemblies. The Voters' Mandate was revived by Nikita Khrushchev as part of his general effort to revitalize local government, and it was continued by Leonid Brezhnev. Since mandates are not answered until after the election, any issues raised are not permitted to influence the election. Because the regime sets aside election period as the time when mandates are solicited, the elections have added impact for Soviet citizens. The continuation of the Voters' Mandate system over the years emphasizes the efforts of the regime to give the Soviet system the appearance of a working democratic system, to both Soviet citizens and outsiders.

Yugoslavia: Collective State Presidency   The unique collective state executive that has exercised the powers of head of state since the death of Josip Broz Tito. The Yugoslav Collective Presidency is composed of eight members, one each elected from the parliaments of the six republics and two autonomous provinces that make up the Socialist Federal Republic of Yugoslavia (SFRY). The Yugoslav Collective Presidency was formally instituted with the 1974 Constitution. It was designed to provide succession to Tito, who served as the country's leader from 1945 until his death in May of 1980. Tito occupied a ninth position on the Collective Presidency, as President of the Republic. Upon his death, that office lapsed and a system was instituted of rotating yearly, in set order, the office of President of the SFRY Presidency, as specified by the Constitution. By 1983, the office had rotated four times. Members of the Presidency are elected for five-year terms, with a two-term limit. Each republican and provincial parliament also elects a deputy President to fill vacancies arising from death or resignation. Since Tito's death, the Presidents of the SFRY Presidency have assumed Tito's functions as commander-in-chief, chief foreign policy officer, and chairman of the Council for National Defense, but only on behalf of the Collective Presidency. The

Presidency is empowered to promulgate statutes by executive order, propose legislation, and convene joint sessions of the federal parliament. The SFRY President presides over the Federal Executive Council, the federal cabinet, and can stay enforcement of FEC regulations with the subsequent approval of the parliament. The Collective Presidency can also declare war if the parliament is unable to act. *See also* FEDERALISM: YUGOSLAVIA, p. 146; YUGOSLAVIA: FEDERAL EXECUTIVE COUNCIL, p. 177.

Significance　　Since Tito's death, the Collective Presidency has functioned smoothly, providing the only constitutional succession to date in a communist-party state. No "little Tito" has appeared, probably because of the federalization and decentralization of power in Yugoslavia. The collective principle of leadership is mirrored by a similar arrangement in the League of Communists of Yugoslavia (LCY). The 23-person LCY Presidency is drawn on the basis of equal representation for the republican and provincial bodies, and elected by them. The Yugoslav army, the only non-federalized entity in the system, is also accorded official representation on the LCY Presidency. The functioning of these collective bodies since Tito's death thus far validates Tito's observation that such bodies would be the most appropriate, if not the only viable, successors in the multinational Yugoslav federation. They may indeed be the only democratic answer in a society of such diversity. Since the 1960s, Yugoslavia has operated much as a confederation, with the powers of the federal government and party organs legally limited and their utilization dependent upon obtaining republican consensus. However unwieldy the collective concept may appear, it reflects the underlying reality of Yugoslav politics.

Yugoslavia: Federal Executive Council　　The executive body of the federal parliament of Yugoslavia. Unlike the Soviet Council of Ministers, the Federal Executive Council (FEC) is a small body that exercises meaningful powers. Members of the FEC are elected for four-year terms (renewable once) from the federal parliament (*Skupština*). The FEC is comprised of a premier (president), four vice-premiers, and seven ministers, each responsible for a specific administrative area, such as defense or foreign affairs. There are no "economic" ministries as in the Soviet Union; in composition and functions the FEC resembles a cabinet of a Western parliamentary system. The FEC is empowered to make legislative proposals, issue regulations implementing legislation, and, in general, is responsible for the day-to-day operations of the federal government. A major function is securing consensus for federal programs from the parliaments of the six republics and two provinces that make up the Yugoslav federation. The members of the upper house of the Skupština, the Federal Chamber, may propose a vote of no confidence, which would then be debated in joint session. The Constitution also provides for the resignation of the FEC president, at which point the entire FEC is dissolved. The republican and provincial parliaments have similar cabinets, with which the FEC works to reach consensus. *See also* ELECTORAL PROCESS: YUGOSLAVIA, p. 141; PARLIAMENTS: EASTERN EUROPE, p. 154.

Significance   Because the Yugoslav parliament meets in regular extended sessions and engages in meaningful debate, the Federal Executive Council little resembles the Soviet Council of Ministers. The FEC is not top-heavy with "economic" ministries; since the state bears no direct responsibility for the operation of the self-managed Yugoslav economy, the only powers the FEC possesses are the usual fiscal and monetary measures. Major policy is undoubtedly decided by the League of Communists; although the FEC may make policy proposals to the parliament, in reality it does not possess independent policymaking powers. It also must share powers with the Collective Presidency, the Yugoslav executive. Judicial review is vested in the federal Constitutional Court, which operates independently of parliament and cabinet. The provision for a vote of no confidence might appear meaningless to a one-party system, but such a provision was exercised by the government of the Republic of Slovenia in the 1960s. The FEC possesses one additional power that is related to its function as consensus-builder for the federation: if it is unable to secure consensus with the republics on matters of national import, the Federal Executive Council with the agreement of the Collective Presidency can approve a temporary one-year measure.

5. The Economic System

Agro-cities   One of the agricultural reforms proposed by Nikita Khrushchev in the 1950s to increase agricultural efficiency by creating urban conditions of life and work in the countryside. Khrushchev proposed that the collective farms (*kolkhozes*) be greatly enlarged through consolidations and that the workers be housed in agro-cities with urban amenities. In effect the goal was to industrialize Soviet agriculture and bring the peasant into the urban working class. Unlike other agricultural reforms of Khrushchev, the agro-city proposal was never implemented. *See also* AGRO-INDUSTRIAL COMPLEX, p. 180; VIR-GIN LANDS, p. 236.

Significance   Despite the abandonment of the agro-city proposal, Khrushchev did succeed in amalgamating the collective farms and increasing the proportion of land in state farms (*sovkhozes*), one of the goals of the initial proposal. In 1953, collective farms totaled 93,300 and embraced 90 percent of acreage, while state farms numbered 4,857. By 1958, collective farms were reduced to 69,000 that included 76 percent of the acreage, while the state farms had increased to 6,002. The greatest increase in state farms resulted from the Virgin Lands project, which opened up vast expanses of Siberia to agriculture. All of the farms in the newly cultivated areas were organized as state farms. The trend of increasing the role of state farms continued after Khrushchev's ouster as Secretary-General: in 1977, for example, 28,000 collective farms accounted for 48 percent of the acreage while state farms numbered 19,636. This development has enhanced party control in the countryside; a smaller number of units makes it possible to staff them with reliable party members. Moreover, Machine Tractor Stations, abolished in 1958, were no longer needed as agents of party control over collective farms. The agro-city proposal, however, was later labeled one of Khrushchev's "harebrained" ideas, and it was used to discredit him after he was ousted from power in 1964. Recently the Bulgarian government has pursued a somewhat similar policy in setting up agro-industrial complexes in the countryside, without, however, the massive capital investment envisioned in Khrushchev's plan.

Agro-Industrial Complex   A form of horizontal and vertical integration that merges collective farms, state farms, and food-related industries into an integrated production conglomerate. An agro-industrial complex typically operates under a unified management board that receives aggregated production targets from the central planning authorities and allocates them among the component units. Management of each component unit is directly responsible to the management board of the agro-industrial complex. The most extensive of such innovations is the Bulgarian Agro-Industrial Complex (APK), currently the organizational form in 90 percent of the Bulgarian countryside. In the Bulgarian complexes, the individual collective and state farms no longer function as separate economic units. They pool assets, land, and responsibilities, and operate essentially as branches of a large agro-industrial conglomerate. The average Bulgarian complex totals 53,127 acres (21,500 hectares) and employs over 6,500 workers. The component units still operate on a cost-accounting basis (*khozraschet*), and members retain their personal farm plots, which the government officially encourages. The Bulgarian complexes are based on food-processing or other agriculturally related industries. At present the Bulgarian agricultural sector includes 153 Agro-Industrial Complexes, 9 even larger Industrial-Agricultural Complexes, and 2 Scientific Production Associations. A Bulgarian complex typically specializes in three to five crops and one branch of livestock production, whereas before an individual collective farm was responsible for producing 50 to 60 different agricultural products. Mono-cropping has increased dramatically; before the reforms Bulgarian grain fields averaged 97 acres (40 hectares); they now average 2,471 acres (1,000 hectares). *See also* AGRO-CITIES, p. 179; KOLKHOZ, p. 205; PRIVATE PLOTS, p. 222.

Significance   Agro-industrial complexes have been most intensely developed by Bulgaria; the other communist-party states have cautiously instituted similar mechanisms but on a smaller scale. In 1976, Romania introduced the Inter-Cooperative Agricultural Councils, which are based on local counties. The Romanian version is smaller, averaging five to seven farms and 24,710 acres (10,000 hectares). East Germany has Cooperative Associations that operate similarly to the Bulgarian complexes but permit the individual components to retain separate economic and juridical identity. In the Hungarian Closed Product System, a leading enterprise in a region contracts directly with the state and collective farms, thus bypassing much of the central planning apparatus. Soviet attempts to institute horizontal and vertical integration in agriculture have concentrated mainly on the Republic of Moldavia, where almost 7,000 farms and food-processing enterprises are grouped into Inter-farm Agro-Industrial Complexes. As with the Bulgarian model, Soviet reforms are mainly administrative, creating a concentration at the intermediate levels but permitting little true decentralization, let alone leeway for market forces, at the lowest levels. Thus far the record is mixed. Bulgaria, which began from a low level of agricultural productivity, appears to have bettered its yields and streamlined the food-processing industry. Hungary is agriculturally self-sufficient, but market forces play a larger role in the Hungarian system and the land is among the best in the communist bloc. The agro-industrial complexes bear some resemblance to the agro-city reform first proposed by Nikita Khrushchev and later branded by his successors as a "harebrained" scheme. Despite this possible ideological taint, the Soviet press frequently praises the Moldavian experiments. Given the endemic problems of Soviet and East European agriculture, it is probable that such reforms will be pursued further. The integration and amalgamation of individual farms and factories appear to offer economies of scale (always a Soviet desideratum), opportunities for specialization, more efficient use of the labor force, and a means of introducing modern industrial methods into the countryside while retaining central control.

Agronomist   A graduate of a Soviet school of agronomy, the equivalent of an American agricultural college. Agronomists were a key feature in the early Soviet attempt to place Soviet agriculture on a scientific basis. In the 1920s and 1930s, the Soviet government attempted to spread the gospel of scientific farming to the countryside through cadres of such agronomists, who were called Michurinites after the noted Soviet horticulturalist I. V. Michurin (1855–1935). The Michurinites were supposed to carry the message of improved quality and productivity in the same way that the Stakhanovites were to be the shock workers of industrial production. These cadres of agronomists played a key role in Stalin's collectivization of agriculture, providing both technical expertise and political surveillance over the peasants. *See also* LYSENKOISM, p. 54; STAKHANOVITE, p. 232.

Significance   The agronomists were part of the massive program of official exhortation to greater productivity during the period of rapid Soviet industrialization in the 1930s. The emphasis on scientism was typical of the faith in technology and central planning so prevalent in the initial era of the Five-Year plans. Michurin himself was one of the early geneticists who influenced Trofim Lysenko with the idea of environmentally determined biological evolution, based on theories first expounded by J. B. P. Lamarck.

Artel'   An association of producers, usually in the professional or service sectors, whose members work cooperatively. *Artel's* originated in prerevolutionary Russia with small groups of laborers in mining, manufacturing, and the skilled trades who collectively contracted with an employer for a fixed wage, which the artel' members shared equally. Under the Soviet government, artel's were organized in most of the formerly free professions, ranging from lawyers to watchmakers and peasants. These groups set their rates and conditions of work collectively and work cooperatively. The largest category of artel' is the collective farms, the *kolkhozes*, which are classified as artel's of agricultural producers with collective ownership of assets. *See also* KOLKHOZ, p. 205.

Significance   Most services in the Soviet Union are rendered through the intermediacy of artel's. Most professionals pursue their chosen profession in an artel'. Collective farmers have been classified as members of artel's since the first artel' charter for the kolkhozes was promulgated by Stalin in 1930. Artel' charters for collective farmers, professionals, and other tradespeople stipulate general work conditions and rules. The artel' itself appoints all officers and sets the conditions of work, but remains under the supervision of local party organs. The artel' form is congruent with the Soviet ideological emphasis on the spirit of collectivity, as embodied in the *kollektiv*, whereby the Soviet citizen is expected to work for the common good of society.

Automated Planning (OGAS)   The unified information system that, using computer technology, is intended to increase the accuracy and efficiency of Soviet economic planning. Automated planning was formally established in 1971 with the establishment of the State Automated System for the Collection, Storage, and Processing of Data for National Economic Planning, Management and Accounting (shortened acronym, OGAS). The central computerized information system receives inputs from all sectors and regions of the economy. The goal is to test all data against appropriately designed plan models for consistency, feasibility, and maximization of policy goals. Some portions of the intended reform are in place; computerized management systems are now the norm in Soviet factories. A large number of variables, however, remain outside the system, and a national computerized system of economic planning is yet to be achieved. *See also* PLANNING, p. 220.

Significance   Thus far, the goal of creating a single national economic plan by computer has not yet been reached. Major problems have become evident in developing indicators, such as what incentives should be selected to raise productivity or which profit levels will best maximize production. These are political decisions requiring more than mere computer capability. There is also disagreement as to how to conceptualize consumer preferences and at what level. For the Soviets, the computer has been a useful tool to rationalize the present system of administrative planning and control, but it has not yet effected a fundamental reorganization of the planning process. Some observers also maintain that the Soviet Union lags behind in computer software technology, impeding full implementation.

Budget of the State   The financial instrument by which the funds of the Soviet Union and other states with centrally directed economies are collected and disbursed according to the planned distribution of income set forth by the national economic plan of each. The Soviet budget of the state is the prototype for most of Eastern Europe. It is the means by which the Soviet government finances and controls the economy as well as all other government operations. The draft national budget is prepared yearly by the Ministry of Finance, approved by the USSR Council of Ministers, and promulgated as law by the Supreme Soviet. The USSR state budget is comprised of some 50,000 subordinate budgets, from local villages to republics; each higher-level budget includes all subordinate government units. The preparation of republican and local budgets is also supervised by the Ministry of Finance, thus ensuring a unified national budget. Expenditures fall into five categories: economic, social and cultural, administrative, defense, and debt servicing. The noneconomic institutions and organizations, such as hospitals and schools, possess their own appropriations budget. The largest portion of the state budget is devoted to financing the economy (an estimated 50 percent), which in turn provides about 90 percent of all budgetary revenues. Revenues derive from direct taxes on citizens (about 10 percent) and from the national economy. The latter includes enterprise profits, tariffs and other payments, turnover (sales) taxes, social insurance payments, and taxes on the income of collective farms. Soviet state budgets are never in deficit. A slight surplus is maintained to form a reserve fund that enables *Gosbank* to issue currency without inflating. *Gosbank* acts as the principal financial officer for the state, executing the budget. All banking institutions, which are the chief source of credit, are part of the state budget, as their resources originate from it and part of their profits accrue to it. The USSR budget of the state functions as the major instrument for redistributing the national income according to the interests of the state and provides a powerful means of centralized control over the economy. *See also* ENTERPRISE, p. 191; GOSBANK, p. 194; NATIONAL INCOME, p. 216.

Significance   The state budget of the USSR derives most of its revenues from the operations of the state enterprises; it thus is far larger than the government budgets of Western states in terms of percentage of national income. The principle of socialist (state) ownership, whereby most of the means of production are controlled by the state, provides the legal basis for the state's right to the profits of the enterprises and cooperatives. By law, the state determines what percentage of the profits accrue to the state; the remainder is available to the enterprises for operating expenses and benefits. The budget is thus the instrument by which thousands of enterprises, cooperatives, and activities are placed under the control of the central authorities. As the state budget is so closely intertwined with the economy, *Gosplan* and the planning authorities play a large role in its drafting, as does ultimately the party leadership. Both the budget and the national economic plan are presented simultaneously to the Supreme Soviet. The budgets of the East European states are similarly centralized and all serve as instruments to ration credit and fund priority sectors of the economy. Yugoslavia remains an exception; much of the budgetary powers of the Yugoslav federation have been devolved to republican and local governments, which possess their own sources of revenues and enjoy autonomy over their distribution. Yugoslav enterprises, as self-managed institutions, also are freed from central government control. Although the USSR state budget indicates the policy priorities of the Soviet state, it is by no means a complete guide. Published budgetary statistics are usually incomplete, particularly in the area of defense expenditures.

Collective Agreement   Agreement between the trade union and the management of an economic enterprise that defines the units of production per worker, the level of output, working conditions, and distribution of benefits. Although in a Soviet-style economy the central planning organs determine the product mix and set production targets, the management and workforce must work out the details of production through the collective agreement (*koldogovor*). The enterprise director concludes the collective agreement with the trade union committee, which acts in the collective interest of the workers. The collective agreement establishes rules for labor discipline and work conditions, allocates housing and benefits funded from the special enterprise for social and cultural activities, and distributes bonuses. *See also* LABOR NORMS, p. 207; TRADE UNION'S, p. 305.

Significance   Actual worker participation in the collective agreement is probably minimal since the workers are represented by the trade union committee, typically staffed and controlled by party members. Critics of Soviet-style economic systems have argued that therefore the interests of the workers are subordinated to the interests of the state. For example, before the independent Polish trade union movement, Solidarity, was suppressed, members frequently charged that the health and safety of workers in key industries such as coal mining had been consistently neglected by the trade union officials, who operate as agents of party policy.

Collectivization   The transformation of agricultural production from private ownership to state-administered collective farms. Collectivization was imposed in the Soviet Union by Josef Stalin in the years 1929–36, resulting in the eradication of the free peasantry and the nationalization of agriculture. Immediately after coming to power in 1917, the Bolsheviks carried out a radical land reform that gave much of the peasantry their own land for the first time. During the Civil War food was mandatorily requisitioned, but requisitions were abandoned in 1921. Russian agriculture remained primitive, being largely unmechanized and divided into small plots. The peasants refused to sell their produce at prices they deemed unacceptable. By the late 1920s, the state faced the possibility of having to import grain. A sharp differentiation had developed between the better-off peasantry, labeled *Kulaks*, and the many marginal peasants. During 1925–29, the total growth of Soviet agriculture was less than 1 percent. By 1929, Stalin had triumphed over his various rivals, and turned to the twin problems of agriculture and industrialization. Collectivization proceeded from two imperatives: the need to secure an agricultural base for industrialization, and Stalin's determination to impose communism on the countryside. Collectivization was both swift and brutal. The instrumentality chosen was the collective farm (*kolkhoz*), a voluntary cooperative in which the peasants pooled labor and resources. Few peasants had voluntarily set up kolkhozes when Stalin announced his drive to collectivize; within six years practically all the arable land in the Soviet Union was collectivized. The peasants were driven by force into the collectives. Those who resisted were summarily executed or sent to almost certain death in prison labor camps. Title to the land was seized by the state. Collectivization was carried out chiefly by the secret police, using such means as impossibly high taxes, deportations, confiscation of all possessions, executions, deprivation of ration cards, and random violence. Famine struck in 1932–33 as the result of the severe disruption in agriculture. In 1932 the internal passport system was reinstated, and most peasants were denied passports and were thus blocked from leaving the collectives. An estimated 3.5–5 million peasants resisted and were sent to prison labor camps. Estimates of the overall death toll vary. Stalin himself admitted casually to 10 million "liquidations." At the end, 25 million small peasant farms had been transformed into about 250,000 collective farms and Soviet agriculture had been permanently transformed. *See also* GREAT PURGE, p. 17; GULAG, p. 259; KOLKHOZ, p. 205; KULAK, p. 24; MACHINE TRACTOR STATION (MTS), p. 211; SOVKHOZ, p. 229.

Significance   Economically, collectivization was a success as it enabled the state to appropriate capital from agriculture for industrialization. In terms of productivity, Soviet agriculture paid a heavy price, from which it is still recovering. Stalin achieved his second major goal, that of Sovietizing the countryside, but at an incredible human cost. Some analysts maintain that the success in breaking peasant resistance may have strengthened Stalin's willingness to use force against the Soviet people, marking the turn of the regime to mass terror. The millions of peasants sent to the labor camps constitute the first great influx into the camps. Collectivization, the purges of the 1930s, and World War II drastically affected Soviet demography. Demographic predictions in the 1920s projected a population of 490 million by 1980, rather than the actual 260 million. When communism was imposed on Eastern Europe after World War II, the new governments were compelled to follow the Stalinist model. Collectivization was carried out with varying degrees of brutality, enforced by police terror. In Hungary, the powerful state security forces, the AVH, enforced it with a vengeance, arresting, executing, and imprisoning hundreds of thousands. Poland, a nation of small peasant landowners, abandoned collectivization after the Polish Uprising of 1956, but the endemic distrust of the peasantry for the Communist Party remains and continues to plague Polish agriculture. Yugoslavia initially attempted collectivization, but after the break with the Soviet Union in

1948 permitted the collectives to disband. Today Yugoslavia, like Poland, is a country of small private farms. Elsewhere collectivization was accomplished with less brutality than under Stalin but with the same result: the transformation of agriculture into a state-administered system.

Command Economy   The Soviet model of state-directed industrialization, instituted by Josef Stalin in 1928. The command economy as a title implies the tight discipline of a military organization. It is essentially a developmental model that relies on tight central control and the mobilization of all resources. It is characterized by (1) state ownership; (2) centrally determined state allocation; (3) mobilization and full utilization of all resources; (4) long-range economic planning that determines priorities and emphasizes heavy industry; (5) high rates of capital investment, usually at the expense of the consumer sector; (6) state enforcement of the economic plans. All control is vested in the central government, and, ultimately, in the communist party leadership. State ministries receive directives ("commands") from the central authorities that they must enforce on the enterprises under their jurisdiction. The economy is organized along branch lines, typically with an administrative ministry or department in charge of the production of a specific branch. The factories function as instruments of the central economic plan; competition is restricted and there is no free market in wages or prices. Only in the area of military production, where the planner and consumer are the same (that is, the state), is there any consumer sovereignty. Otherwise, the command economy is a supply-dominated system rather than a demand system. It rests on a centrally operated and state-owned economy that produces, in essence, a single state monopoly. *See also* COUNCIL OF MUTUAL ECONOMIC ASSISTANCE (CMEA OR COMECON), p. 317; GOELRO, p. 194; NEW ECONOMIC POLICY (NEP), p. 218; WAR COMMUNISM, p. 237.

Significance   The command economy rests on the premise that the well-being of the state depends on rapid industrialization that only central control can create. The Soviet model is thus best understood if treated in a developmental perspective. The Bolsheviks inherited a war-torn, semi-industrialized state surrounded by hostile neighbors. The initial and abortive attempt to institute immediate communism, the period known as War Communism, lasted until 1921, when it was succeeded by the more liberal New Economic Policy (NEP) introduced by Vladimir Lenin. In 1928, Josef Stalin, having consolidated his power, embarked on rapid forced-draft industrialization. The decision to industrialize by harnessing all available resources to the will of the state was both defensive and consistent with the Marxist tenets that socialism is more productive than capitalism, and that communism will be possible only after the mode of production has been radically transformed and consumer goods are plentiful. By placing the state in total control of the economy, Stalin sought to shortcut the lengthy industrialization process carried out in capitalist countries. At the price of incredible hardships and millions of dead, Stalin succeeded in his basic goal. Industrialization was purchased at tremendous human cost. The major source of investment capital was exacted from the peasants and workers. In 1940, the average real wage, based on food prices, was only half of the 1928 level. In addition, millions of prison camp laborers were used to build the industrial base. The record in Eastern Europe, where the Soviet economic model was imposed after World War II, suggests that the command economy is more successful in a relatively underdeveloped economy than in complex industrial systems. The latter, with their increasingly complex variables, demand a much more sophisticated and flexible planning-command system, which has proved difficult to achieve under a centralized political monopoly. The command economy depends on "extensive" development, where rates of planned growth are dependent on increase in inputs rather than in productivity, technology, or modernization of existing plants. The state mobilizes all resources and concentrates them on priority sectors; what it can't do is enforce efficiency. The Stalinist command economy is also inherently autarkic, aiming at self-sufficiency. This aspect has proved especially difficult for the much smaller and resource-poor East European states. As market considerations play little role in a command economy, the East European states were forced to produce by plan, not market, and were compelled by the political power of the Soviet Union to reorient their trade to the communist bloc rather than with their traditional western trading partners. The application of the Soviet model has resulted in varying economic problems in Eastern Europe. The one communist-party state that has avoided many of the economic ills of Eastern Europe is Bulgaria, which is also the least industrialized. Yugoslavia, equally undeveloped in 1946, remains an exception, as it abandoned the Stalinist model in 1950. Under the command economy system of ever-increasing inputs to spur growth, the more developed economic system typically lapses into stagnation. Not surprisingly, Eastern Europe has been in the forefront of bloc economic reform. Reform remains difficult, however, as the economic and political spheres are so closely linked, making economic reform inseparable from political reform. Major attempts to change the politicoeconomic structure and free the economy from political control have generally been suppressed by the Soviet Union, as in Czechoslovakia in 1968. The command economy has created an elite of bureaucrats in charge of the economy. The power structure of the command economy has been resistant to change, as this disturbs the symbiotic relationship between party and administrators, and administrators and managers. While not totally incompatible with political democracy and individual liberty, the command economy has proved inherently intolerant of both. As a model for mobilization and rapid industrialization, however, the command economy remains attractive to undeveloped countries, many of which face conditions similar to or worse than the Soviet Union faced in 1928. To varying degrees, the principle that only the state can plan and guarantee rational allocation of scarce resources has been adopted by many developing nations of the Third World.

Economic Ministry   The governmental organ responsible for the economic management of a specific sector of economy. Soviet productive enterprises operate under the direct administrative command of a government economic ministry. The economic ministries in the Soviet Union are of two types: (1) the all-union, which is responsible for the operation of a specific industrial sector on a national basis; and (2) the union-republic, where administrative authority for a specific sector is shared with or delegated to corresponding ministries in the governments of the 15 union-republics. The chief function of the economic ministries is to ensure implementation of the production targets set by the centrally determined economic plan, which in turn is based on the goals, priorities, and policies determined by the central party leadership. Such ministries are termed economic ministries to distinguish them from the traditional ministerial divisions such as the Ministry of Education or the Ministry of Foreign Affairs; all are grouped into the federal and republican Council of Ministers. Each economic ministry is responsible for a major product or group of related products, such as the Ministry of the Cellulose and Paper Industry, the Ministry of Agriculture, or the Ministry of Chemical Industry. The economic ministries are typically divided into production departments (*glavki*) that direct and administer a specific branch of the economic sector under ministerial jurisdiction. The ministries and departments issue binding directives to the enterprises under their jurisdiction in accordance with the production targets set by the economic plan. Enterprise managers are appointed by the relevant ministry, subject to party approval, and are responsible to the ministry. Enterprises operate under a federal ministry or glavka, a republican counterpart, or, in the case of the least important, under the control of the local soviet, although in the latter case the relevant republican or glavka is ultimately responsible. Economic management in the East

European states is modeled on the Soviet ministerial system, although the organizational structures differ. *See also* COMMAND ECONOMY, p. 187; COUNCIL OF MINISTERS, p. 133; ENTERPRISE, p. 191; PLANNING, p. 220; TARGETS, p. 233.

Significance   The system of economic ministries dates to the 1930s and Josef Stalin's drive to industrialize the Soviet Union under centralized economic control. The Supreme Economic Council or *Vesenkha* (VSNKh) created by Vladimir Lenin in 1918 to direct the war-shattered economy was the predecessor of the system of economic ministries. By 1928, the Supreme Economic Council had become a vast collection of overlapping departments; Stalin reorganized it into three huge commissariats (heavy industry, light industry, and forestry). Subsequently, as the pace of industrialization quickened, the commissariats were in turn divided, eventually into more than fifty such administrative organs designed along branch economic lines; in 1946 the government apparatus was reorganized, and the commissariats renamed ministries. The immense power accruing to the heads of the economic ministries changed the political dynamics of the Soviet Union. Under Stalin, several top decision makers were directors of key industrial sectors rather than high party officials. Analysts of group theory identify the huge economic ministries as a chief focus of competition within the system for favorable allocation of resources. Each economic ministry becomes, in effect, a mini-industrial empire controlling the industry on a regional or national basis. Although the system firmly places the responsibility for meeting production targets on the ministries, it also has negative effects. Each ministry attempts to control as many subsidiary enterprises as possible, that is, those producing the inputs necessary for its sphere of production. Thus, a heavy construction ministry seeks to control the supply of coal and steel necessary for its production, freeing it from dependence on the Ministry of the Coal Mining Industry or other ministries. As success of a ministry is based on plan fulfillment, profits become subsidiary to the system of administrative economic management. While this remains in general a given of the system, the Soviet Union and a number of East European systems have experimented with decentralization of ministerial control, cost-effectiveness, improved research and development capabilities, and administrative reorganization. The major reform has been the creation of industrial associations which replace the glavki. Unlike the glavki, the association is granted greater flexibility in determining how to best meet the assigned production targets and must operate on profit-and-loss accounting. The result is a streamlining of the planning process, as the plan does not have to be disaggregated to the enterprise level, and greater cost-effectiveness. The associations, however, represent decentralization of ministerial control rather than the injection of market considerations. Only Hungary has concurrently decentralized economic management and relaxed governmental control over prices and wages. Elsewhere, the ministerial system has proved to be extremely resistant to any reorganization or reform that appears to diminish its power, as was demonstrated, for example, by the fate of Nikita Khrushchev's *Sovnarkhozy* reform.

Enterprise   The basic unit of production in the vast state-owned and state-directed economy of a Soviet-style economic system. Under Soviet and East European law, the enterprise is a legal entity, or legal person—it can enter into contracts, sue and be sued, and receive legal remedies. Legal personality begins when the enterprise is granted operational management over the state property allocated to it. Comparable to a factory or an industry in a capitalist system, the enterprise is set up by state charter. The charter defines the scope of the enterprise's activities and allocates the necessary capital equipment. The state retains ownership of all assets, determines the distribution of the product, and sets prices. Enterprises are governed by state statutes and regulations—in the USSR, currently, the Regulations on the Socialist Industrial State Enterprise, issued by the USSR Council of Ministers, govern all state enterprises. The primary responsibility of the enterprise is to fulfill the production targets set by the central planning organs; it thus comprises the basic unit in the mandatory economic plans. As economic plans are statutory enactments, they are legally binding upon the enterprise. The central planning authorities determine production, wage allocation, distribution of profits, introduction of new technologies and supply of raw materials. The enterprise is responsible for a technical-industrial-production plan which sets the conditions of production. Enterprises are initiated, reorganized, and dissolved by the state agencies. Enterprises are subordinate to a government ministry. Such ministries are divided into several branch economic departments, called chief directorates (*glavki*). Only the state agency to which the enterprise is responsible can impose new tasks or change the plan. Each enterprise is economically responsible and keeps an account with the State Bank. Performance is evaluated by units produced and costs of production (*khozraschet*). The director is appointed by and responsible to the state agencies. If enterprises are grouped into an industrial association, the association also enjoys legal personage. In the USSR, there are approximately 50,000 state enterprises, ranging from the smallest factory to huge industrial ones employing thousands. *See also* BUDGET OF THE STATE, p. 183; KHOZRASCHET, p. 205; INDUSTRIAL ASSOCIATIONS: OBEDINENIE, p. 199.

Significance   The enterprise is both a legal entity and an agency of the state, charged with fulfilling specific, legally mandated economic activities. Ownership is vested in the state, which according to the tenets of Marxism-Leninism has under socialism ended the exploitation of workers by capitalist owners. The role of the enterprise as the major carrier of the mandatory economic plan has served to limit its activities to implementing the plan targets; management is paid on the basis of production, not sales. Critics have argued that mandatory, detailed central planning stifles innovation, impedes efficiency, and substitutes the inflexibility and irrationality of the planners for the irrationalities of the market. The various attempts at economic reform in Eastern Europe and the Soviet Union have little affected the underlying structure, although Hungary has undergone substantial change. Only the Yugoslavs, by abandoning mandatory central planning and basing their economic system on market considerations, have changed the legal status of the enterprise. While ownership remains vested in the Yugoslav state, control is in the hands of the self-managed enterprises, acting in trust for the state. The Yugoslav enterprise determines its own product mix, purchases inputs on an open market, competes to hire managerial staff, and sells its products at market-determined prices. In essence, the Yugoslav enterprise operates under the principle of usufruct, giving the enterprise the right to enjoy the profits gained from the use of its assets. Since Josef Stalin embarked on a crash program of centrally directed industrialization in 1928, the Soviets have argued that only through scientific allocation of resources by the state can full communism be achieved. Only the Yugoslavs, by retaining socialist ownership over the means of production while abandoning central planning, have freed the enterprise from functioning as a subordinate unit for the administration of state property.

Five-Year Plan   The key component in the system of centrally directed economic planning that over a period of 50 years has transformed the Soviet Union from a semi-industrialized, predominantly agricultural state into a major industrialized economy. The first Soviet five-year plan was initiated in 1928 by Josef Stalin as a blueprint for state-directed crash industrialization. It marked the end of the New Economic Program (NEP) that since 1922 had permitted private agriculture and a measure of market-based activities. The crucial dilemma facing Stalin was how to secure the capital necessary for development. The five-year plan set the pattern: almost all surpluses were channeled back into development, with agriculture contributing disproportionately and consumer needs assigned low priority. Stalin dictated what are now considered to be the essentials of the system:

collectivization of the land, state-directed mobilization of all resources, state control over all production and markets, and a centralized system of economic planning. Since 1928 the Soviet economy has operated on the basis of five-year plans that subject almost all productive forces to direct, mandatory physical planning under tight central control. The five-year plan sets expected growth rates by sector and indicates major capital investments. One-year operational plans detail how the goals are to be reached and disaggregate the targets on a yearly basis and by enterprise. The priorities identified by the five-year plan are policy decisions made by the party leadership, transformed into mandatory targets by the plan. *See also* COLLECTIVIZATION, p. 185; COMMAND ECONOMY, p. 187; MARKET SOCIALISM, p. 212; PLANNING, p. 220.

Significance   The inception of the five-year plan approach and the concept of centralized command over the economy changed the nature of the Soviet system. Since direction is the essence of the plan, the role of the party is paramount. The five-year plan assumes a powerful state apparatus with the power to enforce the commands of the plan and a system of state-directed mobilization through which all resources can be harnessed to the interests of the state. Despite the brutalities of the Stalinist years, in economic terms the period of the first three plans (1928–40) must be judged a success. Forced-draft industrialization under the five-year plans produced an estimated sixfold increase in Soviet industrial output. The costs were incredibly high. Millions of peasants lost their lives during the drive to collectivize the land and personal income remained at approximately the 1928 levels. The structure of Soviet society was transformed. Urbanization proceeded at breakneck speed, private trade was abolished, illiteracy rates fell drastically, and, essentially, the class structure was changed. A powerful state bureaucracy that planned and administered the economy was created. The Soviet five-year plan system remains a major contribution to the theory of economic planning and development. Many developing countries have attempted to duplicate the Soviet success, albeit with less brutality. Such programs are postulated on the idea that, in a situation of scarce resources, it is crucial to plan their use. Soviet five-year plans also exhibit the systematic constants that have negated some of the value of long-range planning: overcentralized decision making, inflexibility, "taut" planning that leads to bottlenecks if one sector fails, and a bias toward heavy industry. Five-year plans were also adopted by the East European states, with minor variations. Yugoslavia, however, abandoned the state command economy in favor of a decentralized, market-oriented system. Most political analysts maintain that the five-year plans illuminate the long-range policy goals of the party leadership. Thus, the tenth five-year plan (1976–80), which assigned heavier investment to defense-related industries, is believed to have been indicative either of the increased aggressiveness of Soviet foreign policy, or of a growing fear of American power. Soviet planners have developed longer-range plans, spanning 10 or 20 years, but the five-year plan remains the key component of the system.

GOELRO   The acronym for the State Commission for the Electrification of Russia, the committee set up in 1920 to bring electricity to the citizens of the new Bolshevik state. Vladimir Lenin utilized GOELRO as a means of dramatizing the advantages of Bolshevism and its concern for the common people. Under GOELRO, the Bolsheviks began a crash program of bringing electricity to the cities and the countryside. The slogan coined by Lenin, "Electrification and power to the soviets equals communism," became shorthand for the promises of communism, even though the soviets (assemblies) themselves were rapidly stripped of autonomous power by the party. *See also* COMMAND ECONOMY, p. 187; PLANNING, p. 220.

Significance   GOELRO constitutes the first instance of long-term economic planning under communism. It thus became the forerunner of the massive centralized planning system instituted by Josef Stalin. The drama of bringing electricity to millions of peasant huts was copied by later communist leaders, including China's Mao Tse-tung. Electrification was viewed by the Bolsheviks as a necessary precondition for industrialization, thus emphasizing the priority the communists placed on rapid industrialization as a means of securing the Revolution.

Gosbank   The national bank of issue, chief source of credit, and central agency of fiscal-monetary policy in the Soviet Union. *Gosbank* regulates the supply and circulation of money and performs all cash transactions for the USSR state budget. Attached to the Council of Ministers in theory, in practice it is virtually autonomous of ministerial control. Consistent with the centralization of key organs in the Soviet Union, Gosbank has no republican analogues; it operates through the central apparatus and about 4,000 regional and local branches. Central Gosbank contains about two dozen directorates and departments, each one of which (such as the Directorate for Loans to the Defense Industry) wields immense power. Each enterprise, collective or state farm, and trading organization must keep its accounts with Gosbank. Gosbank is also charged with collecting the turnover taxes, the chief source of government funds. Some of the assets held by Gosbank are delegated to *Stroibank*, which finances major capital investments, and *Vneshtorgbank*, which handles foreign trade; both are controlled by Gosbank. The 80,000 local savings institutions are also under the control of Gosbank. *See also* BUDGET OF THE STATE, p. 183; GOSPLAN, p. 196; MARKET SOCIALISM, p. 212; PLANNING, p. 220.

Significance   The role of Gosbank is crucial to the Soviet economic system. It is a monopoly institution operating under tight central control. Its functions resemble those of the United States Federal Reserve System as well as those of commercial banks. As the source of short-term credit, it provides working capital to the enterprises, in conformity with their economic plans. Interest rates on short-term credit vary according to who applies and for what purpose, but they are always very low. It is almost always cheaper for an enterprise to borrow from Gosbank than to use its own resources, as working capital pays a higher capital charge. Critics point out that credits are granted according to plan fulfillment, rather than marketability. If an enterprise has met its production targets, even if the goods are not salable, it can obtain the credits necessary to pay its workers and suppliers. Gosbank plays a crucial role in the allocation process, by enforcing rationing of credits. The Polish economic crisis of the early 1980s, however, points out a flaw in the system. If the economic plan is unrealistically ambitious and bank credits must be denied even though the plan requires them, suppliers in essence furnish the credits through delayed payments; eventually such a system will falter. As with all East European and Soviet banking systems, this amounts to one enterprise granting another enterprise credits, which is illegal.

The Yugoslav banking system is almost totally different, resembling a western banking system. The Yugoslav National Bank operates much as the U.S. Federal Reserve System. The commercial banks operate on a profit-and-loss basis and loans are granted to enterprises on the basis of profit-making ability and collateral, rather than on plan fulfillment; interest rates are determined by the market and by the National Bank on the basis of economic conditions. Yugoslav enterprises are free to grant credits to other enterprises, to pool funds, and to seek foreign capital, and they must compete for bank credits. Only the Yugoslav banking system publishes complete financial statistics; Gosbank and its counterparts do not publicly release such figures. The latter served as the basis for one of the criticisms levelled during the Polish crisis of 1980–81, when Solidarity pointed out that when the Polish government began seeking foreign credits, it made the statistics available to foreign banks that it kept secret from its own citizenry.

Gosplan (State Planning Committee)   The supreme planning organ of the Soviet system, responsible for planning and coordinating most of the economic activities of the Soviet state. As almost all of the means of production are state-owned, *Gosplan* functions as the prime determinant of all economic activity in what is essentially a single-state industrial monopoly. Policy decisions as to what economic sectors are given priority status are made by the party Politburo. Gosplan must coordinate these policy decisions with the resources available to the state, and develop both long-range and short-term economic plans to implement them. Despite its formal affiliation with the federal Council of Ministers, Gosplan appears to operate autonomously, its responsibility being one of communicaions and advice-seeking rather than subordination. Based on Politburo policy decisions, Gosplan formulates five-year plans that define the rates of growth for the economy by sectors and products and indicates major capital investment projects. The yearly plans that set production targets for each sector are drawn up in cooperation with the various economic ministries. As each economic sector and its ministry usually wishes to increase its power, the "requests" made to Gosplan must be balanced with the resources available and the priorities set by the party. Gosplan thus also functions as an organ of conciliation and compromise. The politicking is similar to that of cabinet departments, such as education or defense, which compete for a bigger share of federal funding, or the competition among divisions and subsidiaries of a large Western corporation, but on the scale of a single huge national entity. Gosplan both plans the economy and allocates the necessary resources to meet the planned production targets. By the late 1970s, Gosplan was responsible for allocation of production requirements to about 2,000 product groups; below that the republican Gosplans and about 40 ministries allocated needs for much smaller production sectors. Supplies are handled through long-term supply contracts, which may be adjusted if necessary. Gosplan is assisted by several other central organs, such as the State Committee for Building (*Gosstroi*), the State Committee for Supply (*Gossnab*), the State Committee for Labor and Wages, the State Committee for Prices, the State Committee for Science and Technology, and the USSR Academy of Sciences. Gosplan, therefore, occupies the central position in a vast planning bureaucracy that plans and directs the Soviet economy. *See also* FIVE-YEAR PLAN, p. 192; PLANNING, p. 220.

Significance   The plans formulated by Gosplan operationalize in economic terms the priorities and goals of the central party authorities. Gosplan was created by Vladimir Lenin in 1921 to direct the economy; its function became primary to the system when Josef Stalin embarked on a planned program of crash industrialization and instructed Gosplan to develop the first five-year plan for development in 1928. Since then the Soviet economy essentially has functioned under the priorities determined by Gosplan and the party. In the period following the death of Stalin, Gosplan's authority fluctuated, but since 1968 it has operated under a statute that gives it supreme authority for economic planning. East European systems have analogous planning organs, with the exception of Yugoslavia, which does not practice mandatory central planning. Hungary for a short period under the New Economic Mechanism abolished most central economic planning but restored a measure of power to central planning in the mid-1970s. Otherwise, reform of the planning systems that center on Gosplan and its analogues has involved the decentralization of some planning responsibilities rather than on diminution of the core rationale: that only through central economic planning can production best be planned to benefit the state, and resources allocated efficiently. Critics of Gosplan, communist as well as noncommunist, maintain that the emphasis on heavy industry as the "engine" of industrialization has created a planning bias toward the "metal-eaters," the Soviet equivalent of the military-industrial complex.

Gross Industrial Output   The sum of the outputs of all state industrial enterprises and associations in the Soviet bloc countries. The gross industrial output includes all mining and manufacturing, timbering, fishing, and processing of agricultural products, but excludes construction. The total includes much double counting, as the output of each individual enterprise comprises the measurement. Thus, if an enterprise produces machinery, all inputs purchased from other enterprises are counted twice, both in the value of the output of the suppliers and in the value of the final assembled product. If the same enterprise produces both the machinery and all the components, there is no double counting. Gross industrial output is based on wholesale prices, which exclude turnover taxes; however, turnover taxes levied on producers goods purchased by the enterprises are included. *See also* NATIONAL INCOME, p. 216; TURNOVER TAX, p. 235.

Significance   The double counting involved in computing the gross industrial output consistently inflates the measurements of industrial output and thus affects indices of national growth. The extent of double-counting varies over time, with the changing degree of intermediate manufacturing and vertical integration obviously affecting long-term comparisons. Net industrial output figures, which correct for the above, are not made available for the Soviet Union, although some East European systems provide them.

Hard Currency Stores   Stores that offer consumer goods and souvenirs for sale to tourists with hard currencies, which unlike the currencies of the communist bloc states are convertible at exchange rates set by world market conditions. Hard currency stores exist in the Soviet Union, where they are called *Berezki* (pronounced Ber-YOZ-ki) and in all East European states except Yugoslavia. The Soviet bloc states (1) do not permit their currencies to be exchanged on world markets at world market prices; (2) permit foreign currency to be exchanged only at the state banks, which peg the exchange rates artificially low for the foreign currency; (3) do not permit their citizens to use foreign currency for sales transactions. Only Yugoslavia, which maintains a market-based economic system and a freely convertible currency, does not possess a system of restricted hard currency stores. In theory such stores are supposed to be available only to foreign tourists with dollars, francs, marks, and such; in practice the situation varies, with the Berezki being the most restrictive. Hard currency stores should not be confused with the special shops available only to high-ranking party members, although frequently the same items are offered. The hard currency stores sell imported goods, high-quality domestic products and souvenirs, and the most desirable consumer goods produced within the country. Frequently, they are the only retail source of goods such as imported whiskey and cosmetics, locally produced luxury items such as fine jewelry and clothing, or consumer goods such as high-quality toilet paper, over-the-counter medicines, and scarce processed foods. The rates of exchange offered are usually more favorable than those set by the state banks. *See also* SECOND ECONOMY, p. 225.

Significance   The hard currency stores are largely the result of the increased tourism permitted and encouraged by the Soviet bloc states since the 1960s and the inadequacies of some of their production facilities and their consumer sectors. In the 1970s and 1980s, the growing hard currency debts of the bloc states, particularly Poland, Czechoslovakia, and Hungary, may have been a factor in the expansion of the hard currency stores. The hard currency stores form an important part of the Second Economy, all those non-sanctioned economic transactions that take place outside the official state-run economy. As the hard currency stores offer otherwise unattainable goods and better exchange rates, illegal currency transactions and purchases have been made more tempting to local citizens. The hard currency stores constitute an underground distribution system as well as a source of supplies and souvenirs for tourists. The Soviet Berezki are typically more tightly regulated than the East European systems, such as the Polish *Pewex* stores where before 1982 anyone with hard currency could shop with no questions asked. The temptation offered by the Pewex stores was exacerbated by the fact that many Poles have relatives among the 6 million Polish-Americans who regularly send them dollars. As the leaders of the now suppressed Solidarity movement pointed out, the Polish government had "made the złoty worthless" by encouraging the ordinary citizen to obtain hard currency by whatever means possible. The Pewex became the only source of the best of domestic production, such as fine Polish crystal and leather jackets, a situation which further contributed to the alienation of the citizenry. Some analysts have questioned the accuracy of Soviet bloc economic statistics, since the hard currency reserves they report may have entered at the official exchange rate, been exchanged "on the street" at rates up to five times the official rate, or been spent at hard currency stores at yet another rate of exchange. The cynicism implicit in such a system may have deepened the disillusionment of some citizens, who find that the most desirable consumer goods are available only to those with high party positions or access to hard currency. In the 1980s, communist governments have placed even greater emphasis on securing hard currency because of their need to maintain their economies with the purchase of badly needed Western trade items, such as steel pipe, computers, machine tools, food grains, and oil drilling equipment.

Industrial Associations: *Obedinenie*   Large industrial group, usually established as the result of the merger of production enterprises. The number of industrial associations in the Soviet Union increased markedly in the 1970s and early 1980s as the result of the push for administrative efficiency and cost effectiveness. Production in key sectors of the Soviet economy, such as coal, paper, or mining, is now carried out chiefly by the *obedinenie*. Industrial associations take three forms: (1) the *kombinat*, which unites several factories engaged in the same production in a system of vertical integration; (2) the *trest*, which unites several smaller enterprises in the same industrial branch; and (3) the *firma*, a merger of a number of smaller enterprises that are attached to a larger enterprise. Enterprises involved in these mergers may retain their legal identity, or may be reduced to branch status. There are also associations based on territory, controlling all the production of a product on a national, republican, or regional basis. Some of the latter, like the phonograph record association *Melodiya*, predate the newer industrial associations. Frequently the industrial association replaces the production department (*glavka*), or chief directorate, of the economic ministry to which it is responsible, thus streamlining the administrative operation. Unlike the glavki, the industrial associations are economically accountable (*khozraschet*). The industrial association benefits by minimizing costs, unlike the planning authorities and ministerial departments whose main function is to issue orders and ensure that supplies reach the producers. The industrial associations may be compared to a multi-product corporation, or in some cases, a cartel or an industrial complex. The presumed advantages offered by the industrial associations include (1) administrative efficiency; (2) economy of scale; (3) phasing out of smaller, less efficient enterprises; (4) specialization; (5) better coordination of research and development; and (6) streamlining of the planning system. As industrial associations are financed from the profits of their constituent enterprises, cost-effectiveness is enhanced. At present, some 50 percent of the Soviet industrial output is produced by industrial associations; the announced goal is that by the end of the 1980s almost all will be. *See also* INDUSTRIAL ASSOCIATION: VVB, p. 200; INDUSTRIAL ASSOCIATION: WOG, p. 201; MINISTRY, p. 151.

Significance   Although aimed at rationalizing production and instituting better cost control, the industrial associations have not changed the principle of central planning. It is not a market-oriented reform; planners retain control over production targets and supplies. The industrial associations, however, have removed an intervening layer of bureaucracy and relieved the planning authorities of the task of disaggregating the economic plan down to the smallest enterprise; this function is now performed by the industrial associations. The latter may explain why there has been resistance to the industrial associations, as they represent a redistribution of power. The Soviet industrial associations were predated by the East German cartels or VVBs, and, like them, represent the amalgamation of what are assumed to be smaller, less efficient enterprises rather than a move away from centrally directed economic planning.

Industrial Association: VVB   The East German industrial cartel responsible for the production of an enterprise or branch of the economy. The VVB (*Vereinigung Volkseigener Betriebe*, Association of Nationalized Enterprises) operates on a cost-accounting basis, managing the production of most or all of a group of related products produced by its component enterprises. The *Kombinaten*, large industrial associations, typically include several enterprises involved in the same production line, and in most cases have superseded the VVBs. The VVBs possess more autonomy than their Soviet counterparts. The VVBs receive an aggregated national economic plan, determine within the limits of the plan how to best fulfill their portion, and can also negotiate foreign trade contracts without ministerial control. Whereas the Soviet central supply organ, *Gossnab*, controls the supply of materials to Soviet enterprises and associations, the VVBs and Kombinaten have the authority to negotiate contracts with suppliers. The first VVBs were created in 1958 when the economic subministries (in the USSR, *glavki*) were abolished. Unlike the subministries they replaced, the VVBs are economically accountable for their operations. In 1963 the East German government formally adopted further economic reforms that centered on the amalgamation of smaller enterprises, greater priority on incentives, vertical integration, and cost-effectiveness. By the 1980s, much of the East German economy had been organized into industrial associations. *See also* INDUSTRIAL ASSOCIATIONS: OBEDINENIE, p. 199; INDUSTRIAL ASSOCIATION: WOG, p. 201.

Significance   The VVB reforms have influenced other bloc countries, particularly the USSR, where Soviet industrial associations (*obedinenie*) have benefitted from the East German experience with VVBs. The industrial associations and Kombinaten do not represent a fundamental shift in the premise of a centrally planned economy: central control over planning and implementation. The East German system retains macroeconomic planning while devolving microeconomic responsibilities. The simplification of the planning process— vertical integration, and rationalization of industrial production— appear to have benefitted the East German economy, producing higher growth rates, a better quality of goods, and increased capacity to compete in world markets. Despite the apparent economic benefits, even this limited reform has not yet been instituted in full by other bloc countries. The apparent reluctance of bloc states to institute even the limited decentralization of the East German reforms illustrates the major barrier to economic reform in a centrally planned economy, namely, how much economic decentralization can a communist political system permit and sustain?

Industrial Association: WOG   The acronym for *Wielkie Organizacje Gospodarcze*, the large industrial organizations intended to be the key institution in the economic reforms undertaken by the Polish leadership in the 1970s. The WOGs, modeled after the East German industrial associations (VVBs), were formed in 1973 in several key industrial sectors. The WOGs were intended as the first step in a series of economic reforms that would spur growth and raise Polish living standards. The proposed economic reforms grew out of the circumstances that brought Edward Gierek to power in Poland in 1970. In 1970, worsening economic conditions forced the leadership, under Władysław Gomułka, to increase food prices. The Polish workers rioted, Gomułka was forced to resign, and the promise of a better economic deal for the Polish worker was made by Gomułka's successor, Gierek. The growth promised by the WOG reforms was keyed to increasing Polish trade with the West. Unlike the East German government's VVB reforms, the Gierek leadership proved reluctant to diminish the power of the central administrative bodies. Thus, at a time when Poland was seeking world markets, the flexibility of the economy remained limited by the straitjacket of centralization. The economic ministries retained planning power, although plans were supposed to be based on yearly net output rather than on production targets. Wages were pegged to productivity and permitted to rise, but the state controlled prices. The WOGs were then caught between two imperatives: the consumer orientation promised by Gierek and central administrative control. The lines of authority were never clearly defined. Management rules, wages, and prices were in constant flux. The legal status of the WOG and its component enterprises was not changed, so many economic decisions were of an *ad hoc* nature. The formation of the WOGs occurred at a peak period in Polish economic growth. By the mid-1970s, the Polish economy was increasingly buffeted by the increase in energy prices and a worsening world economy. Rather than reform the economic administrative apparatus, the Polish leadership apparently opted for the "quick fix"—increased imports of Western technology financed primarily through hard currency loans from Western banks, with the optimistic assumption that the loans, coming due in the late 1970s and 1980s, would be easily repaid from increased exports. Both this plan and the WOG itself were undermined by worsening economic conditions and the retention of central economic authority. The product lines chosen for expanded export trade were selected by the central authorities with little regard for domestic or international conditions. The WOGs selected to produce these priority items were hamstrung by the central administration. Frequently the production of priority goods was halted by the lack of a small component produced by a low priority enterprise. The production of intermediate goods, which should have been freed to stimulate the productivity of the WOGs, became a roadblock. Foreign firms that entered into hard currency agreements to install new technology and build new industrial facilities were constantly stymied by the muddled lines of authority and delays endemic in dealing with the bureaucracy. An essential portion of the WOG reform, a more rational pricing system, was never enacted. Food prices remained frozen until 1976, when the government simultaneously raised food prices and froze wages, with the result that the workers once more took to the streets to protest. The Gierek government survived the 1976 outbreaks, after rapidly caving in to the workers, only to fall in 1980 when worker alienation coalesced around the movement for free trade unions, Solidarity. Ironically, many of the demands made by Solidarity during its brief legal existence were similar to the proposals first put forth as part of the WOG economic reforms. *See also* INDUSTRIAL ASSOCIATIONS: OBEDINENIE, p. 199; SOLIDARITY, p. 303.

Significance   It would be unfair to single out the abortive WOG reform as the carrier of the Polish economic disaster in the late 1970s and early 1980s. Rather, the fate of the WOGs is best understood as shorthand for all that contributed to the Polish crisis of 1980. The inability of the system to reform itself, even in the face of economic disaster, is not peculiarly Polish. An entrenched planning and administrative bureaucracy, with its symbiotic relationship with management and party, apparently can be reformed only by a determined leadership. This the Gierek leadership lacked, as it also lacked full legitimacy and the ability to enforce decisions. The essential features of the Stalinist command economy imposed on Poland in 1946 were little changed. Once the administrative command system remained in place, the WOG reforms became a self-perpetuating failure when economic downturn hit Poland. Economic reform in Poland may also be inherently more risky than elsewhere. The Polish workers have thrice taken to the streets in protest of government-ordained price increases and brought down the communist leadership—in 1956, 1970, and 1980. The Polish polity also contains other centers of opposition, including the Roman Catholic Church, the intellectuals, and the peasants, all of whom played a role in Solidarity. The imposition of military rule in December 1981, the banning of Solidarity, and worsening economic conditions made economic reform in Poland all but impossible in the short-term future.

Joint Stock Companies   Soviet-controlled economic enterprises set up in Eastern Europe immediately after World War II. The Joint Stock Companies were so-called because they were organized on the principle of assets jointly contributed by the host country and the Soviet Union. Initially, Joint Stock Companies were set up in the former Axis countries (East Germany, Hungary, Romania, and Bulgaria); their contributions or "stock" consisted of assets seized from the defeated Axis Powers. Although a sizable proportion of these assets previously had been expropriated by the Axis from their prewar owners, the Soviet Union treated any assets contributed to the Joint Stock Companies as war reparations. The Soviet Union generally provided managerial and technical aid and some industrial equipment. The assets of the East European states were priced at prewar levels while the Soviet contributions were generally overvalued. Control rested with a Soviet-appointed management board, which prohibited the companies from trading on the free world market. The Joint Stock Companies paid no taxes to their host countries. Although advanced by Josef Stalin as a means of swiftly rebuilding war-devastated Eastern Europe, the Joint Stock Companies were far more an instrument of Sovietization and a means of integrating the East European economies into the Soviet system. Joint Stock Companies were also extended to the non-Axis nations, based on assets seized from the Axis occupiers or "purchased" at artificially low value. Joint Stock Companies were particularly important in the late 1940s in East Germany, where by 1948 they accounted for more than 70 percent of the industrial production, and in Romania, where they constituted more than one-third of the economy. As the assets of the Joint Stock Companies comprised the industrial base of several of the East European states, the Soviet Union thus achieved rapid control over their economies. The Joint Stock Companies were greatly resented by many in Eastern Europe and by 1950, Soviet control having largely been achieved, Stalin began to dissolve the Joint Stock Companies. *See also* COMIN-FORM, p. 313.

Significance   The Joint Stock Companies were a major instrument by which the Soviet Union consolidated its control over Eastern Europe in the immediate postwar years. The only East European state which had liberated itself from Nazi occupation largely through its own efforts, Yugoslavia, was also the only state where such enterprises were successfully resisted. The Soviet attempt to set up Joint Stock Companies in the Yugoslav aircraft and shipping industry in 1947 was used by the Yugoslav communist leadership as one of the justifications for their break with the Soviet Union in 1948. Although the Yugoslavs themselves had pursued a similar course in Albania, setting up six joint Yugoslav-Albanian companies in 1946, Soviet attempts at economic hegemony outraged them. Elsewhere, those East Europeans who criticized the economic exploitation practiced by the USSR in the early postwar years were charged with betrayal by Stalin, and as the Czech Evžen Löbl recounts, many were the victims of the Soviet-inspired purges of the early 1950s. Some analysts have pointed to the series of secret economic and military agreements signed by the Soviets and the Germans between 1921 and 1933 as the predecessor to the Joint Stock Companies. Under these agreements, which dealt with areas expressly forbidden to Germany by the Versailles Treaty, joint German-Soviet factories producing such forbidden items as aircraft and poison gas were set up on Soviet territory. These, however, were not aimed at gaining political control; only the legal arrangements are similar.

When the Joint Stock Companies were dissolved in the early 1950s, the Soviet government required the East European states to buy back their assets, a requirement which cost East Germany an estimated $2 billion. The Soviets retained control of only a few companies, such as *Sovromquartz*, the Romanian uranium mining company. The trading functions of the Joint Stock Companies were assumed by the Council of Mutual Economic Activity (CMEA, or COMECON), on a much more equal basis.

Khozraschet   The system of profit and loss accounting that ensures the economic accountability of a Soviet enterprise. *Khozraschet* rests on the principle of paying operating expenses out of the yield from production. All enterprises, and most industrial associations (*obedinenie*) are subject to khozraschet. Each enterprise keeps its own account with the State Bank; no charge is made for the use of state-owned capital equipment. The expected financial results of each enterprise or association are part of the economic plan. Usually the plan specifies a level of profits for each enterprise. "Profits above plan" are encouraged and rewarded with bonuses. *See also* ENTERPRISE, p. 191.

Significance   The goal of khozraschet is to ensure implementation of the economic plan with the most efficient use of resources. It rests on the power of the state planners to set prices, thus predetermining in effect the level of profits. When Josef Stalin instituted all-out centralization and industrialization in 1928, the underlying principle was that of "one nation, one factory." Enterprises were not held to economic accountability, being reimbursed solely according to plan targets, not for what they actually produced. The practice was quickly abandoned and khozraschet instituted.

Kolkhoz (**Collective Farm**)   The abbreviation for *Kollektivnoe khozyaistvo*, "collective economy," which is the Russian title for the dominant production unit in communist agriculture. *Kolkhoz* land is owned by the state and allocated in perpetuity to each collective farm. All other assets of the kolkhoz are collective property, which communist law treats as a lower form of socialist ownership. Kolkhoz members are not state employees as they are on state farms (*sovkhoz*es), but are considered to be members of self-managing collectives (*artel*'s) under state direction. In theory the kolkhoz is governed by a general meeting that elects a manager and admits and expels members. In practice, the manager is appointed by the party and functions under the direct orders of the state. Each kolkhoz must have a charter, which must be in conformity with the 1969 Model Kolkhoz Charter for the USSR. Until 1958, wages were based on the *trudoden'*, the workday, with points assigned to each job. Days worked were multiplied by the coefficient assigned to each job and wages paid only after all other obligations had been met. Kolkhoz peasants now receive minimum cash wages and since 1970 have been under the state insurance system, although both their wages and benefits lag behind industrial workers. Kolkhoz management and technical personnel, however, enjoy full benefits and much higher wages. State purchase plans dictate what the kolkhoz produces; most are assigned up to 60 different procurement targets. Profits are determined by state-set wages and profit margins are typically kept low. Supplies and equipment are allocated by the central authorities and usually must be purchased by the kolkhoz. Thus the kolkhoz possesses little autonomy, being subject to a multitude of bureaucratic controls. The kolkhoz must operate on a profit-and-loss basis (*khozraschet*), and many are constantly in debt. Other systemic constraints hamper productivity. Soviet agriculture, although based on large-scale farming, is under-mechanized and suffers from a lack of spare parts and repair facilities. Because roads are inadequate, harvests sometimes rot in the field. State orders may require a kolkhoz to repurchase the grain delivered to the state procurement agencies at 2.5 times the price paid the kolkhoz if its procurement targets also include livestock raising. In addition, the kolkhoz is generally responsible for intra-farm roads, schools, and other social improvements that elsewhere are provided by the state. The kolkhoz is thus the least favored form of production in communist-party systems, a situation which has prevailed since the 1930s. *See also* AGRO-INDUSTRIAL COMPLEX, p. 180; ARTEL', p. 182; COLLECTIVIZATION, p. 185; MIR, p. 28; SOVKHOZ, p. 229.

Significance   Soviet doctrine considers the kolkhoz an inferior form of socialism, a lower stage in the evolution to full communism. The kolkhoz became the dominant agricultural organization in the 1930s when Josef Stalin virtually forced the peasants into collectives. Collectivization was achieved at tremendous human costs, the estimated deaths from famine, forced deportation of recalcitrant peasants, and executions ranging past 10 million. Stalin used the kolkhoz to extend party control over the countryside and to exact capital for industrialization. Capital was extracted mercilessly; a kolkhoz might receive 8 rubles for the same amount that would cost the consumer over 300 rubles. Under the "revolution from above" that restructured Soviet society, agriculture became the stepchild, undercapitalized, underproductive, and exploited. Although Soviet doctrine advanced the kolkhoz as the heir to the traditional *mir*, the traditional self-governing Russian village, the result was to bind the peasants to the land as effectively as the serfs had been bound to landlord and state under the Czars. Not until the 1970s were peasants regularly issued the internal passports that would permit them to leave the farm. At Stalin's death, kolkhoz income and productivity were at approximately 1928 levels. Under Nikita Khrushchev and Leonid Brezhnev, the Soviet leadership made major efforts to better the lot of the kolkhozes, and to solve the enduring agricultural problem they inherited from Stalin. Many kolkhozes have been merged or transferred to state farms; in the Soviet bloc, only the USSR now has more land (52 percent) in state farms than in kolkhozes. In Eastern Europe the kolkhoz still dominates. Poland was largely decollectivized after 1956, but the state retains control through pricing and investments. Only Yugoslavia possesses a truly autonomous and private (85 percent) agricultural sector. Both Poland and Yugoslavia limit the size of private farms to about 37 acres (25 hectares). The typical East European kolkhoz is smaller than in the USSR, where the kolkhoz averages 8,450 acres (5,750 hectares) and employs over 500 peasants. Only Hungary, which has freed agricultural pricing and decision making from central control, is agriculturally self-sufficient. Reform of agricultural administration ranges from Hungary's market-oriented approach to Bulgaria's concentrated agro-industrial complexes. Although Soviet agriculture posted a 3 percent yearly growth rate through the mid-1970s, agriculture remains the weakest link in the system. The post-Brezhnev leadership inherited a series of commitments made in 1982 that include (1) provision for state funding of kolkhoz improvements and schools; (2) increased mechanization; (3) forgiving loans to debt-ridden kolkhozes; and (4) increasing investment in agriculture of up to one-third of all state investments. Whether the new leadership can, or will be able to, implement these commitments remains problematical. In all collectivized systems, productivity remains the crucial problem. While the West was able to achieve tremendous productivity with increased capital transfer and outflow of labor, no collectivized system has accomplished this through capital transfer alone, without structural change. Whereas most Western countries employ less than 10 percent in agriculture, communist systems range up to 45 percent, and almost one-third of the Soviet work force is still employed in agriculture. The kolkhoz economy remains overcentralized, characterized by an aging, unskilled, and feminized work force.

Labor Norms   The number of units of output or the volume of work that a worker must produce within a certain time limit. Labor norms are based on the work to be accomplished during a workshift, hour, workweek, or workday; most labor norms are determined by the individual enterprises. The labor norms are proposed by the enterprise management and trade union committee and submitted to the competent state agency under whose jurisdiction the enterprise operates. The state planning authorities specify the production targets, project labor expenditures, and set the amount of the wage fund. The wage fund is based on two indices: (1) the labor norms; and (2) the state-determined minimum wage rate. Jobs are classified, as in the United States Civil Service, and minimum wage rates are assigned by the State Committee on Labor and Wages on the authority of the USSR Council of Ministers. The labor norms specify the amount of work that a worker must produce within a given time period in order to fulfill the plan targets for the enterprise and receive his basic pay. Basic wages in the Soviet Union are therefore determined by physical indicators. The central planning authorities determine only the minimum wage scales, not the conditions and rate of work. Bonuses for overfulfillment are paid by the enterprise. *See also* COLLECTIVE AGREEMENT, p. 184; PLANNING, p. 220; TRADE UNIONS, p. 305.

Significance   Labor norms are a key component of the centralized economic planning process, enabling the planners to estimate future productivity and labor costs. The central authorities enjoy less control over the setting of labor norms than over minimum wage rates; therefore, the minimum wage rates are used to reallocate labor or to guarantee a priority industrial sector an adequate labor force. Typically, transportation, construction, and heavy industrial workers have been paid high minimum wage rates, although their labor norms may be lower or no more than those in less-favored sectors. The centrally fixed wage rates can also act as a determinant of occupational status. If the minimum rate for a certain occupation is low, as with general practice medical doctors, the result is usually a decline in occupational status. Although Soviet wage scales do not discriminate by sex, such occupations as retail sales, research assistants, and medical doctors, which are heavily feminized, are also at the low end of the wage scale. Since 1956 Soviet citizens have been permitted to change jobs voluntarily and many do in an economy of full employment and job security. Other than upping the basic wage scale, the state possesses two ways of providing occupational incentives and preventing maldistribution of labor resources: (1) permitting the labor norms to remain at a low level, or (2) reclassifying jobs at a higher grade. Several East European states, such as Hungary, have experimented with freeing the enterprises from rigid labor norms and centrally determined minimum wages. As in Yugoslavia, where the self-managed enterprise determines wages, the result has been increasing differentials in income. Reform proponents, however, argue that labor norms impede efficiency and innovation, by discouraging any activity that might result in increased productivity and subsequently higher labor norms. As the labor norms are set on the basis of information supplied by the producer, an enterprise benefits from understating labor capacity, thus receiving lower production targets.

Levelling   A theory that proposes that the distribution of material goods in a society be based on a system of equal wages and rewards for all. Levelling presupposes a classless society of sufficient abundance to assure adequate distribution. The idea, which has roots in the early Christian communities, was revived during the English Civil War when the Levellers proposed such a system. Socialist and Marxist thought includes a persistent strain of egalitarian levelling theories, but the concept has been consistently denounced by official Marxist theoreticians as a form of "primitive" or "vulgar" communism. Most communist-party states have attempted to reduce wage differentials but continue to reward the acquisition of higher skills with higher wages. In 1917–18, the Bolsheviks made a brief attempt to peg all administrative and managerial salaries at the average worker's pay, but the effort soon foundered on the realities of waging a civil war and the need to keep the state operating. In 1921 a faction of the Bolshevik party, the Workers Opposition, proposed a drastic levelling in wages and greater intraparty democracy. After Lenin suppressed the Workers Opposition and outlawed all such "factions," levelling came to be associated with treasonable opposition to the Soviet system. *See also* LABOR NORMS, p. 207; WORKERS OPPOSITION, p. 34.

Significance   Although the classless communist society promised by Marxism is congenial with such a distribution system, levelling has been renounced by communist parties in power. The communist dictum, "from each according to this ability, to each according to his needs," as prescribed by Karl Marx in *The Communist Manifesto,* has been amended under socialism to ". . . to each according to his work." Although some maintain that communism has reneged on its egalitarian promise, the major thrust of communism in power has been on industrialization rather than egalitarianism. Levelling is regarded as impossibly utopian for a developing society. Until 1968, the Soviet bloc state with the smallest income differentials was Czechoslovakia, where unskilled workers were frequently paid almost as much as university graduates. This "excessive" levelling was singled out by Czechoslovak economic reformers as a major contributor to the economic stagnation that plagued the country in the 1960s and that helped set the stage for the brief period of liberalization in 1968. Since the Soviet-directed suppression of the 1968 liberalization, income differentials have been brought in line with the other East European states. In practice, levelling policies have been applied mainly to unskilled industrial workers. Farmers traditionally lag behind, favored workers such as miners are paid more, and state bureaucrats are well paid. Communist-party systems also exhibit the sex differentials found in capitalist systems; occupations such as textiles or sales that are heavily female are also the least well paid.

Libermanism   Economic reforms proposed in the 1960s that emphasized the role of market forces and greater autonomy for individual productive enterprises. Libermanism grew out of the realization that the Stalinist system of rigid, centralized economic planning, which emphasized production goals over all else, was increasingly incompatible with an economy of relative affluence and consumer sophistication. The reforms are closely identified with Evsei Liberman, an industrial economist at the University of Kharkov, who in 1962 published a series of proposed economic reforms in *Pravda* that proposed economic decentralization and the partial reinstitutionalization of market forces in selected industries. Liberman's proposals, which became known as the Liberman Plan, centered on incentives to management and workers to reduce production costs and improve quality and product mix. Workers and managers were to be rewarded on the basis of profits, not on fulfilling the Plan. Libermanism proposed essentially that supplies be adjusted to consumer demand, as determined by the profitability of each enterprise, rather than determined solely by the central planning apparatus. Libermanism did not propose to do away entirely with central planning; the goal was to make planning more efficient by relating investment allocation and prices to production costs and sales. In effect, the market mechanism would determine the acquisition of supplies as well as the sale of end products. Khrushchev applied Libermanism to selected textile factories with some success, and, after his ouster, Premier Aleksei Kosygin, who had supported some of Liberman's ideas, continued to press for economic reform. In 1965, the "Statute on Socialist State Productive Enterprises" granted managers greater autonomy in the allocation of capital and long-range planning. Initially, Kosygin and his allies achieved some success in using Libermanism in selected consumer and light industrial enterprises to ameloriate the rigidities of central planning, but as with the *Sovnarkhoz* reforms of Khrushchev, Libermanism was opposed by many party members who were wary of decentralizing power. Key reforms were introduced only hesitantly and mandatory planning remained in force for all basic production schedules. Thus, the Liberman innovations were effectively frustrated; prices continued to be based on cost-plus rather than on market demand and quality. Bureaucrats at all levels resisted any loss of control, and the enterprise managers themselves proved reluctant to trade a sure salary for market-based bonuses. By the late 1960s, the central party bureaucracy had successfully maintained its control over the economy. Although a few Liberman-style reforms survived, as with the earlier Sovnarkhoz reform, Libermanism was essentially finished by the early 1970s. *See also* NEW ECONOMIC MECHANISM, p. 217; SOVNARKHOZY, p. 230.

Significance   Libermanism and its fate typifies the ongoing debate in Soviet society as to the role of market forces vis-a-vis the role of central planning. The crux of the issue is the reluctance of the central authorities to permit any diminution of their power, and the fear of regional inequalities. As long as prices and major investment decisions are centrally determined, Libermanism and similar reforms have little chance. In the Liberman Plan, prices and economic rewards were pegged to economic performance. Soviet authorities felt that this could have the same result that market socialism has produced in Yugoslavia, namely, the diminution of party control and increasing inequities in salaries. Moreover, they felt that, as in Yugoslavia, Libermanism would tend to promote regional inequalities. Any implementation of a market-oriented system would mean the curtailment of central planning and a distinct loss of power for the central authorities. It was feared that Libermanism might stimulate regional and ethnic nationalism, always a touchy issue in the multinational Soviet state. By the 1980s, central planning has come to be conducted with greater flexibility and sophistication, but the basic structure of the Soviet economy remains unchanged, not substantially or permanently affected by the impact of Libermanism.

Machine Tractor Station (MTS)   A state agency, created by Josef Stalin in 1928, that controlled the utilization of agricultural equipment on the collective farms (*kolkhozes*). The Machine Tractor Station was a key element in Stalin's drive to forcibly collectivize Soviet agriculture. It functioned as a central depot for agricultural machinery and repair and served as agent of procurement for the government. Until abolished by Nikita Khrushchev in 1958, the MTS was the chief vehicle of party control in the countryside. Collective farms were obliged to pay for the services of the MTS, frequently in deliveries of agricultural products; by 1952, 68 percent of all grain deliveries to the state were in the form of MTS payments. Added to compulsory deliveries to the state mandated by the economic plans, the system meant that the collective farm was usually in arrears and at the mercy of the MTS. From 1933 to 1953, each MTS included a Political Department charged with general political surveillance over the collective farms on its territory. Directives issued by the MTS were binding on the collective farms. Because the work of the MTS was set by the central planning authorities, the plans frequently were not suitable for local agricultural conditions. See also COLLECTIVIZATION, p. 185; KOLKHOZ, p. 205.

Significance   Khrushchev's abandonment of the MTS system constituted a major step in his de-Stalinization campaign and the effort to place Soviet agriculture on a more rational basis. The initial objective of the MTS was to create a pool of skilled labor and modern equipment for agriculture. Prior to 1928 the government had attempted to mechanize agriculture but with generally disastrous results; most of the expensive imported machinery was ruined for lack of maintenance. Thus, initially, the MTS made economic sense, but as Stalin tightened his grip over the peasantry, the MTS became more a tool of terror, charged with ferreting out local "subversives." The strict centralization decreed by Stalin was especially difficult to apply to local agricultural conditions. Payment to the MTS was set by the party, not in relation to the efficient use of their resources. Their power was such that local organs of government, such as the soviets, atrophied, and few farms contained their own primary party organizations. Khrushchev was determined to create a self-regulating agricultural sector that would increase output. As the MTSs were abandoned and their machinery allocated to the farms, each farm organized its own primary party organization, and today, that, rather than the MTS, is the locus of party control on the farm.

Market Socialism   A form of worker-based industrial democracy in a socialist system that relies on workers' self-management and a free market to determine economic activities. The concept of market socialism was developed by Yugoslavia under Josip Broz Tito as a means of maintaining the country's socialist system while freeing it from Soviet control. The concept eschews the central control of Soviet-style communism for a new form of social and economic decision making based on grassroots participation and control. Market socialism rests on two fundamentals: (1) social ownership of the means of production by the society at large; and (2) management of social property by the workers, operating within the framework of a market

economy in which central control over planning and resource allocation is delegated. The concept developed as a critique of Soviet
practice, centering on the premise that uncontrolled state power,
capitalist or socialist, is inherently dictatorial. In 1948, the Soviet Union
expelled Yugoslavia from the Cominform, the Soviet-controlled association of European communist parties. The expulsion centered on the
refusal of the Yugoslav communist leadership to accept total subordination to Soviet power. The underlying conflict thus concerned national
sovereignty, not ideology, but the Yugoslavs, in developing a rationale
for their refusal to subordinate national interests to the interests of the
Soviet Union, developed a critique that gave theoretical substance to
the Yugoslav insistence on the equality of socialist nations. The
Yugoslav reassessment of the Soviet model focused on the Soviet
party's monopoly of power. Such a critique has roots in the unique
development of the postwar Yugoslav state. Rather than a "revolution
from above," the Yugoslav communists came to power in 1945 by
means of a successful domestic revolution that the communist-led
Partisan Army carried out without help from the Soviet Union. In
terms of historical analogies, it far more resembled the Chinese
communist rise to power than the Bolshevik Revolution. During the
1941–45 guerilla war against the Axis occupiers, the Partisans gained
widespread support and emerged as the only legitimate national force
in the country. The habits of independent decision making developed
in the process of the Partisan War, the careful attention to ethnic
equality, and the fact that most of the core Partisan leadership was
peasant and worker-based gave the Communist Party of Yugoslavia an
independent and egalitarian ethos lacking elsewhere. Although initially the Tito leadership followed Soviet practice by nationalizing what
remained of the meager industrial base and centralizing political
power, when Josef Stalin demanded that Yugoslavia accept total
subordination to the Soviet Union, the Yugoslavs refused. The Communist Party of Yugoslavia was thus forced to justify its existence as a
Marxist socialist state while repudiating the world leader of Marxism.
The instrument selected for this was the concept of self-managed
market socialism. The Yugoslavs argued that by establishing a monopoly of party power over all economic activities the Soviet party had
created a form of "state capitalism." The Yugoslavs proposed to alter
this, by returning to the original ideal of an "association of free
producers" and "self-management by producers." Control of the
socialist property was vested with the workers and the system of
mandatory economic planning dismantled. The linchpin of theory
became a melding of socialism and workers' democracy. In June of
1950, Tito proclaimed the new system in a major speech, "Workers
Manage Their Own Factories." The Yugoslavs claimed that this

represented the first step in the "withering away of the state," thus placing Yugoslavia further along the road to communism than the Soviet Union. They argued that a sovereign socialist nation had the right to "build its own road to socialism," a claim which further infuriated the Soviet leadership. The 1953 Fundamental Law, which replaced the Constitution of 1946, established Yugoslavia as a "socialist democracy" posited on self-management of the means of production and devolving much power to the local units of government. The Yugoslavs thus began a gradual evolution that decentralized and liberalized the system, transferring substantial decision-making powers to the organs of self-management. The term market socialism is best applied to the period between 1963, when a new constitution institutionalized the dramatic changes in the system, and 1974, when the threat of ethnic rivalries and worsening economic conditions brought the Tito leadership to reassert its power. Nonetheless, the underlying premise of market socialism— worker control and the utilization of the market mechanism—has remained in place. Federal intervention in the economy is limited to control over monetary policy, tariffs, investment policy, and currency exchange. Enterprise profits, not plan fulfillment, are the criteria for economic success. The 1974–76 reforms were undertaken in response to national rivalries, which threatened to immobilize the state, and the rise of managerial-technocratic power, which threatened to erode the basic principle of self-management. The devolution of power to republican and local bodies and the market mechanism caused the Yugoslav economy to become one of competition between the republics, a potentially dangerous situation because the constituent units of the Yugoslav federation are based on nationality groups with a long history of hostility. The very success of the market system led to a concentration of power in the largest, most modernized enterprises and thus a usurpation of the rights of self-management by management and technical personnel. The Yugoslav method of preserving the basics of their system was to broaden the workers' right of participation by breaking down the enterprise workers' councils into production units, the Basic Organizations of Associated Labor (BOALs), which became self-managing units with rights of disposal over earned income. Long-range national economic planning remained, but is coordinated by Social Compacts and Self-Management Agreements contracted between enterprises, social agencies, and the organs of local government. The history of market socialism in Yugoslavia has been one of continual evolution and change; the Yugoslavs would be the first to admit that it has not been a coherent theory. The basic principles, however, of a market-guided economy with "socialist" control exercised by the workers, have remained in place. *See also* COMMAND ECONOMY, p. 187; NEW ECONOMIC MECHANISM, p. 217; WORKERS' SELF-MANAGEMENT, p. 239.

Significance   Self-managed market socialism is the foundation upon which the unique Yugoslav system rests. It is the major distinguishing factor between the much more liberal Yugoslav system and its Marxist-Leninist counterparts in Eastern Europe. Economic reform has been the driving force behind the series of reforms that have transformed the Yugoslav state. As economic control was devolved to the enterprise level and the market mechanism instituted, political control was also devolved to local levels. A true devolution of power, not a mere decentralization of central power, resulted. As local and republican governmental bodies assumed substantive powers, the party began to resemble in truth the Leninist description of "a leading force" in society, exercising its power through consensus rather than *diktat*. The dismantling of the central command system has been accompanied by disappearance of secret police terror and most pre-censorship, unimpeded travel to the West, the opening of Yugoslavia's markets to foreign goods, extensive tourism, and a far greater tolerance for pluralism. It has substantially changed the nature of the party and given the institutions of government true substance apart from party will. With the death of Tito in May of 1980, Yugoslavia became the first communist-party state to adhere peacefully to a constitutionally ordained plan of succession. Market socialism in Yugoslavia has exhibited many of the problems associated with western systems: inflation, unemployment, increasing income differentials, and growing regional disparities. The Yugoslav experiment has also been plagued by the situation in which it was applied: an ethnically fragmented and economically backward state; by almost all economic indicators in 1940 it ranked only above Albania in Eastern Europe. Furthermore, the war destroyed most of the meagre industrial base, one-fifth of the housing, and left 11 percent of the population dead. Of the 18 Allied countries involved in the war, Yugoslavia accounted for 17 percent of all Allied losses. That Yugoslavia has prospered under the flexibility of market socialism has been a powerful argument. The Yugoslav system has been attractive to many new nations. Yugoslavia's independence from the Soviet bloc has permitted Yugoslavia to play an international role out of proportion with the state's actual power. Yugoslavia was a founder of the nonalignment movement and has been a leading influence in the Third World. As an alternative to both liberal democratic capitalism and Leninism, market socialism raises troubling questions as it goes to the core doctrine of each: the definition of democracy and the role of the proletariat. Self-managed market socialism has been anathema to the Soviet Union, as illustrated by the fact that attempts to institute some elements of the Yugoslav system have been suppressed either by the Soviet communist party, as in Czechoslovakia in 1968, or by the native power elite. The reaction of the Soviet leadership and its East European counterparts attests to the accuracy of the Yugoslavs' critique of Soviet communism as the entrenched power monopoly of the party elite. Market socialism as a theoretical model lacks coherency; early proponents, such as Oskar Lange, combined enterprise decision making with central planning. Many Western observers still use market socialism to describe the Yugoslav system, but in Yugoslavia itself it is used infrequently.

National Income (NI)   The standard Soviet measurement of the total annual value of the material product of the economy. The national income is the sum of the final sales prices of all material goods produced, less the prices of goods used in production and depreciation of fixed assets. National income, as used by Soviet economists, makes a firm distinction between "productive" and "nonproductive" services, with only the former being considered as generating material production and thus included in national income. Therefore, only those services rendered to direct production are included: typing in a steel factory is included, typing in a government office is not. National income can also be defined as the total consumable material product of the national economy. The total also includes the turnover tax, a tax applied to and included in the final sales price. *See also* GROSS INDUSTRIAL OUTPUT, p. 197; TURNOVER TAX, p. 235.

Significance   National income statistics are not comparable to Western measurements of national income, such as gross national product (GNP), since they exclude most services and include turnover taxes. The distinction between "productive" and "nonproductive" services creates some arbitrary exclusions. For example, postal services to individuals and passenger travel are "nonproductive." Therefore, a railway worker's wages are "productive" only when servicing freight trains. In addition, East European national income statistics may make different distinctions; some, for example, include passenger travel in national income. The turnover tax, included in national income, is applied at varying rates. In contrast, Western statistics exclude sales taxes from national output and adjust for indirect taxation. Also, official measurements of the material product are inherently biased toward overestimation because inflation is usually underestimated in centrally-planned economies. National income statistics for the Soviet bloc countries are useful as a means of detecting yearly changes within the economy but not as a standard of measurement against Western economies.

New Economic Mechanism (NEM)   A Hungarian economic approach that constitutes the most comprehensive departure from the Soviet economic model ever implemented in the communist bloc. The economic reforms undertaken by Hungary in 1968, collectively referred to as the New Economic Mechanism, shifted the nation's economy from the central command model to one of decentralization and substantial market orientation. Under the NEM the Hungarian leadership has instituted decentralization of the economic planning system, freed most prices from government control, awarded incentives for increased productivity, and permitted a greater role for market forces. The new approach was preceded by a series of reforms that were included in the NEM: (1) quality, not quantity, norms; (2) increased profit retention by enterprises and a profit-sharing plan; (3) the reordering of investment priorities from heavy industry to consumer and export goods; and (4) curbing of the powers of the ministerial authorities. The industrial associations, first instituted in 1959, and the individual enterprises were permitted to hire and fire labor, determine production, and negotiate contracts. Under the NEM, agriculture was freed from compulsory state deliveries, agricultural prices were decontrolled, and cooperative farmers were permitted to engage in nonagricultural pursuits (such as machine repair and restaurants) for profit. The private sector was expanded, particularly in the service area. Turnover taxes were slashed and the prices of all but a few basic commodities were decontrolled. Incentive bonuses were awarded for selling goods, not for plan fulfillment. Most annual planning was abandoned in favor of using incentives based on profits; central planning was confined to setting priorities and long-range goals. All of these changes were reflected in new enterprise statutes that legalized the position of the enterprises. The state retains responsibility for long-range planning, general guidelines, credit policy, the prices of a few basic commodities, taxes, and the money supply. Since the formal inception of the NEM, the Hungarian economy has apparently benefitted in terms of higher growth rates (particularly in agriculture), greater consumer satisfaction, and increased trade with the West. As with all of Eastern Europe, Hungary has not been immune to the economic shocks of the 1970s and the worldwide economic slowdown in the 1980s. By 1976, the state had recentralized to some degree, returning to a single comprehensive draft economic plan and restoring centrally controlled allocation for large enterprises. Despite this, the Hungarian economy in the 1980s remains the most decentralized and flexible of the East European systems. It is by far the most successful attempt to reform the centrally controlled economic system inherited from Josef Stalin. *See also* COMMAND ECONOMY, p. 187; HUNGARIAN UPRISING OF 1956, p. 323; MARKET SOCIALISM, p. 212;

Significance   Only Hungary, with the New Economic Mechanism, has been able to shift from the intensive growth model of Stalin to one of improved productivity and decentralization. Opinions vary as to why the Soviet leadership has permitted János Kádár's Hungary to institute the NEM while stifling economic reform elsewhere in Eastern Europe. The most common reasons advanced are (1) the Hungarian leadership itself, under Kádár's direction, undertook the reforms (but so did the Czechoslovak party leadership in 1968); (2) after the Soviets put down the 1956 Hungarian revolt, they felt impelled to permit some loosening of control lest the state erupt once more; (3) the NEM was introduced only after years of preparation, at a time when the Hungarian economy was relatively healthy; (4) Kádár began his reforms when Nikita Khrushchev, who urged such economic reform, was still in power in the USSR; (5) the major reform package, the NEM, was introduced in 1968 when the Soviet leadership was preoccupied with the crisis in Czechoslovakia; (6) 10 million Hungarians are not that crucial to the USSR's self-image of power; and (7) Kádár has very carefully followed the Soviet line internationally, including participation in the 1968 Soviet-led invasion of Czechoslovakia. Whatever the reasons, it is often said that the Hungarians have managed to implement quietly most of what the Czechoslovaks proposed in 1968. The NEM has changed power relationships in Hungary; the power of the managers has increased at the expense of the administrative authorities. Critics from the left charge that the NEM has engendered a "petty bourgeois mentality." Wage differentials have increased, benefitting in particular the workers in agriculture and industry. With the drive to increase productivity, institutions of higher learning now make admissions based on talent rather than on class origins. Thus, for some sectors, upward mobility has declined. Nonetheless, the real gains have evidently both stayed the Soviets' hand and strengthened the Kádár regime. Under NEM, Hungary remains a directed economy operating in a one-party state, but with sizable increments of incentives, indicative planning, and market considerations. For the Hungarians, NEM has functioned possibly as a substitute for political reform.

New Economic Policy (NEP)   Economic reforms begun by Lenin in 1921 in response to the massive opposition aroused by the economic policies imposed by the Bolsheviks during the period of War Communism. The New Economic Policy (NEP), which lasted until 1928, amounted to a substantial reversal in policy and abrogated much of the Bolshevik radicalism of War Communism. Lenin announced the NEP in March of 1921 at the Tenth Party Congress, which met in the face of widespread peasant uprisings, urban riots, and the Kronstadt

Revolt, all of which convinced most of the party that they were in danger of losing control. The NEP abandoned the forced-draft policies of War Communism and the mandatory grain requisitions that so incensed the peasants. It created a mixed economy, with state-controlled heavy industry and banking combined with private agriculture and free trade. The consumer sector was largely freed from central control, a free market in agricultural products was set up, and small private enterprise was permitted. The government attempted to create a stable currency, introduced accounting into industry, and reinstated cash wages for industrial workers. Profit-making became the chief engine of the economy. The state was given no priority in obtaining goods; if a private trader offered a better price, the enterprise could sell goods to him. Such private traders, who became known as Nepmen, flourished under the system and by 1923, 50 percent of all wholesale trade and 78 percent of all retail trade was private. The first years of the NEP were a period of rapid economic recovery. The private sector predominated in agriculture, and the chief goal of the NEP—to conciliate the peasants—was achieved. The relaxation of central planning and economic control increased support for the Bolsheviks. The latter NEP years, 1924 to 1928, coincided with the period of intense political struggle within the party after Lenin's death. Stalin's seizure of absolute power meant the end of the NEP, and in 1928 he announced the first Five-Year Plan, marking a return to tight central control, the end of private enterprise, and the start of the program to collectivize agriculture. *See also* FIVE-YEAR PLAN, p. 192; LEFT OPPOSITION, p. 24; WAR COMMUNISM, p. 237.

Significance   The New Economic Policy represents the highwater mark of Soviet liberalism. Intraparty democracy existed, and the party functioned as the major institution of the Soviet system. The NEP greatly increased support for the new government and gave it time to recuperate from the havoc of the Civil War. It was a purely pragmatic response to the opposition that threatened the party's control; as Lenin termed it, it was a policy of "two steps forward and one step backward." For the peasants in particular, the NEP years before forced collectivization were regarded as their best years. The relative liberalism of the NEP also marked the golden age of Soviet arts. Artistic expression was relatively free of party censorship and much innovation occurred, from Mayakovsky's expressionist poetry to Zamyatin's science fiction. The theater flourished with such figures as Meyerhold and Stanislavsky, who still influence modern drama. The burst of creativity was evident in all forms of cultural activity until stifled by Stalin's demand for total conformity. The NEP for a short period created two Soviet Unions, a relatively free countryside and cultural scene with a socialized, party-controlled industrial sector, both of which managed to coexist and revive the Soviet economy.

Planning   The fundamental principle upon which a Soviet-style or other form of socialist command economy rests. Economic planning and state ownership of the means of production, in Soviet-style systems, have been combined to create a single state monopoly over which the party wields all control. Planning in the Soviet Union is carried out by the central planning agency, *Gosplan*, the regional Gosplans, the economic ministries, and the central party leadership. The plans issued by Gosplan cover several time spans: the long-range 10- or 20-year plans, the 5-year (medium term) plans, and the 1-year operational plans. At the enterprise level, the plan is further divided into quarterly and monthly plans. The most important is the 5-year plan that sets the planned increases for each sector of the economy and indicates the major capital investments for the next five years. Although many governments of the world practice long-range economic planning, Soviet planning differs in that it is not "indicative" as in most other systems, but "imperative"—the production targets set by the plans are legally compulsory because they have been enacted into law by the Supreme Soviet. The relevant government ministries are charged with administering the plans, ensuring that the enterprises and cooperatives under their jurisdiction fulfill the portion of the plan allocated to them. Failure of the "plan carriers" (the enterprises and cooperative) to fulfill their legally mandated responsibilities carry civil and criminal law sanctions. The Soviet planning system is highly centralized; the most crucial decisions, the planned rates of increase by economic sector, are made by the Politburo. Planning begins with the establishment of control ciphers that indicate the planned increases for key sectors of the economy. As the determination of which sectors of the economy are to receive increased capitalization and attention is a political decision, the control ciphers apparently are developed by the party Politburo and Central Committee, on the advice of the Council of Ministers and Gosplan. The setting of control ciphers thus reflects the policy priorities of the party leaders; Gosplan and its coordinating organs (such as the State Committee for Labor and Wages and the State Committee for Supply) develop the overall set of control ciphers. These are handed down to the ministerial departments, the lower planning organs, and eventually to the enterprises and cooperatives, the "plan carriers." On the basis of its share of the control ciphers each enterprise prepares a draft plan that in turn is passed upward through the hierarchical planning system and, after adjustment at each level, eventually reaches Gosplan. Gosplan aggregates the draft plans into a single "State Plan for the Development of the National Economy," which is then enacted as law. The heart of the developmental, or five-year, plan are the indices, which set forth the changes to be effected in each area of the economy; industrial output, national income, state capital investments, labor productivity, profits, turnover of trade, and retail trade. The plan is further divided into sections and indices dealing with each branch of the economy, such as agriculture or transport, and includes sections devoted to planned investment, social welfare services, and regional development. Indices are usually expressed in percentages of expected increase over the previous planning period. Another section of the plan, the material balances, forms the basis of the supply allocations made to various economic sectors. The plan is then disaggregated, first to the ministerial level where each ministry handles that portion of the plan under its jurisdiction (transport, construction, coal mining) and finally to the level of each enterprise or industrial association, to which the ministry assigns a specific percentage of the targeted production. The enterprises and associations develop the technical-production-financial plan (*tekhprom-finplan*), the operational plan necessary to carry out production. The tekhpromfinplan is accompanied by a material balance plan, which when aggregated includes the total national amount of all resources and the uses of every product. Resources include all domestic production, imports, and inventories. The total use includes all intermediate utilization in the manufacturing process, use by the government (civilian and military), and domestic consumption by citizens. This part of the planning process constitutes the authorization for state allocation of labor, wages, and materials necessary to meet each enterprise's production targets. The tekhpromfinplan also details costs, levels of profit, and capital expenditure necessary to planned production. Then, under the direction of Gosplan, and ultimately of the party leaders, the government agencies issue binding directives to the enterprises and cooperatives. These directives, mandated by the plan, specify level of production by units within a specific time period, payments to and disbursements from the state budget, prices, wages, levels of labor productivity (labor norms), the source of supplies, and to whom the product must be delivered. Most output targets are quantitative—so many units of production—but the production targets may include quality norms as well. *See also* COMMAND ECONOMY, p. 187; FIVE-YEAR PLAN, p. 192; GOSPLAN, p. 196.

Significance   Since Josef Stalin initiated the first Five-Year Plan in 1928, central planning has become the hallmark of the Soviet system and its East European counterparts. Undergirding the planning system is the regime-proclaimed goal of building communism. Since Vladimir Lenin, communists have interpreted this as mandating economic industrialization; that only from a position of plenty and power can full communism be achieved. Therefore, from its beginnings Soviet communism has been a developmental strategy as well as a method of governance. The building of communism is also the major legitimating device of the ruling communist party, certifying the monopoly rule of the party as necessary. In addition, Soviet theory maintains that central planning is the solution to the recurring crises of capitalism. Planning in the Soviet Union rests on the following constants: (1) state ownership; (2) administrative control over all economic activities; (3) the party's monopoly of power; and (4) the central planning apparatus. Production for profit and the market are incompatible with socialism. In practice, Soviet planning falls short of the model. As the Soviet Union has industrialized, the number of decisions required are mind-boggling. By one estimate, plan tasks have increased 1,600 fold since 1928. Frequent plan revisions are the norm. In practice, the one-year plans have become adjustments to the previous year's experience, rather than operational plans. There are, moreover, important parts of the economy over which the state agencies have but limited control, such as the labor movement, private agricultural production, and barter and all else included in the Second Economy. East European planning is mainly distinguishable from the Soviet by the degree of disaggregation. In general, the more aggregated the central plan remains, the more flexible and market-oriented the system. In Hungary the plan remains aggregated; the Hungarian enterprise manager negotiates with his own customers and suppliers and bases his plan on the projected results. In East Germany, the industrial associations have substantial responsibility for determining specific economic activities. Yugoslavia has abjured mandatory central planning altogether; economic policy and long-range goals are implemented through cooperative agreements between the government and the individual autonomous enterprises. Other than in Yugoslavia, the planning apparatus and its adminstrative bureaucracy have been the major loci of resistance to economic reform.

Private Plots   Small garden plots allocated to peasants, state workers and employees, retirees, and others for the purpose of raising agricultural produce and livestock for personal consumption. In the Soviet Union, these private plots comprise about 3 percent of the total arable land but account for over one-quarter of the gross agricultural output, according to one recent Soviet estimate. Since the forced collectivization of agriculture in the early 1930s, the private plots have existed within a system of state-controlled agriculture. The state retains ownership of all land but grants the right of usage to individuals and households. The size of the plots is fixed by republican law, varying from republic to republic, and by condition of the land; the size generally ranges from 0.3 to 1.5 acres (0.1 to 0.6 hectares) per plot. Laws also stipulate what type of buildings may be erected on the plots, what improvements may be made, and what types of usage are permissible. The private plots fall into two main categories: those farmed by peasant farmers and those allocated by the enterprises and state agencies to workers, employees, and retirees—such as Nikita Khrushchev who, after his forced retirement from the Soviet leadership, proudly tilled a private plot. The management of the state enterprises (including the state farms, the *sovkhozes*) oversees the allocation of the plots under their jurisdiction. When a worker or employee terminates employment, he loses all rights to the private plot, including any improvements made. On collective farms (*kolkhozes*), the norms for plot size and permissible numbers of livestock are set by each farm's charter. A collective farm household retains the right of usage as long as its members remain in the collective. If they leave or the family dies out, the plot is redistributed among the membership. Compulsory state deliveries from the collective farm plots were abolished by Khrushchev in 1958. Produce from the plots may be sold to the collective, at cooperative markets, or in the peasant markets where prices are allowed to fluctuate. Currently, an estimated 41.6 million Soviet households (about 168 million people) till private plots. *See also* KOLKHOZ, p. 205; SECOND ECONOMY, p. 225.

Significance   Originally the private plots were a concession made by Josef Stalin to the peasants after the brutality of the forced collectivization. When communism came to Eastern Europe after World War II and the new communist leaderships embarked on collectivization, the private plot system was retained. Ideologically, they represent an uncomfortable compromise between the doctrine of full socialization of all means of production and the reality of an agricultural system that frequently has failed to provide an adequate diet. The Brezhnev leadership followed a pragmatic policy toward private plot farming, accepting the crucial role they play, regularizing their position, and providing better marketing outlets. Hungary has progressed furthest in encouraging their use, integrating them into the collective and state farm system. In Bulgaria, where 97.4 percent of the land is nationalized, the private plots are also officially encouraged. In Czechoslovakia, with 90 percent of the land nationalized, and Romania, with 90.6 percent, the private plots exist alongside a small system of private mini-farms. East Germany, where 99 percent of the land is nationalized, also encourages the private plots. Poland and Yugoslavia, where over 80 percent of the arable land is held in private ownership, do not have such a system. Poland, however, retained compulsory state deliveries from private sector agriculture until 1975. Some analysts maintain that the kolkhoz economy would be impossible without the symbiotic relationship that has developed between the collective farm and the intensely tilled private plots. The collective farm provides in-kind payments of fodder and seeds to the private plot tillers and in turn depends upon the private plots to produce feeder livestock and other crops to fulfill its production targets. The private plots are not only a means of subsistence for the collective farmers but also provide a second income for many, with their output constituting an important part of the unofficial, non-sanctioned Second Economy. Thus, within a nationalized agricultural system, an unofficial division of labor exists, with the private plots concentrated on crops and livestock requiring intensive inputs of labor.

Producers' Goods and Consumers' Goods   The two main categories into which all material production is divided. Soviet economics follows Karl Marx's dichotomous classification of all production into producers' goods or consumers' goods, known as Department I and Department II. Department I of the economy produces all goods that are used in the process of production, and Department II, those goods that are consumed. A further refinement has been added by the Soviets: the division of all industrial production into Group A, producers' goods, and Group B, consumers' goods. Groups A and B then deal strictly with industrial production, whereas under the original Marxian scheme Departments I and II include both industrial and agricultural products, according to their end use. Groups A and B should not be confused with so-called "heavy industry" and "light industry." As end use is the determinant, a product such as textiles may be in Group A if manufactured for further processing, but in B if it is sold directly to consumers. *See also* PLANNING, p. 220.

Significance   The respective share allotted to producers' goods and consumers' goods in the Soviet economy has been the subject of ongoing debate. Soviet economic planning often has been accused of neglecting the consumer sector. While the investments allotted to Group B have increased since 1966, those branches of industry that produce producers' goods, frequently the so-called "heavy industry" branches, do receive priority. Such industries are characterized by higher pay rates, higher investment rates, better research and development, and preferential access to transportation and high quality materials. On the other hand, it can be argued that if bottlenecks develop in crucial producers' goods, much of the economy is affected. Defense-related production also blurs the picture. Apparently, most of it is included in Group A, although it certainly may be questioned whether military hardware constitutes producers' goods. Additionally, for Western economic analysis, the inclusion of military hardware in Group A (producers' goods) probably distorts any effort to correlate Soviet economic growth with increased levels of producers' goods.

Regional Wage Differentials   Wage supplements paid to workers in the Northern, Far Eastern, and Central Asian regions of the Soviet Union. The regional wage differentials are intended to attract skilled workers to these remote, harsh regions, and to equalize living standards with those in the European Soviet Union. Wage differentials are paid upon completion of a required term of work; they are thus intended to create a stable work force as well as to attract workers. Soviet wage policy also grants regional wage coefficients (higher base pay rates), which are applied immediately. Most workers in the remote regions receive both. *See also* LEVELLING, p. 209.

Significance   Regional wage differentials represent a continuation of the Stalinist policy of providing material incentives for key sectors of the economy, and a repudiation of the egalitarianism of Marxism. They also attest to the existence of a free labor market in the centrally-planned Soviet economy, emphasizing the fact that Soviet workers may freely change jobs. The wage differentials on the whole have been successful, enticing skilled labor to the remote regions of the USSR. In some Asian areas of the USSR they have led to the Russification of the cities, creating islands of European Russians in an Asian countryside. The opening up of the vast Siberian lands to mining and manufacturing in the late 1960s made such wage differentials necessary, as the post-Stalinist leadership could no longer depend on prison camp labor to develop these remote regions.

Second Economy (Parallel Economy)   The term given to a wide range of unauthorized economic transactions conducted by many citizens in the Soviet Union and Eastern Europe. The Second Economy embraces all economic activity conducted without government sanction for direct personal gain. It may be envisioned as operating parallel to the official "First Economy" where the state controls all production and market operations for the benefit of the state and society. The Second Economy ranges from barter trade and moonlighting to smuggling and bribery. Much of what is included in the Second Economy is based on the exchange of favors and mutual obligations and would not be considered criminal by Western legal norms. The key to understanding the Second Economy lies in the all-pervasive nature of a Soviet-style centralized economic system, which permits almost no private economic activity or ownership of production means. The Russian term, "*na levo*," meaning "on the left," describes the situation well, as so much of these activities involve services and trade considered criminal only because they violate the principle of state control over the economy and means of production. Other than peasant produce markets, there are no free markets in the Soviet Union. The na levo Second Economy thus provides the citizen with a way of circumventing the endemic shortages and inefficiencies of the consumer and service sectors. Na levo is especially prevalent in the service and repair sector. Moonlighting repairmen set up illegal private operations, frequently trading services for other services and favors. Thus a ticket to the Bolshoi can be transformed into a workable television set, or the butcher will save the best cuts for the doctor who can promise an immediate after-hours appointment. A sizable portion of the Second Economy involves *blat,* the Russian term for the art of using connections and influence. Blat may be used to short-circuit the cumbersome bureaucratic system and secure a favorable action from an official. Black market operations, which may involve stolen goods, smuggled goods, or goods produced illegally with state-owned equipment and goods, are especially prevalent in areas of scarcity, such as pharmaceuticals, building supplies, or auto parts. The simple trading of goods between citizens is not considered black market, but is still part of the Second Economy because the official state retail system plays no role in this redistribution of goods. More serious is the use of state property, either after hours, or pilfered from state enterprises and used for illegal production. The peasant farmer is permitted to sell the produce of his household plot but is not permitted the use of water, fertilizer, seeds, or tools from the collective farm to produce his crops. All of these activities frequently involve blat and its more serious forms, bribery and corruption, in order to secure protection from official action. *See also* CRIMES AGAINST SOCIALIST PROPERTY, p. 253; HARD CURRENCY STORES, p. 198; TOLKACH, p. 234.

Significance　　The Second Economy generally results from inefficiencies in the delivery system and shortfalls in the consumer and service sectors, consistently the stepchild of Soviet-style central planning. Other than illegal currency transactions, the Second Economy is less common in other East European states, especially Hungary, which provide more consumer goods and give greater scope to the private sector. All, however, possess underground markets in currency transactions; only Yugoslavia maintains a freely convertible currency. Elsewhere, hard currencies can only be exchanged at the state bank, where exchange rates are pegged artificially low. Since the street rate may be as much as five times the official rate, as in Poland during the late 1970s, many transactions in the Second Economy are carried out in hard currencies obtained from relatives abroad or from tourists. The opening up of the Soviet Union and Eastern Europe to Western tourism has increased this sector of the Second Economy. A sizable unofficial market in food products, much of it barter, exists in those states where most of the agricultural land is collectivized. The equivalent of blat is also present in Eastern Europe; the Yugoslavs call it "VIP" ("connections") and the Romanians, "C.P.R." (a word play on the acronym for the Communist Party of Romania). Some analysts maintain that the Second Economy is far more prevalent in Soviet Asia, Georgia, and Armenia than in the European Soviet Union. Others propose that it has institutionalized graft and bribery at all levels, including the purchase and sale of government posts presumably worth money because of access to bribery. The extent of the Second Economy, estimated at 10 to 20 percent of the Soviet official economy, makes it difficult to accurately assess Soviet or East European living standards, since none of it appears in official statistics.

Socialist Ownership   Ownership of the means of production by society, a fundamental tenet of Marxism-Leninism. Marxist-Leninist theory states that just as private ownership creates capitalism, socialist ownership creates socialism. Socialist ownership then is a necessary precondition for the building of socialism. In practice, socialist ownership has come to mean both ownership and control by the state. Under Marxism-Leninism, the state, as the instrument of the proletariat, nationalizes all land and property, ending the exploitation of the proletariat by the bourgeoisie. In the interests of the proletariat, the state manages the socially-owned means of production. With some deviations, communist systems have firmly adhered to the above principles. Immediately after the Bolshevik Revolution, Vladimir Lenin nationalized banking, industry, and transport. In 1928 Josef Stalin embarked on a massive program of state-directed industrialization that enforced almost universal nationalization of land and property, thus furnishing the prototype for succeeding communist systems. In the Soviet Union, socialist property includes all land, resources, and most real property; citizens are severely restricted as to what they can legally own, particularly property used for individual profit. Although the civil codes of the East European states exhibit some variations rooted in local history and circumstances, all embody the protection and preservation of socialist ownership as a common core. The legal codes establish a hierarchy of property rights, delineated by the degree of limitations set on possession and use. Socialist property is superior to all others; the state is subject to no restrictions in its use. The possession, use, and disposal of the property of social organizations, such as trade unions, cooperative bodies (consumer and housing cooperatives), and collective farms is more restricted. The use of the land and assets of collective farms is guaranteed free to members for perpetual use but may not be transferred and is not returned to farm members should the collective be dissolved. The enterprise acts as manager of the state's assets; the goods produced by the enterprise are state property and may be transferred only as stipulated in the state economic plans. Similarly, planned profits accruing from enterprise operations are also regarded as state property. Socialist property has been acquired through several avenues, including (1) nationalization of land and means of production; (2) state-determined contracts with agricultural producers; (3) tax revenues; (4) foreign trade; and (5) the state's share in revenues from production. In addition, communist civil codes contain provisions for further confiscation of property. Soviet civil law provides for forfeiture of property if property is used "contrary to the intention of these rights in socialist society during the building of communism" or if its usage does not "respect the rules of socialist living and the moral principles of a society building communism." Such provisions permit the Soviet government to confiscate untilled farmlands, underutilized resources, or, as also in the case of the Polish civil code, property suspected of being acquired by illegitimate means. *See also* CRIMES AGAINST SOCIALIST PROPERTY, p. 253; WORKERS' SELF-MANAGEMENT, p. 239.

Significance   The principle of socialist ownership of the means of production and distribution is a distinctive feature of a Soviet-style economic system. The East European states after World War II followed the Soviet model, with certain exceptions. East Germany retained a higher proportion of privately-owned production facilities, which, however, are subordinate to the authority of the central planners. The Polish communist leadership attempted to collectivize agriculture but retreated after the 1956 Polish outbreaks. Polish property law is also among the least restrictive in Eastern Europe. Since the inception of the New Economic Mechanism, Hungary has made more concessions to small-scale private enterprise and farming. The premise of socialist ownership remains in place: what the state concedes, it can also take away. Yugoslav law and theory treat socialist ownership much differently. Yugoslav law also restricts the amount and use of private property, although not as severely. Socialist ownership in Yugoslavia is defined as joint ownership by all members of society, with control vested in those who use the assets of society, the workers, who exercise usufruct, or the right to use property that belongs to all. Society, let alone the state, does not control socialist property. Yugoslav theory separates socialist ownership from control, pointedly maintaining that the power of the state to control the means of production exploits surplus value from the workers as much as does capitalist ownership and control. The Yugoslav critique of Soviet practice thus focuses on the chief source of the Soviet party's monopoly of power, the control achieved through what amounts to almost universal state ownership. Coupled with the principle of workers' self-management, the Yugoslav concept of socialist ownership has given the Yugoslav system a far different dynamic than other communist-party states where socialist ownership equals the state's monopoly of all economic activities.

Sovkhoz (**State Farm**)   The abbreviation for Soviet state farm, a large, state-owned agricultural operation that is organized and operated like an industrial enterprise. Contemporary Soviet leaders prefer the *sovkhoz* form of agricultural organization, which is considered by some ideologues to be closer to the goals of communism than the collective farm, the *kolkhoz*, which is in theory a collectively operated agricultural commune. Instead of delegating responsibility for the land to the members, as in the kolkhoz, the state retains direct ownership of and responsibility for all sovkhoz land and assets. The sovkhoz management is appointed by and is responsible to the ministries of agriculture. Sovkhoz workers are considered employees of the state and unlike the kolkhoz peasants are entitled to full welfare benefits, trade union membership, and a full-time yearly salary. The sovkhoz possesses legal identity and operates under the same laws as a state enterprise. It possesses no assets of its own, exercising only operational management. Many sovkhozes are united into production unions, called *trests* (trusts). The sovkhoz is usually better-equipped and receives substantial inputs of capital and goods from the state, unlike the kolkhoz. Although the sovkhoz must be economically accountable (*khozraschet*), the state frequently covers deficits with subsidies. Many sovkhozes operate as model farms or research institutions; others are devoted to large-scale grain operations. *See also* AGRO-INDUSTRIAL COMPLEX, p. 180; KOLKHOZ, p. 205.

Significance   The sovkhoz was instituted in 1929 as a demonstration of the advantages of fully socialized farming. As Josef Stalin's chosen instrument for the Sovietization of countryside, the sovkhozes have been favored above the collective farms. They proved to be no more productive, however, than the ideologically inferior collective farms, and by 1953 accounted for only 6 to 7 percent of all Soviet agricultural output. Stalin's successor, Nikita Khrushchev, embarked on a "sovkhozization" campaign, implemented through transferral of kolkhoz land to sovkhozes and by placing the newly cultivated "virgin lands" in sovkhozes. These actions greatly increased the percentage of land in the state farms. By 1971, 15,502 sovkhozes cultivated half the arable land, employed one-third of the agricultural population, and produced nearly one-third of the total output. Today, the average sovkhoz contains upwards of 20,000 hectares (49,420 acres) and employs up to 600 workers. Soviet policy continues to favor the sovkhozes over the kolkhozes, which receive a disproportionate share of agricultural investment. There is little proof, however, that the sovkhoz is more productive or efficient than the kolkhoz. Nevertheless, the "socialist transformation" promised by Stalin has developed to some extent. As kolkhozes are transferred to sovkhozes, many traditional peasant villages that form the nucleus of a kolkhoz are slated for extinction. East European systems also follow the Soviet distinction between the state farm and the collective farm with the exception of Poland and Yugoslavia, where most of the land was decollectivized in the 1950s and the remaining state-owned land is held in state farms.

Sovnarkhozy   The acronym for *Sovety narodnogo khozyaistva*, the Soviet regional economic councils set up by Nikita Khrushchev in 1957. The principal objective of the *Sovnarkhoz* reform was to decentralize Soviet economic planning and industrial management, and to replace it with a system of more flexible regional industrial councils. The central economic ministries, which had nationwide responsibility for a specific branch of industry, were abolished and their functions transferred to the Sovnarkhozy. The Soviet Union was divided into 101 economic regions, each corresponding roughly to a province (*oblast'*) or in a few cases, a small republic. The reform was also aimed at ending the system of central ministerial autarky that had frequently led to costly and unnecessary transshipments to facilities thousands of miles apart in order to "keep the business" within the ministry. Each Sovnarkhoz was responsible for managing all the industrial activities on its territory. It was hoped that regionalization would lead to better utilization of planning at all levels, transferring initiative from the central authorities to the local levels where production actually occurs.

Production was to be coordinated regionally, not nationally, by sector. Planning remained under the central control of Gosplan, although the Sovnarkhozy formulated the draft plans for their territory. As with all of the Khrushchev innovations, the Sovnarkhozy were abolished almost immediately after Khrushchev's ouster from leadership and by 1965 the economic ministries were restored. *See also* ANTI-PARTY GROUP, p. 86; LIBERMANISM, p. 210.

Significance   The Sovnarkhozy were part of Khrushchev's effort to improve economic efficiency and reform the party bureaucracy. The replacement of the economic ministries with regionally-based organizations diminished the power of the central bureaucracy and enhanced the powers of the provincial and local party, where Khrushchev's major support lay. As his ouster in 1964 proved, this was not enough to protect him. The Sovnarkhozy reform was followed by a major effort to restructure the party along industrial/agricultural lines, a reform that met a similar fate. Khrushchev also proposed that the Soviet Constitution be redrafted, replacing the federal structure with one based on comprehensive economic regions, an even more unacceptable move. From the beginning the Sovnarkhozy were embroiled in conflict over turf with the state planning apparatus, which proved to be highly resistant to change. The Sovnarkhozy added increased responsibilities for local governments, another of Khrushchev's goals, for which they were ill-prepared after decades of atrophy under Stalinism. In addition to undercutting the power of the central planning and administrative organs, the Sovnarkhozy threatened the military-industrial interests that under central command benefit from their status as high priority industries. The Sovnarkhozy reform was undertaken at the time when the death of Stalin and accession of Khrushchev had loosened the regime and permitted questioning of the central command system inherited from Stalin. The centrally institutionalized bureaucracy in charge of the Soviet economy appeared increasingly unable to cope with the complex economy it had created, while the more productive and flexible Yugoslav system pointed to the advantages of decentralization. Unlike the Yugoslavs, the Soviets were unwilling—or unable—to diminish the power of the central economic bureaucracies. The fate of the Sovnarkhozy illustrates the difficulty of reform in the Soviet Union, particularly reform aimed at decentralization that threatens the status quo power of the entrenched central bureaucracy. The Sovnarkhozy embodied many of the ideas of Libermanism, and, like Libermanism, was doomed. The Sovnarkhozy reform, however, did accomplish some change. Soviet planning was simplified, with fewer production targets planned from the center. When the old system of economic ministries was restored in 1965, some industrial branches that previously had been under direct federal control (all-union ministries) were placed under republican control (union-republic ministries) as a small concession to republican interests.

Stakhanovite   The name given to outstanding Soviet workers who overfulfill their official work quotas and are held up as an example to the rest of the work force. The Stakhanovite movement began in the 1930s as part of Josef Stalin's campaign for an all-out mobilization of the Soviet work force to industrialize the Soviet Union. Also called shock workers, Stakhanovites take their name from Aleksandr Stakhanov, a coal miner supposedly inspired to superhuman efforts by a speech of Stalin's. Stakhanov was typical of the "hero workers" promoted by the regime: an uneducated worker of humble origins inspired by devotion to Stalin and communism. Stakhanov was followed by other such "heroes of socialist labor" in all sectors of the Soviet economy, from collective farmers to a long-distance pilot presented as "the Lindbergh of the Soviet Union." The Stakhanovites became part of the official campaign to encourage overproduction, by singling out selected worker-heroes for praise and material benefits. Such Stakhanovites were presented as the wave of the future, the best example of "the New Soviet Man" who unselfishly bends all his energies to the building of communism. *See also* LYSENKOISM, p. 54; NEW SOVIET MAN, p. 107.

Significance   The Stakhanovite was a much-resented person in many Soviet enterprises in the 1930s. Such overproduction had the effect of increasing the work norms for the coming year, as the central economic planners pressured enterprises to base their production quotas on the best performance rather than on the average. Because Stakhanovites received material rewards as well as honors, the practice increased income gaps. There are reports of Stakhanovites being attacked by their fellow communist workers. Nonetheless, after the communist parties achieved power in Eastern Europe after World War II, similar campaigns were mounted there. Since Stalin's death the Soviets have tended to downplay the material rewards of the overproducer, but the concept is still embodied in official exhortations to the citizenry. For example, the official slogans for the 1982 May Day celebrations issued by the Soviet Central Committee included "Make animal husbandry a shock-work front" and "Shock work is our patriotic and internationalist duty."

"Storming" (*Shturmovshchina*)   The end-of-the-month rush to fulfill production targets, a common feature of the Soviet economy. "Storming" results from tight planning, late deliveries, and a system that measures success in target fulfillment numbers rather than in sales or quality. "Storming" occurs during the last several days of each month, at the end of which the enterprise must fulfill its production targets for that month. *See also* TARGETS, p. 233.

Significance   The effects of "storming" are generally not discussed by Soviet economists. Some do admit that from one and one-half to two and one-half times more goods are produced during the final ten days of each month. The probable result is that much of the Soviet workforce is underutilized at the beginning and overutilized during the final days. Plant managers may overstate labor needs during the planning process in order to have reserve labor capacity on hand for "storming." Some Western analysts also maintain that overtime work without additional pay is common, although work rules require overtime payment. There is probably also a concomitant effect on quality; Soviet "street" lore is replete with warnings not to buy anything produced on the 29th or 30th day.

Targets   That portion of the centrally determined economic plan that lays out the production responsibilities of the enterprises. Targets are usually expressed in units of production to be produced during a given time period utilizing a specified amount of inputs. Inputs are also allocated through the plan; a Soviet-style planning system typically specifies the wages to be paid, investments, operating capital, and the suppliers of intermediate goods for each enterprise as well. Targets are generally quantified, in tangible physical terms—tons produced, kilowatt-hours generated, kilometers of goods transported—and divided by target periods of months, quarters, and years. *See also* LABOR NORMS, p. 207; PLANNING, p. 220.

Significance   Planning by physical targets does not generally allow for additional expenditures for quality or technical improvements during the period of the plan. Such expenditures may raise the cost of production and thus result in nonfulfillment of the plan, as maximum costs of the production targets are usually specified by the plan. Production targeting also results in considerable politicking during the draft plan process. Enterprises typically attempt to keep their production targets low or at previous levels, thus avoiding what is termed the "rachet" effect of ever-increasing targets. Enterprise management has another incentive as well for concealing the true productive capacity of the enterprise. Soviet planning is typically "taut"—the planned utilization of resources is set at the highest possible levels—thus inevitably resulting in bottlenecks when one component falters. An enterprise that conceals some of its productive capacity thus possesses untallied "surpluses" with which to bargain for materials in short supply. Since supplies are so taut, resulting in many later deliveries, and the production targets are mandatory for the enterprises, the result in the Soviet Union is termed the *shturmovshchina*, the "storming" to fulfill the targets during the last days of the quarter or year. In an effort to ameliorate all this, several East European countries have discarded much of the detailed target plan apparatus, setting broad production targets by industrial sector, but leaving their implementation up to the industrial associations; and many of the problems remain. Only the Hungarian leadership, under the New Economic Mechanism, has successfully negotiated a compromise between the "tyranny of the targets" and the Marxian distrust of market incentives.

Tolkach   An employee in the state enterprise whose job is to secure the supplies and raw materials. The *Tolkach*'s official position is usually that of purchasing agent, but his real task is to supply the enterprise with goods frequently not available through regular channels. The Tolkach uses his influence to secure supplies through extralegal deals with other enterprises, usually involving barter, loaning machinery or personnel, or trading favors. Since most Soviet enterprise managers understate their capacity, they usually have supplies and raw materials on hand that can be used by the Tolkach for deals when the regular supply channels fail. In a sense, the "Tolkach economy" represents the leeway in a highly centralized, planned economy. *See also* SECOND ECONOMY, p. 225.

Significance   A Tolkach enables an enterprise to bypass supply bottlenecks to meet production goals set by the economic plan. The "Tolkach economy" constitutes a subterranean marketplace in which barter and favor-trading substitute for cash. While the official connotation attached to the term is negative, the system is tolerated by the authorities because Tolkach deals permit the flexibility needed in a centrally planned economy. Because the Tolkach uses his influence to provide economic favors ranging from providing scarce automobile parts to black marketeering, he may be prosecuted for economic crimes if he oversteps the invisible boundaries of the permissible.

Transferable Ruble (TR)   The unit of accounting used for trade transactions among members of the CMEA (Council of Mutual Economic Assistance). The transferable ruble was established in 1964 for intra-CMEA trade as an "international socialist collective currency." It is, however, anything but an international currency, being non-convertible, non-transferable, and subject to fluctuations in value as determined by the Soviet government as well as by world markets. Theoretically, trade among the European CMEA nations (Bulgaria, Czechoslovakia, East Germany, Hungary, Poland, Romania, and the Soviet Union) is conducted on the basis of world market prices converted into transferable rubles. Several variables, however, influence TR rates. The Soviet government determines exchange rates and there may be little correlation between intra-CMEA TR prices and each country's individual price structure; in 1975, for example, the price per ton of Soviet oil varied from 28 to 41 TRs according to the CMEA importer. Different types of goods, "hard" (the most desirable) and "soft" are valued at different rates, the determination frequently being the subject of political bargaining. TR credits in the CMEA Bank are not transferable to another CMEA country. The debtor state must establish credit with its creditor, not with another CMEA country. Foreign trade in general is hampered in a centrally planned economy because items marked for export, and the means of producing them, must be included in the allocations of the economic plan. Because the Soviet Union and most East European systems follow "taut" planning, that is, the most intensive use of all possible resources, flexibility in trade is extremely limited. Therefore, almost all trade is conducted on the basis of prior bilateral agreements, the transferable ruble being used as a means to clear accounts rather than as a measure of convertible value. In effect, despite the TR, there is no integrated socialist market. *See also* COUNCIL OF MUTUAL ECONOMIC ASSISTANCE (CMEA OR COMECON), p. 317.

Significance   The use of the transferable ruble rather than international monetary measurements insulates Soviet-CMEA trade from the worst effects of world price shifts (as, for example, in the oil crisis) but also serves to isolate the CMEA from the corrective effects of market pricing. Due to the exigencies of taut central planning, intra-CMEA trade continues to be conducted on a bilateral, and frequently on a barter, basis. Within the CMEA, the transferable ruble has not helped to integrate these economies. The transferable ruble is mainly a bookkeeping convenience that helps to preserve Soviet control over intra-CMEA trade. Rather than permit the ruble to be freely exchanged, the Soviet Union has recently chosen to cover its hard currency trade deficits and interest on western loans by sale of gold, tourism, and hard currency arms sales.

Turnover Tax   A tax, similar to a state sales tax in the United States that is levied before purchase and is therefore included in the final purchase price. The turnover tax, in Europe called a Value Added Tax (VAT), constitutes a major portion of the tax revenues of the Soviet Union and most East European states. The turnover tax is equal to the difference between the wholesale price and the final selling price, less handling costs. Most, but not all, turnover taxes are levied on consumer goods, including food. As Soviet economic measurements of national income (NI) are based on final sales price, the turnover tax is included in the national income. If national income is broken down by sector of origin, turnover tax revenue is credited to the relevant industrial sector. *See also* MARXISM: SURPLUS VALUE, p. 72; NATIONAL INCOME, p. 216.

Significance   The turnover tax is frequently used to equalize demand with current supply. Two items may cost the same to make, but one is more in demand by consumers. Therefore, the more wanted item may be taxed at 60 percent; the less desirable at 10 percent, and there will be no incentive for the factory to produce more of the first. The turnover tax can also be used to discourage demand, much as some in the United States have advocated a high tax on gasoline to lower consumption. Prices are set by the central authorities rather than by market conditions; frequently in order to avoid announcing a price hike the turnover tax will be increased. In the early period of industrialization and collectivization of agriculture in the Soviet Union, extremely high turnover taxes on agricultural produce were used to exact capital from both the peasants and the consumers. If no one purchases the goods the payment is still made—in effect, a payment by the financial system to itself. Soviet authorities maintain that the turnover tax is part of the surplus product created in production and is therefore not a tax, enabling them to claim that the state tax burden on the Soviet citizen is extremely low. Because the rates of taxation are generally secret, it is difficult for Western analysts to evaluate the actual value of the Soviet national product or to assess the relative productivity of various industrial sectors. A large part of the economic reforms undertaken in Hungary involved reduction of the turnover tax and more realistic pricing of goods. Hungary's booming economy in the 1970s constitutes some measure of proof that this approach works.

Virgin Lands   A vast agricultural project aimed at expanding the arable acreage of the USSR by sowing millions of acres of idle and unproductive land. The Virgin Lands project was a key part of Nikita Khrushchev's plan to revamp Soviet agriculture. Announced in 1954, the project initially proposed the cultivation of 13 million hectares (32.12 million acres) of untilled land in Kazakhstan, eastern Siberia, the Volga Basin, and the north Caucasus. By 1960, 41.8 million hectares (103 million acres) had been ploughed, most located in areas of marginal rainfall. The first two harvests in the Virgin Lands were successful, but in 1959 yields fell drastically, and in 1963 a severe drought caused widespread crop failure. By 1965 the program of expanding acreage had been abandoned, but much of the land still remains under cultivation, the most productive being devoted to huge grain farms. *See also* AGRO-CITIES, p. 179; ANTI-PARTY GROUP, p. 86; SOVKHOZ, p. 229.

Significance   Khrushchev's grandiose and expensive agricultural experiments, which included the Virgin Lands project, contributed to his downfall in 1964. Assessment of the Virgin Lands project has been mixed; some hold that it drained off capital better spent elsewhere, but other analysts note that where modern dry farming methods are practiced, it has made a sizable contribution to Soviet grain production. The project was also part of Khrushchev's drive to rationalize Soviet agriculture by placing more land in state farms. The Virgin Lands were set up as state farms; today the Soviet Union is the only communist-party state in Eastern Europe that has over half of its arable land in state farms rather than in collective farms. The Virgin Lands project coincided with the plan to increase the consumption of meat in the Soviet Union, using the feedstocks from the Virgin Lands. Although climatic conditions in the Virgin Lands are similar to Canada's Saskatchewan Province, the even more marginal rainfall has made Soviet agriculture particularly vulnerable to weather variations. As part of the project, the leadership of Kazakhstan, the prime area, was reorganized in 1954 and Leonid Brezhnev was brought in as Second Secretary, his first important party post. The Virgin Lands project was promoted by Khrushchev both as a means of increasing agricultural output and as a device to mobilize youth for the "building of communism." The project depended heavily on persuading youth to migrate to Kazakhstan and other inhospitable regions. Although much of the marginal acreage that was ploughed in the enthusiasm of the initial years has since reverted back to grassland, the lure of the Virgin Lands remains; recently Soviet economists and scientists have debated the possibility of reversing the northward flow of the major rivers so as to provide the sorely needed irrigation for these lands.

War Communism   A series of drastic economic measures undertaken in 1918 whereby the new Bolshevik regime attempted to reorganize the war-shattered economy of Russia and institute total state control. War Communism, sometimes referred to as the period of "militant communism," was essentially an effort to hold the country together while fighting a civil war. The period of War Communism lasted from 1918 to 1921, when the anti-Bolshevik forces were defeated. Although frequently described as a comprehensive, long-range economic program aimed at creating communism, War Communism was in reality a series of emergency measures rather than a grand strategy, although the measures themselves were shaped by the millennial nature of Marxism. In 1918 the Bolsheviks controlled a bare one-seventh of the Czarist Empire, inheriting an economy largely destroyed by four years of war. They were faced with two looming crises: (1) a famine in the cities, the result of a drastic decline in agricultural productivity and a war-disrupted transport system; and (2) a semi-industrialized economy where production had fallen to 20 percent of prewar levels. The promises of the Bolshevik Revolution and the destruction of the bourgeois state had encouraged many workers simply to seize the factories, with no direction. In a series of measures, Vladimir Lenin nationalized all industry, transportation, and banking, forcibly requisitioned food from the peasants, instituted strict rationing, abolished most money payments, and conscripted labor. All industry was placed under the control of a Supreme Economic Council, VSNKh (commonly called the *Vesenkha*), directed by the Bolshevik leadership. Lenin modeled this centralized, state-planned economy on the organization of the German economy during World War I, thus the name "war communism." Both systems were shaped by the exigencies of waging an all-out war for survival, characterized by mass mobilization of resources and total central control. The stringent measures were frequently backed by police action, under the newly created CHEKA, the secret police; if necessary, factories functioned under military guard. The forced food requisitions to feed the cities and the Red Army were especially unpopular. The inevitable reaction triggered smoldering resentment, revolts, and black marketeering. By 1921, Lenin had defeated his opponents, the various "white" forces and the interventionist forces sent in by the Allies. The ensuing period of relaxation of central control, known as the New Economic Policy (NEP), lasted until 1928 when Josef Stalin turned once again to the idea of a forced draft march toward full industrialization. *See also* BOLSHEVIK REVOLUTION, p. 12; COMMAND ECONOMY, p. 187; NEW ECONOMIC POLICY (NEP), p. 218.

Significance   War Communism, however drastic and brutal, enabled the new Bolshevik regime to gain enough control over the levers of power to survive and create a power base. In this sense, it was a success. The policies of War Communism shaped many of the fundamentals of the Soviet system—total state control, supremacy of the interests of the party, central economic planning, control by hierarchical superagencies, of which Vesenkha was only the first, and enforcement by police terror—which Stalin later applied to the Eastern European states, however inappropriately. War Communism also marks the first tangible evidence of the Soviet determination to use whatever means necessary, including extralegality and terror, when survival seemed at stake. Despite its abuses, War Communism also revived a war-shattered, semi-industrialized economy. The underlying principle of War Communism—a mandatory method of enforcing, through the power of the state, the most effective use of scarce resources—remains attractive to many a struggling Third World nation today.

Workers' Self-Management The institutional framework within which the modern Yugoslav state has evolved into a unique system embracing Marxist socialism, direct democracy, a ruling communist party and market competition. Self-management is the principle of participation in the work process as the legal and ideological basis for the vesting of economic control in the workers. Workers' self-management, as developed by the Yugoslavs since 1948, rests on two fundamentals: (1) socialist ownership of the means of production, and (2) direct worker control over economic decisions. In practice, it means that only those directly involved in the economic process as workers should make economic decisions. The theory of socialist self-management was applied within the Yugoslav state after the break with the Cominform in 1948, when the Yugoslav leadership refused to subordinate its national interests to those of the Soviet Union. The basic principles of workers' self-management were first spelled out by Josip Broz Tito in 1950, when the Yugoslav leadership realized that the break between Yugoslavia and the Soviet Union was permanent. It was presented as both a critique of the monopoly power of the Soviet party and a justification for Yugoslavia's insistence on developing socialism in its own way. In their critique of Stalinism, the Yugoslavs pinpointed the party's monopoly over the economic process as the cause for the development of a new ruling class whose dictatorial power is based on control of the state-owned means of production. Through self-management, with the workers managing the factories, the Yugoslavs maintained that the process would be reversed and a new socialist society developed compatible with the original tenets of Marx. The thrust of self-management is the devolution of economic decision making power to the lowest levels where decisions can reasonably be made. Society retains ownership of the means of production, but workers are vested with economic control over the utilization of assets and control the distribution of profits. The general membership of each enterprise, acting in trust for society, elects a workers' council and approves the enterprise's governing statutes. The workers' council is vested with the authority to plan production according to demand, hire and fire management, distribute profits, determine further investment, and in general, plan the activities of the enterprise. The elaborate central planning apparatus is dissolved; the powers and risks formerly assumed by the central authorities devolve upon the workers. By definition, self-management excludes decision making by government representatives or management. Self-management theory makes a distinction between the power to govern (vested in the councils) and the power to administer, which the elected councils delegate to management. Management is responsible to the workers. Yugloslav theory views self-management as the form of social organization that will eventually embrace all of society, creating a socialist transformation through widespread participation. The concept, as it was first defined in the 1950s, was limited in application, but it has gradually been extended to all aspects of social and economic activities. In the early years the main focus of the councils was on distribution of profits and welfare issues, not investment; this power still rested with the central investment fund supported by enterprise taxes. By 1965, the process of implementing the self-management principle had proceeded to the point of dismantling almost all central control over investments and banking, freeing prices, and extending the principle of self-management to social institutions such as hospitals, schools and theaters. During the heyday of decentralization, 1965–74, the enterprise became almost totally autonomous. By the early 1970s, the negatives of the system were apparent: rising ethnic competition, economic particularism, grave regional disparities, overconcentration, and a banking system which responded far more to local than national needs. The Yugoslav party leadership reasserted control, and put banking, foreign trade, and investment policies under federal control. The "recentralization" of party power did not, however, involve a repudiation of the principle of self-management. Instead, self-management was further decentralized to the basic units of production (BOALs), within each enterprise. Each such basic unit of production was given the authority to elect its own workers' council, determine its own operating procedures, distribute the profits accruing to it, and, in conjunction with the other production units, elect an enterprise governing board and run the enterprise. *See also* MARKET SOCIALISM, p. 212; MARXISM: HUMANISM, p. 65; WORKERS' SELF-MANAGEMENT: BASIC ORGANIZATION OF ASSOCIATED LABOR, p. 242; WORKERS' SELF MANAGEMENT: WORKERS' COUNCILS, p. 244.

Significance   The institution of self-management is what distinguishes Yugoslav practice from the Soviet model. The postwar development of Yugoslavia is essentially the history of self-management, as it has evolved since 1948, and the vast changes it has wrought in the Yugoslav system. The Yugoslavs view self-management as an operational principle of industrial management, the means of instituting true socialist democracy, and a way of limiting the arbitrary exercise of power. Self-management in practice has also involved a considerable shift in the locus of political power, as government and party power have been devolved to local and regional levels. As self-management developed, a dialectic was set up whereby the devolution in economic power forced a devolution in political power, and changes in the political system further fueled changes in the economic system. As a theory, self-management draws on the writings of Karl Marx and the ideal of direct rule by the proletariat, especially the pre-1848 "humanist" works that center on his concern with alienation. It also borrows from the Marxist humanist critiques of Stalinism, and Western ideals of direct democracy and industrial democracy. Self-management is the reversal of capitalist industrial management, where power is decentralized only at the will of management, within parameters determined by management, and the means of production remain in private ownership. Essentially, workers in the Yugoslav system hold membership, of a participatory and equal nature, in their work organization, and bear responsibility for its governance. The most strident criticism of self-management has emanated from the Soviet bloc, centering on what they perceive as the Yugoslav party's abrogation of its role as the leading element in society, thus diluting the principle of rule by the proletariat. Other such critiques scorn self-management as "anarcho-syndicalism," or "thinly disguised bourgeois capitalism." Such criticism obliquely supports the Yugoslav contention that the biggest bar to economic reform and decentralization in the Soviet bloc is the entrenched bureaucracy that wields a monopoly of control over the economy. Although some East European states, such as Hungary, have cautiously introduced market considerations into their economies and decentralized the planning process, none has been able to institute self-management and its primary institution, the workers' council. Such attempts—Hungary and Poland in 1956, Czechoslovakia in 1968, and Poland in 1980—have been met with political and military suppression, a clear validation of the threat that workers' participation in economic decision making poses to those who wield power in the communist-party states. The Yugoslavs themselves freely admit that self-management has not been implemented without costs, and that they have not developed the perfect system; that self-management requires a great measure of education and self-discipline that the Yugoslav workers may not possess at this time. Nevertheless, the concept has had a profound effect on the entire system. It has been the mechanism through which many liberalizing reforms have been carried out and the chief vehicle for the decentralization and pluralism that so distinguishes Yugoslavia from the Soviet bloc states. The system has undergone a substantial measure of flux, but it has given Yugoslavia scope and room for flexibility, all under the rubric of self-management. It is particularly suited to a state with the remarkable ethnic complexity of Yugoslavia. The vast divergencies in income and resources made it necessary to treat the disparate regions as separate ethnic entities for which one policy directed from the center would not be appropriate. The system has also created its own problems by supporting the growth of particularistic ethnic nationalism, which led to substantial federal intervention in 1971–72. Despite this, workers' self-management has become a distinctive ideology that has had profound influence not only in Yugoslavia but in developing nations as well.

Workers' Self-Management: Basic Organization of Associated Labor (BOAL)   In Yugoslavia, a functional work unit that elects a workers' council and possesses the right of self-management over its activities. The Basic Organization of Associated Labor (*Osnovna Organizacija Udruženog Rada*, OOUR) is the smallest identifiable unit producing a marketable product or service. Under the 1976 Law on Associated Labor, the BOAL is now the fundamental decision making unit within an enterprise or social institute. An enterprise is constituted by BOALs on the basis of an agreement to pool labor and resources, with an agreed-upon pooling of income and risk by members. Each BOAL elects a workers' council that is responsible for organizing its work, allocating wages and investment funds, hiring and firing, and through a Self-Management Agreement, coordinating the work of the enterprise. Management is hired by the BOALs, in joint agreement with the trade union and local county assembly, and is responsible to them. BOALs are set up in all economic enterprises and social institutions such as schools, hospitals, and theaters. A small factory might contain a BOAL for producing the basic components, a BOAL responsible for final processing, and a BOAL for sales. There is no legal size limit on BOALs; they may range from ten to a thousand. Each BOAL is an autonomous legal entity and keeps its own financial records. It must approve the financial statements and working economic plan of the enterprise. Management must present reports at monthly general meetings of the BOALs. BOAL funds are essentially the funds of the enterprise; in an accounting sense they function as cost centers. The BOAL is thus the basic organ of self-management and a method of decentralizing industrial management. A BOAL may leave the enterprise, set up as a separate enterprise, or join another enterprise, providing it does not harm the interests of the other BOALs. The 1976 legislation also set up equivalent organizations in the private sector, the Contractual Organization of Associated Labor (COAL). A COAL may be funded by private capital with an individual contributing 10 percent or more, may employ salaried workers, and upon concluding a self-management agreement will operate similarly to a BOAL and can contract with the public sector. Such COALs are formed of private farmers (who farm 85 percent of the agricultural land), artisans, or small manufacturers. By the 1980s, over 50,000 BOALs and COALs had been constituted as basic units of self-management. *See also* MARKET SOCIALISM, p. 212; WORKERS' SELF-MANAGEMENT, p. 239; WORKERS' SELF-MANAGEMENT: WORKERS' COUNCILS, p. 244.

Significance   The BOAL is the latest in the long series of economic reforms in Yugoslavia aimed at making self-managment viable at the most basic levels of society. The BOALs, or economic units, were introduced in the late 1960s when the increasing concentration and complexity of Yugoslav industries began to call into question the effectiveness of a single workers' council. The 1976 legislation (facetiously called the "little constitution" because it contains 672 articles and is longer than the already lengthy Yugoslav constitution), substantially changed the shape of Yugoslav self-management. After the 1965 economic reforms, successful enterprises and their managers increasingly became centers of autonomous power. In large industrial complexes involving thousands of workers, the workers' council in practice delegated most decision making to management, creating what the Yugoslavs labelled a "technocratic elite." A second catalyst was the 1971 Croat crisis, an assertion of nationalism that brought the heretofore liberalizing party leadership to reassert control. The party leader, Josip Broz Tito, chose to do this by reaffirming the party's leading role as the ultimate arbiter of society, but through the basic units of governance rather than through recentralization. The BOALs offer two advantages by providing the means for (1) bypassing the managerial and technocratic elite; and (2) an enlarged role for the trade unions, which typically contain a high percent of party members. As nominating agency for the workers' council and adjudicator of disputes between BOALs, the trade unions' influence over the workers' councils has increased. The BOALs have also resulted in an increased focus on communications; management is required to communicate with the BOALs and all proposals must be cogently explained to the workforce, as communications between BOALs. The 1976 law accomplished other goals in that (1) it encouraged production in the private sector (which amounts to some 25 percent of Yugoslav production); (2) it reaffirmed the property rights of private farmers and artisans; (3) it provided a means of turning private capital resources into investment; and (4) it increased the capacity of the private service sector. All of these changes were in direct contrast to other communist-party systems. The BOAL reform is consistent with the determination the Yugoslavs have exhibited over the past thirty years to make self-governance a reality.

Workers' Self-Management: Workers' Councils   Representative bodies elected by the personnel of an economic enterprise or production unit that have broad decision-making powers. The workers' council (*radnicki savet*) is the key institution in the unique Yugoslav system of self-management, which vests economic decision making in these bodies. Since 1974–76, large enterprises are broken down into Basic Organizations of Associated Labor (BOALs), or production units, which have assumed most of the duties of the enterprise council. Workers' councils were first instituted in Yugoslavia in 1949 in 215 selected enterprises, as a repudiation of the centralized dictatorship exercised by the Communist Party of the Soviet Union. The 1953 Yugoslav Fundamental Law legally established the right of workers' self-management and transferred the responsibility for managing the means of production from the central government to the workers' councils. In law and in theory, the property of an enterprise remains in public ownership with the workers enjoying the right of usage through the elected councils. They thus represent both the broadest devolution of power in a communist-party system to date as well as the most meaningful form of decentralization. Workers' councils are composed of delegates elected by secret vote of the work force from a list of candidates presented by the trade union. In enterprises or production units of under 30, the entire workforce comprises the council. Members serve two-year terms, renewable for one term. Councils are empowered to elect the director, hire and fire, determine investments, allocate wages, determine the product mix and work arrangements, set production goals, and distribute benefits, thus covering a wide range of managerial responsibilities. The council elects a board of managers that serves as an executive organ and is responsible for day-to-day operations. The director, hired in joint agreement with the trade union and local communal (county) assembly, serves a four-year renewable term, subject to recall; the director is an *ex officio* member of the board of directors. Dismissal proceedings can be initated by the council, the trade union, or the communal assembly. Management is not free to act unless that power has been legally delegated by the council or general membership of the enterprise. Directors are responsible to the workers' councils, not to state organs, for the success of the enterprise. Governance is exercised through the workers' council, the membership of the enterprise meeting in general meetings (*zbors*), the management board, and the councils of the constituent units, the BOALs. Each enterprise or BOAL possesses enterprise statutes, approved by the councils, which set forth operating procedures, rights of members, the basic goals, and policies. The council may also call an all-enterprise referendum on important issues. Income and investment allocation operate within the limits of the Social Compact and Self-Management Agreements, which the relevant workers' councils must approve; these constitute the major instruments for transmitting government economic policy goals to the enterprises. The workers' council can cover costs by retained earnings (since 1965 about 70 percent of revenues after taxes have accrued to the enterprises) from external loans (for which it must compete), from loans from other enterprises, from funds pooled with other enterprises—or it can go bankrupt, in which case the workers' council is dissolved and the enterprise is placed under receivership of the local communal assembly. Workers are provided with insurance against temporary downswings through an inter-enterprise fund that maintains the minimum wage levels, set by the Social Compacts. Workers do not receive a contracted wage regardless of performance; they receive only their share of profits as determined by the workers' council. Therefore, all workers are involved in the operation of the enterprise, at the very minimum participating in its economic success or failure. Salaries of technical and administrative personnel are also set by the workers' council. Economic decisions are made on the basis of market conditions. As part of the massive reform that decentralized economic control and turned the management of factories back to the workers, Yugoslavia dismantled the central planning apparatus. Profits, not plan fulfillment, determine the success of an enterprise. Under the workers' council system, the Yugoslav enterprise is essentially autonomous, operating as Western corporations do within a framework of laws and regulations. Yugoslav enterprises behave much as do Western firms: they advertise, compete for managerial talent, convince banks of their financial soundness, develop new product lines, bargain with suppliers, invest in new equipment and technology, complain about internal communications, wrangle jobs for relatives, and look for good merger possibilities. The workers' council is not analogous to a board of directors: it is legally responsible to the workforce, can fire the management, and by law a majority must be blue-collar workers. All social institutions are organized in the same way. A hospital, cultural institution, school, or social agency operates under a workers' council, with the exception that usually they are paid through government revenues. Recently, workers' councils have been extended to voluntary collectives of private employees. *See also* MARKET SOCIALISM, p. 212;

WORKERS' SELF-MANAGEMENT, p. 239; WORKERS' SELF-MANAGEMENT: BOAL, p. 242.

Significance Yugoslav theory regards the workers' councils as the foundation of the self-management system, through which the Yugoslavs claim to be pioneering a new road to socialism. They also advance the workers' councils as the first concrete step in the "withering away of the state" promised by Marx, thus placing them further along the road to socialism. The Yugoslavs view self-managed socialism as the alternative to the Soviet conception of a bureaucratized dictatorship of the proletariat, which the Yugoslavs term state capitalism. Underlying the institution of workers' councils is the concept of alienation, which the Yugoslavs point out exists when the workers control neither the means or production nor the conditions of their work, including wage distribution. The network of workers' councils has created a new mode of political participation peculiar to Yugoslavia. Every year hundreds of thousands of Yugoslav workers are involved in the institutions of self-management. The work may be time-consuming or performed perfunctorily, but the workers' councils also provide a psychological benefit, giving workers a sense of control over important areas of their lives such as wages, work, and housing. As might be expected, the system appears to work best in enterprises located in the more developed areas. The councils are also criticized for emphasizing short-term goals over long-term, for promoting wage differentials (councils have proven more than agreeable to providing high salaries for skilled management), worsening regional disparities, and pursuing particularistic interests. The institution of workers' councils has inherent attractions for socialist systems, based as it is in Marx's writings and the rule of the proletariat. Workers' councils sprang up spontaneously during the initial days of the Bolshevik Revolution, to be suppressed promptly by Vladimir Lenin once he had gained sufficient control. Their fate in Eastern Europe has been similar, attesting to the threat they pose to centralized party control. All serious East European reform movements, from Hungary in 1956 to Poland in 1980, have included proposals for a workers' council system, and all such attempts have been suppressed by the ruling communist parties.

6. The Legal System

Administrative Offense   In Soviet legal practice, any culpable act, as defined by the authorities, that is not covered by the criminal codes. Administrative offenses include breaches of government regulations, acts that constitute a public nuisance, various forms of negligence, and acts that pose a danger to society. The first category, regulatory violations, constitutes by itself a sizable category since most aspects of Soviet life are covered by regulations, from the workplace to the residence. The many administrative offenses have not yet been codified, being contained in diverse regulations, decrees, statutes, and bylaws issued by various state authorities. Administrative offenses include, among others: (1) licensing violations; (2) breaches of workplace safety; (3) acts committed by 16- to 18-year olds (status offenses) for which parents and guardians are held responsible; (4) violations of environmental regulations; (5) punishable negligence; (6) public disorderliness and drunkenness; (7) violations of the internal passport regulations; (8) minor traffic violations; and (9) failure to fulfill work duties. The State Bank (*Gosbank*) and the Investment Bank (*Stroibank*) may also fine enterprises for economic irregularities. Sanctions are levied by committees of the local soviets, various government agencies, the police, and citizens' groups, such as the Comrades' Courts, the Volunteer Militia (*Druzhiny*), or residence committees. The People's Courts may handle administrative offenses upon request of the authorities; in such case they are considered to be acting administratively and are not bound by the procedural code. Administrative offenses are punishable by public censure, small fines, deprivation of certain rights (such as loss of a driver's license), administrative detention up to 15 days, dismissal from employment, deportation, exile and banishment, corrective labor, and confiscation of property. Thus, while many administrative offenses are relatively minor, in some cases the penalties are severe. The local police have considerable administrative power, especially in the areas of public behavior, traffic violations, and violations of the internal passport laws. Prosecution must be within one month of the commission of the offense. Authorities also have the right to dissolve any association or organization (all of which must comply with the registration laws) if it violates the law or the interests of the Soviet state. This includes religious societies, which may be deregistered and barred from their places of worship. Administrative offenses are imposed through legislative acts, or by administrative decree and regulation. Thus, in the Soviet Union administrative offenses constitute a broad category of punishable acts over which the authorities have considerable interpretive power. *See also* COMRADES' COURT, p. 279; DRUZHINY, p. 283: HOOLIGANISM, p. 260; INTERNAL PASSPORT SYSTEM, p. 261; PARASITE, p. 264.

Significance   Various types of offenses that elsewhere would be considered criminal and thus covered by the legal codes are categorized as administrative offenses in the Soviet Union. The very plethora of rules, regulations, and decrees that stipulate punishable offenses constitute a major instrument of public control. Soviet courts are not clogged with the petty offenses that plague Western court systems as these frequently fall under the category of administrative offenses. In the Soviet system, administrative offenses are also distinguishable by the more severe punishments, which in other legal systems would be applied only by the courts. In recent years, Soviet authorities have made an effort to regularize administrative offenses, spelling out clearly what act is punishable by what sanction. This is probably a corrective measure, indicative of the overall regularization of the Soviet legal system since the 1960s. Abuses under the rubric of "administrative offense" are no longer as common as during the 1930s, when the term "administrative justice" became a catchphrase for the extralegal punishment meted out by the secret police to the millions caught up in the Stalinist purges. Administrative offenses still constitute a sizable body of uncodified law and grant the authorities substantial power to exercise punitive functions.

Anti-Soviet Agitation and Propaganda   The legal charge under which dissidents and nonconformists who question any aspect of the Soviet system are usually prosecuted and punished. Anti-Soviet agitation and propaganda is defined under Article 70 of the Soviet criminal code as any speech or expression that slanders or defames the Soviet state and social system, any propaganda with the same intent, or any such activities intended to weaken the state, including participation in any group with such goals. Article 70 is thus the basic law that controls speech and expression in the Soviet Union. The charge is broad enough that it covers actions as well as expression, and permits the authorities to suppress any activities that they define as dissent. Since the mid-1960s, most Soviet citizens arrested or convicted for political reasons have been charged under Article 70. In 1966, two Soviet writers, Andrei Sinyavsky and Yuli Daniel were convicted of secretly publishing abroad material containing anti-Soviet propaganda. Although the defendants denied any intent to undermine the state, the court ruled that their anti-Soviet intent could be deduced from the content of their writing alone. In the wake of the Sinyavsky-Daniel trial, two new provisions, Articles 190-1 and 190-3, were added to the criminal code. These provisions made it a crime against the state to prepare or circulate statements slandering or defaming the Soviet system, even if direct anti-Soviet intent could not be proved. This has made it possible for the authorities legally to prosecute writers and others whose views are politically unacceptable but not in outright opposition, by maintaining that such activities can be used by "enemies of the Soviet Union." Conviction under Article 70 carries a penalty of up to seven years imprisonment and exile up to five years. *See also* CRIMES AGAINST THE STATE, p. 255; DISSENT AND OPPOSITION, p. 281; GLAVLIT, p. 284.

Significance   The charge of anti-Soviet agitation and propaganda is the main legal instrument used to curb internal dissent. The abolition of the secret police practices and extralegal punishments meted out to dissidents under Stalin left the Soviet leaders with the problem of how to punish those who question the Soviet system. In general they have used three methods: extrajudicial measures such as job denial, administrative confinement to psychiatric hospitals, and punishment under Articles 70 and 190. In practice the legal charge is broad enough for anti-Soviet intent to be inferred from almost any statement or act that suggests change. Prosecutions under the rubric of anti-Soviet agitation and propaganda cover an almost limitless range of activities. These have included, for example, publication of censored works abroad (*tamizdat*), circulating forbidden tapes (*magnitizdat*), taping foreign forbidden broadcasts (*radizdat*), possessing unauthorized films (*kinizdat*), circulating and printing censored manuscripts (*samizdat*), seeking redress for the Crimean Tatars and other national groups, adhering to a forbidden religion, pressing for greater protection of civil rights, and contact with Westerners. Not all Soviet citizens prosecuted under Article 70 are involved in political protest, but by questioning any official policy, be it in religion or art or law, their offense becomes a threat to the state and prosecutable under the criminal code. In essence, the charge of anti-Soviet agitation and propaganda has meant that no one can legally question or criticize the government or party in public. Although some of the most publicized political trials of the Brezhnev regime involved convictions under Articles 70 and 190, the record of treatment of dissenters is immeasurably better than during the Stalinist period. By the mid-1970s, the Brezhnev regime began to replace such convictions with forced deportation abroad in cases of the most prominent dissenters, such as Andrei Amalryk, Zhores Medvedev, Valery Chalidze, and Aleksandr Solzhenitsyn. However, anti-Soviet agitation and propaganda remain the major judicial instrument used to threaten and isolate dissenters.

Arbitration   A quasi-judicial proceeding by which disputes between economic enterprises are resolved. Most of the disputes submitted to arbitration panels involve a breach of contract, such as delays in deliveries or inferior goods. Disputes submitted to arbitration (*arbitrazh*) may involve failure to deliver goods as specified in a contract, refusal to sign contracts required by the state economic plan, or such common breaches as a travel agent who books hotel rooms and fails to produce the guests. An arbitration panel consists of a chairperson, usually a specialist in the area of dispute, and two other arbitrators, each named by one of the parties to the dispute. Arbitration panels are usually organized territorially; their work is monitored by the Court of Arbitration of the USSR Council of Ministers. The arbitration process is both a judicial and an administrative process. Decisions are based on law, especially that provided in the economic plan. Arbitration tribunals were created in 1931 when it became obvious that the ordinary court system lacked the technical expertise to make the economic judgments necessary to operate an almost totally state planned and controlled economy. *See also* ENTERPRISE, p. 191.

Significance   Arbitration proceedings are designed to keep court dockets free of cases requiring specialized expertise and to provide speedy decisions in economic disputes. Procedures are similar to those of courts of law, but while fines and sanctions may be levied, the major aim is to ensure fulfillment of the economic plan. In the Soviet Union and other East European states, arbitration is the routine method for settling civil disputes for which criminal penalties are not applicable. It enforces economic accountability on the enterprises while avoiding lengthy judicial proceedings and the pitfalls of purely administrative control. In many ways, Soviet arbitration procedures are similar to those utilized in Western countries, where arbitration is a voluntary alternative to civil suit action in the courts.

Civil Rights   According to Marxist-Leninist doctrine, those rights of individuals, such as liberty, property, and security, that first appear as the product of the class struggle under capitalism. Used by the bourgeois to defend their rule, communists charge, civil rights are denied to the working class because the bourgeoisie controls the economy and political system. Only when workers exercise economic and political control will they fully possess civil rights. Soviet constitutional treatment of civil rights stems from these Marxist-Leninist assumptions. Communist constitutions emphasize economic rights, such as the right to work, rather than the individual civil rights found in democratic constitutions. In particular, communist doctrine rejects the concept of natural law and innate natural rights. Therefore, state-created law is the only source of civil rights in a communist system. The theory is that socialist law expresses the will of all those who work, and thus the will of the state. If community norms are to be translated into civil rights, they must be sanctioned by the state. Communist legal theorists usually separate civil rights into four branches: (1) socioeconomic rights, such as the right to support in old age, the right to work, the right to education, and the right to leisure. These are emphasized over all other civil rights. (2) equality before the law, uniformity of rights and duties, and ethnic, racial, and sexual equality. Since the Bolshevik Revolution, communist legal systems have strongly guaranteed equal treatment and protection. (3) personal rights, such as the right to privacy, to protection of the person, and to personal property. These rights are observed and protected so long as they do not conflict with the interests of the state. (4) individual political rights, such as freedom of speech, freedom of press, and freedom of assembly. These are the least well-protected and institutionalized. These individual rights of conscience may be exercised only in conformity with the interests of the state, and the state itself will determine what is injurious to its interests. If the exercise of a civil right is viewed as threatening the socialist system, it is not constitutionally or legally protected. There is no independent judiciary to check the lawmakers; the Supreme Soviet itself is the judge of the constitutionality of a law. Communist constitutions place emphasis on the responsibility of the citizen to the state, rather than on the responsibility of state to citizen, and they reject the philosophy that civil rights constitute a limitation on state action. *See also* CRIMES AGAINST THE STATE, p. 255; DISSENT AND OPPOSITION, p. 281; HELSINKI ACCORD, p. 321; HUMAN RIGHTS MOVEMENT, p. 286.

Significance   In the area of civil rights, only the material guarantees are well-developed in communist constitutional law. Many of these are meaningful rights. Although the overall Soviet standard of living generally lags behind Western industrialized countries, Soviet expenditures on socioeconomic rights is considerable. Many Western nations lag behind the Soviet Union in terms of proportionate public expenditures for health, education, and welfare, which in the USSR are considered basic civil rights. Legal protection of all civil rights is dependent upon the interests of the state, as these are treated as privileges granted by the state rather than fundamental, innate rights. Despite the post-Stalin legal reforms, the authorities still enjoy substantial discretionary power to suspend civil rights if their exercise threatens state interests. The underlying political dynamic is that in a highly centralized one-party state, the exercise of civil rights such as freedom of speech almost inevitably engenders pluralism, a threat to the party's domination of the public domain. Although some political dissidents have openly pressed for meaningful implementation of civil rights other than socioeconomic ones, the basic dynamics of a one-party state precludes this. East European constitutions, with the partial exception of Yugoslavia where an independent Constitutional Court exists, follow Soviet practice. Individual civil rights in Yugoslavia have received more protection and the party usually has intervened to abridge such rights as free speech and assembly only in instances of ethnic dissent that they perceive as directly threatening their multinational state. However, in all communist constitutional law, civil rights are viewed as state-created rather than as inherent human rights. Although Western democracies place much emphasis on what the communist states regard as socioeconomic rights, they are viewed as policies and programs determined by social needs rather than as "rights."

Corrective Labor   A common penalty in Soviet criminal law whereby offenders serve work sentences either at their ordinary place of work or in a special corrective labor institutions, instead of being imprisoned in an ordinary penal institution. Corrective labor is the most commonly applied legal sanction in the Soviet Union and operates on the principle that work is the best method of reforming offenders. In theory the emphasis is on reeducation and rehabilitation through participation in the production process rather than on isolation in a penitentiary. Incarceration in penitentiaries is reserved for only the most serious crimes and for the "especially dangerous recidivist," the professional criminal. Thus, most Soviet penal institutions are labor colonies and labor camps, the latter usually in remote regions,

rather than penitentiaries. In 1963, various republics established settlement colonies, where the person sentenced to corrective labor lives
with his family rather than in a labor colony. Within the corrective
labor system there are four "regimes" or gradations in the severity of
work and rules of confinement: general, strict, very strict, and special
(*osobyi*). The latter regime is reserved for the most serious offenses and
usually is carried out in corrective labor camps where the living conditions and work are the harshest. In the case of minor offenses, where
sentences of corrective labor without loss of freedom are usually
substituted for fines or short prison sentences, 20 percent is deducted
from the wages of the offender, who is permitted to remain at his place
of work. If corrective labor is imposed with deprivation of freedom, the
inmate is paid for his labor and the expenses of the labor camp or
colony are deducted. Corrective labor was instituted by Vladimir Lenin
as a means of avoiding the punitive prison sentences of capitalist legal
systems while permitting offenders to be reeducated into socialism.
The concept of work-based compensation for minor offenses was
perverted during the Stalinist era when thousands of innocent people
were sentenced to hard labor in remote regions. Conditions in the
Stalinist labor camps were so harsh that a long sentence was usually
tantamount to the death penalty. Corrective labor was one of the first
areas to be reformed by Stalin's successors, in 1956. The labor camps
were emptied of most of their inmates and a series of laws regularized
the use of corrective labor. The corrective labor institutions are supervised by the Corrective Labor Inspectorate, a branch of the Ministry of
Internal Affairs. *See also* ADMINISTRATIVE OFFENSE, p. 247; DISSENT AND
OPPOSITION, p. 281; GULAG, p. 259.

Significance   Corrective labor is a flexible penalty that can be meted
out for relatively minor crimes while permitting those sentenced to
remain usefully employed. Most of those sentenced are ordinary
criminal offenders, but the fact that the authorities also have used
corrective labor to punish political dissidents, who are frequently sent
to the harshest (osobyi) labor camps, has obscured the fact that many
consider corrective labor to be an improvement upon a penitentiary
sentence. The criticism engendered by this practice has obscured the
basic thrust of corrective labor, which is to avoid long penitentiary
sentences whenever possible. Corrective labor is frequently prescribed by the courts if they feel there are mitigating circumstances,
such as youth, first offense, otherwise good behavior, or a bad social
environment.

Crimes Against Socialist Property   In communist legal codes,
an important category of crime that ranks in seriousness second only to

crimes against the state. Communist legal codes make a clear distinction between offenses committed against state property and those committed against privately owned property. The protection of the first is a priority of all communist criminal codes. Socialist property includes both state property and public property, such as the land and equipment of the collective farms. In the Soviet Union, by law all major resources and means of production are state-owned and controlled; thus socialist property includes practically all but personal possessions. In other communist states, such as Poland where most of the agricultural land is privately owned, or Hungary, which grants far greater scope to private enterprise, less is included under the category of socialist property. Whatever the differing patterns of ownership, however, the underlying principle of the criminal codes is that crimes against socialist property form a special category of serious crime. Generally, the three categories of crime against socialist property are (1) theft of state or public property; (2) criminal enrichment at the expense of socialist property; and (3) crimes that result in the destruction, damage or loss of socialist property. Some actions, such as negligence, are crimes only if committed with reference to socialist property. Misuse or theft of socialist property, embezzlement or fraud, are viewed as actions directed against the state itself, and can be punished severely. Conviction for crimes against socialist property carries heavier penalties than similar crimes against private property. In the Soviet Union, the death penalty may be applied in especially severe cases. *See also* CRIMES AGAINST THE STATE, p. 255; ECONOMIC CRIME, p. 257; SOCIALIST OWNERSHIP, p. 227.

Significance   Crimes against socialist property rank probably as the second largest category of crime in communist systems, although in most countries much of this would be covered by civil law. This is an area where the divergency between official socialization and popular attitudes appears most marked. Despite the emphasis on the seriousness of socialist property crime and the heavy penal sanctions levied, socialist property crime has not abated. Much involves petty pilfering or sheer carelessness. It appears that substantial numbers of otherwise law-abiding citizens regard socialist propety as alien, rather than communal property. Petty pilfering of a kilo of material here, a tool there, may be responsible for inferior quality of goods. The high levels of socialist property crime may also indicate a widespread dissatisfaction with the standard of living, exacerbated by the generally prevailing shortages of many consumer goods. The deemphasis on the rights of personal property ownership, as opposed to state ownership, is consistent with communist doctrine that holds that eventually all private property will disappear. The heavy sanctions levied for socialist property crime contrast to penal practice in the United States, where so-called "white collar" crime such as embezzlement or stock market fraud are punished by relatively light sentences whereas relatively minor theft of personal property can bring heavier prison sentences. Crimes against socialist property are viewed by the communist leadership as threatening to the economic system, and to the state itself. The building of socialism and the evolution of the "new Soviet man" are supposed to inculcate a sense of public responsibility that would virtually eliminate theft of state property. Because this has not occurred, the regime retaliates with penal sanctions against violators. During the Brezhnev era, this category of criminal sanctions has been enforced with less vigilance. The result has been the emergence of a thriving black market and the Second Economy.

Crimes Against the State   The legal charge applied in Communist systems to those actions that the government considers to constitute a danger to the socialist state. Crimes against the state embrace a wide range of actions or presumed intentions viewed as threatening the maintenance of the state. Soviet and East European law is characterized by an emphasis on the protection of the general interests of the state and, in particular, its political and economic interests. Thus, these actions, many of which are not considered criminal under Western legal codes, are defined as crimes because they impinge upon the interests of the state. Early Bolshevik legal codes made a clear distinction between "political" and "nonpolitical," or all "other" crimes. Since its inception, the Soviet legal system has consistently used criminal law for the dual purpose of controlling that behavior normally considered to be criminal and to buttress state control. The latter purpose leads to the definition of any action that supposedly threatens that control as criminal. The effect has been to create a special category of crime almost unique to communist legal codes. Since communist systems usually have insisted on maintaining an ideological monopoly, any expression which the authorities view as questioning or weakening that monopoly is also construed as a crime against the state. The determinant of what constitutes state crime rests on the definition of danger to the system. It can range from circulating unapproved fiction, to falsifying economic plan reports, to leaving the country without permission. Under Stalin, the charge acquired a sinister meaning when it was used to sweep hundreds of thousands of Soviet citizens into the labor camps and prisons during the purges of the 1930s. The post-Stalin legal reforms dropped the term *counterrevolutionary* and defined this category of socialist crime much more precisely, although in application they still remain the most flexible portion of the criminal codes. The RSFSR Criminal Code clearly underlines the priority of Soviet criminal legislation by stating in the first article, ". . . the RSFSR criminal code has as its task the protection of the Soviet social and state system . . ." Crimes against the state are divided into two categories: "especially dangerous crimes against the are labor colonies and labor camps, the latter usually in remote regions, ous" rely on intent to weaken the state as the differential. Thus, damage to communications is a state crime; damage with the intent of weakening the state is "especially dangerous." Some of the major charges defined as state crimes include (1) treason (including flight abroad or refusal to return from abroad); (2) espionage; (3) murdering a public official; (4) sabotage; (5) subverting the economic system through obstruction ("wrecking"), omission, or destruction; (6) anti-Soviet agitation and propaganda; (7) propagandizing war; (8) participation in an anti-Soviet (i.e., unapproved officially) organization; and (9) crimes against other socialist systems. Thus, a great deal of latitude in interpretation still remains; the definition of what constitutes a state crime is largely in the hands of the judicial authorities. While the post-Stalin legal reforms generally operated to limit legal sanctions to specifically described crimes, with state crime the degree of perceived danger to the system remains the determinant. Conviction for crimes against the state carries more severe penalties than " other" criminal acts such as theft of private property. Soviet jurisprudence still generally reserves the death penalty for state crimes. The focus on the supremacy of state interests is illustrated by four other categories of actions also defined as criminal by communist legal codes: economic crime, official crime, crime against the system of administration, and crime against socialist property. With state crime, these categories all share the legal philosophy that preservation of the socialist system is the primary thrust of criminal legislation. *See also* ANTI-SOVIET AGITATION AND PROPAGANDA, p. 248; ECONOMIC CRIME, p. 257; PSYCHIATRIC CONFINEMENT, p. 269; REFUSENIK, p. 298; SOCIALIST LEGALITY, p. 271.

Significance　Singling out actions defined as crimes against the state as a special category of serious crime indicates the manner in which communist legal systems place the interests of the state above other interests. Although since 1960 those accused of state crimes are generally accorded the same procedural rights as other Soviet criminal suspects, the charge itself carries a special burden. In the USSR, pretrial investigation of state crime is carried out by the secret police, the KGB, rather than by the Procuracy as is usual in other criminal cases. Frequently, the attitude and supposed intentions of the accused "state criminal" weigh more heavily than the actual act itself. The broad latitude in defining the various charges subsumed under the rubric of state crime has permitted the Soviet and East European authorities to legally punish any action or expression that they deem to be dangerous to the maintenance of the state. Those whom the Western press refers to as "political prisoners" usually have been sentenced under the charge of crimes against the state. In many cases, their crimes constitute questioning official policy rather than overt actions. Thus, the post-Stalin legal codifications that dropped the old charge of counterrevolutionary crime in favor of more specifically enumerated charges symbolizes the intent of Stalin's successors to establish judicial regularity while retaining the preeminence of state interest.

Economic Crime   Economic activity defined as criminal under communist legal codes. Economic crimes range from "practicing a forbidden profession" to illegal currency transactions. Since almost all economic activity in a communist system is state-controlled, almost all can be legally regulated, and is. Soviet and East European legal codes contain long lists of economic activities defined as crime, usually because they infringe upon the economic interests of the state. Some, such as illegal use of trademarks or false weights, are illegal under most legal codes; other economic crimes are so defined because they impinge upon the state's control over the economy. Economic crime can be construed as any action that impedes the functioning of the economic system; it should be viewed as distinct from property crime, which is generally treated separately in the codes. Private entrepreneurship involving the use of state property, or employing private labor, is strictly forbidden, but occurs nonetheless. Buying and selling outside of state-approved channels is termed "speculation" and is also illegal. Other economic crimes include issuing substandard products, distorting economic plan accounts, poaching, and illegal mining and timbering. The charge "practicing a forbidden profession" can involve some minute distinctions; under Soviet law private craftsmen may repair lampshades everywhere but in Leningrad and Moscow, but private TV repairmen may work only in rural areas. Distilling, supplying, and storing *samogon*, Soviet home-brewed alcohol, is an economic crime. Feeding state-produced bread to livestock is also an economic crime. Despite the range in seriousness of crime, what all these actions have in common is that they are economic activities carried on outside the state-controlled and operated economic system. Penalties for conviction of economic crimes range from minor sentences of corrective labor to several years' imprisonment, or even execution. *See also* CORRECTIVE LABOR, p. 252; CRIMES AGAINST SOCIALIST PROPERTY, p. 253; CRIMES AGAINST THE STATE, p. 255; SECOND ECONOMY, p. 225.

Significance   In the communist legal lexicon, economic crime covers a broad range of activities, many of which are not only legal elsewhere but are often encouraged, and others that are clearly in violation of most legal codes. The common element in all the activities designated as economic crime is that, in a system posited on central state control of almost all economic activity, they in some way violate that control. Much of what are minor economic offenses under Soviet criminal codes are tacitly permitted. Thus, the activities of the enterprise expediter, the *Tolkach*, frequently skirt the permissible but are rarely prosecuted. In those communist systems that permit greater latitude to private economic operations, such as Hungary, fewer activities are designated as economic crimes. In the Soviet Union, one of the most commonly committed economic crimes is currency speculation, the illegal exchange of foreign currency and rubles. Because the Soviet government and most East European systems set the exchange rates of their currencies artificially high, the temptation to change foreign currency outside the State Bank is great. In exchanging dollars for rubles, for example, an American tourist can obtain many more rubles for his dollars on the black market exchange than through the official exchange system. Yugoslavia, which possesses a decentralized economic system and a freely convertible currency, places far less emphasis on economic crime. Soviet criminal theory holds that economic crimes, such as illegal currency transactions, moonshining, cheating on weights, or setting up a business without a license are crimes directed against the state. Thus, the criminal codes have become the main legal instrument used to protect the economic interests of the state and to keep the national economy functioning as intended. The degree to which the laws on economic crime are prosecuted has varied. Today, there is a much greater tolerance of black market activities and private repair professions.

Exile   Legal penalty by which the Soviet authorities can remove someone from their place of residence and resettle them elsewhere, usually in a remote area. Exile and banishment, which means prohibiting someone from staying in specific places, may be imposed for two to five years. Although these punishments are designed to remove people from environments constituting a special risk to them, in practice exile and banishment have frequently been used to punish dissidents and others whom the Soviet authorities wish to remove from public view. Exile and banishment may also be applied in addition to prison terms, in which case they begin after the prison sentence has been served. Those serving terms of exile or banishment are supervised by the local police. *See also* DISSENT AND OPPOSITION, p. 281.

Significance   Exile and banishment are the means by which the Soviet regime isolates minor criminals and those whom it considers political dissidents. Dissidents such as Pavel Litvinov and Larissa Daniel have been sentenced to five-year exile in remote areas, thus effectively cutting them off from public view. More recently the noted dissident physicist, Andrei Sakharov, has been confined to the provincial city of Gorky. The increasing use of such sentences to punish political dissidents represents a marked shift from Stalinist practice when those suspected of dissidence were summarily executed. The practice is a direct carryover from czarist Russia when political dissidents were frequently sentenced to exile in Siberia. Such Bolshevik leaders as Lenin and Stalin were alumni of the system of exile to Siberia. In addition to exile and banishment, Soviet dissidents who apply for permission to emigrate are often refused exit visas (*refuseniks*). Another form of exile has been meted out recently to prominent dissidents— being forced into exile abroad after being stripped of their citizenship.

Gulag   The Russian acronym for Chief Administration of Corrective Labor Camps, the vast prison labor system set up by Josef Stalin in 1930. The term *Gulag* came into common usage with the publication in the West of Aleksandr Solzhenitsyn's *Gulag Archipelago*, the first reliable account of the extent and horror of Stalin's prison labor camps. The Gulag is an integral part of Soviet history, absorbing millions of innocent people in successive waves of repression. As Solzhenitsyn documents, the first wave comprised peasants caught up by Stalin's collectivization drive; successive waves embraced millions sentenced during the purges of the 1930s and the postwar repression, which included returning Soviet prisoners of war, labeled "traitors to the Fatherland" for their involuntary exposure to the West as POWs. Most were sentenced by administrative measures, by the secret police (NKVD). Sentences of up to 25 years or indefinite sentences, tantamount to death sentences given the harsh conditions and starvation diets, were the rule. The Gulag became a part of the Soviet economic machinery; huge amounts of convict labor built up Siberia, Central Asia, and the Far North. Prisoners were frequently taken, not for any transgressions, but to fulfill the NKVD's labor quotas. By the testimony of Solzhenitsyn and others, an estimated 13 to 25 million people perished in the labor camps. *See also* COLLECTIVIZATION, p. 185; GREAT PURGE, p. 17; THAW, p. 305; ZEK, p. 274.

Significance   A major signal that de-Stalinization was underway in the Soviet Union occurred when Nikita Khrushchev released millions from the Gulag, among them the prisoner Aleksandr Solzhenitsyn.

Khrushchev's famous "secret speech" before the 1956 (20th) party congress detailed Stalin's atrocities and focused on the Gulag and the purges as proof of Stalin's crimes. In 1962, Khrushchev permitted the publication of Solzhenitsyn's *One Day in the Life of Ivan Denisovich,* the first public admission that the prison camps had existed. Shortly afterwards Khrushchev tightened controls and Solzhenitsyn, banned from further publishing in the Soviet Union, was eventually stripped of his citizenship and forced into emigration. Successive Soviet leaderships have not reconstructed the Gulag, now redesignated GUITU, nor relied on prison camp labor for massive industrial projects, but dissenters are still sentenced to corrective labor camps and prison camp literature is still banned. Although Stalin justified the camps as necessary to carry out the class struggle and build communism, the record remains. Although other systems have used prison labor including, as Solzhenitsyn documents, the early Bolshevik regime, none has used it on the scale of the Soviet Union from 1930 to 1956.

Hooliganism   The legal charge applied by Soviet authorities to any public behavior considered to be criminally antisocial and disruptive to the social order. The term hooligan developed as English slang connoting "ruffian" or "hoodlum." As defined under Article 206 of the Soviet RSFSR Criminal Code, hooliganism constitutes "actions rudely violating the social order and expressing obvious disrespect for society." Although similar to the Western concept of "disturbing the peace," hooliganism is a much more sweeping and elastic charge, and carries a more pejorative meaning. Behavior punishable as hooliganism ranges from public drunkenness and swearing to resisting the authorities, fighting, inflicting physical injury, and malicious vandalism. Unlike more specific criminal offenses, hooliganism is as much a kind of attitude and behavior as it is criminal activity. The concept is flexible enough so that it is one of the most frequently applied articles of the criminal codes. Soviet authorities estimate that 20 to 30 percent of all criminal acts fall under the rubric of hooliganism, most involving drunkenness. A charge of hooliganism involves both a violation of public order or public interests and a violation of socialist morality, as defined by the authorities. Thus, the charge is applied to a wide range of public behavior and is considered a crime against society itself. Minor hooliganism is punishable by administrative action, by short-term detention or corrective labor, or fines, and there is no appeal. More serious offenses carry a sentence of up to seven years imprisonment or corrective labor. Many minor cases of hooliganism are referred to the authorities by the *Druzhiny*, the citizens' militia, and involve drunkenness, disturbing the peace, and resisting authorities. *See also* COMRADES' COURT, p. 279; DRUZHINY, p. 283.

Significance   The definition of hooliganism changes from locale to locale, and from time to time, according to how tightly the authorities wish to control public behavior. The current articles covering hooliganism date from 1966. Prior to that, hooliganism had been included in the criminal codes since 1926 but was much less well defined, and even more sweeping in application. Under Khrushchev, the concept of hooliganism was used to enforce conformity in a wide range of situations. Evidence of nonconforming behavior, i.e., hooliganism, ranged from excessive contact with Westerners to wearing conspicuous clothing and listening to Western music. Despite the fact that the 1966 law tightened up the definition, the concept is still flexible enough to cover a wide range of behavior, some of which would not be considered criminal under Western legal codes. Moreover, there are marked differences among the criminal codes of the various republics in definition and treatment of procedural details. The fact that the concept involves a breach of "socialist morality," as defined at will by the authorities, also makes hooliganism a sort of residual crime. It is frequently applied in cases where the authorities wish to control public behavior, yet where a more specific crime might be difficult to prove. The term itself is used to ensure conformity to acceptable behavior; to label someone a "hooligan" is to charge that they are unacceptable by public standards.

Internal Passport System   A method of controlling the movement and residence of Soviet citizens. Under the internal passport system, every person over age 16 must carry a personal identity booklet and be registered at their place of residence. Issued by the Ministries of the Interior in the various republics, the internal passport contains such personal information as current address, military status, occupation, work record, ethnic origin, date and place of birth, and a current photo, which must be updated at set intervals. Soviet citizens are required to present their identity papers on request to any competent authority and must register with the police whenever they spend the night in a public accommodation in another city, or stay with another family or friends for an extended period. Free movement to urban areas in the Soviet Union is restricted with a permit required for permanent residence in a city. The internal passport system existed in czarist Russia, was abolished in 1917, and was revived by Stalin in 1932 in order to control the *kulaks* and "counterrevolutionaries." *See also* KOLKHOZ, p. 205.

Significance   The internal passport system is not unique to the Soviet union, as many Western European nations require similar documents and similar registration procedures for travelers. However, the uses to which the Soviet system is put are more restrictive. It is used as a method of control over the citizenry and as a way of curbing unwanted migration to the cities, especially to Moscow, Leningrad, Kiev and Odessa. Thus, the Soviet Union has been spared the dilemma of many developing countries whose cities are strained beyond their resources. The requiring of permanent resident permits has led to a subterranean "black market" in arranged marriages, since marriage to a legal city-dweller permits the spouse to acquire a permanent residence permit. The Soviet government has been able through residence permits to allocate manpower to developing areas and maintain a stable agricultural population. The requirement that nationality be listed has particularly affected persons of Jewish ancestry, since Soviet law requires that in this one case the religion rather than area of birth be listed. Many Soviet Jews have maintained that this requirement typifies an endemic antisemitism of the Soviet regime, and permits Soviet authorities to keep track of Jewish dissidents.

Lay Assessors   Nonprofessional citizen judges who serve as representatives of the citizens in all Soviet courtrooms of original jurisdiction. Lay assessors, also called people's assessors, were first instituted by Lenin, and since the 1958–1960s Soviet legal reforms have become a fully institutionalized part of Soviet legal procedure. Soviet courtroom legal practice uses a panel of judges, as in continental law, rather than the citizen jury of British common law systems. Soviet practice is to use one professional judge and two lay assessors. The lay assessors are selected from a list to serve for two-week periods in all courts of original jurisdiction, including military courts. Since the bulk of original jurisdiction is handled by the local People's Courts, lay assessors play the largest role in these local courts and are responsible for determining the procedure and outcome of all civil and criminal cases. Although the lay assessors receive rudimentary legal training and each possesses a vote equal to that of the professional judge, they rarely dissent from the professional judge. Lay assessors are also used in original jurisdiction (trial) cases in the higher courts, up to the republican and federal Supreme courts. In the People's Courts, lay assessors are elected to an assessors' list for five-year terms by popular vote; above that level they are selected by the appropriate governing legislature. They participate in trial preparation, including the decision of what charge is to be levied, and in the trials in all criminal and civil cases of original jurisdiction. *See also* PEOPLE'S COURTS, p. 265; SOCIALIST LEGALITY, p. 271.

Significance   The concept of lay assessors is consistent with the socialist legal theory that the administration of justice should be shared by the citizens, thus permitting broad popular participation in the maintenance of the social order. Since Soviet courts do not use the jury system, some analysts have equated the function of lay assessors with that of juries in Western, common law systems. However, since the lay assessors are treated as judges rather than as a lay jury of citizens, they are as judges bound to administer the law, in all its intricacies, rather than simply determine guilt or innocence. Although since Stalin the Soviet system has made a determined effort to educate lay assessors, they are nevertheless required to be familiar with technical legal processes for which they have had little preparation. This is especially problematical if they wish to question the positions taken by the professional judge. Understandably, few are willing to argue with the judge, although if both lay assessors do take issue their vote is considered binding.

Liquidation   The extralegal practice of removing individuals or groups from important state and party posts for political reasons. The term liquidation is also frequently used to denote the actual physical execution or exile of those who fall out of political favor. Stalin used physical liquidation as an instrument to instill fear and ensure political conformity, dubbing those subjected to liquidation as "enemies of the people." Since Stalin's death, with the dismantling of the worst excesses of the system of terror, liquidation has come to mean imprisonment for political enemies. Liquidation of oppositional groups and individuals in the form of execution or imprisonment is characteristic not only of the communist states during the Stalinist period but of many fascist regimes and of colonial and Third World governments. *See also* GREAT PURGE, p. 17.

Significance   Liquidation is a vicious political instrument used to intimidate potential opposition and instill fear of those in positions of power. In totalitarian systems it has come to be associated with the secret police who are given extralegal powers to deal with so-called "enemies of the state." Although political opposition may be either real or imagined, the effect is to institutionalize terror as a method of political control. During the period of Stalinist terror, hundreds of thousands of Soviet citizens were liquidated. Many just disappeared, their families never learning of their whereabouts or what had happened to them.

Official Crime   Crimes committed by Soviet state officials in the exercise of their duties. A separate chapter of the RSFSR Criminal Code is devoted to official crimes, which include abuse of authority, neglect of duty, taking bribes, giving bribes, and forgery. "Official" in Soviet terms covers a broad range of persons: soldiers on guard duty, policemen, enterprise managers, teachers, sea captains, voluntary militia members, and in general, any representative of authority or anyone in the administration of a public or state institution. "Substantial harm" must be proved; if the harm is not substantial, the offense will be a disciplinary offense. "Substantial harm" also includes loss of profits, which applies to economic enterprises. Such crimes must be intentional, involving the use of an official position, so defined, for mercenary or personal purposes that damages the interests of the office and the state or public interests. Official crimes may be committed either by deliberate action or by omission, the nonperformance or improper performance of duties. The maximum penalty is eight years imprisonment. *See also* ADMINISTRATIVE OFFENSE, p. 247; CRIMES AGAINST SOCIALIST PROPERTY, p. 253.

Significance   Almost all modern legal codes contain provisions directed at official crimes, including the United States Constitution, which prescribes the impeachment process for a President so charged. The scope of official crimes in the Soviet legal code is particularly broad, including as it does everyone from volunteer militiamen to enterprise managers. In effect, it extends criminal responsibility to the entire public sector, which in the Soviet Union is almost all-encompassing.

Parasite   In communist law, an able-bodied adult who deliberately avoids work, enjoys unearned income from exploiting others, or in general leads "an antisocial parasitic way of life." The definition of the so-called parasite as a criminal rests on several tenets of Soviet communism: (1) that every citizen is under the obligation to work to build socialism; (2) that the system has the right to define how citizens may earn income; and (3) that all the citizens must contribute to the building of socialism by following a socialist life-style. Antiparasite laws first appeared in 1957 in several republics as part of Nikita Khrushchev's campaign to mobilize the population and ensure social conformity through the application of administrative and social sanctions. Under an all-republic 1961 edict, the deliberate refusal to engage in "meaningful labor" was made an administrative offense subject to the penalty of resettlement and forced labor. The 1961 edict also included "leading a parasitic way of life," a category so broad that it enabled the authorities to punish dissident intellectuals with sentences of up to five years forced labor in remote regions. In 1970, parasitism was made a crime, under Article 209-1 of the Criminal Code, and the definition of what had been an administrative offense was tightened. The offense of parasitism was thus regularized, with the court process defined, and arbitrary action against those accused lessened. Citizens and state and public organizations may report a suspected parasite to the police. If upon investigation the police sustain the complaint, the accused parasite is warned. The person so accused must be offered work; if the parasite refuses to carry out the work assigned, he or she will be prosecuted, because failure to carry out assigned work is a criminal offense. The 1970 law excludes housewives, the temporarily unemployed, disabled, pensioners, and others. The second portion of the law, following "a parasitic way of life," has been applied to those who enjoy unearned income from "nonlabor" activities, such as speculation, price-fixing, bribery, extortion, kickbacks, illegally employing hired labor, black market operations, and begging. In such cases, the court also confiscates all property gained. The 1970 antiparasite law is still subject to arbitrary use by the authorities since it also applies to those who commit antisocial acts that could lead them into parasitism. *See also* HOOLIGANISM, p. 260.

Significance By labeling the deliberate non-worker a parasite and making him subject to criminal sanctions, the Soviet system has changed the right to work concept to a legal duty to work. As the law against parasites applies to behavior and life-styles as well as to overt acts, it constitutes an important element of official control over individual behavior. Parasitism may be either a deliberate act or a life-style, since the law also makes it a crime to engage in "antisocial" acts that could possibly lead to "a parasitic way of life." The Soviet antiparasite laws are an example of punishing behavior that in the West would not be considered illegal or criminal. As a result, the inclusion of parasites in official Soviet criminal statistics distorts their meaning for Western analysts. In 1981 the Polish military regime promulgated similar antiparasite laws, aimed at punishing those involved with the suppressed trade union movement, Solidarity.

People's Courts General court of original jurisdiction (trial of first instance) for almost all civil and criminal cases. The People's Court (*narodnyi sud*) is the lowest level court in the four-tiered hierarchy of teritorially-based Soviet courts. It handles over 95 percent of all violations of law. In the People's Court, and in all cases of original jurisdiction at higher levels, cases are heard by a panel of one elected professional judge and two lay judges, or lay assessors. The judges of the People's Courts are elected at the district general election, at which they run unopposed, for five-year terms and are subject to recall. The number of judgeships assigned to these district courts depends upon the case load. As is common in continental law, the judicial panel issues a unanimous decision; there are no dissenting or minority opinions. The Soviet judicial system does not clearly delineate the rules of original jurisdiction. The Procuracy or the court itself may send a case to a higher court for its first trial; such cases usually involve crimes against the state or issues that the authorities wish to publicize. People's Courts may issue declaratory statements, such as declaring a person missing or dead. They are also empowered to issue legally binding supplementary directions to citizens or organizations. For example, if a person is convicted of filching goods from his enterprise, the enterprise may also be directed by the court to take steps to prevent further thievery. All decisions of original jurisdiction may be appealed to a higher level court, at the territorial or Republican level, or to the USSR Supreme Court. In addition, the Procuracy may protest decisions. *See also* LAY ASSESSORS, p. 262; PROCURACY, p. 266; SOCIALIST LEGALITY, p. 271.

Significance   For most citizens in a communist state, the People's Court is the judicial organ that most affects their lives. As the workhorse of the communist judicial system, it handles everything from minor infractions of the law, administrative disputes, and civil issues to minor and major crime. Communist legal theory emphasizes the educative as well as the punitive function of the judiciary. The work of the People's Courts is well publicized. Judges may be recalled and some are, usually after a well-orchestrated media campaign that documents their socialist shortcomings. The name itself, which dates from the early days of the Bolshevik Revolution, signifies the intent to distinguish the courts closest to the people from bourgeois court systems. As with all courts in communist legal systems, the independence of the People's Courts is severely limited. Judges are empowered only to administer existing law rather than to set precedent through judicial interpretation. As the major legal instrumentality of the system, the People's Courts are subject to tight supervision, from the local Soviet, all higher courts, the Procuracy, the Ministry of Justice, and ultimately, the Party. All issue regulations and instructions that are binding upon the courts. Thus, because party policy decisions in the legal area can be transmitted immediately to the People's Courts, shifts in communist legal practice can be deduced frequently from the actions of the People's Courts.

Procuracy   The uniform, centralized system of powerful state attorneys, headed by a federal Procurator-General, which is responsible for overseeing and ensuring uniform compliance of all state agencies with the law. The Procuracy, which operates independently of administrative supervision, is the key institution in Soviet and other communist legal systems. Its broad-reaching functions include supervision (*nadzor*) over every government action as well as involvement in every stage of the judicial process. In the courtroom, the Procurator functions as a prosecuting attorney, with greatly expanded powers. Procurators are empowered to detain, arrest, conduct pre-trial investigations, determine cause, indict, initiate trial, transfer a case, release an accused, recommend sentences, appeal decisions, and supervise detention. Much of the power of the Procuracy derives from its centralization and freedom from supervision. The Soviet Procuracy and the KGB (secret police) are the only governmental organs exempt from the principle of dual subordination to both higher and local government agencies. Although technically supervised by the Council of Ministers, the Procuracy is effectively subordinate only to its own hierarchy and ultimately, to the party leadership. Thus, the federal principle does not apply to the Soviet Procuracy. Every administrative level of government contains a procuracy, headed by a Procurator and staff, who are responsible for ensuring legal conformity of the actions of all government agencies on its territory. The local procuracy of the *raion* (county) oversees the work of the local People's Courts and the executive committee of the local soviet (assembly), whereas in Moscow the federal procuracy monitors the work of the federal Council of Ministers. Since, in addition to government administration, all state-owned economic enterprises are controlled by the various ministries at federal or republican levels, in essence the Procuracy monitors all aspects of Soviet public life. The structure of the Procuracy is highly centralized. Each Procurator and staff are responsible only to their superiors in the procuratorial hierarchy. The central apparatus of the Procuracy includes the military department, the department of general supervision, the bureaus of investigation, the department for supervising penal institutions, the departments of criminal and civil supervision, and various support departments, such as finance, administration, statistics, and criminological research. All subordinate units of the Procuracy are structured similarly. The final arbiter is the Procurator-General. The Procurator-General also appoints the Chief Military Procurator, the Procurators of the union-republics and higher territorial units, and confirms the appointments of lower units. Local procuratorial officials are not appointed by the relevant republican legislatures, as with other local officials, but by the Procurator-General of the republic. The functions of the Procuracy may be divided into (1) criminal investigation and prosecution; (2) "special" supervision of the legality of all actions of the courts, penal institutions, and police; and (3) "general" supervision over all administrative bodies. The General

Supervisory Department of the Procuracy is the key unit that monitors all government actions. At any administrative level, the Procurator is the dominant judicial official. If at any stage in the judicial process the Procurator becomes convinced of the innocence of the accused, he must inform the judiciary that the case is halted. The Procuracy may appeal court decisions to higher level courts, including the federal Supreme Court. Although pretrial investigations involving suspected crimes against the state are conducted by the KGB, they are supervised by the Procuracy. In addition, the military Procuracy is also under the direct supervision of the central Procuracy and the Procurator-General. If the Procuracy decides that a civil case involves state interests, it may enter the case. Although constitutionally responsible to the federal Supreme Soviet and its Presidium, the Procuracy operates essentially under the supervision of the Department of Administrative Organs of the central communist party hierarchy and is thus subordinate only to the central party organs. The Procuracy is organized along military lines by hierarchical rank and its members wear uniforms that denote their rank. The approximately 15,000 members of the Soviet Procuracy comprise the most prestigious sector of the legal profession. *See also* DUAL SUBORDINATION, p. 137; PEOPLE'S COURTS, p. 265; SOCIALIST LEGALITY, p. 271.

Significance   The Procuracy is a unique institution, both administrative and judicial in its responsibilities, and functionally independent of all but the party leadership. Although European legal systems based on Roman law frequently include a procuratorial institution, the Soviet Procuracy and its East European analogues are distinguished by their extensive powers and freedom from administrative control. By instituting an independent, centralized monitoring body, the party ensures that party policy will be executed. In the judicial process, because the Soviet legal system has no equivalent to habeas corpus, the supervision of the Procuracy is crucial. The Procuracy also acts as an ombudsman. Citizens can and do complain to the appropriate Procurator, from protesting a local administrative decision to providing information leading to a criminal investigation. The Soviet Procuracy also serves to restore centralization to a federalized system of administration. Thus, the Procuracy is a powerful instrument for enforcing conformity. The Soviet Procuracy is the direct lineal heir of the czarist procuracy that Peter the Great established in 1722 as a means of creating a centralized administrative system under imperial control. Abolished with the Bolshevik Revolution, the Procuracy was reinstituted by Lenin in 1922 almost in its earlier form. During Josef Stalin's rule, the functions of the Procuracy were usually limited to executing the instructions of the secret police. With the post-Stalin legal reform and regularization of the Soviet legal system, the Procuracy regained its role as a key institution. East European communist systems, with minor differences, follow the organizational structure and functions of the Soviet Procuracy.

Psychiatric Confinement   Confinement in a mental hospital of political and religious dissidents in the Soviet Union as a form of extralegal punishment. Although the overwhelming majority of Soviet citizens confined to psychiatric institutions are committed for medical reasons, in the West the term has come to refer to those few who have been compulsorily committed for non-medical reasons. Citizens can be committed by a civil process, a judicial procedure, or by transfer from an ordinary penal institution. Commitment must be confirmed by a panel of three psychiatrists. In the case of a political dissident, the usual practice is that the police simply inform the health agencies that a suspect is mentally ill or a potential threat to himself or society. Once committed, the only appeal is to the Ministry of Health, which oversees all commitments. The use of an administrative procedure with limited right of appeal rather than punishment through the judicial system has enabled the authorities to avoid public trials and publicity in the case of especially determined political dissidents. The use of psychiatry for political purposes dates to the 1930s and was revived in 1961 when the post-Stalin legal reforms greatly circumscribed the criminal charges under which persons could be tried for political reasons. Commitment for political reasons increased after 1970 when it became legal to commit persons for "preventive reasons." The criteria for involuntary psychiatric confinement is vague, using such diagnoses as "delusional condition" or "incipient schizophrenia," which can be interpreted to mean that anyone who persistently opposes or questions the regime is insane or about to become so. *See also* ANTI-SOVIET AGITATION AND PROPAGANDA, p. 248; DISSENT AND OPPOSITION, p. 281; HUMAN RIGHTS MOVEMENT, p. 286.

Significance   Involuntary psychiatric confinement for political reasons has generally been applied to dissenters who refuse to recant. The practice has generated much criticism in the West as well as conflict within Soviet scientific circles. Most such compulsory psychiatric commitments rely on the opinion of the Serbski Institute of Forensic Psychiatry that a link exists between political protest and mental illness. The assumption is that only a mentally ill person will criticize the socialist system and refuse to conform. Under this definition, only a dramatic change in views indicates that the person has been "cured." During the 1970s and 1980s, public outrage in the West, vigorous self-defense, and the refusal of some Soviet psychiatric commissions to cooperate has won release for some dissidents. The highly selective use of this method of punishing political dissent is a clear sign that the Soviet authorities are unwilling to return to the Stalinist practice of disregarding the legality of the criminal process in cases of perceived political dissidence.

RSFSR Criminal Code   The codified criminal law of the largest Soviet republic, the Russian Soviet Federated Socialist Republic, on which all other republican criminal codes are modeled. The RSFSR Criminal Code of 1961 is based on the reforms in criminal law and procedure spelled out by the Federal Basic Principles of Criminal Law enacted by the Supreme Soviet in 1958. The Basic Principles and the RSFSR Code together represent the culmination of the post-Stalin effort to codify Soviet criminal law and procedure and remove extralegal abuses committed under Josef Stalin. The underlying principle for post-Stalin Soviet legal jurisdictions is that a specific punishment is provided only for conviction of a specific crime, as spelled out by the criminal codes. Thus, the 1958 and early 1960s legal reforms in the Soviet Union brought Soviet law in line with the common practices of continental legal systems based on Roman and Napoleonic law. Soviet law consists of both federal law and the laws of the 15 union-republics, but unlike the state law of the United States, there is little difference among republican legal codes. The RSFSR legal codes serve as the model for all other republican codes, with only minor differences stemming from the cultural traditions of the various Soviet nationalities. The general procedure is for the Supreme Soviet to enact All-Union Fundamental Principles, which then form the basis for the more detailed republican legal codes. All republican law must conform to federal law. *See also* SOCIALIST LEGALITY, p. 271.

Significance   The RSFSR Criminal Code is the major expression of the post-Stalin legal reform that regularized Soviet law. One of the most important consequences of the legal reform was the dropping of "social danger" as a reason for criminal punishment. Under the prewar criminal codes, for example, it was legal to punish a citizen for merely seeming to embody, as a person, "counterrevolutionary" (i.e., anticommunist) tendencies. Other actions which were not crimes in and of themselves were punishable if the courts considered them a "social danger." Social danger and counterrevolutionary crime were the rubrics under which the most flagrant abuses of legality had occurred under Stalin. The new criminal codes abandoned the principle of analogy, inherited from czarist practice, under which a judge could convict a person of a "crime" not specifically enumerated in the criminal codes if the court determined it to be "analogous" to a specified crime. The RSFSR Criminal Code also stipulated that confessions must be corroborated by other evidence of guilt, thus removing one of the worst abuses of Stalinism where prisoners were tortured, confessions extorted, and the victim summarily executed. The RSFSR Criminal Code constitutes a landmark in the regularization of Soviet legal practice. Unlike Anglo-Saxon common law, which is based on precedents established by the courts and various collections of laws, modern civil law like the RSFSR code is based on the continental civil law tradition of comprehensive legal codes containing a systematic outline of general principles and specific crimes, procedures, and punishments. This the 1961 RSFSR Criminal Code accomplished. Because all Soviet legal codes are similar, the common practice of citing the RSFSR Criminal Code, as in "conviction under article 70," is factually an error but a convenience resorted to by many, since the RSFSR code serves as the model for all other republican codes.

Socialist Legality   The Soviet legal theory that distinguishes between socialist and bourgeois legal systems. Socialist legality is viewed as a force that supports the construction of socialism, in contrast to bourgeois legality which protects the rule of the bourgeoisie. According to Marxism-Leninism, law is determined by the economic base of society. Each class structure, from feudal to capitalist to socialist, gives rise to a specific type of law. All but socialism are based on the private ownership of the means of production and all but socialism are designed to protect it. Socialist law is based on the social ownership of the means of production and expresses the will of the working class. Socialist legality also emphasizes the role of law as educator, as a means of public instruction in the norms of socialist behavior. The socialist state creates socialist law and in the interests of preserving the socialist order, elevates the rights of the state over those of the individual citizen. The state is the sole source of law. As Andrei Vyshinsky, a leading legal theorist of the 1930s stated, socialist legality "is a creative force promoting social development, helping workers in the advance toward the construction of a classless socialist society." *See also* CIVIL RIGHTS, p. 251; COMRADES' COURT, p. 279; CRIMES AGAINST THE STATE, p. 255; GREAT PURGE, p. 17; RSFSR CRIMINAL CODE, p. 270; SOCIALIST OWNERSHIP, p. 227.

Significance   The newly victorious Bolsheviks faced a dilemma which the concept of socialist legality solved. Marxism postulates that courts and laws will "wither away" with the state once communism is achieved. Having repudiated all czarist law as bourgeois and having dismantled the czarist court structure, the Bolsheviks were faced with the necessity of maintaining public order and securing the Revolution. Vladimir Lenin instituted the Revolutionary Courts which administered "revolutionary justice," their main purpose being to safeguard the Revolution and to punish its suspected opponents. During the chaos of the Civil War (1918–22) such revolutionary tribunals were frequently arbitrary and brutal, and all operated extralegally as no Soviet legal codes were published until 1922. They did establish the precept that the goal of socialist legality is to safeguard the socialist order. Legal codes and courts were established as a necessary component of the building of socialism, rather than as temporary institutions due to shortly "wither away" with the approach of communism. The idea of citizen-based justice was retained with the institution of the lay assessors, two lay judges who sit on the three-person judicial panel on all People's Courts, the courts of original jurisdiction which replaced the revolutionary tribunals. During the 1930s socialist legality was gravely compromised by Josef Stalin's use of the concept to justify the mass deportations and executions of the Great Purge. After Stalin's death in 1953, Nikita Khrushchev's de-Stalinization campaign focused on restoring the legitimacy of socialist legality, through a codification of the legal codes, an emphasis on procedural regularity, and the abandonment of Stalinist terror. Khrushchev also emphasized the educative function of socialist legality, setting up citizen-based Comrades' Courts and the volunteer militia (*Druzhiny*). Despite the institutionalization of legal norms accomplished since 1958, Soviet socialist legality retains its central thrust, the primacy of the state. Law is viewed as a means of directing the power of the socialist state, not as a limit on government, and violations of legality continue to occur, particularly in cases of perceived opposition to the state.

Supreme Court of the Soviet Union   The highest judicial body in the Soviet legal system. The Supreme Court of the Soviet Union is the only federal, or all-union, court; unlike the federal judiciary of the United States, there are no lower federal appellate or district courts. The only other nationally based courts are the military courts, set up by military districts rather than on administrative districts. All other Soviet courts operate within the jurisdiction of the 15 union-republics; each republican court system culminates in the republican Supreme Court. The Supreme Court of the USSR is headed by a Chairman and a Vice-Chairman and is divided into three panels: civil, criminal, and military. Members are appointed by the Presidium of the Supreme Soviet for five-year terms and the Chairmen of the republican supreme courts are *ex officio* members. Total membership is usually 31. Despite its title, which may be misleading to North American students, the Supreme Court of the USSR has no power of judicial review over legislative or executive actions; it exercises supervision only over the judiciary. The court exercises both appellate and original jurisdiction. In appellate cases, protests are brought to the Supreme Court of the USSR by the Procurator-General or by the Chairman of the Supreme Court, but the Supreme Court will hear a protest against the decision of a republican court only if it is in possible violation of federal law or with the interests of another republic. Only in rare cases does the Supreme Court act as the court of original jurisdiction, confined largely to those in which the leadership seeks to publicize cases by trying them in the highest court. Two such cases were the espionage trials of the American U-2 pilot Gary Powers in 1960 and the Soviet officer Oleg Penkovsky, convicted in 1963 of spying for the United States. The most important function of the Supreme Court lies in the area of judicial interpretation and instructions to all other courts. The Supreme Court is empowered to issue general instructions (*rukovodyashchie razyasneniya*), interpretations of laws, and applications that are legally binding. Thus, the Supreme Court is quasi-legislative since these general instructions carry the force of law and are frequently used to instruct the courts as to how relevant legislation should be interpreted and applied. The Procurator-General and the Minister of Justice attend plenary (full) sessions of the Supreme Court and the Minister of Justice is empowered to propose draft general instructions to the plenum. In its major functions, the Supreme Court (1) issues binding general instructions and interpretations of legislation for all other courts; (2) hears cases on protests by the Procurator-General or the Supreme Court Chairman (appellate function); (3) reviews the decisions of the republican courts; (4) resolves conflicts between republican supreme courts and lower courts, and between republican supreme courts and federal legislation; and (5) advises the Presidium of the Supreme Soviet on draft federal legislation. *See also* PROCURACY, p. 266.

Significance　　The Supreme Court of the USSR is the chief instrumentality for imposing uniformity in judicial practice, interpretation, and application in an otherwise republic-based judicial system. Through its power to issue binding instructions, it assures uniformity in judicial practices. Working closely with the Procuracy, the Supreme Court supervises the actions of all courts. Since communist legal doctrine rejects the principle of a fundamental law to which the state is subordinate, the Supreme Court cannot rule on the constitutionality of executive and legislative acts, but it can expand and explain their meaning to the courts that must implement them. Also, as a legal system based on continental, Roman law, Soviet law does not operate on the principle of judicial review as do common law systems. Some of the difficulties Americans have with understanding the Soviet Supreme Court arise from the fact that although it is the highest court in a federalized judicial system, that judicial system is not based on common law and judicial precedent and it operates within the context of a tightly centralized political system.

Zek   Russian prison camp slang for prisoner. *Zek* is derived from ZK, the official abbreviation for *Zaklyuchennyi* (pronounced Za-klyu-CHON-nyi), prisoner, used on all official prison camp documents. *See also* GREAT PURGE, p. 17; GULAG, p. 259.

Significance   The term Zek received wide publicity from the writings of Aleksandr Solzenitsyn, Nobel Prize–winning author living in forced exile in the United States. Solzenitsyn's works, particularly *One Day in the Life of Ivan Denisovich* and *Gulag Archipelago*, contain vivid descriptions of the life of the Zeks in Stalin's prison camps. Because of the influence of Solzenitsyn, Zek is now frequently used to refer to political prisoners who have been imprisoned for their opposition to the Soviet regime.

7. Citizen and State

All-Union Knowledge Society (*Znanie*)   A Soviet educational organization founded in 1947 as the successor to the League of the Militant Godless. As the name of its predecessor indicates, the main function of the All-Union Knowledge Society is to propagate atheism. It is, however, much less heavy-handed than its predecessor in pursuit of creating the atheist society proper for a Marxist-Leninist state. *Znanie* has developed into a multipurpose educational society. It publishes a monthly journal, *Science and Religion*, and copious educational material, much of it designed for trade union and youth group members. Soviet statistics claim a membership of 3 million for Znanie; most are party workers, educators, and government officials. *See also* ATHEISM, p. 37.

Significance   The All-Union Knowledge Society springs from the inherent hostility of Marxism-Leninism to rival belief systems, including specifically religion. Eastern European attempts to inculcate atheism are generally lower key. In staunchly Roman Catholic Poland, where the Polish Communist Party can at best hope only to neutralize the church, the party has preferred to work through captive organizations, such as PAX, which simultaneously profess Catholicism and communism.

Citizen Participation   The involvement of individual citizens in collective activities that relate to the functions of the political system. Citizen participation in communist-party systems is neither pluralistic, in the sense of interest groups that articulate interests and influence policy, nor totalitarian, in the sense that there is no citizen input.

275

Communist citizens' organizations do not help select leaders, define policy objectives, or question authority. None exercises countervailing power in terms of the Communist Party. Instead, participatory modes are structured so as to permit the citizen a role in the implementation and monitoring of policy. At the minimum, a communist citizens' organization must transmit desired values. The party determines the scope and nature of permissible activities for each group; none may operate openly without official approval. In communist states, the usual primary groups—peer groups, social clubs, and the like—do not operate independently of the state. Citizen participation in communist-party states has changed substantially since Josef Stalin defined the proper role of the trade unions as "transmission belts" for party policy. As the use of terror declined in the post-Stalinist era, citizens' organizations came to play a substantive role. Marxist doctrine includes a strong commitment to the role of the citizen in governance. The 1919 Bolshevik party program, for example, stated: "All the working masses without exception must be gradually induced to take part in the work of the state administration." The Stalinist concept of citizen participation as an instrument for mass mobilization has given way to a more meaningful policy where millions of Soviet citizens are actively involved in monitoring the activities of the authorities and overseeing the implementation of decisions. Soviet citizen participation is especially impressive at local levels, comparing most favorably with Western nations. Soviet citizens serve as volunteers in deputy's offices, monitor the local social welfare organs, trust residence committees to maintain social standards, and make numerous demands on local authorities. Participatory modes may be divided into roughly four categories: (1) job-related, such as trade unions and training organizations; (2) administrative support; (3) monitoring and control; and (4) hobby, social, and peer groups. The last, which ranges from sports clubs to youth and women's groups, provide officially approved leisure activities and serve as agents of official socialization. The second and third groups involve citizens' groups, mainly at the local level, that help determine how policy shall be implemented; these range from the residence committees to the volunteer militia. Control is carried out by a vast army of "citizen inspectors," comprising an amazing 22 percent of the total Soviet population. These voluntary organizations also serve as a conduit of information for policymakers. Once past the policy-making stage, Soviet authorities expend tremendous energy in soliciting the input and advice of the myriad citizens' groups; for example over 4,000 citizen-initiated amendments were offered to the draft 1977 Soviet Constitution. What is not permitted, however, are interest groups that make counter-policy proposals. Nonetheless, citizen participation, especially in the Soviet Union, possesses meaning in terms of personal efficacy, giving the citizen a sense of control over some aspects of life. Citizen participation was expanded by Nikita Khrushchev, who saw it as the first stage in the "withering away of the state" promised by Marxism. While the Brezhnev leadership dropped the phrase "the state of the people," which Khrushchev substituted for the dictatorship of the proletariat, the emphasis on citizen participation has been maintained. *See also* DISSENT AND OPPOSITION, p. 281; DOSAAF, p. 282; DRUZHINY, p. 283; MASS ORGANIZATIONS, p. 291; SOVIET, p. 160; TRADE UNIONS, p. 305.

Significance   The citizens of no other state are so regularly involved in participatory activities as those of the Soviet Union. A huge network of organizations blanket the land and countless public meetings are held to discuss every political decision. Nonetheless, there is no recorded instance of a major government proposal being rejected. Thus, Soviet-style participation does not meet the Western definition as activity aimed at aggregating interests, articulating these to policy-makers, and influencing policy outcomes. Some political analysts, such as Jerry Hough, argue that Soviet participatory activities fall within the general understanding of citizen participation, as both personally efficacious and as an instrument of citizen input. Others maintain that the Soviet Union and its Eastern European counterparts are totalitarian systems that by definition exclude participation. Theodore Friedgut argues that participation must be voluntary, which describes most Soviet citizen participation, since many obviously still feel free not to participate in organized citizens' activities. Still others term communist citizens' organizations "institutionalized interest groups," providing genuine citizen involvement in policy implementation. Patterns of participation vary among the communist-party states; most observers agree that the Soviet system is probably the most institutionalized and widespread. Yugoslavia stands outside this model of directed participation. Its unique self-management system is based on decentralization and a commitment to self-government; the Yugoslav citizen is offered a totally different mode of participation through direct self-management bodies. The "zone of political indifference," as some analysts term it, is also far broader in Yugoslavia. Even the more liberal Yugoslav regime, however, has retreated since 1972 when it discovered, via the Croat nationality crisis, that opening up the political process to local interest groups enhanced the centrifugal tendencies of the multinational Yugoslav state. Elsewhere, the ruling communist parties determine the limits, modes, and scope of activity. This was underlined recently when a miniscule group of Soviet citizens mounted a public demonstration against nuclear arms escalation. Although they were in general articulating official Soviet policy toward the danger of nuclear holocaust, their sin lay not in content but in lack of official permission; they were promptly repressed. How much actual personal efficacy is transmitted through the officially approved forms of citizen participation is an open question. Events in Eastern Europe indicate that many official organizations may be viewed as meaningless. In Czechoslovakia in 1968, all traditional citizens' groups suffered a swift change, from the Czechoslovak youth movement, the ČSSM, which simply distintegrated, to other groups such as veterans' clubs and even sports clubs, which became active proponents of reform. Poland in 1980 evinced an even more dramatic repudiation of managed participation. The Polish workers renounced the trade unions, and in what became their major demand, formed a coalition of independent trade unions which they called Solidarity. Party control over citizen participation is buttressed by its control over all information, which in democratic societies is the basis of informed participation. Although the Lake Baikal case may be an exception, most Soviet citizens are not acquainted with the extent of environmental damage nor the health risks involved, and thus cannot effectively question government on environmental matters. In contrast, in the much more open Yugoslav society the citizen has access to such information, and indeed in one case informed citizens blocked the construction of a proposed nuclear power plant. Thus, citizen participation in communist-party states includes one crucial constant: the party controls and defines the scope of participation. Instances such as the formation of Solidarity indicated that the party's monopoly of power has been breached, and the essential Leninist tenet of democratic centralism weakened.

Collective (*Kollektiv*)   A Russian word to which the Soviets have attached an ideological meaning that emphasizes the necessary subordination of individual interests to the needs of society in the building of communism. *Kollektiv* is a term that every Soviet citizen, from school age on, is familiar with. School children are taught that they are responsible to their classmates for their behavior, and this socialization is continued through organizations such as the Young Pioneers and the Komsomol. As the Soviet citizens mature, they become involved with a multitiered system of collectives. The collective to which the citizen is responsible may be a work unit within the factory, an army unit, an apartment house committee, a mass political organization, or indeed the entire Soviet population. The "spirit" of collectivity implies mutual responsibility and conformity to the values of the system, as well as cooperation and altruism toward fellow members. *See also* NEW SOVIET MAN, p. 107.

Significance The tactics of mass mobilization pursued by the Soviet communist party include emphasis on obedience to the norms of the collective. Every citizen is expected to be politically active and to subordinate personal interests to the good of society. The spirit of collectivity is part of the vision of the new Soviet man, that new human who will be shaped by the socialist environment into a virtuous, unselfish being willing to bend all energies to the task of fulfilling the promise of communism. In recent years, the Soviets have deemphasized the new Soviet man theory, but the party still promotes the collective as a means of ensuring conformity and teaching responsibility. Today the most frequent point of reference is the "working collective," which may be found anywhere from the shop floor to an authors' group.

Comrades' Court The quasi-judicial, locally based citizens' tribunal which is responsible for enforcing public morality and conformity to communist values in the workplace and place of residence. The Comrades' Court (*tovarishcheskii sud*) acts as an informal tribunal conducting public hearings in matters generally involving "antisocial behavior" and petty crime. Comrades' Courts are established in workplaces, residences, neighborhoods, collective farms, and schools. First set up in 1918 to deal with disciplinary problems during the period of the Civil War, they were subsequently downgraded during Stalin's rule. The Comrades' Courts were revived by Nikita Khrushchev in 1959. Each court consists of a panel of elected lay judges who rotate as the three judges who preside during court sessions. Although Soviet doctrine states that the Comrades' Courts are a voluntary creation of the residential or workplace collective rather than an official institution of the state legal apparatus, the Comrades' Courts have legal status under the law. The Courts may levy social sanctions or minor fines for "antisocial behavior" but, except for minor and first-time infractions, they are not permitted to deal with cases covered by the criminal code. "Antisocial behavior," by which is usually meant any behavior that is contrary to the precepts of communism and injurious to the Marxist-Leninist social order, may involve cases ranging from alcoholism and prostitution to domestic quarrels, violation of work rules, and nonpayment of rents. Comrades' Courts generally deal with three types of cases: (1) cases involving a violation of morality and community standards (swearing in public, failure to provide for aged parents, public drunkenness, for example); (2) minor

crimes and first offenses (distilling alcohol, poaching); (3) cases referred by the local courts (usually minor matters of civil and property
law). Comrades' Courts based in the workplace usually deal with such
infractions as violation of work rules, repeated absences, and refusal to
obey directions. Any citizen, organization, or the court itself can initiate
a charge. Cases may also be referred to the Comrades' Courts by the
local Office of the Procurator, the volunteer citizens' militia (*druzhiny*),
the residence committees, or the local People's Court. The hearing in a
Comrades' Court is conducted on an informal, *ad hoc* basis as charges
are brought, with the three judges determining the penalty. In
addition to minor fines and/or damages, the Comrades' Courts may
issue warnings, demand an apology, or reprimand the accused. In
areas of severe housing shortages, the residence-based Comrades'
Courts are often concerned with disputes over apartment allocation.
There is no right of appeal although complaints may be made to the
local assembly or trade union, which oversee the Comrades' Courts in
their areas. *See also* CITIZEN PARTICIPATION, p. 275; DRUZHINY, p. 283;
RESIDENCE COMMITTEES, p. 299; SOCIALIST LEGALITY, p. 271.

Significance   Comrades' Courts are a significant part of the widespread network of voluntary citizens' groups through which the Soviet
Communist Party encourages conformity and promotes loyalty to the
system through citizen participation. The courts basically rely on peer
pressure and minor penalties to ensure social conformity, but they also
provide a fast and informal method of resolving family disputes and
minor social infringements. The system makes everyone responsible to
their neighbors and instills a sense of collectivity in the citizenry. The
work-based Comrades' Courts inculcate labor responsibility; the other
courts monitor the citizens' social behavior. The success of the Comrades' Courts in involving substantial numbers of citizens is attested to
by their rapid increase since 1960. It is estimated that around 300,000
formally recognized Comrades' Courts exist in the Soviet Union.
Comrades' Courts are also used in Bulgaria, Hungary, the German
Democratic Republic, and other socialist states. The Comrades' Courts
were a major part of Khrushchev's post-1959 attempt to transfer some
of the functions of the state to public organs based in mass citizen
participation. Much of the work of these courts has come to be as
concerned with education and prevention, through peer pressure and
criticism, as with the punitive aspects of their work. During the
Brezhnev era, such "populist" approaches were deemphasized and a
greater emphasis placed on bureaucratic autonomy. Many Soviet
citizens apparently remain suspicious of the Comrades' Courts because
the judges do not have legal training and the proceedings are more
susceptible to popular and party pressure.

Crimean Tatars   A small nationality group, numbering about 200,000 who were accused of collaborating with the Germans and were forcibly resettled in Central Asia in 1944. The Crimean Tatars were one of eight such small nationalities who were exiled en masse from their traditional homelands by Josef Stalin. Others exiled include the Ingush, Chechens, Kalmyks, Khemsin, Karachi, Balkars, and Volga Germans. Although since cleared of the charge of collaboration, successive Soviet leaderships have refused to permit this people to return to their homes. *See also* HUMAN RIGHTS MOVEMENT, p. 286.

Significance   The Crimean Tatars have become both a cause and a symbol of communist injustice for human rights activists in the Soviet Union. The leading proponent of redress for the Crimean Tatars has been General Piotr Grigorenko. Grigorenko was declared mentally incompetent and incarcerated in a psychiatric hospital until massive protests from the West effected his release and eventual exile abroad.

Dissent and Opposition   The all-inclusive term applied to activities which either question the policies of the ruling communist parties or directly advocate change. Defining dissent and opposition is difficult; Western constructs are imprecise in the Soviet context and in Soviet terms, the two are virtually indistinguishable. Basically, any questioning of the party's authority, whether or not it posits systemic change, is treated as opposition by the Soviet authorities. Dissent and opposition in Soviet-style systems surfaced only after the death of Josef Stalin. Prior to 1953, the massive terror system imposed on the citizens of the communist-party states stifled any such inclinations. The brief post-Stalin period of the Thaw, the publication of Aleksandr Solzhenitsyn's *One Day in the Life of Ivan Denisovich*, and the removal of the worst of police terror, emboldened some to believe that within-system evolution was possible. An ever-shifting spectrum of dissent and opposition has arisen in the Soviet Union and Eastern Europe. The belief in within-system evolution peaked with the efforts of the Czechoslovak liberalizers to create a "socialism with a human face," suppressed by Soviet tanks in August of 1968. In 1970 the Fifth Directorate of the KGB, charged with suppressing dissent, was created. Despite this, dissent and opposition continued, culminating in the Polish events of 1980–81, when over 10 million Poles united under the banner of Solidarity. Within the Soviet Union, dissent appears to have been almost silenced. The accession of Yuri Andropov, former head of the KGB, to the party leadership, indicates that there will be no softening on the part of the Soviets toward dissent and opposition. *See also* DEVIATIONISM AND REVISIONISM, p. 45; HELSINKI ACCORD, p. 321;

HUMAN RIGHTS MOVEMENT, p. 286; PRAGUE SPRING, p. 295; SOLIDARITY, p. 303; WORKERS OPPOSITION, p. 34.

Significance   Suppression of dissent and opposition has been embedded in communist-party systems since Vladimir Lenin outlawed intraparty democracy in 1921. The actions of the Brezhnev regime forced many dissenters into opposition, an explicit questioning of the very legitimacy of the ruling communist parties. Despite severe repression, dissent and opposition now appears to be a constant in the Soviet bloc. The dissent of the 1960s and 1970s is characterized by two distinctions: (1) dissenters increasingly appealed to the West, and to communist parties outside the bloc for support; and (2) dissenting and oppositional groups have made common cause across national boundaries. In the 1970s, particularly after the signing of the Helsinki Accord, much dissent has focused on the area of civil liberties. Dissent in Eastern Europe possesses a further commonality, the desire for freedom from Soviet dictate. This is equally impermissible by Soviet standards; the Soviet Union will no more tolerate pluralism and erosion of party control in Eastern Europe than it will within its own borders. The Eastern European communist parties remain dependent upon Soviet power for their continuing existence. Their identity as communist-party states is a function of their subordination to the Soviet Union. Whatever deviations from the Soviet model may occur —a New Economic Policy in Hungary, a quasi-independent Romanian foreign policy—exist only with the implicit permission of the Soviet Union. Any dissent or reform that calls into question the leading role of the national communist party, and by extension that of the Communist Party of the Soviet Union, is out. Whether dissent is repressed by the national government, as with the imposition of military rule in Poland in 1981, or directly by the USSR, is unimportant; the Soviet Union still determines the limits of dissent and opposition. Despite the rising ferment, there has been little fundamental change in these systems.

DOSAAF (Voluntary Association for the Assistance of Army, Air Force, and Navy)

A Soviet mass organization that provides paramilitary training and recreation for the civilian population. First set up in the 1920s as *Osoaviakhim*, DOSAAF's membership is now estimated at some 80 million citizens, who provide the Soviet Union with a ready pool of semi-trained military manpower. DOSAAF is not subject to formal military control; it operates independently of the Ministry of Defense and is under the control of local party organizations. Although military officers serve as instructors, the basic management of activities is provided by school, party, and youth group personnel. DOSAAF embodies elements of a volunteer militia, a home guard, a civil defense network, athletic training, and ROTC; anyone who has reached age 14 is eligible to join. Paramilitary training in such areas as marksmanship, guerilla tactics, and physical training is offered and DOSAAF also serves as the medium for sports activities, such as glider training, parachute jumping and pilot training, which are not otherwise permitted in the civilian sector. All Soviet amateur radio operators must be DOSAAF members. Through DOSAAF, veteran pilots, paratroopers, and other ex-service personnel can maintain their military skills. The 50 percent of new army conscripts who have DOSAAF experience are usually promoted more rapidly than other conscripts. *See also* MASS ORGANIZATIONS, p. 291.

Significance   DOSAAF provides the Soviet Union with an immense ready reserve of semi-trained military manpower and reinforces the image of a nation in arms, ready to respond to military emergencies. Because so many of its activities are intrinsically appealing, DOSAAF enlists a sizable proportion of the population. Thus the Soviet population is undoubtedly one of the most militarily well-trained populations. However, formal control of DOSAAF and most day-to-day responsibility are under civilian control. This, some analysts maintain, has enabled the party to restrict the scope of the military. Every communist state in Eastern Europe, including Yugoslavia, has an organization similar to DOSAAF. DOSAAF, and its counterpart organizations, is valuable in that it gives a large portion of the population a sense of participation in the defense of the system and promotes a sense of nationalism. Some Sovietologists also maintain that DOSAAF indicates an increasing militarization of Soviet society.

Druzhiny   Volunteer citizens' militia who are part of the party-sponsored network of community self-help organizations intended to involve citizens in the control of public behavior. *Druzhiny* units provide neighborhood patrols for protection against street crime and direct traffic, and provide crowd control at such events as May Day. Druzhiny members may stop anyone suspected of "antisocial behavior," which can be broadly interpreted as ranging from eccentric dress to "parasitism," which usually covers charges of trading with foreigners or earning income from minor illegal transactions. In addition, they may provide the manpower for raids on dissidents, illegal meetings, religious meetings, or any group that offends community norms. The volunteers, called *Druzhinniki*, can refer such persons to the local Comrades' Courts, quasi-legal citizens' courts, for reprimands or sanctions. In other words, the Druzhiny function as a voluntary adjunct to the authorities, enforcing regime-determined norms of behavior and meting out punishment through the Comrades' Courts if necessary. Druzhiny members are usually students drawn from the Komsomol units, pensioners, or workers, who "donate" their time. Known as Volunteer Popular Detachments (*Dobrovol'nye narodnye druzhiny*), the Druzhiny were set up by Nikita Khrushchev in 1959 by the resolution, "On the Participation of the Working People in the Preservation of Public Order in the Country." As the resolution implies, the goal is to broaden the base of public support for the party by involving citizens in social control, and to ensure social conformity to the party. Although initially under direct party control, since 1974 the Druzhiny have been supervised by local governments. *See also* CITIZEN PARTICIPATION, p. 275; COMRADES' COURT, p. 279; MASS ORGANIZATIONS, p. 291.

Significance   The Druzhiny serve two functions: (1) they involve masses of citizens at the local level and build support for the system through voluntary participation; and (2) they provide control over people's public behavior. The creation of the Druzhiny coincided with the period in Khrushchev's rule when the extrajudicial powers of the security forces were curbed. By placing control of public behavior in the hands of local volunteer units, control was enhanced while the party's role became less obvious. Because peer pressure more than police pressure tends to ensure conformity, the system works. The trade unions and similar workplace organizations supervise the citizen at work; the various residence committees supervise him at home, and the Druzhiny supervise his public behavior. Thus, the Druzhiny serve as an institutional element for social control, imposing conformity on those whose behavior, while not in violation of the legal codes, is still not in accord with party dictates. The Druzhiny also serve to mobilize the population for the building of a communist society, a function they share with other community-based voluntary organizations such as the residence committees and the Comrades' Courts. Soviet theory holds that when communism is achieved, the state will wither away and state functions will be fulfilled by social organizations; the Druzhiny are promoted as a step toward the ultimate realization of communist self-government. Their success is evident from the fact that most Soviets appear to accept the role of the estimated 7 million Druzhinniki.

Glavlit   Abbreviation of an early title for the Chief Administration for the Protection of State Secrets in the Press, the censorship agency through which the Soviet regime ensures that only those materials it deems acceptable reach the public. *Glavlit* regulates all public information and literature in accordance with the goals of the party. Glavlit also can permit only a limited edition or restrict circulation. All information is categorized into (1) mass consumption; (2) foreign consumption only; (3) restricted circulation; (4) for top officials only; and (5) total suppression. Glavlit may also permit publication only if stipulated deletions are made. Emigré reports indicate that the list that Glavlit has determined cannot be printed includes works that (1) are anti-state; (2) question the dictatorship of the proletariat or Marxism-Leninism; (3) reveal anything that the system considers a state secret; (4) are pornographic; (5) contain positive references to capitalist countries; (6) foment religious or ethnic hostilities; and (7) are "mystical," "ideologically weak" or do not conform with the tenets of socialist realism. Any criticism of the Soviet system and its leaders is forbidden, plus events that might demean the USSR, such as airplane crashes, environmental pollution, or disasters. Since the list of censorable items also includes any admission that Glavlit exists, its actual operation is difficult to pinpoint. It is supplemented by *Glavrepertoire*, the Chief Administration for Control over Performances and Repertoires. All entertainment must register and submit programs for approval. Control extends to phonograph records (thus Western rock and roll is banned), radio, television, ballet, and theater. The agencies of censorship have branch offices throughout the country and work closely with the "ideological officials" at the various territorial party levels. All are ultimately responsible to the Central Committee and the Ministry of Culture. Party organs also determine what events and themes require obligatory publication, the major goal being to glorify the party and the system. *See also* MEDIA, p. 293; SAMIZDAT, p. 300; SOCIALIST REALISM, p. 301.

Significance   The authority of Glavlit and its adjuncts extends over all forms of public expression, from books to ballet to circus acts and musical groups. Its stifling effect on artistic expression has caused many famed musicians and ballet stars to seek artistic freedom in the West. Glavlit's power is largely self-regulating; most who must operate within the system understand the ground rules. Eastern European systems, with the exception of Yugoslavia, have analogous censorship agencies, as, for example, the Polish Main Office for the Control of Press, Publication, and Public Spectacles. Censorship in Yugoslavia is much less rigid, being confined mainly to works that the government feels might increase national tensions, or those that question Yugoslavia's existence as a socialist state. Yugoslavia also permits the circulation of Western journalism and literature and is far less puritanical about pornography. Reform movements in Eastern Europe have frequently sought a loosening of censorship. One of the most dramatic—and to the Soviets, threatening—acts of the 1968 Czechoslovak reforms was the brief abolition of censorship. Similarly, the Polish regime in 1980 found Solidarity's demand for an end to censorship one of the most difficult to permit, cutting as it does to the very core of the party's monopoly of power.

Hero of Socialist Labor/Hero of the Soviet Union   The highest awards in the elaborate system of public honors used in the Soviet Union to confer both status and material benefits. The Hero of Socialist Labor and the Hero of the Soviet Union are part of some 30 different honorary ranks and awards that are used to reward behavior considered beneficial to the Soviet State. These top two awards are accompanied by the Order of Lenin, the highest honorary rank, whose recipients are entitled to better housing, monthly payments, and other benefits. Another high status award is the Lenin Prize, granted for outstanding scientific, cultural, and technical achievements, which the Soviets put forward as the socialist counterpart to the "capitalist-controlled" Nobel Prize. The awards stand at the apex of a complex profusion of merit-based awards, ranks, orders, medals, and insignia that are conferred by all levels of Soviet government. For example, women who have borne several children may be awarded the rank of Heroine Mother. Awards may also be conferred on institutions, military units, groups, social organizations, and even cities. Only the highest awards carry special privileges, however.

Significance   The granting of awards such as the Hero of Socialist Labor and the Hero of the Soviet Union stems from the Soviet conception of the building of socialism as heroic, similar to an all out war effort. Those who contribute "above and beyond" the ordinary are considered heroes. Such awards and prizes are increasingly utilized to reward achievement in nonparty areas, such as science or the arts. Because the highest awards carry special privileges, from better pay to access to the special party stores, they serve to further distinguish the elite from the average Soviet citizen.

Human Rights Movement   A loosely organized protest movement in the Soviet Union and Eastern Europe that focuses on demands for the implementation of individual civil liberties. The human rights movement maintains that Marxism, in theory a doctrine of human liberation, in practice has resulted in the suppression of fundamental human liberties. Many human rights activists remain avowedly

Marxist, pointing out that the constitutions of the communist-party states, which guarantee basic civil liberties, have been violated by the communist regimes. The movement appeared in Moscow in 1965 with the Constitution Day demonstrations protesting the violation of rights guaranteed by the Soviet Constitution. It was furthered by two events: the Soviet-led invasion of Czechoslovakia in 1968, and the signing of the Helsinki Accord in 1975. In 1968 the Group for the Defense of Human Rights in the USSR was formed. The Soviet human rights movement has drawn on such groups as the Crimean Tatars and other dispossessed nationalities, the Baltic Catholics, the Baptists, and Jews. In 1976 the Civic Group to Assist the Implementation of the Helsinki Agreements was formed. Most of the movement's leaders have been expelled, imprisoned, incarcerated in psychiatric hospitals, or otherwise punished. Similar groups have arisen in Eastern Europe, particularly after the suppression of the Czechoslovak liberalization movement. All such groups have been repressed by the East European counterparts of the KGB. *See also* CIVIL RIGHTS, p. 251; CRIMEAN TATARS, p. 281; DISSENT AND OPPOSITION, p. 281; HELSINKI ACCORD, p. 321.

Significance   The human rights movements demand that their governments obey their own laws and the laws of the international treaties to which they are signatories, a demand that goes to the very heart of the relationship between citizen and state in a communist system. The movement differs somewhat between the Soviet Union and Eastern Europe. The Eastern European states generally possess more experience with such freedoms as an uncensored press, fair trials, the right to association and to petition the government, and the freedom to emigrate. In the Soviet context, those who advocate human rights are advocating a political form that is essentially at odds with Russian political culture. The handful of Soviet human rights activists are far more isolated from the masses than those in Eastern Europe, where human rights activists are more a part of the political culture. The Eastern European states are also more permeable, despite censorship and police control. In East Germany, an estimated 200,000 citizens applied for exit visas after the signing of the Helsinki Accord. In Romania, a small but determined group of intellectuals continue to press for civil liberties. Human rights activists have been particularly active in Czechoslovakia and Poland, the former typified by the Chapter 77 Movement, and the latter by a host of groups that helped coalesce Polish dissidence around Solidarity in 1980. The human rights movement has been more explicitly political in these countries. Most Polish and Czech activists deliberately label themselves oppositionalists rather than dissenters, pointing out that the suppression of reform in Czechoslovakia in 1968 and the imposition of military rule in Poland in 1981 demonstrate the futility of working within the system. Repression has been severe. The Soviet Union is apparently determined that no state within its ambit can permit the questioning of the party's authority.

KGB   Abbreviation for *Komitet Gosudarstvennoi Bezopasnosti*, the Committee for State Security of the USSR, the secret police agency charged with preserving state power and maintaining surveillance over the Soviet population. The KGB is also a dual-function agency, with responsibility for foreign operations and intelligence. Thus, it combines the functions of an FBI and CIA, and, in addition, enjoys a preeminent position in Soviet politics. The KGB is the latest in a long line of Soviet secret police agencies, beginning with the CHEKA (the All-Union Extraordinary Committee to Combat Counterrevolution and Sabotage), created by Vladimir Lenin almost immediately after the Bolshevik Revolution. Its later incarnations, in order, were the GPU, OGPU, NKVD, NKGB, and MGB. Through all these transmutations, the secret police has functioned as an instrument of the central party authorities. The KGB's functions, in addition to maintaining party control, include (1) espionage (both foreign and domestic, including the recruiting of agents); (2) intelligence gathering and analysis; (3) counterintelligence and surveillance of the military; (4) domestic control over the population (including responsibility for investigating all political crimes); (5) protecting the borders of the USSR; and (6) disinformation and covert activities. It directs a sizable army of over 200,000 border guards, numerous security troops, and a secret service that guards high officials, totaling somewhere over 500,000 forces. The principle of dual subordination does not apply to the KGB; it is subordinate only to the highest party levels. KGB officials are included in all government bodies, party committees, army units, and in most enterprises. The Communist Party has its own organizations within the KGB. The KGB has representation on the Central Committee, the central committees of the union-republics, the party secretariat, and the politburo. The KGB representative and head for many years, Yuri Andropov, succeeded Leonid Brezhnev as secretary-general of the party in 1982 following Brezhnev's death. The KGB is organized along military lines, with officials having military designations (General, etc.) and is divided into Directorates, and into Departments. For example, these include (1) the First Directorate, which includes the Disinformation Department; (2) the Second Directorate, which operates the domestic informant network; (3) the Third Directorate, in charge of military counterespionage (known as SMERSH during World War II);

and (4) the Fifth Directorate, in charge of controlling dissidence. The KGB plays a key role in foreign policy implementation, probably outranking the Ministry of Foreign Affairs. Recent analysis of Soviet affairs maintains that the KGB and two key Central Committee organs, the International Department and the International Information Department (created by Brezhnev in 1978) are major actors in formulating foreign policy. Reportedly, the head of the KGB has also been a member of the secretive Defense Council, thus placing the KGB in a central position in Soviet affairs. *See also* ACTIVE MEASURES, p. 309; CRIMES AGAINST THE STATE, p. 255; DEFENSE COUNCIL, p. 136; DUAL SUBORDINATION, p. 137; POLITBURO, p. 118; PROCURACY, p. 266.

Significance   The KGB represents a constant in both Russian and Soviet political history, since the KGB is the lineal heir of the *Okhrana*, the czarist secret police, and the CHEKA. Since the inception of the CHEKA, under Felix Dzerzhinsky, the Soviet secret services have been characterized by extralegality and close cooperation with the ruling oligarchy. Lenin created the CHEKA to "protect the Revolution." Under the CHEKA, a "Red Terror" began; during the Civil War and beyond, executions were carried out on a mass basis, administered by Revolutionary Tribunals that operated outside any existing laws to punish all who were suspected of opposing the Revolution. The CHEKA acquired the first secret service army, the Troops of Internal Security of the Republic. Under Josef Stalin, the secret service became an instrument of personalized terror and the epitome of the totalitarian police state, responsible only to Stalin. As the major implementor of the collectivization of the peasants and the purges of the 1930s, it was responsible for sending millions to their deaths. Nikita Khrushchev is generally credited with circumscribing the powers of the secret police, but his goal was to ensure the subordination of the KGB to the party, not to curb its extralegality or role as the "action arm" of the party. Under Brezhnev, the KGB appeared to increase its status. KGB representation on all major party and government bodies increased, whereas under Khrushchev the KGB was not even accorded full membership on the Central Committee. The Brezhnev regime appeared to make greater use of the KGB in foreign affairs, particularly in the area of "active measures" and "destabilization" activities, such as support of international terrorists and other covert activities aimed at foreign governments. It is assumed that the KGB works closely with the counterpart secret services of the bloc countries, using them when feasible to mount covert operations as well as a means of maintaining control over the East European countries. Yugoslavia is an exception; one of the catalysts to the 1948 Yugoslav-Soviet break was the Soviet Union's attempt to control the Yugoslav secret police, the UDBa.

Yugoslavia has also curbed the autonomy of its secret police. The KGB draws heavily on the *Komsomol* for recruits, called the *"Chekisty,"* and rewards them well. They operate in a system that imposes markedly fewer restraints, both domestically and internationally, than the secret services of democratic systems. Under Brezhnev, the KGB continued to act as the primary agent of party policy, a relationship made explicit by the accession of Yuri Andropov to the party leadership.

Komsomol   The organization for Soviet youth that serves as the main agency of political socialization for Soviet youth. The *Komsomol* (*Kommunistecheskii Soyuz Molodezhi*) enrolls youth between the ages of 14 and 28, serves as the youth wing of the Communist Party, and functions as the main agent of recruitment for future party members. Komsomol units are organized in schools, farms, places of work, and military units, and are under direct party supervision. The organizational structure of the Komsomol is modeled on the party organization and replicates the hierarchical institutions of the party. At each level, from local through district to republic and federal, Komsomol units are directly supervised by the analogous territorial units of the party. At the federal level the Secretariat of the Central Committee, through the Department of Organizing Party Work, is responsible for Komsomol policy and activities. At the district (*raion*) or higher levels, all Komsomol secretaries must be party members. The overt party control exercised over the Komsomol is indicative of the importance with which the party views the Komsomol. While the Pioneer Movement, the official organization for 7- to 14-year olds, is recreational in nature, stressing entertainment, good citizenship, and physical fitness, the Komsomol concentrates on political activities. Members are assigned political duties such as serving in the citizens' militia units (*Druzhiny*) or overseeing the Young Pioneers. Komsomol activities are meant to fill much of the free time of young people, channeling them into organized political activities and socializing them into the participant values espoused by Marxism-Leninism. Komsomol activities are distributed along functional lines; party secretaries guide Komsomol activities in sport, culture, education, industry, and military. In institutions of higher learning, a substantial proportion of the teachers are Komsomol leaders. Membership runs fairly high, although not all are by any means activists. In 1968, about 38 million young people were enrolled; in 1974, an estimated 63 percent of the 15- to 17-year olds were members. In addition to career advancement, one of the inducements for joining the Komsomol are the activities, which range from inexpensive skiing trips to dances. The Komsomol also publishes a widely circulated daily, *Komsomol'skaya Pravda. See also* CITIZEN

PARTICIPATION, p. 275; MASS ORGANIZATIONS, p. 291; PRIMARY PARTY
ORGANIZATION (PPO), p. 122.

Significance The Komsomol is the main avenue of recruitment for
the Communist Party and the primary training ground for future
party members. In addition to selecting the best prospects for party
membership, the Komsomol in general socializes the youth into the
prevailing party values and trains them for participation in the system.
Up to age 23, all candidate members of the party must be Komsomol
members; most of the candidate members enter the party dirctly from
the Komsomol. For the party, the Komsomol is indispensable as the
pool from which the party elite can select future party members. Thus,
those who are asked to join the party have been preselected in a careful
screening process that begins in their teens as Komsomol members.
However, many Komsomol members are far from active. For many,
membership in a Komsomol unit is viewed as the minimum political
commitment required for admission to higher education or career
advancement, much as the American businessman will join the local
Rotary or Jaycee Club. Applicants to universities and other institutions
of higher education must submit a character reference from either
their Komsomol unit or place of work. The Komsomol also represents
the interests of youth in policymaking and its input is frequently
solicited by the party. The exremely high levels of Komsomol membership in the military ranks gives the party built-in control, and it is
estimated that upward of 80 percent of the officers have been members. One of the major criticisms of Komsomol is that it has become
ossified, with many leaders well past the age of "youth." At the very
least, membership signifies external compliance with socialist norms,
but for the ambitious, Komsomol work is a major path to upward
mobility and success.

Mass Organizations Voluntary associations open to both party
and nonparty members that offer the opportunity for the masses to
become active in the system. In communist states party membership is
highly selective; without the mass organizations the bulk of the
citizenry would have no formal affiliation with the state. In a Leninist
system, the party must be restricted to an avant-garde of people who
manifest extraordinary dedication to the communist cause. Members
are carefully screened and party membership is deliberately kept low,
in the Soviet Union averaging about 10 percent of the adult population. Soviet doctrine also states that, as full communism approaches,
the role of the citizens' organization in the management of the state
increases. Thus, mass organizations are perceived both as a mobiliza-

tional device and as an instrument for developing a communist society. The trade unions, youth groups, volunteer militia (*Druzhiny*), and paramilitary organizations (DOSAAF) are leading examples of Soviet mass organizations. Participation is voluntary; all activities are supervised by the party and government. Draft bylaws must be approved by the government, which also has the power to dissolve any organization if it deems its activities harmful to the interests of the state. Party members form the nucleus of the mass organizations; frequently such work is part of a member's party assignment. All mass organizations are subject to party control (*rukovodstvo*) and to legal supervision by the Procuracy. Their functions are defined by the party and they operate under democratic centralism. The primary mass organization is of course the Communist Party, which according to the Soviet Constitution is ". . . the leading and directing force in Soviety society." *See also* CITIZEN PARTICIPATION, p. 275; PARTY ASSIGNMENT, p. 110.

Significance   Belonging to a mass organization is usually the minimum requirement for participation in public life. Active membership also provides a means of upward mobility, and frequently constitutes an avenue of access into party membership. Membership is in effect a pledge of support for the system, enabling the ruling communist party to claim almost universal support. Although the modes of participation are structured by the party, membership is voluntary. The political aims of the mass organizations are usually less overt than their socialization and mobilization objectives; they do however provide the public with a means of involvement in community life, especially in such organizations as the residence comittees or volunteer militia units. In addition to the Soviet range of mass organizations, the East European states also possess national front organizations, umbrella organizations open to all. The national front organizations reflect the different historical means by which communism came to Eastern Europe, having been set up after World War II as supposedly universalistic organizations comprised of all non-fascist elements of these societies. Their only substantive function is to conduct elections, preserving the fiction that communism is voluntary. A major function of all communist mass organizations is to control citizen involvement and prevent deviant behavior, as defined by the party. Communist systems have an unyielding hostility to the formation of any organizations that are not sponsored and approved by the party. The party is charged with carrying out the will of all the people; the role of the mass organization is to assist the party in its mission by involving the broad citizenry in supportive functions.

May Day   The International Day of Labor and Labor Solidarity, celebrated on the first of May in the Soviet Union and Eastern Europe as a mass reaffirmation of communism and as a national holiday. May Day became an international holiday in 1890, on the basis of a resolution of the Paris Congress of the Second International. It was initiated as a sign of solidarity with the Haymarket strike in Chicago in 1886, which had ended in bloody police repression. Early May Day demonstrations called for an eight-hour working day and better working conditions. In the 1930s, May Day demonstrations assumed an antifascist nature. In many countries, socialist and nonsocialist, the First of May is an international holiday.

Significance   May Day in the communist-party states is a key holiday, marked by parades and celebrations that honor the successes of the system and serve to reaffirm the allegiance of the masses to the goals of communism. In some years, the May Day parade in Moscow is the occasion to show off the latest in military armaments and crack military units. In others, the theme is peace, achievements, and solidarity. The United States is one of the few countries that does not acknowledge this international labor holiday. The American Labor Day in September and the May 1 "Law Day" were established as rivals to the socialist-inspired May Day, which most of the world continues to observe.

Media   The system of public information that in a communist system fulfills two functions: (1) gathering and dissemination of news, and (2) propagandizing. Although Soviet and East European constitutions guarantee freedom of the press, the media is actually under tight party control. The media is directed by trusted party officials and its practitioners are well-trained in professional schools and controlled by the various professional associations to which they must belong, such as the Union of Journalists. Most media journalists are party members, bound by party discipline; usually censorship is thus self-applied rather than direct. Direct supervision is carried out by the Propaganda Department of the Central Committee, with corresponding sections at every party level. East European media systems, with the exception of Yugoslavia, operate in the same way. Communist systems place great importance on the media as a tool of socialization and mobilization; typically, they rank high in per capita publication of newspapers and periodicals. News is the responsibility of three types of "publishers": party, government, and mass organizations. Each has its own press; there is no such thing as a newspaper, magazine or radio station without official affiliation. Thus, in the Soviet Union, *Pravda* is the newspaper published by the Central Committee; *Izvestiya*, by the

Presidium of the Supreme Soviet; *Trud*, by the Trade Unions; *Komsomol'skaya Pravda*, by the youth organization Komsomol; and *Literaturnaya Gazeta*, by the Union of Soviet Writers. Distribution is supervised by the All-Union News Agency. Dissemination of news to foreign countries is controlled by the Soviet Press Agency, TASS, and its Eastern European counterparts. *See also* DISSENT AND OPPOSITION, p. 281; GLAVLIT, p. 284; SAMIZDAT, p. 300.

Significance   Since the Bolshevik Revolution, ruling communist parties have controlled the media. Vladimir Lenin abolished freedom of the press in November of 1917 with the Decree on the Press, which authorized the Council of People's Commissars (*Sovnarkom*) to ban all "bourgeois" press organs hostile to Soviet power. All printing equipment was nationalized and news dissemination became a party monopoly. As radio and then television came to the communist bloc, party control was similarly exacted, with greater difficulty in Eastern Europe where proximity to the West permits many citizens to "eavesdrop" on Western broadcasting. In some countries, the authorities try to ferret out those looking at Western television by the direction of their TV antennas, or by quizzing their children about favorite programs. The Soviet media in particular is notable for "non-reporting"; the party generally bans news that casts the system in an unfavorable light. Thus, Soviet citizens know about Love Canal and the Michigan PBB scandal but not the nuclear waste accident in Siberia, nor the dumping of untreated chemicals in Soviet lakes; major forest fires go unreported until the smoke reaches Moscow; airplane disasters are not mentioned unless someone prominent is killed. Yugoslavia remains an exception to the party-controlled media and generally "gray" content of communist media. Yugoslav media, under self-management, must turn a profit and their content is consequently much livelier and less controlled. In Yugoslavia, Western publications, ranging from *Playboy* to the *Herald Tribune*, are sold. Elsewhere, control over the media is a yardstick for measuring party orthodoxy. Any loosening of party control, as in Czechoslovakia in 1968, constitutes a striking reversal of Leninist practice. Thus far, the threat to party monopoly is so obvious that no communist-party state outside of Yugoslavia has permitted even a semi-free press.

People's Control Committee (*Komitet narodnogo kontrolya*) The volunteer organization through which Soviet citizens exercise public supervision of state activities. The "citizen inspectors" of the People's Control Committees ensure that government orders are properly implemented and expose official malfeasance. Frequently they perform an ombudsman function, mediating between citizens and state authorities. Consistent with the Marxist commitment to worker control over production, many operate in the factories. Such citizen monitoring dates from the earliest days of the Bolshevik Revolution; the first Workers' Control Committee was created in November 1917. In 1920 Vladimir Lenin instituted the People's Committee for Workers' and Peasants' Inspection (*Rabkin*), the predecessor of the People's Committees. Nikita Khrushchev revived the citizen inspectors as part of the effort to enhance local citizen participation. The functions of the citizen inspectors include (1) supervising the implementation of party and government orders; (2) improving economic and bureaucratic efficiency; and (3) identifying those officials who fail to carry out their responsibilities. They also handle citizen complaints and make suggestions to the authorities. The 9.5 million citizen inspectors are the core of an even larger public compliance system that includes 10 million volunteers attached to the trade unions, 13 million to the local soviets, and 4 million with the youth groups, a total of 36.5 million or about 22 percent of the adult population. *See also* CITIZEN PARTICIPATION, p. 275.

Significance   The People's Control Committees constitute a major form of directed citizen participation in the Soviet Union. It should be noted that in Russian, *kontrol'* means *verification* or *audit*, not, in the English sense, to exercise power. The citizen inspectors are intended to resemble the elements of citizen control present in pluralistic societies, such as interest groups, party competition, and a free press. Their scope is limited by the party, and they have no authority over the party itself.

Prague Spring   The name given to the 1968 reform movement in Czechoslovakia that culminated in a broad-based attempt to democratize Czechoslovak political life. The Prague Spring was abruptly terminated by the Soviet-led military invasion in August 1968. The Soviets replaced the reforming party leadership with pro-Soviets, forced the negation of the legally mandated reforms, and effectively returned Czechoslovakia to satellite status. The Prague Spring grew out of the unique circumstances of Czechoslovakia, the most westernized and industrialized country to fall under communism, and the only functioning democracy in Eastern Europe before World War II. Communism in Czechoslovakia, possibly because it was so incompatible with the political culture, remained Stalinist long after the Khrushchevian reforms loosened controls elsewhere. The initial impetus for reform was the economic stagnation of the early 1960s, which many attributed to the orthodox leadership's insistence on slavishly copying Stalinist methods. Other pressures for reform emerged: (1) the demand for coequality by the Slovaks; (2) the demand for rehabilitation of those punished in the Soviet-instigated purges of the 1950s; and (3) a generalized demand for a freer cultural life. By December of 1967, reform-minded intellectuals had gained enough ascendency in the party to force Antonín Novotný out of the leadership, replacing him with Alexander Dubček. During the succeeding eight months until the Soviet invasion the Czechoslovak party presided over the most far-reaching reform yet proposed by a ruling communist party. The most important elements of the reform included (1) the removal of democratic centralism; (2) curbing the police; (3) reinstating meaningful parliamentary debate; (4) publication of party debates; (5) abandonment of the *nomenklatura* system; (6) federalism; (7) economic reform; (8) removal of censorship and the guarantee of civil rights; and (9) the right of citizens to form associations and petition the government. In essence, Dubček proposed a responsible party, operating openly with intraparty democracy and meaningful participation of the citizenry. Censorship simply withered away and countless groups formed to discuss the reforms; by one count, 135 groups were active by August 1968. Despite Dubček's assurances that Czechoslovakia would remain a loyal socialist member of COMECON and the Warsaw Treaty Organization, 500,000 troops of the Warsaw Treaty Organization invaded on August 21, 1968. *See also* BREZHNEV DOCTRINE, p. 311; DISSENT AND OPPOSITION, p. 281; HUMAN RIGHTS MOVEMENT, p. 286; SOLIDARITY, p. 303.

Significance   The Soviet repression of the Prague Spring clearly defines the limits of reform in the Soviet bloc; no communist party can permit any diminution of its "leading role," nor tolerate incipient pluralism. The *ex post facto* rationalization of the invasion, the Brezhnev Doctrine, states that the Soviet Union will intervene wherever "socialism is threatened," by their definition. The Soviets imposed "normalization," their Orwellian term for a return to party orthodoxy, a massive purging of the party membership, and a negating of the reforms, including all the actions taken by the 14th Czechoslovak party congress, held secretly in Prague in August under the Soviet occupation. The effects of the Prague Spring and its fate continue: (1) The Czechoslovak party lost most legitimacy and today rules over a demoralized citizenry; repression of intellectuals has been especially harsh. (2) The remaining unity of the communist world was shattered; the Western European communist parties were particularly alienated. (3) Most dissenters have concluded that intraparty reform is impossible as long as the Soviets retain control. (4) The West has realized that it has no viable means of restraining Soviet action in Eastern Europe without risking war. The Yugoslavs, whose pioneering path outside the bloc the Czechoslovaks hoped to emulate, reassessed their defenses and strengthened them vis-à-vis the Soviet Union, and in turn reversed their liberalization of the 1960s. Perhaps ironically, the most lasting effect of the Prague Spring is the Brezhnev Doctrine, which clearly and openly enunciates the Soviet policy of maintaining its Eastern European satellite empire.

Professional Associations Professional unions and societies that in communist systems are the sole legal means by which creative artists can exercise their professions. The professional associations of actors, artists, film makers, musicians, writers, and others are the major method of party control over cultural life. Unlike other voluntary associations, the professional associations must have special government authorization, not just approval of bylaws, and operate under stricter party surveillance. The output of each creative artist must be in conformity with the party line on artistic expression—as a 1982 Soviet Central Committee resolution states, ". . . the tasks of artistic creation are inseparable from the tasks that face the people as a whole in their struggle to build communism." Any artist who deviates from party-approved forms is subject to expulsion from his professional association. Direct control is exercised by various state committees, as Soviet filmmaking is supervised by the State Committee for Cinematography. The general guidelines are that all artistic expression must show the system in the best possible light and help mobilize the people for the building of communism. *See also* DISSENT AND OPPOSITION, p. 281; MEDIA, p. 293; SAMIZDAT, p. 300; SOCIALIST REALISM, p. 301.

Significance The professional associations have generally served to project the image desired by the party at the cost of creativity and freedom of expression. They constitute a "closed shop" system under party control. The party determines admissions and orders expulsions. As all are required to work, an expelled artist who persists in his creative work may be charged with parasitism and imprisoned, as was the Soviet poet Josef Brodsky. Since Josef Stalin created the Soviet Writers' Union in the 1930s, the professional associations have ensured that the party determines the permissible limits of creative expression. Party control is extensive, ranging from the banning of rock groups to bulldozing unauthorized exhibitions of non-realistic paintings. Professional associations have been and are a foci of dissent, especially in Eastern Europe. In 1967, a major proponent of liberalization was the Czech Writers' Union. Such party-controlled unions impose party conformity over the dead as well; the Czech writers began their dissent with a move to "rehabilitate" Franz Kafka and restore him to his rightful place in Czech literature. The price of party conformity has been to drive many of the best creative artists into opposition; intellectuals in Eastern Europe have generally been in the forefront of reform movements. The list is almost endless, from the Petőfi Poet's Circle in Hungary in 1956 to the Polish writers in 1980. Others chose to conform publicly, frequently performing mundane tasks such as translation while continuing to produce privately, in the Soviet expression, "writing for the drawer." Recently the Soviet Union and the more repressive regimes, such as Czechoslovakia and East Germany, have preferred to force their troublesome creative artists into exile abroad. The conformity exacted by the professional associations is in essence the price for exercising one's chosen profession. Artists ranging from the Czech rock group "Plastic People of the Universe" to Ukrainian folksingers and Nobel prizewinner Aleksandr Solzhenitsyn have all been banned from the public through the mechanism of the professional association.

Refusenik   A Soviet citizen who applied for and was denied permission to emigrate from the Soviet Union to another country. Many Soviet *refuseniks* are Jews who have applied for permission to emigrate to Israel, but the term refers to all those refused an exit visa. Soviet legal doctrine maintains that emigration is a state-granted privilege, although the 1975 Helsinki Final Act of the Conference on Security and Cooperation in Europe, to which the Soviet Union is a signatory, guarantees emigration as a right. In the 1970s, the government began to require that an applicant also renounce Soviet citizenship. Renunciation of citizenship must be approved by the Presidium of the Supreme Soviet and can be denied on the grounds of damage to the interests of national security and to the interests of the state. In practice, most of those forced to renounce their Soviet citizenship have been Jews wishing to emigrate to Israel. The issue became highly sensitive in the 1970s when increasing numbers of Soviet citizens, perhaps encouraged by the spirit of détente and the signing of the Helsinki Final Act, applied for permission to emigrate. Since 1970 over 250,000 Soviet Jews have been granted permission to emigrate, but many others have been refused. These refuseniks, labeled political dissidents by the authorities, are frequently persecuted by loss of jobs, harassment of family members, and, occasionally, legal action. The most celebrated case is that of Anatoly Shcharansky, a mathematical engineer repeatedly refused permission to emigrate. In 1978 Shcharansky was eventually tried and imprisoned for treason and anti-Soviet agitation and propaganda, on the ground that his actions constituted hostile activity against the Soviet Union. *See also* CIVIL RIGHTS, p. 251; HELSINKI ACCORD, p. 321; HUMAN RIGHTS MOVEMENT, p. 286.

Significance In essence the refusenik is a stateless person created by the Soviet Union's denial of the right to emigrate. The existence of this category of political dissidents attests to changes in Soviet politics since the 1950s. Under Stalin, the merest indication of a wish to emigrate was treated as treason and summarily punished; the fact that hundreds of thousands of Soviet citizens have dared apply for permission to emigrate emphasized the change. The case of the refuseniks illuminates Soviet theories of international law and civil rights. The Soviet Union maintains that international treaties to which the state is a signatory, such as the Helsinki Accord, are binding upon the state in the area of international law but the state itself will determine whether a treaty creates binding domestic law. The refuseniks' challenge to the official doctrine that civil rights are privileges granted by the state apparently resulted in the decision to make the issuance of an exit visa conditional upon permission to renounce citizenship. The case of the Jewish refuseniks, the largest group, is tied both to Soviet interpretation of international law and civil rights and to Soviet foreign policy interests. The dilemma for the Soviet leadership has been whether to refuse most such applicants and thus be charged with official anti-Semitism and violation of the Helsinki Accord, or risk antagonizing Arab leaders. The number of exit visas that have been issued indicates that the Helsinki Accord and the Jackson-Vanik Amendment, which tied United States cooperation to observance of Helsinki, has had some effect. As the refuseniks attest, however, the USSR has yet to observe all of the provisions of the Helsinki Accord and to apply them in a nonarbitrary, nondiscriminatory way.

Residence Committees Part of the network of officially sponsored local organizations through which Soviet citizens are encouraged to participate in community affairs. Residence committees are set up in places of residence and serve as a form of self-help and community self-government. Committee functions include controlling deviant behavior, such as alcoholism, handling residents' complaints, mobilizing the neighborhood for various self-help projects, overseeing building maintenance, and representing their community in outside events. The residence committees report to the executive committee of the local soviet. As with all forms of political participation in the Soviet Union, their activity is structured by the party, but they influence community life and give the citizens some direct control over their living conditions. The committees work closely with the *Druzhiny* (the volunteer citizens' militia) and the Comrades' Courts, to which they frequently refer cases. They organize volunteer work days (*subbotniki*) in which teams of citizens do everything from repairing sidewalks to landscaping the neighborhood. Involvement in residence committees is extensive; Moscow reportedly has between 2,500 and 3,500 such committees enrolling upwards of 50,000 citizens. They serve as an adjunct to the local authorities, constituting what the Soviets term "public self-administration." In all, membership in such volunteer citizen organizations is impressive: participation in the residence committees, Comrades' Courts, volunteer militia, parents' groups and other such organizations was recently estimated at over 30 million. *See also* CITIZEN PARTICIPATION, p. 275; COMRADES' COURT, p. 279; VOLUNTEER REPAIR SQUAD, p. 307.

Significance   Residence committees encourage masses of people to join local community organizations that enhance the sense of participation in the system and give many citizens a sense of personal involvement. The committees are tangible evidence that the Soviet system maintains its Leninist objective of mass participation. Such part-time volunteer activity often serves as an entry into a political career or to professional promotion. Although the residence committees have more freedom to articulate citizens' complaints than to make policy changes, they still constitute an important avenue of interest articulation for the average person. Since they handle complaints that are transmitted directly to the local soviet, they may also help to create a "public opinion" that may influence local decision makers. By involving masses of citizens, they build a sense of participation and grassroots community, mitigating the anomie of a large-scale industrial society.

Samizdat   Literally, "self-publication," the hand-to-hand circulation in the Soviet Union of unapproved manuscripts. *Samizdat* is a contraction of *sam* (self) and *izdatel'stvo* (publishing house), a Russian word play on *gosizdat*, the popular abbreviation for the government publishing house and sole printer in the Soviet Union. Since any work published must be approved by the state censors (*Glavlit*), anyone wishing to circumvent censorship must resort to samizdat. Soviet samizdat relies on typing carbon copies or photographing manuscripts; permits for the use of photocopying or duplicating machines must be issued by the police. Samizdat operates on the chain letter principle, with each recipient passing copies on to friends who duplicate the process. Legally, the production of samizdat is not a crime, but the authorities generally assume that such material is inherently damaging to state interests and therefore punish its dissemination under the charge of circulating anti-Soviet propaganda. Initially, the samizdat of the early 1960s was chiefly literary material, as writers, encouraged by the brief period of the Thaw, found themselves blocked once more by the censors. Such major works as Aleksandr Solzhenitsyn's *Gulag Archipelago* and Roy Medvedev's *Let History Judge* have been circulated only in samizdat. As the Brezhnev leadership tightened controls, samizdat emphasis shifted to political themes. A major contributor was *The Chronicle of Human Events*, a periodic samizdat which focused on political and religious dissent and detailed the repression of free thought. Soviet samizdat has been particularly prevalent among religious believers and nationalists—the Baptists, Seventh-Day Adventists, Baltic Catholics, Ukrainians, Jews, and others. In Eastern Europe, samizdat has been more outrightly political. An extensive underground samizdat apparatus in Poland helped to create the nationwide reform movement, including a widely distributed worker newspaper and an entire publishing enterprise assembled from illicitly acquired printing equipment. *See also* ANTI-SOVIET AGITATION AND PROPAGANDA, p. 248; DISSENT AND OPPOSITION, p. 281; GLAVLIT, p. 284; MEDIA, p. 293.

Significance   Samizdat has publicized violations of the Helsinki Accord and detailed the repression of those deemed dissidents by the various communist regimes. Much of what Western analysts know about dissidence in the communist countries is due to samizdat. Although those who engage in samizdat are always liable to punishment under the elastic definitions of antistate propaganda, the communist regimes have recently preferred to force their most prominent dissidents into exile. Technology and human ingenuity have created a host of related activities. *Tamizdat*, "over there (*tam*) publication" involves the publication abroad of unapproved material. *Magnitizdat* is the illegal taping of such events as speeches, poetry readings, and nationalist folk songs. *Kinizdat* involves illegal motion pictures, and *radizdat* the taping of Western radio broadcasts. Yuri Andropov, Leonid Brezhnev's successor, headed the KGB suppression of Soviet dissidents for many years, and samizdat has continued to be a key concern of the Soviets under his leadership.

Socialist Realism   A doctrine imposed by Stalin in 1934 that elevated the communist party line as the ultimate standard against which all literary and artistic creativity had to be measured. Socialist realism subordinated individual creativity to the political aims of the party and the state. During Stalin's rule all creative works were obliged to glorify the achievements of "socialist construction" and to stress the positive aspects of Soviet life. One of the constant themes was the glorification of the "new Soviet man." By tightly controlling the dissemination of all creative works through official channels art or culture that did not accord with the precepts of socialist realism was banned. This was accomplished through censorship or the creation of such party-dominated artists' associations as the Union of Soviet Writers, the Union of Soviet Composers, or painters' artel's. Andrei Zhdanov, who held the Politburo post that gave him control over all policy dealing with science and culture, followed the Stalinist dictum that defined artists as "engineers of human souls." The term socialist realism was in part derived from the realist school of French literature that flourished at the beginning of the nineteenth century. The representatives of this school maintained that writing should represent a "slice of life." Stalin interpreted this as a dictum that all Soviet art must be accessible to the masses and reflect the current party line. This dictum frequently had the effect of vulgarizing much of Soviet cultural output and playing havoc with the creative talents of individual artists. The outpouring of avant-garde creativity that so distinguished the Soviet Union in the 1920s was stifled. Painting became little more than poster art, glorifying Stalin and socialist achievements. Architecture, which had created some remarkable works in the 1920s, ceased to be experimental and conformed instead to the Victorian preferences of Stalin. Realism in literature was perverted into a glorification of every aspect of the system. Ballet, theater, and painting lost their vitality and were frozen into artistic forms that have been superseded elsewhere. Soviet culture has never recovered the reputation that it enjoyed in the 1920s. See also GLAVLIT, p. 284; MEDIA, p. 293; SAMIZDAT, p. 300.

Significance   Although the doctrine of socialist realism is applied less rigidly today, most of the original strictures remain. Most forms of Soviet culture remain less creative and innovative than their counterparts elsewhere. Nonrepresentational artists seldom are permitted official showings; any creative activity dealing with uncertainty, pessimism, or the mystical is suspect. The tight censorship maintained over all forms of culture has created a long line of dissident creative artists. Some, like Boris Pasternak, have elected to stay within their country; others like Mikhail Baryshnikov have emigrated in search of the artistic freedom their country denied them. Since the precise standards of socialist realism have never been clearly stated, many Soviet creative artists have found it impossible to stay within the letter of the definition even if they so desired. Thus, the musician Dmitri Shostakovich and the abstract artist Wassily Kandinsky were charged with "formalism," which essentially meant that their art was not comprehensible to Stalin. The charge was applied to any art that seemed tainted with modern Western trends, as determined by party censors. Most of the major figures of Soviet culture during the 1920s were unable to conform to the straitjacket imposed by socialist realism, and were silenced or liquidated during the purges. The almost endless list includes such artists as Isaak Babel', Evgeny Zamyatin, Boris Pilnyak, Mikhail Bulgakov, Osip Mandel'shtam, Anna Akhmatova, and Boris Pasternak. Since Stalin's death, the system has relied on self-censorship as much as on outright oppression. It is difficult for a creative artist to pursue his or her profession without membership in one of the professional organizations. If the work breaches the code of socialist realism, the artist is denied membership. The original intent of Zhdanov's policy still applies: socialist realism is essentially a tool of control over the entire community of creative artists in the Soviet Union.

Solidarity   The worker-based movement for reform that culminated in 1980–81 in a mass demand for the reform of the Polish economic and political system. Solidarity takes its name from the federation of free trade unions set up in August 1980 by striking Polish workers in the Baltic shipyards. In the 16 months between the formation of Solidarity and its suppression by martial law, Solidarity politicized the entire country, from peasants who formed their own independent unions to party members who joined Solidarity. After the workers mounted nationwide work stoppages, the government permitted the registration of Solidarity as an independent trade union. At its peak, Solidarity, loosely organized under the direction of Lech Wałęsa and a core of worker and intellectual activists, embraced about one-third of the entire population. Some of Solidarity's demands were granted initially—a loosening of censorship and police control, travel abroad, and the right to form independent associations. From the beginning, however, it was obvious that the ability of the Polish Communist Party to make accommodations was severely circumscribed by Soviet policy toward any incipient pluralism in Eastern Europe that threatened the party's monopoly of power and by implication, Soviet control over Eastern Europe. In December of 1981, martial law under General Wojciech Jaruzelski was imposed, Solidarity was disbanded, and all concessions were revoked. A year later, Wałęsa and other Solidarity leaders were released, confinement without conviction was ended, and martial law rule was lifted, but massive cleavages remained in Polish society, and the economy verged on collapse. *See also* BREZHNEV DOCTRINE, p. 311; DISSENT AND OPPOSITION,

p. 281; PRAGUE SPRING, p. 295; TRADE UNIONS, p. 305; INDUSTRIAL ASSOCIATION: WOG, p. 201.

Significance   To date, Solidarity represents the most serious challenge to the legitimacy of Marxist-Leninist rule, challenging the very basis of its claim to rule in the interests of the working class. The suppression of Solidarity starkly underlined the Soviet determination to retain control of Eastern Europe, in particular the Polish nation that forms its western borders. No evidence exists that the Communist Party of the Soviet Union seriously considered permitting the Polish Communist Party to share power with a mass worker movement, let alone institute reforms that would permit free speech and association. Solidarity also represents the culmination of successive waves of dissent in Poland—in 1956, 1968, 1970, and 1976—that on two occasions toppled the party leadership, as did Solidarity in 1980 when Edward Gierek was replaced by Stanisław Kania. In 1980, the mainsprings of Polish rebellion—workers' disgust over the inability of the party to manage the economy, the nationalism and anti-Russianism of the Poles, the intellectuals' demands for human rights, and the powerful role in society of the Polish Catholic Church—all converged. In an officially atheistic communist country where the preponderant majority are practicing Catholics, the support of the church gave Solidarity an unsurpassed moral base. Solidarity also represents the first time that workers and intellectuals in Eastern Europe have made common cause effectively. Intellectual dissident groups like KOR (the committee for Social Self Defense) and the Flying University (the underground system of education) gave their full support to the workers. Although initially the workers' demands centered on economic reform and free trade unions, in the end Solidarity was distinguished by the fact that the workers put their jobs on the line for democratic reforms. The 16 months of Solidarity's existence were marked by many "firsts." A nationwide Solidarity Congress was held, Poles were permitted to travel abroad, and in Gdańsk, the scene of a 1970 government repression of strikes in the shipyards, a massive memorial to the slain workers was erected, with the party attending the unveiling. With the imposition of military rule, Solidarity has gone underground, but Poland remains a nation divided into a ruling elite and alienated masses. The consensus is that the regime currently in charge has little hope of attaining legitimacy or solving Poland's seemingly incurable economic problems.

Subbotnik   Volunteer workday during which teams of Soviet citizens plant flowers, clean up parks, lay sidewalks, and in general improve their conditions of living. The *subbotnik* is usually organized by local community organizations, such as the residence councils and schools. *See also* CITIZEN PARTICIPATION, p. 275.

Significance   The subbotnik is part of the extensive network of voluntary activities through which the Soviet system inculcates a sense of community responsibility. It constitutes probably the minimum public activity; even the most inactive citizens are drawn into subbotniks. If evaluated in terms of improving local living conditions, the efforts of subbotnik teams can be considerable. Such voluntary community efforts are vital to the Soviet concept of citizen participation, which involves self-help and building a sense of responsibility to one's neighbors.

Thaw   The term used to describe a period of relaxation in the early post-Stalin years, lasting to the early 1960s. The Thaw takes its name from a novel of the same title by Ilya Ehrenberg, published in 1954. The pace of de-Stalinization quickened after Nikita Khrushchev's secret speech before the 1956 20th Party Congress, which revealed Stalin's inhumanities. Khrushchev released millions from the penal labor camps and dismantled the ubiquitous terror system, embarking on legal reforms that have made Soviet justice repressive but not arbitrary. Artistic controls were also loosened. Works such as *One Day in the Life of Ivan Denisovich*, by the recently released prisoner Aleksandr Solzhenitsyn, appeared and Soviet culture experienced a brief flowering. Deteriorating relations within the Soviet bloc, in particular after the Hungarian and Polish uprisings of 1956, eventually terminated this period of internal relaxation. By the early 1960s, controls over artistic expression were tightened and Soviet dominance over Eastern Europe was reaffirmed. *See also* DE-STALINIZATION, p. 318.

Significance   The Thaw is typical of the alternating periods of control and relaxation that characterize Soviet-style political systems. Even Stalinist Albania, for a short period in 1970–74, experienced a minor thaw. These fluctuating periods of relaxation appear conditioned by both international and domestic circumstances. The Thaw coincided with the relaxation in international relations following the Geneva Summit between Khrushchev and President Dwight Eisenhower. Conversely, Soviet-directed repression of East European movements has been accompanied by tightened controls within the Soviet Union.

Trade Unions *(Sindikaty)*   Government-sponsored workers' associations that operate under close party supervision in communist-party states. Trade unions are organized along branch production lines, not by profession or occupation as in the West. Each enterprise or state institute has a single union, whose general membership elects a factory, plant, or local committee. In larger enterprises and industrial associations, the shop committees are the primary organizational unit. Union organization is similar to party organization, with the branch unions merged into the All-Union Congress of Trade Unions, which elects a Central Council. Democratic centralism and strict subordination to all higher bodies are the basic rules for these organizations. Membership is voluntary and open to all, including management; practically all workers are at least nominal members. Communist doctrine maintains that the state, which rules in the interest of the workers, protects their interests. Therefore the function of the trade unions is not to "represent" the workers or to articulate their demands, but to resolve disputes and ensure fulfillment of the common interest of workers, state, and management, thereby increasing productivity. At the factory or shop level, the trade union works out how best to implement the plan targets. Its major functions include (1) drawing up, with management, the yearly collective agreement on wage and bonus distribution and labor conditions; (2) maintaining responsibility for labor discipline; (3) organizing a factory grievance committee; (4) maintaining safety standards; and (5) administering social benefits. Union officials, although "elected," must be preapproved by the party. Grievances involving such topics as work conditions, discipline, and firings are initially handled by the grievance committee and union committee. Decisions may be appealed to the local courts. Disputes frequently are settled in favor of the workers. Trade unions at the factory or shop level have a bargaining role, but in general their existence is based on workers' common interest with management and government in securing a better life. *See also* MASS ORGANIZATIONS, p. 291; SOLIDARITY, p. 303; WORKERS' SELF-MANAGEMENT, p. 239.

Significance   Trade unions form a key part of the system of total mobilization that characterizes communist-party systems. Recent Soviet practice has been to involve the unions more closely in decision making; unions can submit legislative proposals, and their input is sought in economic decisions. Josef Stalin once referred to unions as "transmission belts," after breaking all independent union power. His view was accurate because their essential function remains that of transmitting party policy. While they may give the workers a sense of participation, they do not permit them a role in management or policymaking. Given the trade unions' inability to provide this, it is not surprising that demands for free trade unions have been prominent in practically all East European reform movements, from Hungary in

1956 to Poland in 1980. The Polish Solidarity movement was worker-initiated and eventually united much of the country behind the demand for independent trade unions and democratization. A particular area of contention is worker safety. Coal miners in Poland, in Romania, and in the Soviet Donbas area have all charged the unions with endangering workers for the sake of fulfilling production targets. Unions in Yugoslavia occupy an ambiguous position. With workers' councils, Yugoslavia possesses an independent mechanism for articulating workers' interests, yet it has retained the traditional union structure. The frequent strikes that the Yugoslav government tolerates have placed the trade unions in a dilemma as yet undecided—do they assume leadership of the strike or exhort the workers to return to work? Recently, the Yugoslav government has given the trade unions a larger role in factory affairs, but the basic contradiction remains.

Volunteer Repair Squads   Residentially based voluntary maintenance squads that carry out routine repairs and maintenance in city apartment buildings and dwellings. The volunteer repair squads (*remontnaya druzhina*) repair windows, fix electricity, plaster cracks, and make other simple repairs. Most contain a core of skilled workmen who direct the work. *See also* CITIZEN PARTICIPATION, p. 275.

Significance   Given the generally low availability of state maintenance services, the volunteer repair squads fill an important function. In Moscow, volunteer repair squads enrolling thousands of workers regularly perform maintenance on city dwellings. The squads are part of the vast network of local volunteer organizations in the Soviet Union. Their main function, in addition to the maintenance they perform, is to socialize citizens into a sense of community responsibility for the neighborhood, creating what in the West is called community development and neighborhood organization.

8. Foreign Policy

"Active Measures"   According to the United States Department of State, a term used by the Soviets to cover a broad range of their activities aimed at achieving Soviet foreign policy objectives. The Soviets allegedly include in the term "active measures" (*aktivnye meropriyatiya*) such actions as disinformation, the use of communist parties and front groups around the world, the manipulation of the media in target countries, operations to expand Soviet political influence, forgeries, and other techniques and tactics designed to undercut opponents of the USSR. The purpose of spreading disinformation is to gain public acceptance for something that is not true, but is in the Soviet interest. With the recognition that Soviet sources are suspect and questionable, the State Department alleges that the approach used is to achieve publication of false news in reputable noncommunist media. Soviet media, such as TASS or Radio Moscow, are then able to quote reliable sources in the capitalist world with the expectation that their news stories will be picked up and circulated by other noncommunist media. *See also* KGB, p. 288.

Significance   "Active measures," as alleged by the United States government, are part of the propaganda war waged between the two camps, East and West. Political influence operations, especially those using agents held in high regard as in the case of disinformation, are difficult to detect and counter. Individuals are able to disguise their KGB connection while taking an active role in public affairs. Examples of "active measures" undertaken by the Soviets abound. In Angola, Zaire, and South Africa, for example, the Soviets have spread stories that the United States is trying to oust the government of Angola, that the United States was supporting "2,000 specially trained gunmen"

309

based in Zaire to attack Angola, and that American agents had met with South African and Zairian representatives to conspire against the Angolan regime. In another case, the Soviets spread a story that the CIA-financed antimalaria research program carried on in Pakistan was involved in an attempt to breed a special mosquito that would infect their victims with a deadly virus. Such examples of Soviet duplicity and "dirty tricks" abound, since they have become a common pattern in global propaganda and ideological warfare. Similar activities are also allegedly carried on regularly by American agents, particularly those in the Central Intelligence Agency, aimed at destabilizing existing communist systems and preventing communism from spreading to other societies.

Annexation of Territory   A means of territorial acquisition, rejected by Soviet international legal doctrine as an instrument of capitalist imperialism. Nonetheless, Soviet legal doctrine recognizes, and practices, territorial annexation by socialist states as justified under certain circumstances. These include (1) the principle of national self-determination; (2) the recognition of the historic rights of the peoples of diverse territories; (3) deprivation of an aggressor's territory as reparation; and (4) voluntary adherence to specific annexations. The various territorial acquisitions of the Soviet Union have been justified under one or more of these rubrics. *See also* NATIONAL FRONT, p. 325; SALAMI TACTICS, p. 333.

Significance   The official rejection of annexation as a means of acquiring territory has had little actual impact, since the history of the modern Soviet state is marked by sizable territorial acquisitions. The doctrine of historical rights of the peoples was applied at the end of World War II when the Soviet Union seized Polish, Czech, Romanian, and Hungarian territory. The most commonly used rationale has been that of "voluntary adherence," setting up a puppet government supported by military occupation, followed by a referendum that always has been in favor of joining the Soviet Union. In the prewar period, such republics as Azerbaidzhan and Georgia were added by this method. In the postwar period, the same method was followed in the Baltic states (Estonia, Latvia, and Lithuania). Some analysts maintain that Soviet intentions in Afghanistan are based on the same scenario, for annexation of all or part of the present Afghanistan state.

Berlin Wall   An action taken at the instigation of Nikita Khrushchev in August 1961 to fortify and seal off East Berlin from West

Berlin. The building and military fortification of the Berlin Wall were rapidly extended to the entire border between West Berlin and the surrounding East German territory, and to the entire East German–West German border. The intent, which was successful in that it evoked only a verbal protest from the West, was to stop the flow of East German trained manpower across the border and to bolster the East German regime by removing the exposure of its people to the West. The building of the Berlin Wall left only 13 heavily guarded official crossing points. Anyone attempting to cross illegally the concrete wall and barbed wire reinforcements was arrested or shot. Limited pass agreements between the West and East German governments were negotiated in the late 1960s, but the entire border and the Wall itself remain heavily guarded. *See also* EAST GERMAN UPRISING OF 1953, p. 320; OSTPOLITIK, p. 327.

Significance The building of the Berlin Wall and the border fortifications between East and West aided the industrial expansion of East Germany by stopping the general exodus into West Germany. Because the building of the wall evoked only a verbal response from the West, the Soviets could assume that it amounted to a tacit agreement of the post–World War II division of Europe. The treaties later signed between East Germany and West Germany regularized policies on border crossings and millions of Germans could visit across the wall. The Berlin Wall itself remains for many a symbol of Soviet intransigence.

Brezhnev Doctrine A doctrine developed by Leonid Brezhnev and the Soviet leadership that declares that the Soviet Union and Eastern European socialist states are committed to defend, by force of arms if necessary, the integrity of the socialist system whenever and wherever it is threatened. The Brezhnev Doctrine was developed and invoked in 1968 as an after-the-fact rationale to justify the Soviet-led invasion and occupation of Czechoslovakia by troops of the Warsaw Treaty Organization. In effect, it rejects extreme internal liberalization as well as subversion by the West as policies and actions that can be permitted in socialist states. *See also* PRAGUE SPRING, p. 295; SOCIALIST INTERNATIONALISM, p. 335.

Significance The Brezhnev Doctrine was developed as a justification for intervention in communist states by communist states. Like the Monroe Doctrine, the Brezhnev Doctrine is a policy expounded by a major state that seeks to maintain a degree of hegemony within its regional sphere of influence. Leonid Brezhnev presented it as part of the doctrine of "socialist internationalism," which enunciates the principles of solidarity and unity among socialist nations. For Brezhnev, all socialist states have a responsibility to protect and preserve socialism, by force of arms if necessary. The Brezhnev Doctrine clearly limits the sovereignty of East European states. It is a continuation of the Soviet policy carried on since the end of World War II that held that the Soviet Union must unilaterally determine what policies and actions are politically acceptable in bloc states. Brezhnev in effect made a distinction between communist and capitalist states in proclaiming his doctrine. United States' intervention in Vietnam or the Middle East, for example, would be contrary to international law and the principle of sovereignty, but in the case of socialist states, the interest of the Soviet Union and the socialist movement take precedence over the sovereignty of individual states. Brezhnev justified this view by holding that countries like Czechoslovakia can maintain their sovereignty only under conditions of socialism. Thus, Soviet intervention in a socialist state is a domestic rather than a foreign matter, and Western criticism of violations of sovereignty should be rejected outright. Coming as it did at a time when the Soviets were promoting a policy of détente with the West, the Brezhnev Doctrine emphasizes the priorities of the Soviet leadership. In 1979, the Doctrine was given new meaning with the Soviet invasion of Afghanistan and the application of the principle of "socialist solidarity" to a nonbloc country. The potential threat of intervention that characterizes the Brezhnev Doctrine was apparent in Poland during the early 1980s when many observers feared that the Soviets would intervene militarily to suppress the independent trade union Solidarity. Although the Polish army took military control of the state through martial law decrees by declaring that an internal "state of war" existed, the threat of Soviet intervention remained.

Capitalist Encirclement   The plight of the Soviet Union as a socialist state surrounded by hostile capitalist states pursuing political, military, and economic policies aimed at securing its destruction. This world view developed as the Bolshevik Revolution succeeded. One Soviet leader, Leon Trotsky, expounded the view that the only effective means of dealing with the capitalist encirclement was to lend strong support to revolutionary movements in all capitalist states aimed at ending the threat by winning the battle for world socialism. Vladimir Lenin, and later Josef Stalin, argued that the Soviet Union must build itself into an impregnable bastion of power able to discourage attack or turn back all invaders. With Stalin's victory in the intraparty power struggle in the late 1920s, the Soviet Union embarked on a massive program to implement the latter course of action. After

World War II and the accession of China and East European communist states to the communist bloc, Stalin declared that the condition of capitalist encirclement had ended. *See also* CONTAINMENT, p. 315.

Significance   Stalin utilized the concept of capitalist encirclement as a justification for ruthless internal policies during the 1920s and 1930s. Industrialization was regarded as the highest priority during the Stalin era, a vital means to survival of the Soviet state. After Adolf Hitler's rise to power in Germany, Soviet citizens and the left-wing parties of the West tended to accept the idea that Soviet behavior was conditioned and justified by capitalist encirclement. Repressive policies used to quash all opposition within Russia were based, according to Soviet propaganda, on the hostile encirclement of fascist states, with fascism judged to be the highest stage of capitalism.

Cominform   The acronym for Communist Information Bureau, the international organization of European communist parties created by the Soviet Union in September 1947 as a means for maintaining control in those countries where communist parties had already, or were expected to, come to power. The Cominform included the parties of Albania, Bulgaria, Czechoslovakia, France, Hungary, Italy, Romania, the Soviet Union, and Yugoslavia. The prewar predecessor of the Cominform, the Comintern or Communist International, had been used by Josef Stalin to dominate other communist parties. The Comintern was dissolved in 1943 as proof of Soviet cooperation with the Allies. Postwar Europe confronted Stalin with a new situation. The Soviet Union was no longer the sole communist-party state. In Yugoslavia, a nationally based communist party had come to power with little help from the Soviet Union. Elsewhere in Eastern Europe the communist parties were either newly installed in power by the Red Army or well on their way to achieving power with Soviet help, but the question remained as to whether they would retain full loyalty to the Soviet Union. In Italy and France, the large communist parties were competing in free elections, with the possibility that they might owe their seats in government to electoral power rather than to Soviet power. Stalin's purposes in creating the Cominform were to (1) consolidate Soviet power over Eastern Europe; and (2) extend Soviet control over states, such as Czechoslovakia, where full communist power had not yet been achieved. *See also* COMINTERN, p. 314; POTSDAM CONFERENCE, p. 332; YALTA AGREEMENT, p. 343; YUGOSLAV PARTISAN WAR, p. 35.

Significance   The creation of the Cominform marked the further deepening in the Cold War between the West and the communists.

Poland was immediately forbidden by the Soviets to accept the American offer of inclusion in the Marshall Plan. Czechoslovakia was similarly sanctioned when the Czechoslovak Communist Party took over by a coup in March 1948. As a means of total Soviet control, however, the Cominform was less than a success. Its most momentous decision occurred in June 1948 when at Soviet instigation the Cominform expelled the Yugoslav Communist Party. The Yugoslav communists and their leader, Josip Broz Tito, were accused of every ideological sin in the Marxist lexicon, but their essential sin was that they refused to accept Soviet political and economic domination. The expulsion from the Cominform harmed Yugoslavia economically but unified the country behind Tito, and the state survived.

National communism of the Tito type, that is placing national interests above Soviet interests, became a bête noire of Stalin's. In the subsequent wave of Soviet-directed purges that hit the East European parties in the early 1950s, anyone suspected of harboring "Titoist" or "nationalist" leanings was summarily jailed or executed. Subsequent decades have little to offer as proof that the Soviet party has developed much more tolerance for independent communist parties. The Yugoslav expulsion also created much dissension within the Greek Communist Party and contributed to the defeat of the communists in the Greek Civil War of 1949. In fact, the most lasting effect of the Cominform was that it created a new kind of communist party: a party, namely the Yugoslav, that remained avowedly Marxist, operated a one-party communist state, and refused to accept the dominance of the Soviet Union. With Stalin's death and the signing of the Belgrade Declaration in 1955 signalling a cautious opening of relations between Yugoslavia and the Soviet Union, the Cominform ceased to exist in 1956.

Comintern   The acronym for the Communist International, the Soviet-dominated international organization of communist parties founded in 1917 by Vladimir Lenin. The Comintern was initiated as the communist successor to the International Association of Socialist Parties, founded in 1889. The creation of the Comintern crystallized the division between the radical left wing of Marxist socialism and the mass-based socialist parties of Europe, which maintained that socialism could be achieved by working with the parliamentary process. Most of the communist parties of Europe were born out of the conflict between revolutionary communism and what became socialist democratic parties. The Comintern immediately issued a manifesto to all workers to support the Bolshevik regime. Lenin dictated the tactics to be followed by the new communist parties, including infiltration of the trade unions and support of all bourgeous nationalist movements that threatened the colonial empires of the European powers. By exacting ruthless discipline, the Soviets dominated the Comintern parties, and the Comintern served largely as a tool of Soviet foreign policy. The Comintern was structured as a centralized, Leninist organization over which the Soviets wielded control; the membership was organized into sections that were viewed as branch establishments of the international communist movement, headquartered in Moscow. The Comintern was formally dissolved in 1943, as it made little sense for the Soviet Union to continue to support the overthrow of the very governments with which it was allied against the Axis powers. Moreover, it was fighting to preserve its very existence, and desperately needed the support of Western societies, especially the United States. *See also* COMINFORM, p. 313; INTERNATIONAL BRIGADES, p. 20.

Significance The Comintern was characterized by the complete subordination of all other communist parties to Soviet interests, even at the expense of a member communist party. Thus, the Comintern ordered the Chinese Communist Party to subordinate itself to the Kuomintang, even though this almost destroyed the Chinese party in the interwar period. In the 1930s, the Comintern became a tool for the propagation of Stalin's personal dictatorship. The member parties and sections were repeatedly purged and many of their officials lost their lives. This created lasting ill will between the Soviet Union and other communist parties, especially the Yugoslav and Polish, whose Comintern sections suffered greatly during the purges, and contributed to Stalin's suspicion of any "native-based" communist party. The most lasting effect of the Comintern occurred in 1921 when Lenin set forth the tactics and organization for all member parties, an organizational structure that is followed by all ruling communist parties to this day.

Containment The basic post–World War II United States foreign policy aimed at discouraging Soviet expansionist initiatives. Containment doctrine was first expounded in 1947 by George F. Kennan, Chief of the Policy Planning Staff of the Department of State. For Kennan, Soviet policymakers functioned under the imperatives of a Stalinist dictatorship influenced by communist ideology and Russian history. Kennan further reasoned that the Soviet regime, to retain public support, must either give the Russian people "bread or circuses," meaning either the economic rebuilding and planning program must succeed, or, in its absence, foreign ventures must be undertaken. He concluded that the Soviet system was unlikely to succeed in the former, and therefore the West must do all possible to discourage the latter. The Truman Administration accepted Kennan's basic assumptions and undertook a two-phase policy to implement the containment approach. Phase I instituted the Truman Doctrine, which called for halting Soviet expansion by drawing a "geopolitical shatter zone" from Northern Europe to Southeast Europe, and from the Middle East to South and East Asia. Phase II called for implementing the policy by building "situations of strength" through countervailing American power allied with other Free World nations. Having thus established a perimeter, the United States would be able to react to any Soviet attempt to break the ring at a time and place and in a manner of its own choosing. By frustrating what Kennan assumed to be Soviet policy objectives, internal pressures on the Soviet regime would be intensified and dissatisfactions with the Stalinist dictatorship would increase. In time, according to Kennan, Soviet leaders would realize that Soviet interests would not be served by intimidation, disorder, subversion, and insurrection, and that accommodations could be worked out through peaceful diplomacy. *See also* CAPITALIST ENCIRCLEMENT, p. 312.

Significance   The containment doctrine in its general guidelines accepted as fact the hostility of the former World War II allies and their continuing competition in the postwar world. To make the containment doctrine effective, the Truman Administration began a massive program of rearmament, established military bases around the world, especially in the perimeter area around the Soviet Union, and entered into military alliances with over 40 nations. As supplementary policies aimed at strengthening the containment strategy, the United States undertook a vast program of economic aid to rebuild the war-shattered economies of Western Europe (Marshall Plan), and instituted a global program of providing aid to the underdeveloped countries (Point IV Program) where communist movements had become an increasing problem. The United States also sought to rally the United Nations peacekeeping machinery and use it as a means for coping with any future Soviet aggressions. The containment doctrine was not completely successful in its stated objectives, however. Although the Soviet Union has not expanded its territory, countries in Europe, Asia, Africa, the Middle East, and Latin America have, with Soviet aid, adopted the communist system since the containment approach was implemented in 1947. George Kennan and other early supporters of the containment doctrine have, in retrospect, determined that the policy may have been counterproductive in its approach to the Soviet Union. Instead of stability and peace, the implementation of the doctrine has led to implacable hostility between the Soviet Union and the United States, and to a mutual fear that has encouraged a massive arms race. The ultimate purpose of containment was not war but accommodation. During the 1960s and 1970s, it appeared that the containment doctrine had finally succeeded by encouraging the Soviets to join with the United States in a general détente. The Soviet incursion into Afghanistan in 1979 and the Reagan Administration's arms buildup in the 1980s, however, contributed to a return of the cold war.

Council of Mutual Economic Assistance (CMEA or COME-CON)

A regional group organized in 1949 by the Soviet Union to integrate the economies of Eastern Europe and to provide for national specializations. COMECON's original membership of Czechoslovakia, Bulgaria, Hungary, Poland, and Romania was broadened in time to include Albania (since withdrawn), East Germany, Cuba, and Mongolia. COMECON's machinery for eliciting cooperation among members is headed by a Council that functions as the main decision making body except on matters of basic policy, wherein it is empowered only to make recommendations to member governments. A permanent Executive Committee implements policy decisions, a Secretariat headquartered in Moscow operates under Council direction, and more than 20 standing commissions carry out planning and operations in commodity fields. Major economic policies are decided outside the COMECON structure at conferences of the first secretaries of the national communist parties. During its early years, COMECON did not become an instrument for integrating the economies of Eastern Europe. Each country retained its full economic sovereignty in formulating economic plans and carrying on foreign trade. A web of trade treaties was developed among its members, however, and most trade was carried on among bloc members. When Nikita Khrushchev assumed power in the Soviet Union in the late 1950s, he at once began to try to revive the ideal of economic integration through the building of a "socialist commonwealth" based on free cooperation rather than on Soviet domination through forced bilateral agreements, as developed earlier by Josef Stalin. The new approach, according to the Soviets, was based on "equal rights," and "fraternal cooperation in the sphere of politics, economics and culture." By permitting a certain amount of diversity, the Soviets aimed at achieving greater bloc unity as a response to growing political and economic unity in the West. The basic guideline for the new approach was a planned specialization so that each member would concentrate on those products that it could produce with greatest efficiency. *See also* TRANSFERABLE RUBLE, p. 234.

Significance The Council of Mutual Economic Assistance was created to emulate the success of the European Community's economic integration approach. Just as the Warsaw Pact was somewhat of a carbon copy of the North Atlantic Treaty, so, too, COMECON was an attempt to copy the successes of the European Economic Community. Although the "grand design" for an integrated world socialist economy never materialized, COMECON has accomplished much since it was revitalized during the Khrushchev era. Although it is no longer completely controlled by the Soviets, the other active members are still dominated by the political power and the sheer economic weight of the Soviet Union. Some members have rejected the planned specialization of production for each country. The less-developed countries, such as Romania, have refused to accept the implications of the division of labor since it relegated them to an inferior status of suppliers of raw materials and farm products. Romania's plans for a well-rounded economy with heavy industry at its core remain the national goal, thus removing the country from active participation in most COMECON programs. The failure to achieve high levels of economic integration relates also to the difficult economic development problems faced by each member, and the desire of each to retain a high level of freedom of action in its political and economic actions. Gains promoted by COMECON in addition to increased inter-bloc trade include common projects, such as the Eastern European "friendship" oil pipeline, a power grid linking members, and a common freight car pool. COMECON members have also agreed to switch from oil to nuclear power by 1990. In recent years, growing nationalism in Eastern Europe has further weakened the basic premises of COMECON, and the natural tendency of socialist states with planned economies to strive for national self-sufficiency has hampered efforts to achieve integration, but the organization remains useful as a forum for open debate on common economic problems.

De-Stalinization   The process in the Soviet Union and in most Eastern European countries of renouncing the Stalinist model of communism that imposed government by institutionalized terror. De-Stalinization provided for governmental and legal reforms and a general liberalization. De-Stalinization began in the period following Josef Stalin's death in 1953, encouraged by revolts in Czechoslovakia and East Germany. Soon dramatic changes in the political climate occurred in Hungary and Poland, followed by slow but steady reform progress in Bulgaria and Romania. Only Albania and East Germany retained the Stalinist model, with few changes in their political and legal systems. The reform movements were encouraged in 1956 by Nikita Khrushchev in his famous speech attacking Stalin and Stalinism before the 20th Congress of the Communist Party of the Soviet Union.

Polish and Hungarian intellectuals seized upon this opportunity to seek drastic change in their political systems, leading to a major military intervention in Hungary by the Soviets who feared that reforms had gone so far that the very existence of communism was threatened. See also HUNGARIAN UPRISING OF 1956, p. 323; STALINISM, p. 78; THAW, p. 305.

Significance   The main pressures for political liberalization throughout Eastern Europe during the 1950s and 1960s came from Khrushchev's attack on Stalinism and changes that were subsequently made in the Soviet legal system. Leaders in other communist states recognized that they could no longer depend on terrorism and the support of the Soviet Union to remain in power, leading to a general relaxation in the exercise of power. Khrushchev's charge that Stalin had debased the basic nature of communism by developing a cult of personality led to changes aimed at reducing the previously dominant role of individual leaders, such as that of Bolesław Bierut in Poland, Klement Gottwald of Czechoslovakia, Mátyás Rákosi of Hungary, and Gheorghie Gheorghiu-Dej of Romania. In many cases, one individual held the top posts in both party and government, but the de-Stalinization campaign with its attack on the cult of the individual resulted in a temporary abandonment of the dual role. Reforms during the period of de-Stalinization mainly took the form of reduced power for the state security system, ending a period in which the secret police had enjoyed unchecked authority over all citizens. The impact of de-Stalinization and its liberalizations remain today in the Soviet Union and in most Eastern European countries. When compared with Western democratic systems, however, the communist states in the region are still harshly governed with little freedom enjoyed by the individual.

Détente   A condition in international politics that denotes a climate of reduced tension in the relations between two or more countries. Although détente is a common diplomatic term, it has been applied particularly in recent years to describe the relationship between the Soviet Union and the United States that emerged in the 1960s and lasted until the Soviet intervention in Afghanistan in 1979. Détente was based on a recognition that peaceful coexistence was an essential ingredient in American-Soviet relations, and that in its absence the cold war and an expanding arms race could lead to the calamity of a nuclear war. *See also* PEACEFUL COEXISTENCE, p. 329; SOVIET ARMS CONTROL AND DISARMAMENT STRATEGIES, p. 335.

Significance   In the field of foreign policy, it is a matter of decision makers' judgment as to whether a state will pursue a conciliatory policy of détente or utilize a confrontational system of diplomacy in the hope that the opposition will back down. After two decades of confrontational, cold war politics, the two superpowers began to negotiate their differences in the 1960s as a result of the military situational factors and the pressures of world and domestic opinion. The period of détente produced a number of arms limitation agreements, increased East-West trade, the Helsinki Accord aimed at obtaining a general agreement to the post–World War II European status quo, and a great increase in tourism and cultural exchanges. Many of the diplomatic gains achieved during the period of détente were wiped out as a result of Soviet penetrations in Africa, Latin America, and Asia, and its incursion into Afghanistan. Also, despite détente, the arms race continued in full force during the 1960s and 1970s, with the result that by the 1980s both sides were engaged in a massive buildup of nuclear warheads and delivery systems that made all previous arms races in recorded history pale into insignificance. With the death of Leonid Brezhnev in 1982 and the coming to power of Yuri Andropov, the Soviets gave some indication that they would be amenable to working out a new era of détente in Soviet-American relations.

East German Uprising of 1953   Anticommunist demonstrations and riots that broke out in East Berlin and other cities of Soviet-controlled East Germany in June 1953. The East Berlin uprisings mark the first time that communist authorities in postwar Eastern Europe were faced with a mass, worker-supported protest against communism and Soviet control. The disturbances quickly spread to the major cities of East Germany and involved tens of thousands. The East German People's Police lost control and regular Soviet military units were called in. The demonstrations were especially severe in East Berlin, which at the time was not sealed off from West Berlin. Soviet and Western tanks confronted each other across the border while unarmed demonstrators stoned the Soviet tanks. *See also* BERLIN WALL, p. 310; PRAGUE SPRING, p. 295; SOLIDARITY, p. 303.

Significance   The East German uprising was the first popularly supported protest against the Soviet-imposed communist governments of postwar Eastern Europe. The Soviet authorities proved willing to use armed force, as they did in later events, such as the Hungarian Revolution of 1956 and the Prague Spring of 1968. Mass arrests and executions by the Soviet military followed, but in the wake of the uprising the Soviet Union initiated more liberal policies in East Germany, which were followed by liberalization throughout Eastern Europe after Stalin's death. In turn, this liberalization may have contributed to the Polish and Hungarian uprisings of 1956.

Great Patriotic War   The name commonly given to World War II in official Soviet literature and commentary. The official use of *Great Patriotic War* to denote the Soviet Union's role in the Allied victory over the Axis reflects a change in values that occurred under the stress of the German invasion. Josef Stalin recognized in the darkest days of the war that the populace could be much more effectively mobilized to fight for the survival of the Russian homeland than for the survival of the international working class and Marxist socialism. Russian patriotism became a respectable force to be drawn upon for the war effort. This constituted an implicit acknowledgment that Soviet citizens could hold allegiances other than to the international working class and communism, and that these allegiances could be both potent and useful. Symbols from the past were resurrected, such as the creation of Cossack units, and the Suvorov and Kutuzov military orders, named for czarist generals who fought Napoleon in 1812. *See also* IDEOLOGY, p. 48.

Significance   The title Great Patriotic War implies that the war was a struggle of all Soviet peoples for the basic survival of the state. The war was the single most traumatic event in the history of the Soviet state, resulting in some 20 million dead, immense destruction, and a heroic defense effort marked by such battles as Stalingrad and the siege of Leningrad. The Great Patriotic War is still used as a rallying device, and much Soviet cultural activity relates to themes derived from the war. The continued appeal of such themes reflects the power of nationalism in the Soviet Union and emphasizes the primacy in many situations of nationalistic values over ideological values in human motivation.

Helsinki Accord   Major agreements concluded at Helsinki at the conclusion of the Conference on Security and Cooperation in Europe aimed at achieving détente and an acceptance by all parties of the post–World War II status quo in Europe. Also known as the Helsinki Final Act, the Accord was signed by 35 nations, including the 15 NATO countries, 7 Warsaw Pact nations, and 13 neutral and nonaligned European states. Agreement was reached in four areas, with the Accord thereby divided into four sections referred to as "baskets."

Basket I is concerned with security in Europe. It proclaims basic principles to guide relations among European states, and it calls for the resolution of specific security problems through the adoption of confidence-building measures. Basket II calls for various forms of cooperation in dealing with problems created by science and technology, economics, and the environment. Basket III provides for international cooperation in promoting humanitarian ventures in the fields of human rights, education, and culture, and it calls for the free flow of people, ideas, and information throughout all of Europe. Basket IV of the Accord, procedural in nature, provides for the holding of periodic review conferences in which participating states are called upon "to continue the multilateral process initiated by the Conference" to reduce hostility and increase understanding and common programs. Two review conferences have been held, the first at Belgrade (1977–78), the second in Madrid (1980–82). *See also* DÉTENTE, p. 319; HUMAN RIGHTS MOVEMENT, p. 286; SOVIET ARMS CONTROL AND DISARMAMENT STRATEGIES, p. 335.

Significance The Helsinki Accord was an effort to end the Cold War and to restore good relations between East and West throughout Europe. The Accord, however, was merely a diplomatic agreement, not a treaty that created international law. It was considered to be only a beginning step in a multilateral process that would engender cooperation and understanding among all European nations and foster a new spirit of détente between communistic and capitalistic Europe. Following the 1975 conference, the Soviets showed good faith by permitting greatly increased emigration, especially of Jews going to Israel, and the German Democratic Republic declared an amnesty and released many political prisoners. Participating European states also signed a convention that provided for joint action in dealing with problems of air pollution in Europe. The ultimate objective of the Helsinki agreements was to tear down barricades, walls, and fortifications and let people and ideas move freely throughout Europe. The review conferences were to be the instrument for this continuing multilateral diplomacy. The Madrid review conference, however, indicated how the political climate had changed since the Helsinki conference in 1975. Delegates from 35 countries—the United States, Canada, and all European states except Albania—met in 1980 against a background of deterioration in East-West relations. By 1982, the conference was still in session despite lengthy recesses and growing vituperation in the discussion, producing charges and countercharges concerning such matters as the internal crisis in Poland. The major issue—whether a European disarmament conference should be called to negotiate confidence-building and security-promoting measures from the Atlantic to the Urals—was strongly but unsuccessfully pushed by the neutral and nonaligned European countries. Although Helsinki could be judged a success in some ways, the end of détente, return of the cold war, and the great acceleration in the arms race nullified much of its potential.

Hungarian Uprising of 1956   A major revolt against Stalinism and Soviet control that broke out in Hungary in 1956. The Hungarian Uprising began on October 23, 1956, with widespread demonstrations and demands for the withdrawal of Soviet troops from Hungarian soil. It progressed to the formation of spontaneous workers' councils, the revival of the prewar democratic parties, and the announcement of Hungary's intent to withdraw from the Warsaw Pact and seek neutral status. The revolt ended on November 4 as Soviet troops reentered Budapest. The reformist leader, Imre Nagy, was taken captive and executed by the Soviets, who broke their promise of a safe conduct for him. János Kádár was installed as leader and Soviet control reaffirmed. *See also* DE-STALINIZATION, p. 318; BREZHNEV DOCTRINE, p. 311; NEW ECONOMIC MECHANISM, p. 217; SEPARATE ROADS TO SOCIALISM, p. 77.

Significance   The Hungarian Uprising of 1956 was the first nationalistic, mass-backed revolt in Eastern Europe. Hungarian demands for freedom from Soviet control were fueled by several factors that converged in 1956: (1) worsening economic conditions in a country where communism had been imposed with the greatest brutality; (2) the seemingly successful attempt of the Poles to ameliorate Stalinism (the Polish October) through mass demonstrations; and (3) the continuation of the hated regime of Mátyás Rákosi. It occurred against the backdrop of a confusing period in international relations. In 1952 the Republican leadership under President Dwight Eisenhower appeared ready to jettison the policy of containment of communism for one of actively encouraging revolt in Eastern Europe. The American-sponsored Radio Free Europe (RFE) launched Operation FOCUS, which campaigned for "nationalist opposition" to communism in Eastern Europe. Simultaneously, the post-Stalin Soviet leadership cautiously began to de-Stalinize, which included permitting limited reforms in Eastern Europe. All this encouraged the nationalistic reform movement in Hungary, where the imposition of an essentially alien system was particularly resented. Despite the apparent American support, there was never any likelihood of aid from the West, particularly as the Uprising coincided with the 1956 Suez Crisis and the landing of French and British troops in Egypt. The inability of the

West to free Eastern Europe from Soviet control became an admitted fact and the West began to seek bettered relations through a policy of détente. János Kádár subsequently has carried out many of the economic reforms demanded in 1956 but has kept Hungary a loyal member of the Warsaw Pact.

In Poland in June 1956 a similar uprising appeared probable as Polish workers in the seaport towns demonstrated against the government. The "Polish October," however, did not develop into a full-blown rebellion. Władysław Gomułka was asked to return to the party leadership, the agricultural collectivization drive was halted, and the party effected a compromise with the Polish Catholic Church, releasing Stefan Cardinal Wyszynski from prison and restoring him to his position as head of the Church. Gomułka managed to persuade the Soviet leadership that he could defuse the Polish situation, and a showdown with the USSR was averted.

Institute of the USA and Canada (ISKAN)   Soviet research institute charged with policy-related analysis of American-Soviet relations. The primary function of the Institute of the USA and Canada is to study the formulation and implementation of American foreign policy. In addition, it analyzes American domestic politics. Headed by Georgi Arbatov, the Institute was formed in 1967 out of the Institute of World Economics and International Relations (IMEMO). It is a key institution in Soviet national security policymaking, maintaining close relations with the top leadership. The Institute has a permanent staff of about 300 and employs many top politicians and military officers as consultants and instructors. It is also a degree-granting institution; many of the Soviet diplomatic corps hold degrees from the Institute.

Significance   Although the influence of the USA Institute is difficult to assess, much official policy toward the United States is shaped by the Institute's policy analysis. Recently, much of its effort has centered on analyzing American nuclear policy. The *Amerikanisty*, as the institute specialists are called, are a favored group, provided with access to Westerners, travel abroad, ample salaries, and much prestige. It has become known as a favored place for the children of the elite; both V. M. Molotov's son and the son of party leader Yuri Andropov have been employed there.

International Adjudication   The peaceful settlement of international disputes through impartial third-party adjudication. Although the Soviet Union has participated in international bodies of adjudication, it refuses to accept any settlements unless it has explicitly agreed in advance to adjudication. The Soviet concept of sovereignty holds that no nonsocialist state can adjudicate over a socialist state. Thus, the Soviet Union prefers to work through direct negotiations or special commissions in which it participates. Although it is a member, the Soviet Union has never accepted the compulsory jurisdiction provided by the Optional Clause of the Statute of the International Court of Justice (ICJ). Before 1945, the Soviet Union refused to participate in any international adjudication; it did not, for example, become a member of the Permanent Court of International Justice even though it joined the League of Nations in 1934. In 1945, the Soviet Union ratified the Statute of the ICJ upon joining the United Nations and there has always been a Soviet judge as one of the 15 judges that comprise the Court. The Soviets, however, have refused to submit to the Court's compulsory jurisdiction, preferring to directly negotiate adjudicatory and arbitral rights in major treaties, such as the Helsinki Accord. *See also* CIVIL RIGHTS, p. 251; HELSINKI ACCORD, p. 321.

Significance   The Soviet policy of abjuring international adjudication has not meant that the Soviet signature on an international agreement is worthless; in general the Soviet leadership has fulfilled its international obligations, with the general proviso that no agreement with a nonsocialist state can override the interests of the socialist state. Similarly, capitalist states will reject adjudication when their primary national interests are adversely affected. With the Soviet accession to international bodies, such as UN specialized agencies like the International Labor Organization (ILO), an area of conflict has arisen. The USSR, for example, has accepted the jurisdiction of the ILO labor conventions, but Soviet trade unions have refused to apply them to Soviet workers. The ILO has become periodically a battleground between the American labor unions, who seek to expel the Soviets, and the Soviets, who maintain that such actions are "imperialist" conspiracies against socialist workers. The Soviet attitude makes it unlikely that Soviet participation in international adjudication will increase; the Soviet leadership continues to insist on direct involvement rather than adjudication by third parties.

National Front   A political device utilized by the Soviet Union and national communist parties to forge an alliance between communist and noncommunist groups to achieve some mutual objectives. The Soviets have used the national-front approach for national security purposes, and in foreign policy to try to promote a unified approach to a common enemy. In Third World countries, the local communist party has often used the approach to form an alliance aimed at securing independence or in protecting the nation's independence once gained. Typically, a national front engenders political and military cooperation among various parties, groups, and individuals, and it usually has been motivated by a common fear and hatred of fascism, which communists define as the highest stage of capitalism. Communists have often held prominent leadership positions in national front movements, along with others from socialist and democratic movements and groups. *See also* FASCISM, p. 47; INTERNATIONAL BRIGADES, p. 20; SALAMI TACTICS, p. 333.

Significance   The communist use of the national front technique began in the 1930s with the rise of fascism in Western Europe. In the democratic countries of Europe threatened with fascism, antifascist "popular front" coalitions were forged with the blessing of the Soviet Union. The Popular Front, for example, became a ruling coalition in France from 1936 to 1938 under the leadership of Leon Blum, and a national front was formed in Spain but was destroyed by the fascist Falangist party under Francisco Franco in the Spanish Civil War. During World War II, national front coalitions in Europe helped to carry on a common struggle against fascist occupation forces in their efforts to liberate their countries from the invaders. In Yugoslavia, for example, the communists succeeded in attracting many prominent noncommunists to the banners of the Partisan Movement, which continued the war against the invaders through guerilla operations. Since World War II, the Soviets and indigenous communist parties in Asia, Africa, and Latin America have made effective use of the national front device in their anticolonial and independence struggles. The National Liberation Front (NLF) of Vietnam, for example, proved effective in driving the French and, later, the Americans, out of Vietnam and securing independence for the state. Once the objectives of a national front arrangement have been achieved, there is a natural tendency for the coalition to dissolve, and competition for power among the democratic, socialist, and communist elements that comprised the front resumes.

Nonalignment   A policy of many countries to avoid military alliances with either the West or the Soviet bloc. Nonalignment as a state policy of "Third Force" nations emerged from the first meeting of neutralist leaders of 29 African and Asian nations held in Bandung, Indonesia in 1955. Seven nonaligned summit conferences have followed: Belgrade (1961); Cairo (1964); Lusaka (1970); Algiers (1973);

Colombo (1976); Havana (1979); and New Delhi (1983). At its first formal Conference of Nonaligned Countries in Belgrade, Yugoslavia in 1961, a nonaligned country was defined as one that must "(1) pursue an independent policy based on peaceful coexistence; (2) not participate in any multilateral military alliance . . . ; (3) support liberation and independence movements; and (4) not participate in bilateral military alliances with the Great Powers." By agreement reached at Belgrade in 1961, a Conference of Nonaligned Countries will usually be held "every three years." In 1983 there were 101 members in the non-aligned movement. *See also* SEPARATE ROADS TO SOCIALISM, p. 77; WARSAW PACT, p. 340.

Significance Only two communist countries—Yugoslavia and Cuba—currently follow a neutralist foreign policy and are members of the Conference of Nonaligned Countries. In Eastern Europe, although Albania and Romania do not participate in the Warsaw Treaty Organization, they have not joined the nonaligned world bloc. Yugo-slavia under Marshal Josip Broz Tito pioneered the policy of non-alignment in Eastern Europe and in the world after being expelled from the Cominform. Along with Tito, cofounders of the nonalign-ment movement included such luminaries as Jawaharlal Nehru of India, U Nu of Burma, and Achmed Sukarno of Indonesia. The nonaligned movement became a major force in world politics during the 1960s and 1970s as increasing numbers of colonies gained their independence and opted for nonalignment, referring to their foreign policies by such descriptive terms as "neutralism," "neutrality," "posi-tive neutrality," "isolationism," and "nonalignment." In recent years, the nonaligned movement has been weakened as a result of territorial, political, and military conflicts among some of its members. One of the most important results of nonalignment is that it permitted a com-munist state, Yugoslavia, to take the leadership in a world movement for disarmament, peace, and stability, and to receive international support for its rejection of Soviet military, political, and economic hegemony. At the 1983 Conference of Nonaligned Countries in New Delhi, the mantle of leadership was passed from Fidel Castro to Indira Gandhi for the next three-year period. Ninety-nine nonaligned coun-tries attended the New Delhi conference.

Ostpolitik A major West German initiative aimed at securing a détente and normalization of relations with East European commu-nist states. *Ostpolitik*—the first major German initiative of global scope since World War II—was a policy initiated by the Social Democratic Party (SPD) under the leadership of Willy Brandt. Brandt's chance to put his ideas into action came as foreign minister of the Grand Coalition government, and later as Chancellor, after the SPD came to power. The German proposals were put forward in a general mood of détente, which at the time permeated the leaderships of both East and West. Ostpolitik was essentially aimed at doing away with the burdens left over from World War II. The policy aimed at the normalization of relations with the several East European states with which the German Federal Republic did not have peace treaties, and at the establishment of normal diplomatic and economic relations. It was also intended to normalize relations with East Germany (German Democratic Republic) through direct negotiations, which previous German governments steadfastly had refused to do for fear of legitimizing the postwar division of Germany. The 1968 Soviet invasion of Czechoslovakia temporarily interrupted the process, but the will to decelerate armaments among the principal powers was such that talks were resumed soon after that event. Negotiations led to a reestablishment of relations and to peace treaties with Poland and Czechoslovakia. These meant the abandonment of major territorial claims by the German Federal Republic and the acceptance of the removal of major German populations from the territories of those states as final. The treaty with Poland was ratified in 1972. West Germany also signed a treaty committing Germany to a pacific settlement of outstanding disputes with the Soviet Union in August 1970. The final seal on the Ostpolitik was negotiated in Helsinki in 1975 and is covered by the Helsinki Accord that emerged from that Conference on Security and Cooperation in Europe (CSCE). It was envisioned that the Ostpolitik would continue and that the results would be reviewed periodically by international conferences, the first of which was held in Belgrade in 1977. By then, a new chill had set in because of the alleged Soviet non-performance of their treaty obligations in several areas ranging from the violation of civil rights of Soviet citizens to Soviet restrictions on the emigration of individuals to the commitment undertaken in the treaty to permit freer circulation of Western publications and journalists with the Soviet bloc. *See also* DÉTENTE, p. 319; HELSINKI ACCORD, p. 321.

Significance   Ostpolitik denotes a period of détente in West German–communist bloc relations ranging from 1966 to the late 1970s. Its results have placed the final *de jure* seal on the conditions that existed as a result of the post–World War II settlements in Europe. For the first time, the territorial changes and population shifts were recognized as permanent. The German Federal Republic in effect accepted the bitter fruit of defeat in World War II. Ostpolitik, however, provided West Germany with broad leadership opportunities within the NATO alliance. It was accepted by her allies as a bold new initiative that would contribute to easing tensions as well as opening boundaries to trade and freer communication. On the other hand, the modernization of the Soviet and East European armed forces and their substantial numerical superiority over NATO have placed the fruits of Ostpolitik and détente into question. In addition, the 1979 Soviet invasion of Afghanistan weakened both détente and Ostpolitik, although increased East-West trade in the 1980s and the laying of a natural gas pipeline from Siberia to Western Europe have helped keep the idea of Ostpolitik alive. Ostpolitik also laid the groundwork that eventually led to the recognition by the Federal Republic (West Germany) and the GDR (East Germany) of each other's sovereignty, and to the admission of both Germanies into the United Nations as two independent countries.

Peaceful Coexistence   A policy by which countries with diverse sociopolitical systems, religions, and ideological orientations renounce war and cooperate with one another. The idea of peaceful coexistence of communist and capitalist states was first proclaimed by Vladimir Lenin when he took Russia out of World War I and sought to buy time to build socialism. In the contemporary world, peaceful coexistence recognizes the suicidal nature of nuclear war. Soviet Premier Nikita Khrushchev emphasized in a speech before the 20th Party Congress in 1956 that major war was unthinkable, but that competition between states with different social systems should continue in all nonmilitary areas. For Khrushchev, this meant that communism would prove itself to be the superior social system and would preside over the burial of capitalism. Without a major war, communists believe that the doom of capitalism actually will be speeded up. Current Soviet leaders have accepted the dictum that peaceful coexistence is in the interest of the Soviet Union and the world communist movement, that a nuclear war would threaten the survival of communism and the Soviet state. *See also* DÉTENTE, p. 319; LENINISM, p. 51.

Significance   The proclamation of the policy of peaceful coexistence by Soviet leaders was a recognition that the threat of nuclear annihilation required a new tactical approach for communism to win the ideological struggle with capitalism. Peaceful coexistence in time ripened into a general policy of détente between the two major power blocs, but by the early 1980s conflicts and misunderstandings between the Soviet Union and the United States had shattered détente and led to a major escalation in the arms race. For many years Chinese leaders rejected peaceful coexistence, criticizing the Soviets for engaging in "appeasement." By the 1970s, however, China adopted its own peaceful coexistence doctrine and used it as a basis for a Chinese-American détente. Despite its emphasis on peaceful coexistence, the Soviets have continued to give major support to liberation movements in the developing world. They insist that the policy applies to relations between states and should not be interpreted as meaning ideological coexistence in the world. Pacifism, however, is rejected since "just wars" of national liberation fought by indigenous peoples with Soviet support are regarded as the means for achieving communism in the Third World. Thus, the Soviets claim the right to provide economic and military aid to revolutionary movements to offset the support given by capitalist countries to prop up reactionary regimes opposed by the masses. To the Soviets, these actions are compatible with the doctrine of peaceful coexistence. Except for the emphasis on the dangers of nuclear war, most of the ideas expounded by the communists concerning peaceful coexistence are reiterations or reinterpretations of Lenin's and Stalin's interpretations of Marx.

People's Democracy   The title applied by the Soviet Union to the communist regimes that came to power in Eastern Europe after World War II. The designation of "people's democracy" signified that the Soviet-dominated communist parties had taken control, purged the government of bourgeois politicians, and instituted central economic planning. Originally, the people's democracies included all of Eastern Europe except Yugoslavia, where an independent communist movement achieved power without the aid of the Soviets. The designation denotes a transitional stage between bourgeois capitalism and socialism, the title preserving the fiction that these regimes were "popular democracies," i.e., based in the working class. Doctrinairely, people's democracies are dictatorships of the proletariat without the soviets (assemblies); thus, only the Soviet Union could claim to have surpassed the proletarian dictatorship and entered full socialism. *See also* BREZHNEV DOCTRINE, p. 311; SATELLITE, p. 334.

Significance   The people's democracy is an inferior form of socialism, thus of necessity under the tutelage of the Soviet Union. The people's democracies are obliged to follow the Soviet interpretation of Marxism-Leninism; any deviation from the Soviet model is regarded as revisionism, a point reinforced by the Brezhnev Doctrine. The people's democracy formulation was first introduced by the Soviet Union in 1924 in Outer Mongolia, after its invasion and occupation by the Red Army. The East European states have gradually abandoned the designation, preferring to title themselves socialist republics or states.

Polycentrism   The principle and practice in the world of politics of having more than one decision-making center. In international affairs, polycentrism refers to a balance-of-power system characterized by a number of power centers. Polycentrism can be distinguished from a bipolar system in which there are two dominant superpowers that monopolize decision making. In a bipolar system, each superpower's sphere of influence incorporates a number of satellite states that must follow the lead of the superpower because they have no other options. In the balance of power, a bipolar system tends to produce a rigid, unyielding relationship between the two camps, whereas under polycentrism there is a flexible balance with many active participants. *See also* DÉTENTE, p. 319; SOCIALIST INTERNATIONALISM, p. 335.

Significance   The rigid Soviet-American bipolar balance system that emerged after World War II slowly gave way to the emergence of a polycentric system of many power centers. The idea of polycentrism in the communist world was first advanced by Palmiro Togliatti, head of the Italian Communist Party, following the Hungarian revolution of 1956. Until Hungary sought to go its own way, the general assumption in the communist camp was that Moscow should give direction to the international communist movement, and to the communist states of Eastern Europe. All communist states, parties, and movements were expected to accept Soviet leadership without question. In the West, polycentrism also took hold, with the European allies of the United States increasingly pursuing their own political, military, and economic policies. By 1982, polycentrism in the Western camp had led to many conflicts among alliance members, including those concerning the emplacement of new missiles in Western Europe, the building of a Soviet gas pipeline from Siberia to Western Europe, and the basic question of détente. In East Europe, the Yugoslavs have given special emphasis to polycentrism by taking their separate "road to socialism" and refusing to join the Warsaw Treaty Organization. In addition, Poland, Hungary, Romania and Czechoslovakia have redefined their roles vis-à-vis the Soviet Union, and Albania has remained completely aloof from Soviet policies. The Soviet Union has recognized its inability to retain full hegemony over these states, but it has proclaimed the right through the Brezhnev Doctrine to intervene in any communist state whose actions, by Soviet definition, threaten socialism.

Potsdam Conference   A major conference of the representatives of the United States, Great Britain, and the Soviet Union held near Berlin in the summer of 1945 to reach agreement on treatment of defeated Germany and how to bring about the defeat of Japan. The Potsdam Conference was presided over by the leaders of the Big Three (President Harry S Truman, Premier Josef Stalin, and Prime Minister Winston Churchill, who was replaced at the midpoint of the Conference by his newly elected successor, Clement Attlee). The major agreements concluded at Potsdam were (1) abandonment of the policy developed at Yalta to dismember Germany, and agreement to reduce the reparations demanded from Germany; (2) adoption of a compromise concerning the borders of Poland, with the Oder-Neisse rivers established as the Polish-German boundary; (3) provision for an "orderly and humane" transfer to Germany of several million Germans from Poland, Czechoslovakia, and Hungary; (4) a reaffirming of the Yalta policy of total defeat for Germany and the division of the country into four occupation zones, with each governed by one of the Big Four (the Big Three plus France); (5) division of Berlin into four zones of occupation with an Allied Control Commission formed to govern the city as a four-power authority, with each power responsible for administering policies in its zone; and (6) the complete demilitarization of Germany, the destruction of the Nazi party, the liquidation of the German armaments industry, and holding Germany legally responsible for the war by establishing an international tribunal to put German leaders on trial for war crimes. Various postwar problems were discussed, but most were relegated to the newly created five-power Council of Foreign Ministers, which included the Big Three plus France and China. Other matters discussed but turned over to the Council of Foreign Ministers for future consideration included the question of violations of the Yalta Agreement requirement that there be free elections in Eastern Europe, a United Nations trusteeship for Korea, and Turkish control over the Dardanelles. *See also* YALTA AGREEMENT, p. 343.

Significance   Although the Potsdam Conference agreements were intended to be provisional measures only, the division of Germany into occupation zones and other decisions taken at Potsdam have left their imprint on history in the absence of a general peace treaty. The occupation zones, for example, have led to the emergence of two Germanies; West Germany or the Federal Republic emerged out of the British, French, and American occupation zones, and East Germany or the German Democratic Republic was formed out of the Soviet zone. Already at the Potsdam Conference charges and counter-charges were exchanged, especially between Stalin and Churchill, concerning the critical question of the establishment of new postwar political regimes in Eastern Europe, and whether the Red Army was permitting the "free elections" guaranteed by the Yalta Agreement. As a result of the Potsdam Conference, all former German territory east of the Oder and Neisse rivers was annexed by Poland and the Soviet Union, and approximately 10 million Germans were forced to migrate to East Germany, from which many of them ultimately fled to West Germany. The Potsdam Conference was in effect a recognition that the threat of Nazi Germany that had held the allies together during the war period no longer existed, leading to growing suspicion of each other's motives and competitive policies. Shortly, by 1947, these were to harden into a cold war between the East and West that would continue for many years. While the Soviet promise to enter the Far Eastern war against Japan was reaffirmed at Potsdam, a promise that was kept, President Truman's experience of negotiating with Josef Stalin at Potsdam and the alleged violations of Yalta led him to reject sharing the occupation of Japan with the Soviets. Although historians disagree over which side contributed most to the deterioration of relations between the East and West that began at Potsdam, it is obvious that old suspicions and new opportunities for all participants emerged to dampen their wartime ardor.

Salami Tactics   The method by which Soviet-backed communist parties of Eastern Europe gained power in the postwar Eastern European states. Salami tactics refer to the communist strategy of "slicing off," one piece at a time, the noncommunist power positions within the coalition governments of national unity constituted under the Yalta Agreement of 1945. Communist parties participating in the governing coalitions usually insisted on holding the Ministries of Defense and Interior, which gave them control over the secret police, the army and the flow of information. This domination of key ministries permitted them to force all noncommunists into opposition. By using a combination of strikes by communist-dominated unions, police terror, and a denial of newsprint to stifle all opposition, they forced the noncommunist parties first out of the coalition, and then into conformity or extinction. The process generally evolved in three stages. The first, a working government coalition in the Western sense, differed only in that the communist domination of the police and media permitted them to squelch any criticism of the Soviet Union. As the communists secured their power, the parties that initially had been tolerated within the coalition were driven out and denounced in the communist-controlled press as agents of imperialism or Nazi sympathizers. Representatives of the noncommunist parties permitted to remain within the government were handpicked by the communists. The chief targets during this second stage were usually the peasant parties and the bourgeois parties, especially the social democrats. In the final stage, the communists fused the remaining rump parties into a united party. In essence, they thus established one communist organization, and liquidated or drove into exile the remaining oppositional leaders. Ultimately, all individuals and groups capable of opposition were crushed or integrated into the communist power bloc. *See also* NATIONAL FRONT, p. 325; YALTA AGREEMENT, p. 343.

Significance   Salami tactics were used by the communists in all East European states where the Allied Powers, by terms of the Yalta Agreement, agreed upon a power-sharing arrangement between communists and noncommunists in the postwar governments. The initial ability of the communist parties to dictate which ministries they held was buttressed by the fact that the Soviet Army had liberated and occupied Eastern Europe. In Yugoslavia, where the indigenous communist party was dominant, such tactics were hardly necessary, but even there the Western Allies insisted that the Yugoslav London-government-in-exile be permitted to share power. The scenario differed from state to state. Yugoslavia, where the communist party constituted a genuine popular movement with its own police apparatus, achieved one-party status almost immediately upon the dissolution of the short-lived Tito-Subasić Agreement. The struggle was much more pronounced in those states, such as Czechoslovakia and Poland, where the prewar peasant parties or social democrats were strong. By 1948, the communists had consolidated their power in all of Eastern Europe, in violation of the spirit of the Yalta Agreement. They secured this monopoly of power because of the presence of the Soviet Army, the disorganization of war-ravaged Eastern Europe, shrewd political actions, such as salami tactics, and, in some cases, the strength of the indigenous communist party.

Satellite   A pejorative term applied to the nations of Eastern Europe governed by ruling communist parties. Satellite was used to describe the status of the East European states during the 1950s period of the Cold War. A satellite nation was assumed to be completely subordinate to Soviet control, particularly in international affairs. As the era of détente opened, and the West began to recognize the differences among these nations, the term passed into disuse. *See also* SOVIET BLOC, p. 337.

Significance   The use of the term *satellite* implies that these states had been deprived of all elements of national sovereignty and were mere "puppet states" of the Soviet Union. As the Yugoslav, Albanian, and

Romanian leaderships distanced themselves from Soviet policy, the term lost most of its descriptive power.

Socialist Internationalism   The requirement that all Marxist socialist parties support Soviet foreign policy and accept Soviet interpretations of Marxism-Leninism. Socialist internationalism also applies to the relations among socialist states, mandating that they subordinate their national interests to those of the Soviet Union. *See also* BREZHNEV DOCTRINE, p. 311; POLYCENTRISM, p. 331.

Significance   Although the Soviet leadership continues to insist that the Soviet Union is the recognized center of the international communist movement, the doctrine of socialist internationalism has been severely eroded. In essence, the doctrine rested on the Soviet Union's self-proclaimed superiority as the first country of communism, a claim repudiated by Yugoslavia, Albania, the People's Republic of China and its Asian communist allies, and several other communist parties. Since Yugoslavia's split with the Soviet bloc in 1948, many national communist parties have rejected the Soviet interpretation of socialist internationalism. The major defection occurred in 1960, when the People's Republic of China refused to accept Soviet hegemony. Within the bloc, Romania has rejected the concept and has pursued an independent foreign policy. The Soviet-led invasion of Czechoslovakia in 1968, carried out under the rationale of "restoring socialism" to Czechoslovakia, stripped the doctrine of any remaining ideological legitimacy and revealed it as an instrument to perpetuate Soviet power. In the wake of the invasion, the "Eurocommunists" of Western Europe, led by the Italian Communist Party, explicitly rejected socialist internationalism. Most of the communist states of Eastern Europe remain securely bound by the doctrine, obliged to support Soviet foreign policy and to acquiesce to Soviet control.

Soviet Arms Control and Disarmament Strategies   The positions taken by the Soviet Union concerning the reduction of or control over armaments. Although communists generally blame capitalism and the competition for economic advantage for war and the continuation of the arms race, the Soviets have expounded a policy of peaceful coexistence for capitalist and communist states in the nuclear era. The standard posture of the Soviets has been one of seeking to conclude a nonaggression pact with the West before implementing any tangible disarmament plans. The West, particularly the United States, has demanded that a foolproof inspection system and an effective control system be established and proved workable before any meaningful disarmament occurs. For the Soviets, onsite inspection within its borders smacks of espionage as part of preparations for an attack, and consistently has been rejected out of hand by Soviet negotiators. The Soviets and the West have engaged in various kinds of negotiations since the end of World War II in their efforts to bring the arms race under control or to end it. Many forums have been utilized in the search for agreement, including those of the United Nations in New York and Geneva, and in the Strategic Arms Limitation Talks that have been carried on in Helsinki and various other sites. *See also* PEACEFUL COEXISTENCE, p. 329; STRATEGIC ARMS LIMITATION TALKS (SALT), p. 338.

Significance Soviet delegates have participated in hundreds of arms control and disarmament conferences and bilateral negotiations. Some of these negotiations have been concerned with the topic of "general and complete disarmament," an idea first presented to the world by Premier Nikita Khrushchev when he placed the question on the agenda of the 14th General Assembly of the United Nations in 1959. On disarmament, substantial disagreement continues to exist between the superpowers on such questions as force levels, timing, inspection, control bodies, and enforcement systems. Agreement to dissolve all armies and weapons' systems may have to await such unlikely events as the resolution of all major political issues that divide the East and the West, an end to the political-economic-ideological struggle for supremacy, and an honest and complete recognition by both sides that nuclear war spells absolute catastrophe for all. Both nations, however, have been willing to negotiate and to conclude arms control agreements so long as they do not interfere too arbitrarily in the development of new weapons' systems and the continuation of the arms race. Specific treaties and agreements concluded by the Soviet Union and the United States include (1) the Antarctic Treaty of 1959 that prevents the militarization of the Antarctic continent and provides for its removal from superpower conflicts; (2) the Partial Nuclear Test Ban Treaty of 1963 that bans nuclear weapons' tests on the ground, in the atmosphere, in outer space, and underwater, permitting only underground tests; (3) the "Hot Line Agreement" of 1963, a Soviet-American Memorandum of Understanding by which a teletype communications link was established between Washington and Moscow as a means of avoiding nuclear war through accident, miscalculation, or misunderstanding; (4) the Outer Space Treaty of 1966 that bans nuclear weapons and prohibits any form of militarization in outer space or on any planet; (5) the Non-Proliferation Treaty of 1968 that prohibits nuclear weapons' states from assisting, encouraging or otherwise helping non-nuclear states acquire a nuclear weapons' capability; (6)

the Seabed Treaty of 1971 that bans nuclear weapons from the seabed of the world's oceans outside of each state's territorial waters; and (7) SALT I agreements to limit the quantity and quality of nuclear warheads and delivery systems of the Soviet Union and the United States. In addition, several SALT II treaties were signed but the United States Senate refused to consent to their ratification. Both countries, however, accepted Protocol II of the Treaty of the Prohibition of Nuclear Weapons in Latin America of 1967 by which they agreed not to inject nuclear weapons of any kind into that region. The Helsinki Accord of 1975, although not an arms control measure, sought to scale down the chances for war and reduce the level of hostility between the East and West by getting all European nations and the United States to agree to the post–World War II status quo in Europe, and to promote cooperation and understanding among all signatories. The record thus indicates that, while no tangible progress has been made in securing arms reduction, numerous arms control measures have been agreed to and have been scrupulously observed by both superpowers.

Soviet Bloc   Those states of Eastern Europe that acknowledge the primacy of the Soviet Union's leadership in foreign policy and in the basic tenets of their commonly held ideology. Originally, the Soviet bloc included all the states of Eastern Europe: Albania, Bulgaria, Czechoslovakia, East Germany, Hungary, Poland, Romania, and Yugoslavia. In 1948, Yugoslavia refused to comply with what was considered the common bond of the bloc, acknowledgment of Soviet hegemony. The Soviet-controlled Cominform, the association of European communist parties, expelled the Yugoslavs in 1948. Subsequently, in the early 1960s Albania sided with China in the dispute between the Soviet Union and China, and became a nonmember. *See also* COMINFORM, p. 313; SATELLITE, p. 334.

Significance   Membership in the Soviet bloc is generally defined as including those East European states that are members of the Warsaw Treaty Organization (WTO), and the Council of Mutual Economic Assistance (CMEA), that is, Bulgaria, Czechoslovakia, East Germany, Hungary, Poland, and Romania. If the term is taken as implying total Soviet control over the domestic and international affairs of these countries, its application becomes far more questionable. Romania has pursued a foreign policy independent of the Soviet Union, maintaining good relations with China and Israel, while internally remaining a tight dictatorship. Romania also has distanced itself from the CMEA and refused to participate in the 1968 WTO invasion of Czechoslovakia. Czechoslovakia, Hungary, and Poland have all attempted to break with Soviet control at various periods. Nonetheless, the Soviet bloc countries retain enough unity under Soviet control that they are considered one of the two major power blocs in the international community.

Strategic Arms Limitation Talks (SALT)   Negotiations carried on between the Soviet Union and the United States aimed at securing agreement on the control of strategic nuclear weapons and their delivery systems. SALT discussions began in Helsinki in 1969 and have continued since then, interspersed with occasional breakdowns in negotiations. The initial objective was to limit or eliminate construction of Anti-Ballistic Missile (ABM) systems, which both countries planned at that time. Negotiations since have covered the whole range of strategic weapons' systems. These include efforts to control nuclear testing with a comprehensive ban, limits placed on the numbers and types of strategic nuclear delivery systems, limits on the building of ABM sites, denuclearization of specific geographical areas, and the problem of avoiding nuclear war through agreement on confidence-building measures and by providing each other with information concerning military activities. In the initial negotiations from 1969 to 1972, usually referred to as SALT I, agreements were reached whereby the ABM systems were limited to two in each country, and the total number of missile-delivery systems with nuclear warheads was limited. Attempts to limit MIRVing—that is, controlling the number of independently targeted nuclear warheads in each delivery system—failed. In 1973, at the Nixon-Brezhnev summit meeting in Washington, guidelines were worked out for SALT II discussions aimed at establishing further control over strategic weapons. These included provisions for (1) establishing permanent ceilings on offensive strategic forces; (2) controlling certain qualitative aspects of strategic weapons; and (3) working out plans for ultimate reduction of strategic weapons, both warheads and delivery systems. Subsequent negotiations led to a 1974 Nixon-Brezhnev summit in Moscow at which two SALT II agreements were signed. These agreements sought to place additional limitations on the building of ABM systems, and to limit underground testing of nuclear devices. In late 1974, agreement was reached between President Gerald Ford and President Leonid Brezhnev at the Vladivostok summit to place a ceiling on the total number of delivery systems with nuclear warheads, and a limit of 1,320 missiles that each nation can arm with MIRVs. By 1979, a comprehensive SALT II treaty providing several types of arms control procedures and limits was signed in Vienna by President Leonid Brezhnev and President Jimmy Carter. The United States Senate balked, however, and refused to bring the

SALT II treaty out of the Foreign Relations Committee for a vote. President Ronald Reagan, shortly after taking office, announced to the world that he would not seek to obtain the Senate's consent to ratification, holding that SALT II gave an unfair advantage to the Soviets, that actions under the treaty could not be completely verified, and that the treaty was weak because it permitted a Soviet arms buildup and did not include arms reduction provisions. *See also* DÉTENTE, p. 319; SOVIET ARMS CONTROL AND DISARMAMENT STRATEGIES, p. 335.

Significance   Strategic Arms Limitation Talks have been striking failures in their announced objective of bringing the United States–Soviet Union strategic arms race under control. No actual reduction in strategic weapons has occurred. Both parties have been willing to agree to certain limitations concerning the quantity and quality of strategic weapons so long as those provisions did not interfere with their plans for developing new and improved strategic weapons' systems. The SALT I agreements and SALT II treaty emerged out of a period of détente between the two superpowers. When détente ended as a result of Soviet intervention in Afghanistan and Soviet support for the Polish regime in its repression of the Solidarity union, so did progress toward agreement to limit superweapons. Soviet efforts to achieve a position of parity in the arms race, and its political and military involvement in Asia, Africa, and Latin America, combined to weaken the potential of SALT as a bargaining forum. Fears in the United States that the Soviet Union has gained an advantage in the arms race have led to an end to détente, the restoration of controls on exports to the Soviet Union, a boycott of the 1980 Moscow Olympic Games, and a tremendous increase in the budget to rebuild an American posture of military superiority. As a result, hopes that SALT negotiations in the 1980s could bring about agreements to help restore détente and bring the arms race under some measure of control appear to be dashed by new strains in the relations of the major nuclear states.

Titoist Purges   The Soviet-orchestrated offensive against "Titoism," "bourgeois nationalism," or "revisionism," all code terms for the Soviet Union's determination to maintain control over Eastern Europe. The Titoist purges, carried out in Eastern Europe immediately after Yugoslavia's expulsion from the Cominform, were obviously inspired by Josef Stalin's determination that no other communist state would successfully challenge Soviet domination. The period of the purge trials, 1949–53, coincided with what is termed the "satellization" of Eastern Europe, marked by subservience to the Soviet Union. *See also* ANTI-SEMITISM, p. 5; COMINFORM, p. 313; GREAT PURGE, p. 17; TITOISM, p. 80.

Significance   The Titoist purges embittered Eastern European relations with the Soviet Union. Ample evidence now exists that the Soviet Union directed the purges through the KGB and its Eastern European counterparts. The purges hit especially heavily at party leaders with a national following, Jews, Spanish Civil War veterans, and communists with Western experience. Many "nationalist" leaders, in particular the Slovaks of Czechoslovakia, were jailed and/or executed. The Titoist purges destroyed many prominent communists, among them László Rajk of Hungary, Lucretiu Patrascanu of Romania, Traicho Kostov of Bulgaria, and Rudolf Slánský and Vladimír Clementis of Czechoslovakia. Władysław Gomułka of Poland escaped death, emerging from jail in 1956 to lead the Polish party's reform movement. The resentments engendered by the purges from a backdrop to many Eastern European reform movements. Demands for rehabilitation of the victims was an issue in Hungary in 1956 and Czechoslovakia in 1968. Many victims have since been "rehabilitated," the most bizarre case being the reinterment of László Rajk in Hungary in 1956, which helped fuel the Hungarian Uprising.

Warsaw Pact   A series of bilateral mutual aid treaties established by the East European communist bloc in May of 1955. Signatories of the Warsaw Pact include Albania, Bulgaria, Czechoslovakia, the German Democratic Republic, Hungary, Poland, and Romania, each of which signed a bilateral treaty with the Soviet Union. Albania, however, has been anti-Soviet and has refused to participate in Pact activities since the early 1960s, Czechoslovakia withdrew briefly during its "Prague Spring" period of liberalization, and Romania has refused to permit the Soviets to station their troops on its territory. Yugoslavia has remained aloof, preferring a policy of nonalignment. China, North Korea, Mongolia, and Vietnam have observer status, but China ceased to participate following the Sino-Soviet schism. Labeled a treaty of "friendship, cooperation, and mutual assistance," the Warsaw Pact was largely a reaction to the Western action of rearming and permitting the inclusion of West Germany in the North Atlantic Treaty and NATO, and the text of the bilateral treaty arrangements borrowed heavily from its North Atlantic counterpart. To implement the common defense provisions of the Pact, a Warsaw Treaty Organization (WTO) emerged as the East European counterpart to the North Atlantic Treaty Organization (NATO). Decisions of the WTO are made by a Political Consultative Committee that meets irregularly, with each active member of WTO represented on the Committee by a high-ranking governmental or communist party delegate. Between sessions of the Committee, policy matters are resolved by the Joint Secretariat located in Moscow and dominated by the Soviets. The most important military agency is the Joint Armed Forces Command, headed by the commander of the united forces of the WTO, a position regularly filled by a Soviet marshal. The Joint Chiefs of Staff, composed of the Chiefs of Staff of member countries or their deputies, functions under the direction of the Joint Command. Under the Warsaw Pact, if a hostile attack occurs against any member state, all signatories are pledged to go to the immediate aid of the country under attack. The Pact also obligates its members to resolve their internal disputes by negotiation and to refrain from the use of force, solving all outstanding problems by peaceful means. *See also* CONTAINMENT, p. 315; PRAGUE SPRING, p. 295.

Significance The Soviets have always maintained that the Warsaw Pact was strictly a defensive and belated response to the North Atlantic Treaty and the formation of NATO. There can be little question that fear of another devastating German attack led the Soviets to conclude the Warsaw Pact treaties and to develop the joint military command structures. West Germany's inclusion in NATO meant for the Soviets that the division of West and East Europe into Western and Soviet bloc states was irreversible, and that the Cold War would continue indefinitely. The boundaries to be protected were delineated in the Warsaw Pact and the North Atlantic Treaties, and in each case they tended to define the extent of each superpower's sphere of influence in Europe. Most key positions within WTO have been held by the Soviets over the years since 1955, but this dominance over the alliance decision-making machinery and military command structure has not gone unnoticed in Warsaw Pact countries, which have increasingly resented the dominant Soviet role. Under the alliance and WTO, the Soviets currently station troop units in all East European states except Romania, Albania, and Bulgaria. Romania has been under great pressure in recent years to sign a new status-of-forces agreement that would permit Soviet troops to be stationed in the country, but a rising tide of Romanian separatism and nationalism under the leadership of Nicolae Ceauşescu has encouraged Romania to resist these demands. The only collective military action undertaken by the WTO collective force has been the invasion of Czechoslovakia in 1968 to keep that country in the communist camp. The invasion of Hungary in 1956 and the Soviet incursion into Afghanistan in 1979 were both actions carried out solely by the armed forces of the Soviet Union. Although the Warsaw Pact and Warsaw Treaty Organization have helped to restore some semblance of equilibrium to the East-West imbalance following German rearmament, growing polycentrism in Eastern Europe has prevented its full development as a regional political organization and an integrated military group. Mainly, dissatisfaction with Soviet domination of the alliance has weakened its structure and role. Increasingly, it has functioned as a forum to give formal approval to Soviet foreign policy initiatives.

Wars of National Liberation   Revolutions, civil wars, and anti-colonial uprisings aimed at liberating Third World nations and territories from the imperialistic control of Western nations. Wars of national liberation as a doctrine was expounded first by Vladimir Lenin, who enlarged upon Marxist theories concerning the key role of the urban proletariat by suggesting that the masses of Asia, Africa, and Latin America could also rise up to throw off their oppressors. The contemporary definition was formulated by Premier Nikita Khrushchev in 1961. He held that the Great Powers must live in "peaceful coexistence" because war between the East and West was unthinkable, but insurgencies undertaken against the established order in other regions of the world were "just wars" to liberate the enslaved masses from the political and economic bondage imposed upon them by Western elite groups, or their lackeys. *See also* KHRUSHCHEVISM, p. 49; LENINISM, p. 51; PEACEFUL COEXISTENCE, p. 329.

Significance   The contemporary concept of "wars of national liberation" is an attempt by the communists to justify and rationalize violence to gain political objectives in the nuclear age. Accepting the assumption that a nuclear war would be suicidal, Soviet leaders recognized that the denouement of the Marx-predicted historical process of social evolution needed violence, and so they developed a justification for "their" kind of war. Although the Soviets have not become directly involved in fighting such wars, they have accepted an obligation to provide money, economic aid, military supplies, and other forms of help to insurgents in many countries. From the communist perspective, the West "exports counterrevolution" and communists therefore have a right to aid the insurgents while continuing to hold that revolution is "indigenous" and "cannot be exported." Soviet leaders have described many modern conflicts as "wars of national liberation." These include the Cuban Revolution, the Vietnam War in both Phase I (the French effort to maintain colonial rule) and Phase II (United States involvement), Ethiopia, Algeria, the guerrilla wars in the Portuguese colonies of Angola and Mozambique, the insurrection in El Salvador, and the struggle for Namibian independence. Under Mao, the Chinese also expounded a doctrine of national liberation wars, calling for an uprising by the peasants in all class-dominated societies.

Yalta Agreement A major executive agreement concluded during World War II at a summit conference of the Big Three (President Franklin Roosevelt, Prime Minister Winston Churchill, and Premier Josef Stalin) held at Yalta in the Russian Crimea in February 1945 to develop joint strategy in the final stages of the war against Germany and Japan, and to resolve postwar political problems. The Yalta Agreement included a number of important decisions concerning war strategy and postwar policies, including those relating to the nature of the proposed United Nations organization. War-related decisions included in the Agreement were (1) a guarantee that there would be free, democratic elections in the liberated countries of Eastern Europe implemented by coalition governments composed of communists and noncommunists; (2) a decision that Poland would be compensated for land lost to Russia by annexing all German territory up to the Oder and Neisse rivers, with the subsequent transfer of millions of Germans out of the area; (3) an agreement that there would be an Allied occupation of defeated Germany, reparations would be exacted, war criminals would be brought swiftly to justice, and a vigorous de-Nazification program would be carried out; (4) a commitment of Soviet entry into the war against Japan within three months of the end of the European war, in exchange for certain benefits, including Soviet annexation of the Kurile Islands and the southern part of Sakhalin Island, a recognition of Soviet hegemony over Mongolia, and a guarantee of railroad and port rights in China; and (5) a promise by Stalin to recognize Chiang Kai-shek as the sole spokesman for China by concluding a treaty of alliance with him. Major decisions concerning the proposed United Nations organization included (1) original membership in the new world organization would be open to all states that declared war against the Axis Powers by March 1, 1945; (2) the Soviet Union would receive three memberships, one each for the Soviet Union, the Ukraine, and Byelorussia; (3) the veto power in the Security Council would be limited to use on substantive but not procedural questions, and it could not be used by a party to a dispute to block Council consideration; and (4) a trusteeship system would be established to replace the League of Nations mandates system. *See also* POTSDAM CONFERENCE, p. 332; SALAMI TACTICS, p. 333.

Significance The Yalta Conference and the Agreement reached by the Big Three helped to reshape the power structures and spheres of influence in Europe and Asia. In many ways the Yalta Agreement took the place of a general peace treaty at the end of World War II, as a basic instrument to harmonize the policies of the Allied Powers toward the defeated Axis Powers. Many in the West, however, consider the Yalta Agreement to be a "sellout" to the Soviets. They point out that the main Anglo-American objective—to prevent Soviet domination and communization of the Eastern European states occupied by the Red Army—failed because the Agreement permitted the Soviets to manipulate the "free, democratic elections" to secure communist victories in the 1946–48 postwar period. Other critics charge that it was a mistake to bring the Soviet Union into the war against Japan to share in the spoils when the war was already being won by the United States, even before the first atomic bomb was dropped on Hiroshima. President Roosevelt, it is charged, was ill and too weak to stand up to Stalin's demands. Other observers note, however, that the objective at the Yalta Conference was basically that of trying to develop a world community of interests on which to build a stable peace, and that cooperation and compromise among the Great Powers was essential for achieving that objective. The problems, they emphasized, grew out of the situational factors of that day rather than out of Western concessions to Stalin. The communization of Eastern Europe, for example, could have been prevented only by military actions that evicted the Red Army, a course of action that could have produced World War III. In fact, most portions of the Agreement were implemented by the signatories. Ten million Germans, for example, were forced to migrate out of the territories east of the Oder-Neisse rivers as the borders of Poland were moved westward. The Soviets lived up to their agreement and entered the war against Japan within the stipulated three-month period. "Free" elections were held in Eastern Europe, but Soviet machinations resulted ultimately in communist victories. Finally, the compromises on United Nations membership and voting procedures made it possible for that organization to come into existence and function as a world peacekeeping body, albeit sometimes imperfectly. Although the controversies continue concerning the impact of Yalta on world affairs, its failure to achieve President Roosevelt's anticipated objectives is evidenced by the continuation of the cold war and arms race, and the enfeeblement of the United Nations as world peacekeeper.

INDEX

Cross-references to dictionary entries are located in the text at the end of each definition paragraph. Page references in BOLD type indicate dictionary entries. For individual countries, consult the *Guide to Countries* on p. xiii.

345